PERL
PROGRAMMER'S

INTERACTIVE WORKBOOK

VINCENT LOWE

Prentice Hall PTR
Upper Saddle River, NJ 07458
http://www.phptr.com/phptrinterative

ISBN 0-13-020868-X

Editorial/production Supervision: *Kathleen M. Caren*
Acquisitions editor: *Mark L. Taub*
Development editor: *Ralph E. Moore*
Marketing manager: *Dan Rush*
Manufacturing manager: *Alexis R. Heydt*
Editorial assistant: *Audri Anna Bazlen*
Cover design director: *Jerry Votta*
Cover Designer: *Anthony Gemmelaro*
Art director: *Gail Cocker-Bogusz*
Series design: *Meryl Poweski*
Web site project manager: *Yvette Raven*

Printed in the United States of America
10 9 8 7 6 5 4 3 2 1

ISBN 0-13-020868-X

Prentice-Hall International (UK) Limited, *London*
Prentice-Hall of Australia Pty. Limited, *Sydney*
Prentice-Hall Canada Inc., *Toronto*
Prentice-Hall Hispanoamericana, S.A., *Mexico*
Prentice-Hall of India Private Limited, *New Delhi*
Prentice-Hall of Japan, Inc., *Tokyo*
Prentice-Hall (Singapore) Pte. Ltd., *Singapore*
Editora Prentice-Hall do Brasil, Ltda., *Rio de Janeiro*

To Dudley and Joan Lowe.

You filled my childhood home with books.

Now you can see where that leads.

CONTENTS

FROM THE EDITOR

Prentice Hall's Interactive Workbooks are designed to get you up and running fast, with just the information you need, when you need it.

We are certain that you will find our unique approach to learning simple and straightforward. Every chapter of every Interactive Workbook begins with a list of clearly defined Learning Objectives. A series of labs make up the heart of each chapter. Each lab is designed to teach you specific skills in the form of exercises. You perform these exercises at your computer and answer pointed questions about what you observe. Your answers will lead to further discussion and exploration. Each lab then ends with multiple-choice Self-Review Questions, to reinforce what you've learned. Finally, we have included Test Your Thinking projects at the end of each chapter. These projects challenge you to synthesize all of the skills you've acquired in the chapter.

Our goal is to make learning engaging, and to make you a more productive learner.

And you are not alone. Each book is integrated with its own "Companion Website." The website is a place where you can find more detailed information about the concepts discussed in the Workbook, additional Self-Review Questions to further refine your understanding of the material, and perhaps most importantly, where you can find a community of other Interactive Workbook users working to acquire the same set of skills that you are.

All of the Companion Websites for our Interactive Workbooks can be found at `http://www.phptr.com/phptrinteractive`.

Mark L. Taub
Editor-in-Chief
Pearson PTR Interactive

ABOUT THE AUTHOR

Vincent Lowe is Vice President of Business Development for Aqueduct Information Services. In addition to his regular duties, he still frequently finds time to serve as a technical trainer, teaching Perl and Java for clients around the US. A nationally recognized speaker, Mr. Lowe frequently appears at industry trade shows where he presents his hard-headed views on technology and engineering. In his spare time, Mr. Lowe enjoys hiking with his furry best friend, Apollo, and occupying a comfortable seat at the ballpark when the weather and schedule permit.

INTRODUCTION

AN OPEN LETTER TO FUTURE PERL PROGRAMMERS

I want to tell you about some of the things I've learned during the time that I've been teaching and working with Perl. That's why this book is here.

First of all, someone once told me, "If you want to learn a programming language, you have to do two things. You need to read a lot of code and you need to write a lot of code." We've tried to make that process inevitable with this book. You will not get to the other end of this book successfully until you've read and written a number of programs.

It follows that you can't learn Perl by simply reading a book. You can look at the information, understand it, but you can't KNOW it until you try it with your own hands. (If you want to *grok* it, you have to DO it.) It doesn't matter if the book title says "Instant" or "Made Easy"; you will not learn the language from a book, you learn it through an effort of your mind.

If you'll lend me your mind for a little while, I'll try to drive your effort along a path that exposes you to the power of the Perl programming language. Your part of the bargain is to complete the exercises and answer the questions along the way, even if the topic doesn't seem related to the burning problem you want to solve. If you pay attention to the scenery on the way, you'll end up a more capable programmer.

TO GET STARTED

So what do you need to get started with this book? You will need a system with Perl installed. If you need help with this step, you might find information relevant to your platform in Appendix B. Otherwise, you'll want to check the book's companion website, which you can find at http://www.phptr.com/phptrinteractive/.

The next thing you'll need is a command processor (or a shell). UNIX programmers can use any of the traditional shells. Win32 programmers can use your native OS command processor (COMMAND.COM or CMD.EXE) or an aftermarket shell (such as 4DOS, Korn shell, or Bash). For the type of work we'll be doing here, there's very little point-and-click. If you don't find enough information in Chapter 1, "Getting Started," look for additional help with setup and choosing a shell at the companion website.

Another thing you will need is the Perl documentation. You can get it from the same place you got Perl itself. This documentation will make your work with this book much easier. Everything you need to know to solve the exercises is in this book, but you may find that you can come up with more creative or bulletproof solutions if you learn to search the documentation. Before you tear into the exercises, make sure that you have the documentation properly installed in a convenient fashion.

AT FIRST, A BRISK TOUR

In the first two chapters, we take you rapidly through a number of techniques that you will use in your subsequent Perl programs. Don't worry too much if you can't understand why we do things a certain way in the first couple of chapters. Everything you see there will be explored in detail later in the book. But when you get to Chapter 3, "Scalar Variables," you'll already know enough Perl to do some interesting exercises.

Every book has at least one formal structure. That is the beginning-to-end or sequential structure. Sometimes a book will have another structure. It will be available through an index that describes the book in an associative fashion. A dictionary or encyclopedia is like this. The book you hold in your hand will also have this structure. But there is another. A "narrative structure" is also present.

Through the narrative that associates your study with each of four fictional characters, you will watch (and help build) each of four different projects in Perl. Later on in this introduction, I'll tell you more about the characters themselves and their final objectives.

CONFIDENTIALLY, YOU SHOULD KNOW...

One more word to the wise: If you currently plan to run your Perl programs in a UNIX environment, don't just let your eyes glaze over when we talk about what it takes to get the programs to run on a Win32 box. If you plan to become an accomplished Perl programmer, there is a good chance that you'll have to face this sooner or later. Those of you who are currently using a Microsoft operating system and imagine that you always will, don't ignore the parts of this journey that apply to UNIX systems. By knowing how it works in the UNIX world, you'll open a new vista for yourself, maybe even discover a new way of thinking about how your programs should be designed.

TELLING THE WHOLE TRUTH

Sometimes, there is a distinction drawn between concepts such as *function*, *operator*, *command*, *expression*, *keyword*, and *modifier*. Each of these terms has a formal meaning in Perl, but you needn't worry about that while you're learning the language. If it looks like a function, smells like a function, and tastes like a function, you can call it that, even if some erudite Usenet snob tells you that it's really an operator. He may be right, but so are you.

So we will avoid worrying too much about the "inner secrets" until we need to know them. If it looks and smells like a two-dimensional array (or a function), then I'll let you call it that and I'll expect the same forgiveness from you.

THE PEOPLE YOU'LL MEET

As you pursue your studies here, you'll run into some interesting characters.

Uncle Larry: Everybody called him Uncle Larry and almost no one could remember his full name. (One of his friends once said, "His real name? Why, I call him Uncle Larry and he responds. I speak of him by that name to others and they know who I mean. I guess that would make it his real name.") He claimed to be nothing more than a simple storyteller, but most of the people who knew him thought Larry was a prophet. He told stories, yes. But he also served as a mentor for most of the people he knew. He lent a hand when people had questions, and he always had a ready answer when someone found themselves at a dead end with a programming problem. (Larry develops a Storyteller's program that demonstrates pattern substitution and file I/O techniques.)

Major Ellie: Victim of an inexplicable temporal accident, Major Ellie found herself cast into the pre-spacefaring society of 21st century earth. (Yes, this is a pre-spacefaring society that we live in today.) Ellie knew that Arthur Clarke's prediction would one day be accurate. (Clarke said, "If mankind persists as long as even the shortest lived species of dinosaur, the word ship will, for all but a brief time at the dawn of history, mean a vessel that carries people between the stars.") Ellie thrust herself into the work of helping to drag mankind into space, and later to the stars. (Ellie works on a Solar System model that explores Perl data structures.)

Coach Randal: Randal knew something that many sports fans, and everyone who hates sports, didn't know. If you watched for a while, you'd usually see someone exceed their potential and do something extraordinary. That was what made it worthwhile. Never mind the money, the publicity, the personalities, and the egos. Sport was about the players, small or large, who found a way to dig deep into their souls and find their absolute best. This is what caused them to take less money, work the long days, live with the pressure and, sometimes, the heartbreak. Those golden moments of heroism made everything worthwhile. (Randal works on a couple of tools that explore the use of stacks and queues in Perl.)

Barber Tom: Nobody feels the pulse of the community more surely than a good barber. Sooner or later, everyone had to come and see him. When they felt comfortable with him, people told Tom their secrets and concerns. He knew this and believed that it obligated him to share the benefit of his insight whenever it was required. This he did cheerfully, even on those rare occasions when he was the only person who realized that his insight was a benefit. (Tom works on an interactive program that maintains a list of "To Do" items.)

CONVENTIONS USED IN THIS BOOK

The following typographical conventions are followed in this book:

`perl -v`	A command you should enter into the computer

`$ echo $LOGNAME`
 	
`johnmc`
	An example of interaction with the computer. Notice that the parts you would type are bold, the output from the computer is in the plain style.

`ls(1)`	The names of UNIX utility programs will look like this. The parenthesized number is a manual page section reference. If you read the man page on your system for the utility, you'll see that it's in the section referred to by this number. Some versions of UNIX use a different method of referring to the various sections. This is the traditional approach. Our primary interest here is that the name is that of a UNIX utility and that there is a man page for the utility.
`chop()`	The name of a Perl function.
`for()`, `foreach()`, or `while()`	In this book, we present the names of loop constructs with trailing parentheses. This is simply a visual reminder that the reference is to a construct that does expect a parenthesized clause.
line 37	Line number references are italicized to help make it easier to follow the discussions that follow a code example.

SET YOUR COUNTDOWN CLOCKS

Well, you're still here, so I think it's time you got started. Go pay for this book if you haven't already and make sure you have a comfortable chair in front of your keyboard. If we do this right, you're going to be spending a little bit of time in that chair. My hope for you is that you'll have some fun and learn something while you're seated there.

ACKNOWLEDGMENTS

Thanks are due first to Ralph Moore for the encouragement, guidance and polish he lent the project. Mike Faurot earned a big vote of thanks for his heroic efforts in review. Many things in this book are better because of Mike and there are probably a couple of things that would have been better if I'd listened to him a little more. Ashley Fraser deserves thanks for the inconvenient questions, the countless trips up the stairs with a cup of hot tea, and for enduring the many sacrifices inevitable in any successful effort. Mark Taub, Bob Ray, Maggie Wing, and Marc Loy all lent moral support. My morals haven't changed folks, but the book is finished.

C H A P T E R 1

GETTING
STARTED

In this chapter, we'll start by running Perl from the command line. There are two good reasons for doing this. First, it is important to understand how the Perl interpreter is run. You may run Perl and supply the name of a program you've written, or you may create a program that starts Perl by itself. Either way, you should be familiar with the options that are available.

The other reason it's good to understand the use of Perl from the command line is that you may often need to do simple jobs that can be accomplished with little enough code that you can type it into a single command.

LAB 1.1

RUNNING PERL FROM THE COMMAND LINE

LAB OBJECTIVES

After this Lab, you will be able to:

✓ Check your Perl Version Number

✓ Run a Simple Script from the Command Line

✓ Use Perl to Process a File

Before you can write Perl programs, you need to confirm that Perl itself is properly installed and functioning on your system. The simplest method of doing this is to ask for the Perl version number. As you do this, we'll talk a little bit about the operating system shell that provides the execution environment for your programs.

Once you're sure that Perl is installed and working properly, you'll try to run a simple program embedded directly into the command line. Our primary objective in this Lab is to see that we can get a simple instruction to run. That will be additional proof that Perl is installed and working properly.

One good reason for specifying a script on the command line is to use Perl to process a stream of input from a pipe, or to loop through the lines of a file and print certain lines in much the way that the UNIX grep(1) and sed(1) commands can. We'll see how to do this and try a couple of experiments that may spark your imagination.

VALIDATING YOUR DEVELOPMENT ENVIRONMENT

**LAB
1.1**

Our first step is to be sure that Perl will run. To do that, we need to talk for a moment about the command interpreter, or, as it's called most commonly, the *shell*. Most texts about Perl assume that you'll be working on a UNIX system and that you will use the shell to run your Perl program. Once upon a time, this was a valid assumption for most people; Perl earned a great deal of its early popularity within the UNIX community. But today you might find yourself writing Perl programs for a variety of systems, including various breeds of UNIX, Windows NT, some other breed of Windows, or even MS-DOS.

If you begin by understanding a little bit about your command interpreter, you'll be able to make sense out of the things you have to do to get your Perl program to run.

Our base assumption is that you are looking at a prompt from your command interpreter. On your UNIX system, that prompt will look something like **$** or **%**, depending upon the shell you get when you log in. On Windows systems, your prompt will look more like **c:\>** when you set up an MS-DOS prompt.

The Whole Truth

If you use Windows exclusively, you may not use the MS-DOS prompt very often. That's okay, there are two ways you might get it to start.

The first is to pull up your "Start" menu and look for an option labeled "Run." Choose that and a dialog box will appear. In the text field you see there, type the word "command" and press the Enter key.

The other way you might do this is to look on your "Start" menu for the "Programs" option. You'll usually see an option near the bottom of the Programs menu called "MS-DOS Prompt" which you can select and you'll get what you need.

Here's what you should see:

When you type the name of a program from your command line, it will run if it can be found according to an environment variable called $PATH. That variable contains the names of directories that hold programs you might want to run. You can inspect this environment variable by using the echo(1) command.

■ *FOR EXAMPLE*

To see the current setting of your $PATH environment variable, you might say:

```
$ echo $PATH
/bin:/usr/bin:/usr/local/bin:/opt/perl5/bin:.
$
```

If you are running MS-DOS or Windows, type the following at your command prompt:

```
C:\> ECHO %PATH%
C:\BIN;C:\WINDOWS;C:\WINDOWS\COMMAND;C:\PERL5
C:\>
```

In this example, programs located in the \bin (or c:\bin) directory can run no matter what directory you currently happen to be in. So, as long as you have the Perl executable file somewhere in the path, it should run for you.

"THIS IS PERL"

There are several ways to check this, but the simplest way is to ask Perl to print the version number. If it gives us an answer, we can tell that it's also ready to run our programs. The command is:

```
$ perl -v
```

You should probably make it a habit to run this any time you are working in a new or unfamiliar environment.

SAY HELLO TO PERL

Once you know that Perl is installed and will respond to your requests, you can try a simple command. In order to give Perl an instruction to execute, we use the option to indicate that the next command-line argument is the actual Perl program.

■ FOR EXAMPLE

For our first try, let's see what happens when we make Perl print out a short message.

```
$ perl -e 'print "Hi Larry!"'
Hi Larry!$
```

Notice that we used single quote marks around the command. We put double quotes around the message to be printed by our command. If you are running Perl from an MS-DOS prompt, you'll have to reverse the way you use the quotation marks.

```
C:\> perl -e "print 'Hi Larry!'"
Hi Larry!
C:\>
```

The UNIX shell recognizes both the single quote mark and the double quote mark. The single quote (sometimes called the "bulletproof quote") tells the shell, "Hands off until you see another single quote mark. Don't interpret any special symbols, don't substitute variable values, just don't mess with it!"

It's a good idea to encase your script in single quotes so that the UNIX shell doesn't misinterpret any special symbols that are meant for the Perl interpreter. The MS-DOS prompt, on the other hand, recognizes only the double quote mark. This means that you have to surround your script with double quotes. You can use single quotes inside the script because the command processor sees them as just another character.

If you need to put double quotes inside your script when you're using the MS-DOS prompt, you might find it handy to know that whenever you want to quote a string like:

```
print "This is a quoted string"
```

Instead, you could say:

```
print qq{This is a quoted string};
```

Our command from above could be written as:

```
C:\> perl -e "print qq{Hi Larry!}"
Hi Larry!
C:\>
```

Throughout the remainder of the book, I'll show you how to do things when you are using a Bourne shell. This Lab is your best chance to figure out how you'll have to change the instructions to work on your system.

 Check the Prentice Hall Interactive site associated with this book for a chart that may help you decide how Perl is supposed to work on your system. Instructions for using the PH site appear in the introductory material. Point your browser at:

http://www.phptr.com/phptrinteractive/

SIFTING THROUGH A FILE WITH PERL

You can use Perl to sort through a collection of text files, dealing only with the lines that you designate. This is somewhat similar to how you might use grep(1), sed(1), or awk(1). You do this by using the -n option to Perl and by naming the text files after the script on the command line. Here's what it would look like:

```
perl -n -e 'script to process lines' file1 file2
```

This would go through each line in all of the named files, executing your script once for each line.

When you use the option instead, your instructions will be performed once for each line of the input files and then the line will automatically be printed.

You may combine two Perl options, as:

```
perl -ne 'script' file1 file2
```

■ FOR EXAMPLE

Let's suppose we have a file called `names.txt` that contains the following:

NAMES.TXT
```
Phil Greenbelt,MD
Bill Washington,DC
Mike Vienna,VA
Larry Sebastopol,CA
Tom Mountain View,CA
```

If we want to print out the lines that contain the string "CA", we could use the *match operator* to find lines that contain the target phrase. The match operator looks like this:

```
m/pattern/
```

To get the job done then, we could run the Perl command:

```
perl -ne 'm/CA/ && print' names.txt
```

This will print only the last two lines of the file for us because those are the only lines that contain the phrase "CA". Don't worry too much at this point about the `&&` operator and the `print` command. We'll explore those in detail before we're finished.

If you wanted to make some changes to the lines in the file, you could have Perl print out every line but change a few things before the lines are printed. This is where `perl -p` comes in handy. Each line will be printed, but our Perl instructions can be used to alter the text in some of the lines before they are printed.

We can see how this might work if we use the *substitution operator*. It allows us to specify a pattern to be found, and then change it to another value. It looks like this:

```
s/oldpattern/newpattern/
```

Let's suppose we still have the `names.txt` file. If the District of Columbia (DC) achieved statehood and was renamed to Barrytown (BT), we could write the following Perl command to change the addresses appropriately:

```
perl -pe 's/DC/BT/' names.txt
```

This would print out each line from the file with the addresses updated. We'll explore the match and substitute operators in greater detail when we get to Chapter 6, "Tests and Branching." For now, this is enough to get us started.

REVIEW

Table 1.1 provides an overview of the Perl options and operators that you will explore in the Lab Exercises.

Table 1.1 ■ Perl Options and Operators

Element	Definition	Example/ Explanation
-v	Print the version number.	`perl -v` This command-line option instructs Perl to print the version number and some associated information.
-e	Execute statements presented on the command line.	`perl -e 'print "Hello!"'` This results in the string "Hello!" (without the quotes) being printed to your screen.
-n	Execute your instruction once for each line of the input file(s).	`perl -ne 'm/CA/ &&print' input.file` This results in Perl printing all lines from `input.file` that contain the word "CA" (without the quotes.)
-p	Execute your instruction once for each line of the input file(s) and then print each line.	`perl -pe 's/old/new/' input.file` This causes Perl to examine each line from `input.file` searching for the string "old" and replacing it with the string "new" and then printing the line whether a substitution was made or not. (See Chapter 6, "Tests and Branching," and Chapter 7, "Regular Expressions," for more information on this.)

LAB 1.1

`m/pattern/`	Match operator: instructs Perl to match lines that contain the pattern. Used in conjunction with other instructions. (See additional details in Chapter 7, "Regular Expressions.")	`m/Vienna/ && print;` A Perl program containing this instruction will print a line that contains the word "Vienna."
`s/pat1/` `pat2/`	The substitution operator instructs Perl to search for a pattern and change it to another value.	`s/Vienna/Tyson's Corner/` A Perl program containing this instruction would substitute the phrase "Tyson's Corner" for the word "Vienna".
`\n`	The newline metacharacter.	`print "hello\nworld\n";` A Perl program containing this instruction would print the word "hello" and then move to the following line before printing the word "world".
`\t`	The tab metacharacter.	`print "hello \t world";` A Perl program containing this instruction would print the word "hello" followed by a tab and then the word "world."

LAB 1.1 EXERCISES

1.1.1 CHECK YOUR PERL VERSION NUMBER

From your shell prompt (or MS-DOS prompt), run `perl` to see your version number. Then answer the following questions:

a) What version of Perl do you have?

_____

_____

b) Who owns the copyright to Perl?

_____

_____

c) Where can you obtain the license agreement?

_____

_____

1.1.2 RUN A SIMPLE SCRIPT FROM THE COMMAND LINE

In the Lab text examples, you saw the `print()` function used to send a message to the console screen. Inside the string that `print()` displays, you may insert the special characters `\n` and `\t` to get the newline and tab characters, respectively. Use that technique to accomplish the following tasks:

a) Run a Perl script from the command line that prints a blank line, then the word "Hello" followed by two tabs, then the name Larry and another blank line.

_____

_____

b) Modify the command line from the last question to produce two lines of output that looks like:

```
Hello        Larry
Hello        Randal
```

Be sure that there's a blank line at the beginning and end of your output.

1.1.3 USE PERL TO PROCESS A FILE

Use the match and substitute operators along with `perl -n` and `perl -p` to create solutions for the following problems.

> **a)** Print out all of the lines from the `names.txt` file that contain the pattern "`il`".

_____

_____

> **b)** For each line that contains the pattern "`en`", change the pattern to "`un`" and then print only those lines.

_____

_____

> **c)** Print every line in the file, changing the lines that have "`CA`" to read "`Republic of California`".

_____

_____

LAB 1.1 EXERCISE ANSWERS

1.1.1 ANSWERS

> **a)** What version of Perl do you have?
>
> *Answer: I don't know the answer to this question (it's different for each implementation of Perl). But this is the output I got from the command on my system:*
>
> ```
> This is perl, version 5.004_02
> Copyright 1987-1997, Larry Wall
> ```

```
Perl may be copied only under the terms of either the
Artistic License or the GNU General Public License, which
may be found in the Perl 5.0 source kit.
```

From this, you can see that I have Perl version 5.004. At the time of publication, this was not the latest version, but it is a good stable one.

b) Who owns the copyright to Perl?

Answer: Larry Wall, the creator of Perl, retains the copyright.

Many people contribute to the growth of the language now and everyone is encouraged to suggest improvements and contribute new code. Larry acts as an arbiter to ensure that changes to the language do not lead it astray and that Perl is used in a fair and equitable fashion.

You may make your own copy of Perl to use it. You may use the things you create with Perl for whatever purpose suits you. You may even redistribute Perl as long as you include the license and copyright information. If you redistribute Perl, you must also make the source code available or provide information about where the source code can be obtained. This arrangement has made Perl a trust of the programming community and has contributed to its growth and popularity.

In essence, if you want to use Perl, you can. If you have an idea that will improve it, you are encouraged to submit it. If you submit a change that is adopted and becomes useful to the Perl programmers' community, you will be recognized for your contribution.

The success of this approach with Perl and Linux and other GNU projects forms the basis of the *"Open Source Software"* movement.

c) Where can you obtain the license agreement?

Answer: The Perl source kit contains both the Perl Artistic License and the GNU General Public License. Everyone is encouraged to read both of these, particularly if you find Perl useful. It's a small price to pay for a programming language that allows you to build so many useful things.

**LAB
1.1**

1.1.2 ANSWERS

a) Run a Perl script from the command line that prints a blank line, then the word "Hello" followed by two tabs, then the name Larry and another blank line.

Answer: You would do this differently on a UNIX system than you would do it from an MS-DOS prompt. We'll show you both solutions here. If you are running your Perl scripts from an MS-DOS prompt, be sure you understand how to modify the UNIX example to get the solution that will work on your system. In future exercises, we'll show only the UNIX answer and you'll have to modify it for your own machine.

For UNIX:
```
perl -e 'print "\nHello\t\tLarry\n\n"'
```

For the MS-DOS prompt:
```
perl -e "print qq{\nHello\t\tLarry\n\n}"
```

To make this work under the MS-DOS prompt in the chapter, we put double quotes around the entire script and single quotes around the printed string. The single quote won't work in this case because it prevents the \n and \t characters from being interpreted by Perl. Perl treats the single quote as a "bulletproof quote," just like the UNIX shell.

These differences will become less pronounced as we move on to more complex programming examples (and as we spend less time running our scripts from the command line). It is important, however, to understand how to run Perl from the command line because you'll do that often as a subordinate part of the program development cycle.

 If you want to make life easy on yourself, visit the Prentice Hall Interactive site to learn how to get a Bourne shell that you can run on your MS-DOS machine. There are other benefits beyond those that affect your Perl development cycle. The companion website is located at:

```
http://www.phptr.com/phptrinteractive/
```

b) Modify the command line from the last question to produce two lines of output that look like the example shown in the Exercise.

Answer: This isn't much different from the answer to the last example, it's just longer. Here are the UNIX and MS-DOS prompt versions:

UNIX:

```
perl -e 'print "\nHello\t\tLarry\nHello\t\tRandal\n\n"'
```

MS-DOS prompt:

```
perl -e "print qq{\nHello\t\tLarry\n\Hello\t\tRandal\n\n}"
```

1.1.3 ANSWERS

a) Print out all of the lines from the names.txt file that contain the pattern "il".

Answer: To do this, the command would be:

```
perl -ne 'm/il/ && print' names.txt
```

Don't forget that if you're running your command under the MS-DOS prompt, you have to use double quotes. This command should print all of the lines that contain the string "il", which is just what you wanted to do.

b) For each line that contains the pattern "en", change the section containing the pattern to "un" and then print only those lines.

Answer: You have to use perl -n to get only the lines you change. You have to use the substitute operator to make the changes to the lines. Your command line should look like this:

```
perl -ne  's/en/un/ && print' names.txt
```

c) Print every line in the file, changing the lines that have "CA" to read "Republic of California".

Answer: This time you'll have to use perl -p *to get each line to print. On the other hand, you won't have to issue an explicit* print() *statement. Here's what your command will look like:*

```
perl -pe 's/CA/Republic of California/' names.txt
```

We don't need a print statement because the -p switch indicates that you want Perl to print each of the lines that it encounters in the named file(s).

All we have to do here is set up the substitution. This sort of operation is similar to the `sed(1)` program often used by UNIX administrators and developers.

Incidentally, the most common reason for using Perl from the command line, the way we have here, is to accomplish things that are commonly done with other UNIX utilities. If you are not accustomed to working from the command-line prompt, these Exercises may have been a struggle, but don't worry. If you didn't do this sort of thing a lot in the past, you probably won't have to do it in the future either. Just come back to this chapter after you've been using Perl for a few months and see if there's anything here that you can use. We're going to run Perl from the command line very infrequently after this Lab.

LAB 1.1 REVIEW QUESTIONS

1) What option prints the Perl version information?
   a) _____ `$ perl -version`
   b) _____ `$ perl -v`
   c) _____ `$ perl -o version`
   d) _____ `$ perl --version`

2) What option allows the Perl program to be stated on the command line?
   a) _____ `$ perl --execute 'program instructions'`
   b) _____ `$ perl -e 'program instructions'`
   c) _____ `$ perl -p 'program instructions'`
   d) _____ `$ perl --run 'program instructions'`

3) What option allows each of the instructions in the Perl program to be performed once for every line of an input file?
   a) _____ `$ perl -ne 'program instructions' input.file`
   b) _____ `$ perl --iterate input.file`
   c) _____ `$ perl --readloop input.file`
   d) _____ `$ perl -i input file`

4) What option processes an input file by reading each line, running the program instructions using the current line, and then printing the current line?
   a) _____ `$ perl -ne 'program instructions' input.file`
   b) _____ `$ perl --iterate input.file`
   c) _____ `$ perl -pe 'instructions' input.file`
   d) _____ `$ perl -i pgm.pl input file`

5) Which Perl instruction can be used to display a message?
   a) _____ `println "message";`
   b) _____ `display "message";`
   c) _____ `print "message";`
   d) _____ `system->out "message";`

6) What special code allows a message to include tabs and newlines?
   a) _____ `"\r"` is a newline, `"\t"` is a tab
   b) _____ `"\n"` is a newline, `"\t"` is a tab
   c) _____ `"\r"` is a newline, `"\b"` is a tab
   d) _____ `"\n"` is a newline, `"\007"` is a tab

7) What Perl operator can be used to match a pattern in a text string?

   a) _____ `find "pattern";`

   b) _____ `match "pattern";`

   c) _____ `m/pattern/`

   d) _____ `f/pattern/`

8) What Perl operator can substitute one pattern for another in a text string?

   a) _____ `replace ("old", "new");`

   b) _____ `substitute ("old", "new");`

   c) _____ `r/old/new/`

   d) _____ `s/old/new/`

Quiz answers appear in Appendix A, Section 1.1.

L A B   1.2

WRITING YOUR FIRST PERL PROGRAM

LAB OBJECTIVES

After this Lab, you will be able to:

✓ Save and Run a Perl Script in a File

✓ Make the Script Self-Executable

It is useful to be able to specify a Perl program right on the command line, but for anything other than the simplest of programs, this is not how we usually prefer to work. Trying to write a complex Perl program on the command line is like trying to deliver a murder trial summation standing on one leg atop the high dive. We really need a better way to do things.

In this Lab, we'll see how to save your Perl program in a file and what you have to do to run the program. Then, we'll manipulate the file so that it can become a stand-alone program in its own right. Along the way, we'll take a look at how you can put comments into your programs to document them for the next programmer who has to work on your code.

When your Perl program consists of more than one command, you'll need to put a semicolon (;) at the end of each command. Several commands can be put on one line as long as you put a semicolon at the end of each one. A single command can span several lines; the semicolon tells Perl that the command is complete. You'll see examples of each of these techniques before we've finished our study of the language.

A PERL PROGRAM IN A FILE

As a first step, let's take your first program from Lab 1.1 and save it in a file in the current directory.

HI.PL
```
print "Hi Larry!\n";
```

Notice the file name we've chosen. By convention, many programmers give the extension .pl to their Perl program files. This is not required, nor does it have any bearing upon how easy it is to run the program. The custom simply makes it easier to pick out the Perl programs when you are looking at a directory listing. We will employ this convention throughout this book, but you can name your programs in any fashion that suits you.

Here's something similar to the substitution program from your last Lab exercise:

SECEDE.PL
```
# this program should be run with perl -p
s/CA/Republic of California/;
```

Two things to note here. First, line 1 begins with a # symbol. In Perl, this means that the line is a comment. Except when it appears in a quoted string, the # symbol tells Perl to ignore the remainder of a line. In fact, let's look at that program again:

SECEDE2.PL
```
# this program should be run with perl -p
s/CA/Republic of California/; # don't forget, supply a filename
```

A WORD ABOUT COMMENTS

I won't belabor this, you might have heard it elsewhere: _comments are very important._ Some programmers will tell you that they add nothing to the program because the computer knows what to do whether you supply comments or not. Others will tell you that if you write your code clearly, you needn't comment. Most programmers who try to convince you of this are those who were poorly trained.

In today's programming world, we know that the time a programmer spends staring at code trying to figure out what it means is much more important than the time a computer spends executing the code.

Programmer time is expensive, processor time is cheap.

Something that seems obvious to you now might not seem obvious to the programmer who will try to maintain your program sometime in the future. Something that seems obvious to you today may not seem so when you look at your own program in six months. (In fact, if you're a good programmer and *if* your skills evolve, you won't even be able to look at your six-month-old code without squirming, even if you thought it was terribly clever when you originally wrote it.)

EXECUTING YOUR PROGRAM

From the command line, you can run your program simply by starting the Perl interpreter with the name of the program as the only argument. You may also use options to Perl just as we did in the previous Lab.

■ *FOR EXAMPLE*

To run the programs we just saw, you might try this:

```
$ perl hi.pl
Hi Larry!
$ perl -p secede.pl names.txt
Phil Greenbelt,MD
Bill Washington,DC
Mike Vienna,VA
Larry Sebastopol,Republic of California
Tom Mountain View, Republic of California
```

In essence, we replace the occurrence of -e 'script instruction' with the name of a file that contains the instructions. Because we put the instructions into a file, we can easily include any number of them. Also, because the instructions are contained in a file, they are not subject to misinterpretation by the command processor. Your program will run the same way no matter what operating system platform you are using when you execute it. Remember how much fun we had with quote marks in Lab 1.1?

PERL STANDS ALONE

You can fix your program so that it will run _stand-alone_ just like the applications on your system such as Netscape or vi. The key is to add a special sort of comment line at the very beginning of your program file. The comment looks like this:

```
#!/usr/bin/perl
```

A number of things have to be true for this to work. First of all, it must be the very first line in the file. Also, that path to Perl must be correct for your system. The example shown here works fine when Perl is installed in the /usr/bin directory. On many systems, Perl is installed in the directory /usr/local/bin. This would give us:

```
#!/usr/local/bin/perl
```

Once you know where Perl is installed on your system, you can set up the first line of your program to make the program ready to run in stand-alone mode. There is another step that we'll talk about in a moment.

Now there may be times when you want to use some of Perl's special options as we did in the secede.pl program from the last Lab. This is no problem. You simply include the options when you set up the first line of the program.

■ FOR EXAMPLE

Let's rewrite secede.pl for stand-alone operation:

SECEDE3.PL
```
1   #!/usr/bin/perl -p
2   #
3   # $0: reads the database named on the command line
4   #
5   s/CA/Republic of California/;
```

After we take one more step, this would allow us to run the program as:

```
$ secede3.pl names.txt
```

This approach works when you are going to invoke your program from a UNIX shell (Bourne, C Shell, Korn Shell, or one of the near-emulations of these). There are some older UNIX systems that still won't react correctly to this, and if you are running your program under the MS-DOS prompt, you'll have to do something differently.

For the older UNIX systems (and when you run your program on a number of other platforms), you'll need to provide a little snippet of code that will start Perl and feed the remainder of the script to it. For MS-DOS operation, you'll need to make the program look like a batch file and have it start Perl for you.

■ FOR EXAMPLE

Perhaps the easiest way to show you how this works is to supply you with some models. You can use these as templates for your programs. (These templates may be obtained from the companion website: `http:// www.phptr.com/phptrinteractive/`.)

For a traditional UNIX shell, use:

UNIX.PL
```
1  #!/usr/bin/perl
2  #
3  # $0 -program does something interesting
4
5  # --- your program goes here ---
```

For older UNIX systems, and other OS platforms, use:

OTHER.PL
```
1  :
2  #
3  # $0 - program does something interesting
4  #
5  eval "exec /usr/bin/perl -S $0 $*"
6      if $running_under_some_shell;
7
8  # --- your program goes here ---
```

In both of our first two examples, we use *line 3* to act as a reminder to maintenance programmers about the operation of the program. If you use either of these templates, you should be sure to modify this line to say something meaningful about your program. You'll see some good examples as we look at more code in this text.

To run your program under the MS-DOS prompt:

DOSPERL.BAT
```
1  @echo off
2  perl -x -S %0 %1 %2 %3 %4 %5 %6 %7 %8 %9
3  goto endofperl
4  #!perl
5
6  #  --- your program goes here ---
7
8  __END__
9  :endofperl
```

This last example is the trickiest and you may need to tweak it a bit to get it to work for you. For instance, if your command line to this program has more then nine arguments, the batch file will not pass all of the arguments to the Perl program.

Check the Prentice Hall Web Interactive site for more information on other ways to get your DOS Perl program to work stand-alone. Direct your browser to:

```
http://www.phptr.com/phptrinteractive/
```

GRANTING PERMISSION

For the UNIX platform, we still have another step to perform to enable stand-alone execution of the program. We must turn on the "execute permissions" for the program file. The simplest way to do this is to issue the following command:

```
$ chmod +x somefile.pl
```

This will grant execution privilege to all users of the system, but that's probably not terribly harmful in most cases. If you are writing your program on a large multi-user system, you want to be precise with file permissions, particularly with programs. But if you are working on a personal workstation or a small workgroup server, you needn't be as diligent with permissions. If you need more information about file permissions, check your system documentation, particularly the `chmod(1)` man page.

CHECKLIST

In summary, these are the steps you would conduct to create your own Perl program:

1. Put your Perl commands into a plain text file.
2. Insert the Perl invocation line at the beginning of the file (or wrap your script in the appropriate template shown previously for your system).
3. Name the file *something*.pl if you want to comply with convention. (Name it *something*.bat if you're planning to run it on an MS-DOS or Windows system and if you've used the template shown previously.)
4. Turn on the execution permissions for the file. (This step is necessary only on UNIX systems.)

LAB 1.2 EXERCISES

1.2.1 SAVE AND RUN A PERL SCRIPT IN A FILE

We could put any of our programs from the first lab into a file and execute the file instead of typing the program in at the command line. We'll start with the simple "Hi Larry" program and proceed to a couple of more complex ones.

In Exercise 1.1.2, Question b, you wrote a program that printed two lines of text. Put the program instructions into a file called `hello2.pl` in the current directory. From your command prompt, run Perl with the name of your program as the only command-line argument.

a) Did the output look the same as before?

_____

_____

Write a program (`hello6.pl`) that prints six lines of text. Save the program in the current directory and run it. The message can say whatever you want.

b) Will the program still run properly if you name it `hello6.perl`?

_____

_____

Rewrite your `hello6.pl` program so that it still prints out six lines, but uses only one program instruction to accomplish this.

c) Record the program here.

_____

_____

1.2.2 MAKE THE SCRIPT SELF-EXECUTABLE

We can take any of the programs we've written so far and make them work in stand-alone mode. (If you're programming for an operating system other than UNIX, read through the steps here, but then move on to the next Lab question.)

First, open the `hello2.pl` file with your text editor. Add an invocation line similar to the one we saw in the Lab discussion at the very beginning of the file. (Something like "`#!/usr/bin/perl`".)

Save the file and exit your editor. When your prompt appears, mark the file as executable with the `chmod()` command, as shown in the discussion.

Now when your prompt appears again, simply type the name of your new program file.

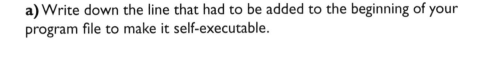

a) Write down the line that had to be added to the beginning of your program file to make it self-executable.

In the Lab discussion, we saw three template files that can be used to form the foundation for a Perl program. Choose the one that's appropriate for your system and make a copy. Name the copy by following your first initial with "template.pl" (for example "`vtemplate.pl`") and then open it with your text editor.

Change the initial comment to describe what the program really does. (This program will simply print a message and exit. Its real purpose is to act as a customized template for your future programs.)

At the appropriate location, insert a program instruction that prints a greeting message with your name. Have a second instruction that prints the message "Add your program here." Save the file and quit your editor. Now take any additional steps that you believe might be necessary to render the new file self-executable. Run the program to be sure that it executes properly.

b) Once you have your program running, record three things: first, the name of your new template; second, the name of the template you used for your system; third, what steps (if any) you used to make the template executable.

LAB 1.2 EXERCISE ANSWERS

1.2.1 ANSWERS

In Exercise 1.1.2, question b, you wrote a program that printed two lines of text. Put the program instructions into a file called `hello2.pl` in the current

directory. From your command prompt, run Perl with the name of your program as the only command-line argument.

a)   Did the output look the same as before?

Answer: Here's how that program might look:

HELLO2.PL

```
print "Hello\tLarry\nHello\tRandal\n";
```

Or you might have written it like this:

HELLO2A.PL

```
print "Hello\tLarry\n";
print "Hello\tRandal\n";
```

In either case, the output should look just like what we did in the earlier
Lab Exercise. The primary difference at this point is that we can run this
procedure now with a lot less typing. We type the program in one time,
and we can reuse it many times.

On the other hand, sometimes as you develop Perl programs, you may
want to try an experiment with a feature of the language without taking
any risks to the program you are writing. One way to do the experiment
would be to save the experimental instructions in a program file and run
it. Sometimes it is more efficient to simply try a command line that performs the experiment for you.

Write a program (hello6.pl) that prints six lines of text. Save the program
in the current directory and run it. The message can say whatever you want.

b)   Will the program still run properly if you name it hello6.perl?

Answer: Your program may bear only a mild resemblance to this one:

HELLO6.PL

```
print "Hi Larry!\n";
print "Hi Randal!\n";
print "Hi Joe!\n";
print "Hi Mom!\n";
print "Hey, it looks like I'm going\n";
print "to be on Terry's show today.\n";
```

No matter how close your program is to this one, and no matter what you name it, you can expect it to run the same. Perl doesn't care what you call your program file. One thing to remember, though. When you run a program the way we're doing it here, you need to be sure that the program file is in the current directory. You can certainly run a program file that resides in a different directory, but on your command line you'll have to provide the full pathname to the location of the program file.

**LAB
1.2**

Rewrite your `hello6.pl` program so that it still prints out six lines, but uses only one program instruction to accomplish this.

c) Record the program in the space provided.

Answer: There are several ways to do this (there are always several ways with Perl), but your program might look like one of the following:

HELLO6A.PL
```
print "line 1\nline 2\nline 3\nline 4\nline 5\nline 6\n";
```

Not a very imaginative program to be sure, but it prints six lines. Here's my favorite way to do the job:

HELLO6B.PL
```
print "
line 1
line 2
line 3
line 4
line 5
line 6"
;
```

This program does have the side effect of printing an extra blank line at the beginning, but we can live with that. The point I want to make here is that you can open a quoted string and allow it to span several lines. This is perfectly legal and very convenient.

1.2.2 ANSWERS

a) Write down the line that had to be added to the beginning of your program file to make it self-executable.

Answer: The program might look something like this:

HELLO22.PL
```
#!/usr/bin/perl
print "Hello\tLarry\nHello\tRandal\n";
```

The first line (in this case "`#!/usr/bin/perl`") will probably work on your system if you're running an operating system that installs Perl in the `/usr/bin` directory. Many systems have Perl installed in `/usr/local/bin` or some other location. (for instance, `/opt/bin/perl` is another common spot.)

You'll have to figure out the answer to this before we go much further. Fortunately, there are some handy utilities that can help you with this. Try these commands:

```
$ which perl
```

or try:

```
$ type perl
```

Usually, one of those commands will report back to you to tell you where the Perl executable file is located. If you're using MS-DOS or another operating system other than UNIX, you're going to have to use the steps we explore in the next Exercise question.

b) Once you have your program running, record three things: first, the name of your new template; second, the name of the template you used for your system; third, what steps (if any) you used to make the template executable.

Answer: If you are working on a traditional UNIX system, you could have used the "`unix.pl`" template.

VTEMPLATE.PL (FOR **UNIX**)

```
1   #!/usr/bin/perl -n
2
3   # $0: template for Perl programs
4   #
5   print "Hello Vincent.\n";
6   print "Add your program here...\n";
```

For those of you who use this template, there is one additional step before your program will be self-executable. You have to run chmod(1) to alter the permissions on the program file. In the Lab discussion, we showed you one quick and easy way to run that command. Here are three other ways you might do it:

```
$ chmod u+x vtemplate.pl # executable only by program owner
$ chmod 755 vtemplate.pl # executable by everyone
$ chmod 700 vtemplate.pl # readable/executable only by owner
```

If you are running an older version of UNIX (like XENIX, early versions of SCO UNIX, and some others), you might need to use the "other.pl" template.

VTEMPLATE.PL (FOR OLDER **UNIX**)

```
1   :
2   #
3   # $0 -template for Perl programs
4   #
5   eval "exec /usr/bin/perl -S $0 $*"
6       if $running_under_some_shell;
7
8   print "Hello Vincent.\n";
9   print "Add your program here...\n";
```

Just as with the previous example, you'll have to run chmod(1) if this is the template you'll be using. The good news is that once you get your template permissions set correctly, you can simply copy the template file whenever you want to start a new program and the new program file will have the right permissions before you begin programming.

The Whole Truth

You can simply use the `other.pl` template without worrying too much about what it means, but in case you're curious about why this works, this explanation may help.

In `other.pl`, the Perl interpreter is started in *line 5* by using the shell command `exec()`. This is a legal shell command as well as a Perl command. When *line 5* is seen by the shell, it starts Perl and tells it to run the program named by `$0` (which is the name of "the *current program*"). Perl will start and of course it also reads *line 5* and finds that it's a legal command. But for Perl, the instruction on line 5 is not complete. Perl continues to read at *line 6* and that line tells Perl to ignore the instruction unless a variable called `$running_under_some_shell` is set to a value other than 0. Well, the variable has never even been defined, so Perl won't run *line 5*. And that's okay because we wanted that line to really be there onlyfor the benefit of any shell that is trying to run our program as a shell script.

If you are running under MS-DOS, Windows, or Win32, you will have to use "*dosperl.bat*" for your template.

VTEMPLATE.BAT (FOR **MS-DOS**)

```
 1 @echo off
 2 perl -x -S %0 %1 %2 %3 %4 %5 %6 %7 %8 %9
 3 goto endofperl
 4 #!perl
 5
 6 #  template for Perl programs
 7 print "Hello Vincent.\n";
 8 print "Add your program here.\n";
 9
10 __END__
11 :endofperl
```

When you use this template, you don't have to take any special action to turn it into an executable file. The reason for this is that you'll name it in a special way. When you use the MS-DOS prompt, the name of your program identifies it as executable. A file that ends with `.bat` will be treated as a program by the MS-DOS command processor. So you're ready to go as soon as you save your file and exit from your editor.

LAB 1.2 SELF-REVIEW QUESTIONS

1) Perl program statements should be terminated with which of the following?
   - **a)** _____ a "#" character
   - **b)** _____ a comment
   - **c)** _____ a ";" character
   - **d)** _____ an environmental impact statement

LAB
1.2

2) Comments in Perl are preceded by which of the following?
   - **a)** _____ a "#" character
   - **b)** _____ a pair of "//" characters
   - **c)** _____ a ";" character
   - **d)** _____ a 21-gun salute

3) To make a Perl program self-executable on most UNIX systems, what line must appear at the very beginning?
   - **a)** _____ `#perl --run`
   - **b)** _____ `#!/usr/bin/perl`
   - **c)** _____ `perl program run thyself`
   - **d)** _____ `!#/usr/bin/perl`

4) When a Perl program is set up to invoke the interpreter this way, you may not use any command-line options.
   - **a)** _____ True
   - **b)** _____ False

Quiz answers appear in Appendix A, Section 1.2.

C H A P T E R   1

TEST YOUR THINKING

In this chapter we learned that Perl can be invoked with the -n or -p options to process the lines of text from an input file. Those options can also be used to process a series of lines that come from the output of another program. When you omit the input filename, your Perl program will read any data that has been piped to it.

For instance, if you run the ls(1) program under UNIX, you might see output that looks like this:

```
$ ls -l
total 15
"
-rwxr-xr-x   1 500    everyone    164 Nov  1 18:33 dosperl.bat
"
-rw-r--r--   1 510    everyone     91 Jan  1 20:41 findperl.pl
-rw-r--r--   1 510    everyone     39 Oct 28 20:23 hello2.pl
-rw-r--r--   1 500    everyone     57 Nov  1 20:29 hello22.pl
-rw-r--r--   1 510    everyone     49 Dec 28 20:22 hello2a.pl
-rw-r--r--   1 500    everyone    177 Oct 28 22:00 hello6.pl
```

(For MS-DOS systems, you can use the DIR command, or get a copy of the fls.pl *program from the website. This project will work with either of those programs.)*

You can feed that output of ls(1) to a Perl program with a line that looks like this:

```
$ ls -l | perl -ne 'perl instructions'
```

Your program will treat the output lines from the ls(1) command as if they were in an input file. Use this technique to accomplish the following tasks.

1) Write a command line that will print only the lines from the output of `ls(1)` that contain the pattern "Oct". (You may have to choose a different pattern depending upon the files that are on your system.)

2) Write a Perl command line that takes the output from `ls(1)` and prints any line that contains "Oct" or "Nov".

3) Write a Perl command line that prints every line of output from `ls(1)` but changes any occurrence of the pattern "Nov" to "11 ". (The trailing space in the substitute pattern will keep the output lines aligned.)

CHAPTER 2

THE
NICKEL TOUR

<table>
<tr><td colspan="2" align="center">CHAPTER OBJECTIVES</td></tr>
<tr><td colspan="2">In this chapter, you will learn about:</td></tr>
<tr><td>✓ Comments, Command Line, Environment</td><td>Page 38</td></tr>
<tr><td>✓ Keyboard and System Commands</td><td>Page 52</td></tr>
<tr><td>✓ Reading Quickly from a File</td><td>Page 67</td></tr>
</table>

I want to give you a taste of Perl without making you wait until you learn all of the syntax. So we're going to take a whirlwind tour of several Perl features in this chapter before we work with the language in earnest. As we go through the examples that follow, don't worry if some of the demonstrations don't make perfect sense to you. Everything you see here will be explained in detail later in the book at some time or another. If you see something here that allows you to accomplish a task before I explain it formally, you can use it right away.

This works because Perl is more like a natural language than just about any other programming language you'll encounter. You might know only a few things about Perl now, but you will be able to do some things, sometimes even powerful things, right away.

So snap on your protective headgear and let's get started with the "nickel tour" of Perl.

LAB 2.1

COMMENTS, COMMAND LINE, ENVIRONMENT

LAB OBJECTIVES

After this Lab, you will be able to:

✓ Use Comments, Two Types

✓ Use Command-Line Arguments

✓ Use Environment Variables

In this Lab, we'll enhance and extend our simple first program from Chapter 1, "Getting Started." We'll begin by looking at two different ways to add comments. We'll also find out that comments have three distinct uses.

We'll see how a program can use the arguments from the command line and variables that have been set in the environment.

We'll wrap up by doing some simple things after we read from files.

THREE TYPES OF COMMENTS

We talked a little bit about using comments in Chapter 1. You saw that a # symbol can be used to force the interpreter to ignore anything that follows it on the line. This mechanism can be used for each of the three primary purposes of comments. I characterize these as:

- Incidental comments
- Block comments
- Structural comments

Incidental comments are those that accompany a line of code and explain it tersely. Mostly these are put in place to serve as quick reminders for a programmer later on, especially if the intent of the code is not clear. A little secret here: I find that most incidental comments are added to a program after it has been sitting around for awhile. The original author (usually) or a maintenance programmer (sometimes) will look at the code after it has aged awhile and decide that a particular phrase or stretch of code needs to be documented. This pragmatism is usually the result of someone's having stared for 5 or 10 minutes at the code without being able to imagine what the original programmer was thinking about.

Block comments are those that introduce a program or a major section. They attempt to explain its important characteristics. Appropriate things to include in a block of comments can include a description of the program's operation, its purpose, revision and authorship information, and maybe even a "to do" list for future enhancement of the program.

Structural comments are not really comments at all. They are simply lines of code that have been disabled by rendering them as comments. By this I mean that we put a comment symbol at the beginning of such a line and it no longer executes as a program instruction. It is placed "on hold" instead, until we are ready to turn it back into part of the program.

■ FOR EXAMPLE

The following program shows comments used in all three of these ways:

MULTICOMMENT.PL

```
 1 #!/usr/bin/perl -n
 2 # $0: Scans a file for entries from California or Texas
 3 #
 4 #     This program uses "perl -n" mode to scan a file and
 5 #     print the appropriate lines.  We will print lines
 6 #     for California addresses intact, and print lines
 7 #     for Texas addresses after changing them to reflect
 8 #     the new name.
 9 #
10 # print lines that contain the string "CA"
11 /CA/ && print;
12 s/TX/Republic of Texas/g && print; # help Texas secede
13 #s/,TX$/,Estado de Tejas/g && print # change language
```

In this program, _lines 2-9_ illustrate a comment block. This is a reasonably common way to start a new program. We haven't discussed it before, so it bears mention here that the symbol $0 is a shorthand used in Perl to mean "the current program."

Line 10 presents an incidental comment that applies to the following line. The incidental comment in _line 12_ applies to its own line. Both of these are fairly typical examples. You should place these wherever you feel that they are helpful.

Line 13 forms a structural comment. (It also includes an incidental comment at the end.) This line is in the program in the event that we want an alternative to the code we run in _line 12_. If we decide to use _line 13_, then we'd probably "comment out" _line 12_ (by placing a # at the very beginning) and remove the first character from _line 13_ to activate it instead.

COUNTERFEIT POD CONTENT

Perl provides another way to embed human-readable information in your program. This mechanism is called POD (for Plain Old Documentation) It allows you to embed special comments in your program that have an important side effect. Programs provided with Perl can read this type of comment and turn it into any of several forms of documentation.

For instance, you might include a descriptive paragraph at the beginning of your code to explain the operation and behavior of your program. When you're finished writing your code, you can use a program called "pod2html" that will sift through your code, reading only the POD content, and use that to create a web page. Another program "pod2man" can do the same thing to produce a man page.

We'll see how to use POD for its intended purpose in Chapter 11, "Functions." Right now let's see how we can take advantage of POD content to comment out a large block of code.

Because every POD directive begins with an = sign at the beginning of the line, the interpreter treats any line that begins with an = sign as a POD markup, even if it's not necessarily a supported instruction. This means that you could comment out a block of code with fake POD. The Perl interpreter would ignore the block of code, thinking that it is documentation. The filter programs (like `pod2html`, for instance) would also ignore the block because it isn't legal POD content.

To make this work, we put a "simulated POD" instruction at the beginning of the block we want to deaden, and the real POD instruction "=cut" at the end.

■ *FOR EXAMPLE*

This program will print only two lines of output even though the three lines in the middle of the program are legal Perl code.

DEADBLOCK.PL
```
1  #!/usr/bin/perl
2
3  # $0: program demonstrates use of fake POD markup
4  # to comment out a block of code
5  #
6
7  print "This is a normal section of code...\n";
8
9  =debuggingNow
10
11 print "This is code in the dead block.\n";
12 print "This is more code in the dead block.\n";
13 print "This is the last code in the dead block.\n";
14
15 =cut
16
17 print "This is code after the dead block.\n";
```

READING INFORMATION FROM THE COMMAND LINE

Your program can read the arguments typed in by the user on the command line. You've probably already noticed the use of the special symbol $0. This represents the name of the current program.

You use the Perl `shift()` function to get the first argument from the command line. If you use `shift()` again, you will get another command-line argument each time until the list of arguments is exhausted.

Suppose you run your program with the following command line:

```
$ helloarg.pl Larry Tom Randal
```

If your program prints $0, you would see `helloarg.pl`. If your program calls `shift()` and prints the result, you would see "Larry" the first time it happens. The second time you do that, you would see "Tom," and so forth.

MULTIPLE ARGUMENTS TO `print()`

So far we've given only one argument at a time to the `print()` statement, but there's no reason we have to stop there. We can provide an arbitrary number of arguments, separated by commas.

■ FOR EXAMPLE

You can write a `print()` statement to look like this:

```
print "the party of the first part",
    "wishes to kiss the party of the second part",
    "in the presence of the party of the third part.\n";
```

We'll explore more variations on this later in the chapter. For the moment, it means we can write a program that prints our program name plus a greeting directed toward each of the names from the command line. Let's look at such a program.

HELLOARG.PL

```
1   #!/usr/bin/perl
2
3   print "Program name: $0\n";
4   print "first arg: ", shift, "\n";
5   print "second arg: ", shift, "\n";
6   print "third arg: ", shift, "\n";
```

Here is what happens when we run it:

```
$ helloarg.pl Larry Randal Tom

Program name: helloarg.pl

first arg: Larry

second arg: Randal

third arg: Tom
```

This program works correctly only if we happen to find three arguments on the command line. In Chapter 6, "Tests and Branching," we'll look at how you can test for the presence of arguments before you try to print them.

HELLO $USER—READING THE ENVIRONMENT

Another source of information that your program might utilize is the shell environment. (Our discussion here will suppose a UNIX shell, but even the MS-DOS prompt shell maintains an environment; you access it in the same manner.)

The shell environment consists of configuration information for use by the programs that you run. The shell itself uses an environment variable called $PATH to figure out where your executable programs are stored. Many programs that manipulate the screen [such as vi(1), emacs(1), and pine(1)] depend on an environment variable called $TERM that helps them determine which control codes should be sent to the screen.

You may want your program to take advantage of information stored in the environment. This is easy to do when you program with Perl. We'll look at the issue in detail when we get to Chapter 5, "Hashes." For now, we can simply use a simple syntax that looks like this:

```
$ENV{'VARNAME'}
```

This will work for an environment variable called $VARNAME. So we can write a program that prints a customized greeting as long as we believe that the current user's name is stored in $USER. It might look like this:

HELLOUSER.PL
```
1   #!/usr/bin/perl
2   print "Hello ", $ENV{'USER'}, "\n";
```

LAB 2.1 EXERCISES

2.1.1 USE COMMENTS, TWO TYPES

Starting with the code in the program `deadblock.pl`, move the `=debug-gingNow` token so that the second print statement (the one that says "This *is code in the dead block.*") will execute. For this Exercise, make sure that a blank line appears both before and after the `=debuggingNow` token.

a) Does the program work as expected if you simply move the token?

_____

_____

b) Move the token between the remaining two dead statements. Make sure that there's no blank line before or after the token. Does the program now produce four lines of output?

_____

_____

2.1.2 USE COMMAND-LINE ARGUMENTS

In the discussion for this Lab, we saw a program (`helloarg.pl`) that could print out the value of up to three command-line arguments. Run that program with only one command-line argument.

> **a)** Did the program refuse to run, did it fail, or did it simply print lines with no value in place of the shift()-ed arguments?

_____

_____

The program prints the program name in its first line of output. Run the program by using the full path to the program. If your program is in `/src/perl/PWB/ch02/helloarg.pl`, then run it as:

```
/src/perl/PWB/ch02/helloarg.pl Larry Joe Tom
```

> **b)** Does the value printed by `$0` reflect the complete pathname?

_____

_____

> **c)** Run `helloarg.pl` with each of the following arguments and describe what you see:
>
> -v
>
> "Raymond J. Johnson Jr."
>
> --

_____

_____

2.1.3 USE ENVIRONMENT VARIABLES

To see how an environment variable can be useful in your program, we'll have to set up some dummy variables and observe a program that uses them. Here are some things for you to try:

Use the `set` command to print out the contents of your current environment. (This works in the UNIX shells as well as at the MS-DOS prompt.)

Create a new variable that doesn't currently exist in your environment. (You'll probably be safe if you set up $OPERATOR as a variable.) One of the following should work for you. Remember that case is significant in the UNIX shells, so enter the command exactly as you see it here.

```
Bourne Shell
$ OPERATOR=Joe; export OPERATOR

C Shell
% setenv OPERATOR Joe

Korn Shell (and BASH)
$ export OPERATOR=Joe

MS-DOS Prompt
c:> set OPERATOR=Joe
```

a) Write a short Perl program that prints a greeting addressed to the name represented by the OPERATOR environment variable.

_____

_____

b) Revise your program so that it prints a greeting from a name given on the command line to the name held in the OPERATOR environment variable.

LAB 2.1

———————————————————————————

———————————————————————————

Uncle Larry was beset nearly every afternoon by requests from the town children who demanded that he tell them a new story. They were seldom satisfied with a story that he'd already told them. So he decided to write a program that would help him generate new stories when his mental well ran dry.

He thought that he'd begin by writing a program that expected him to create several environment variables. For example, he might set up the environment like this:

```
CREATURE="German Shepherd"
NAME="Max"
KINGDOM="Timbuktu"
MONSTER="Dragon"
PROFESSION=Mailman"
KITCHEN_UTENSIL="Ice Cream Scoop"
TOOL="Garden Hoe"
export CREATURE NAME KINGDOM
export MONSTER PROFESSION KITCHEN_UTENSIL TOOL
```

His program would then print a story that used the values stored in the environment. As an example, the program might say:

"Once upon a time there was a German Shepherd named Max who decided to take a vacation in Timbuktu. While he was there, he met an evil Dragon who threatened the very kind Mailman with a gigantic Ice Cream Scoop. Max took out his trusty Garden Hoe and battled the evil Dragon. Soon the evil Dragon was defeated and he fled with a promise never to return to Timbuktu again."

c) Write a program like Larry's that prints a story using the environment variables shown above. You can use the story shown here if you cannot think of your own.

———————————————————————————

———————————————————————————

LAB 2.1 EXERCISE ANSWERS

2.1.1 ANSWERS

a) Does the `deadblock.pl` program work as expected if you simply move the token?

Answer: It works fine if you move the `=debuggingNow` marker. You can use this approach any time you want to "comment out" a section of code.

This solves a big problem for most programmers. If you want to comment out only one line of code, it's a simple matter to insert a "#" sign at the beginning of the line. This approach continues to be practical when you want to comment out a small number of adjacent commands.

When you want to comment out a large block of code, it's difficult to insert the correct symbol at the beginning of every line in the block. A good text editor will reduce the pain slightly, but it's an inefficient process, at best. Using "counterfeit POD" to simulate block comments is a much easier approach.

b) Move the token between the remaining two dead statements. Make sure that there's no blank line before or after the token. Does the program now produce four lines of output?

Answer: The approach still works. Beware that the filter programs will all expect POD command paragraphs to be preceded by a blank line. We'll learn more about this in Chapter 11, "Ends and Odds."

The Perl interpreter, on the other hand, looks for only those things that appear to be POD directives. When it sees what it believes to be one, it ignores source code content until it sees an `=cut` marker.

2.1.2 ANSWERS

a) Did the program refuse to run, did it fail, or did it simply print lines
   with no value in place of the shift()-ed arguments?

   Answer: The program ran without complaint. It printed an argument when `shift()`
   found one, but it printed nothing when `shift()` *failed to find any remaining com-*
   mand-line arguments.

b) Does the value printed by $0 reflect the complete pathname?

   Answer: When the program is run with a full pathname, printing $0 will print the fully
   qualified name of the program.

c) Run `helloarg.pl` with each of the following arguments and
   describe what you see.

   Answer: When the program is run with the following arguments, here is the result:

`-v`	`first argument: -v`
`"Raymond J. Johnson Jr."`	`second argument: Raymond J.` `Johnson Jr.`
`--`	`third argument: --`

As you can see, Perl prints whatever arguments you feed it on the command line. We'll talk about the command line a lot in this book because it's a wonderful way to control a program.

When you write a program that can be controlled from the command line, it can be run as part of an automated procedure. This is common for UNIX utilities, and sadly missing from most MS-DOS utilities. As a Perl programmer, you can take advantage of the strong tradition established by UNIX tool builders. If you do this, your programs can be run by a task scheduler (see the `cron(1)` man page) or kicked off by another process (especially a server like `httpd` or `inetd`, both of which are important to an Internet/Intranet host).

**LAB
2.1**

2.1.3 ANSWERS

a) Write a short Perl program that prints a greeting addressed to the name represented by the OPERATOR environment variable.

Answer: Your program might be slightly different, but it should function in a fashion similar to this one:

HELLOUSER2.PL

```
1  #!/usr/bin/perl
2  print "Hello ", $ENV{'OPERATOR'}, "\n";
```

b) Revise your program so that it prints a greeting from a name given on the command line to the name held in the OPERATOR environment variable.

Answer: Your program might be slightly different, but it should function in a fashion similar to this one:

HELLOUSER3.PL

```
1  #!/usr/bin/perl
2  print "Hello ", $ENV{'OPERATOR'},
3    ", from your friend ", shift, "\n";
```

c) Write a program like Larry's that prints a story using the environment variables shown above.

Answer: Your program may be very different. This one meets the requirements for the lab:

NEWSTORY.PL

```
1   #!/usr/bin/perl
2   print "Once upon a time, a friendly $ENV{'CREATURE'} \n",
3   "went on a vacation to far away $ENV{'KINGDOM'}. \n",
4   "While he was there, he saw an evil $ENV{'MONSTER'} \n",
5   "attacking a nice $ENV{'PROFESSION'} with his giant \n",
6   "$ENV{'KITCHEN_UTENSIL'}.  He beat the $ENV{'MONSTER'} \n",
7   "mercilessly about the head and shoulders with his trusty \n",
8   "$ENV{'TOOL'}.  Soon the $ENV{'MONSTER'} apologized to \n",
9   "the $ENV{'PROFESSION'} and rode away with a promise to \n",
10  "be nice from now on.  --The End--\n";
```

In order to run this program, you'll have to set up the environment variables first. Your commands might look like this (for Korn/BASH shells):

```
$ export CREATURE="Rabbit" KINGDOM="Atlantis"
$ export MONSTER="Sea Serpent" PROFESSION="Meter Maid"
$ export KITCHEN_UTENSIL="Meat Tenderizer" TOOL="Drill"
```

Then if you simply run the program shown above, you'll get a story that can be redirected to a file, piped to the print queue, or simply shown on the screen. We'll use this program later in a Lab that will allow us to work with it more flexibly.

LAB 2.1 REVIEW QUESTIONS

1) How can you print the first from the list of command-line arguments?
   a) _____ print "@ARGV[0]\n";
   b) _____ print "$ARG1\n";
   c) _____ print shift, "\n";
   d) _____ print getarg(1);

2) How can you print an environment variable called "OS_TYPE"?
   a) _____ print env(OS_TYPE);
   b) _____ print $ENV{'OS_TYPE'}, "\n";
   c) _____ print env('OS_TYPE');
   d) _____ print ENV(OS_TYPE), "\n";

3) How many arguments can the print() statement accept?
   a) _____ a maximum of 256.
   b) _____ a maximum of 1024.
   c) _____ as many as your patience will allow.
   d) _____ no more than eight.

Quiz answers appear in Appendix A, Section 2.1.

L A B   2.2

KEYBOARD AND SYSTEM COMMANDS

LAB OBJECTIVES

After this Lab, you will be able to:

✓ Read Input from the Console Keyboard

✓ Run a System Command

✓ Read Input from a System Command

In the last Lab, we saw how to get input to our program from the command line and from the environment. In this Lab, we'll see how to read input from the keyboard and how to run system commands for their own sakes as well as how to run commands so that your program can process the output.

Most UNIX utility programs read their input from the "standard input stream" (sometimes abbreviated STDIN). This usually means the console keyboard, but it could be a pipeline that contains the output of another program, or it could be the content of a file read in through redirection.

Your Perl program can take this same approach and there are several advantages to doing things this way. If you design your program well, the same program can be used by someone who intends to feed it information from the keyboard, from a pipeline, or from a file.

The ability to write a program that serves in each of these capacities is what keeps us writing new programs that read from STDIN.

INPUT FROM THE CONSOLE

Let's start by looking at how you might get input from the system keyboard. It's not very difficult at all. You can do it with a phrase like this:

```
$line = <STDIN>;
```

LAB 2.2

After you've done this, you can print the value typed in by the operator simply by putting $line in a print() statement.

■ *FOR EXAMPLE*

Consider the following fragment of code:

```
1  print "Please enter your name: ";
2  $name = <STDIN>;
3  print "Well, Hello ", $name;
```

This allows us to conduct a dialog with the operator of our program in a fairly straightforward fashion. There's only one little problem that remains. Look closely at *line 3* in this example. Did you notice that there is no newline (\n) character?

If you run the code as shown it will work and probably will do what you want it to do. But that is a side effect of the fact that the value stored in $name includes the newline character typed in by the program operator. Sometimes that fact works out to our advantage (as in this example) and sometimes it is merely tolerable. Other times you'll find that the extra character gets in the way. This is why Perl offers us the chomp() function. It simply removes the trailing newline character from a text string.

So you can update the preceding code to read:

```
1  print "Please enter your name: ";
2  $name = <STDIN>;
3  chomp ($name);
4  print "Well, Hello ", $name, "!\n";
```

Now our message is a little more emphatic.

RUNNING A SYSTEM COMMAND

Another thing that you might want your program to do is to start a program that already exists on the local system. This is pretty easy to do. You simply put the command line for the program you want to "kick off" inside a call to the system() function.

■ *FOR EXAMPLE*

Imagine that you want to have your program run something like "ls " on the current directory. This is how you do it:

```
system ("ls -1.");
```

The ls(1) program will run immediately. If the command you run changes anything about the underlying system, that change will take effect. If the program produces any output, it will be seen by the program operator. Redirection is allowed, so we may pipe the output from one program to another just as we would do from a shell prompt.

So if you wanted to have your program print a file listing for the current directory in sorted order, you could set up the command this way:

```
system ("ls -1 | sort -n+4");
```

That causes the output of ls(1) to be sent to the sort(1) program with the instructions that the sort be numeric and that the data should be sorted according to the information seen in the fifth column. (On an MS-DOS system, you'll have to substitute DIR for the ls(1) command, and your sort program works a little differently.)

If there is a program error, you can detect it by inspecting the special variable $?. The grep(1) program provides us a good way to see how this works. Normally, you run grep(1) by providing a pattern and then a file-name on the command line. If the pattern appears in any of the lines in the file you name, those lines will be printed out for you.

■ *FOR EXAMPLE*

If you wanted to search for the string "shoulders" in one of the programs from the current directory, your command line would look like this:

```
$ grep "shoulders" newstory.pl
```

If the pattern exists within the file, you will see the lines that contain the pattern printed on the console. If you inspect $? at this point, you'll find that grep(1) exited with a code of 0. That means that everything went okay. (To inspect the exit value from the shell prompt, use the command "echo $?" if you use the Bourne, Korn, or BASH shells; use "echo $status" if you're using the C shell. From our Perl program, of course, we'll simply "print $?" when we want to see the result.)

If grep(1) runs and doesn't find the pattern within the file that you name, it will emit an exit code of 1. If it cannot find the file that you name, it will emit an exit code of 2. We'll experiment with this in the Exercises to see how the system() function works in Perl.

CAPTURING INPUT FROM A SYSTEM COMMAND

Sometimes you'd like to run a system command, not so that you can see the output, but so that your program can process the information. You can run a system command and trap the input for use by your program by including the command line for the system command in backward quotes. (These are also called "grave quotes" or sometimes "backticks.")

■ *FOR EXAMPLE*

So if we want our program to store the name of the local system, we could use a line like this:

```
$system  = `uname -n`;
```

Perl will see the output of the "uname" command on that program line as if you'd typed in the value yourself. (Users of the MS-DOS prompt can try this too, but you don't have a uname(1) command. Use the VER command instead.)

With this in mind, we could write the following program:

HELLOALL.PL
```
1  #!/usr/bin/perl
2  print "Hello ", shift,
3     " from $ENV{'USER'} on system ", `uname -n`, "\n";
```

As you might guess from inspection, this program prints a greeting addressed to the name found on the command line, from the name identified in the environment, and includes the system name as found in the `uname(1)` command.

LAB 2.2 EXERCISES

2.2.1 READ INPUT FROM THE CONSOLE KEYBOARD

With the ability to read operator input from the keyboard, you can start to write programs that conduct simple two-way dialogs. Let's try a few things that will illustrate exactly what we're getting when we say <STDIN>.

Here's a simple program that you can easily type in for yourself:

READKEY.PL
```
1  #!/usr/bin/perl
2  print "WHAT is your name? ";
3  $name = <STDIN>;
4
5  print "Well [$name], WHAT is your favorite colour?\n";
6  $color = <STDIN>;
```

Run the program and observe the output. Then answer these questions:

a) After the operator types in a name, the program prints that value within square brackets. What purpose do the brackets around $name serve in this program?

_____

_____

b) Insert the following code after line 3. How does this change the result?

```
chomp ($name);
```

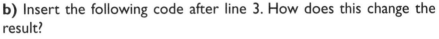

Uncle Larry ran his `newstory.pl` program a few times and decided that it held promise. He felt that a logical extension would be to prompt for values each time the program ran instead of requiring that a bunch of environment variables be set up in advance.

It's possible to revise the `newstory.pl` program from Exercise 2.1.3. Instead of reading the values from the environment in your new program (`newstory2.pl`), prompt the operator to type them in from the keyboard.

For example, the program run might look like this:

```
$ newstory2.pl
Type in the name of a creature: Gila Monster
Type in the name of a kingdom: Montana
<...etc...>
```

c) Write the new program `newstory2.pl`.

2.2.2 RUN A SYSTEM COMMAND

Because you know how to run a system command, it's easy to create an interactive user shell of your own with Perl. Here's a simple program that takes the first step:

NEWSHELL.PL
```
1   #!/usr/bin/perl
2   print "Contents of the current directory:\n";
3   system "ls -CF"; # use "dir" for MS-DOS prompt
```

```
4   print "\nEnter the name of a file to display: ";
5   $fname = <STDIN>;
6   chomp $fname;
7   system "cat $fname"; # use "type $fname" for MS-DOS
```

**LAB
2.2**

Run this program and observe its behavior. Then answer the questions.

> **a)** What change must be made to the program in order to allow it to remove a file instead of simply dumping its contents to the screen?

_____

_____

> **b)** Using the ideas illustrated in `newshell.pl`, write a program (`newshell2.pl`) that allows the operator to type in any command and then submit that command to be executed by the shell.

_____

_____

From what we've discussed, it should be possible to write a program that prompts the operator for a directory name and then creates a directory with that name. The name typed in might be an absolute pathname or it might be relative to the current directory. (Remember that names beginning with / are assumed to be absolute pathnames.) Your program can use the exit code from the system command ($?) to determine whether the operation succeeded or failed. For now, simply print a message that includes the exit code.

> **c)** Write a program (`newdir.pl`) that prompts for a directory name and then creates a directory with that name. Print the exit code.

_____

_____

Test your program with each of the following directory values and report the results. (Information after the # sign is for your benefit. It should not be typed in.)

d) `newdir #directory that doesn't exist`

_____

_____

e) `/tmp/gooddirectory #legal absolute pathname`

_____

_____

f) `/badparent/newdir #bad parent directory`

_____

_____

g) `/etc/newdirectory #parent directory inacces-sible`

_____

_____

2.2.3 READ INPUT FROM A SYSTEM COMMAND

There will be a time when you want your program to use information that can be retrieved from a system command. You saw in the Lab text that you can do this by using the "backtick operator."

There are a couple of simple system commands that you can use to see how this works for yourself. On a UNIX system, you can use the `pwd(1)` command to print the value of the current working directory. You can use the `uname(1)` command as we saw above to print the name of the current host. (If you are running MS-DOS, then substitute the CD command for `pwd`. Substitute VER for `uname`.)

a) Write a program (`identity.pl`) that stores the value for the current working directory in a variable called `$work` and the value for the system name in `$hname`. Print those values out in a message.

_____

_____

b) Write a program (`dinfo.pl`) that stores information about files in the current directory in a variable called `$files`. Print that variable as part of a message.

_____

_____

LAB 2.2 EXERCISE ANSWERS

2.2.1 ANSWERS

a) After the operator types in a name, the program prints that value within square brackets. What purpose do the brackets around `$name` serve in this program?

Answer: The square brackets don't have any programmatic effect on the variable. They are used to allow you to see when the variable doesn't have any content, or when the content is an "invisible" character like a tab or newline.

If you get into the habit of printing your experimental output inside some visible delimiter characters like the square brackets, you'll often be able to immediately see why something didn't turn out exactly the way you intended.

b) Insert a call to the `chomp()` function after line 3. How does this change the result?

Answer: This fixes our little problem from the original version of the program. Now the name is available in the program without a trailing newline character. For the most part, when you get a simple bit of input from the user in this fashion, you should habitually `chomp()` *the result so that the trailing newline is removed.*

You probably added a line that looks like this:

```
chomp ($name);
```

This is just fine. Later on, you may be tempted to try something like this:

```
$name = chomp (<STDIN>); # Bad Code!!
```

It's really okay to combine the read operation and the `chomp()` into one statement. But this instruction assigns the value 1 into `$name`. If you want to do this, your code should look like this:

```
chomp ($name = <STDIN>); # Good Code!!
```

c) Write the new program `newstory2.pl`.

Answer: The program you wrote might be slightly different from this one. It is presented here simply to give you an example of a working model.

NEWSTORY.PL

```
 1  #!/usr/bin/perl
 2
 3  print "Enter the name of a creature: ";
 4  chomp ($CREATURE = <STDIN>);
 5  print "Enter the name of a kingdom: ";
 6  chomp ($KINGDOM = <STDIN>);
 7  print "Enter the name of a monster: ";
 8  chomp ($MONSTER = <STDIN>);
 9  print "Enter the name of a profession: ";
10  chomp ($PROFESSION = <STDIN>);
11  print "Enter the name of a kitchen utensil: ";
12  chomp ($KITCHEN_UTENSIL = <STDIN>);
13  print "Enter the name of a tool: ";
14  chomp ($TOOL = <STDIN>);
15
16  print "\nOnce upon a time, a friendly $CREATURE \n",
17  "went on a vacation to far away $KINGDOM. \n",
18  "While he was there, he saw an evil $MONSTER \n",
19  "attacking a nice $PROFESSION with his giant \n",
20  "$KITCHEN_UTENSIL.  He beat the $MONSTER \n",
21  "mercilessly about the head and shoulders with his trusty \n",
```

```
22   "$TOOL.  Soon the $MONSTER apologized to \n",
23   "the $PROFESSION and rode away with a promise to \n",
24   "be nice from now on.  \n--The End--\n";
```

Although this might look like a lengthy program listing, there are really only three things going on here. First, the program prompts the operator for a response (as in *line 3*), then it gathers and runs chomp() on the response (as in *line 4*). At last, it prints a story (starting in *line 16*) using the values gathered from the initial dialog with the operator.

Note that the program uses a combined read and chomp() operation as we discussed earlier. Also notice that the story is printed with one long program instruction. We'll be working with this program again later in the book, so be sure that you're happy with your version at this point.

2.2.2 ANSWERS

a) What change must be made to the program in order to allow it to remove a file instead of simply dumping its contents to the screen?

Answer: To do this, you need to change the line that says:
```
system "cat $fname";
```

It needs to say:
```
system "rm $fname"; # or use "del $fname" for MS-DOS
```

This is not the "definitive" way to remove files in Perl, but it suits our purposes here. The point is that you can make your Perl program do anything you know how to do from the command-line prompt. As you continue your study of Perl, you'll learn many ways to do things with internal commands that are normally done with external programs in your shell scripts.

The only time you need to worry about whether to use an external command (that you already know) or search for a way to do it with a command that is built into Perl, is when you are planning to perform some task many times in quick succession. It's almost always faster to use Perl's built-in commands, but it matters only when you have a high repetition count.

b) Using the ideas illustrated in `newshell.pl`, write a program
(`newshell2.pl`) that allows the user to type in any command and
then submit that command to be executed by the shell.

Answer: This program meets the requirements.

NEWSHELL2.PL

```
1   #!/usr/bin/perl
2   print "What command?> ";
3   chomp ($cmd = <STDIN>);
4   system "$cmd";
```

*BEWARE: This is a very dangerous technique. As written, this program
doesn't present any more danger than giving the operator a login account
and a shell prompt. Whatever they can do with this program, they could
also do from the command line. But you should get an uneasy feeling any
time that your program is designed to execute instructions that are supplied by an outside source. In more complex programs, we are going to inspect any input for ques-
tionable patterns before we allow it to be executed.*

Visit the website for more information about this if security is
one of your concerns.

`http://www.phptr.com/phptrinteractive`

c) Write a program (`newdir.pl`) that prompts for a directory name
and then creates a directory with that name. Print the exit code.

Answer: Here's a program that meets the specs.

```
1   #!/usr/bin/perl
2   system "ls -CF";
3   print "\nName of new directory: ";
4   $dir = <STDIN>;
5   chomp $dir;
6   system "mkdir $dir";
7   print "Result code: [$?]\n";
8   system "ls -CF";
```

As a courtesy, this program begins by showing the contents of the current
directory. Then, in *lines 4-5*, it gathers and processes a directory name

typed in from the keyboard. Finally, it attempts to make the directory and then prints the result code.

Hopefully, this gives you some ideas about things that you can do with this technique.

Test your `newdir.pl` program with each of the following directory values and report the results.

d) `newdir`

> *Answer: This should have worked fine. Result code was 0. If you tried it a second time with the same value, it would fail with a result code of 1.*

The first time you run your program with this value, the program should succeed at creating the new directory. The result code of 0 tells us that nothing went wrong. If you try it again now, it should fail since the attempt to make a new directory cannot succeed if the directory already exists.

e) `/tmp/gooddirectory`

> *Answer: This should also have worked fine. Result code was 0. If you tried it a second time with the same value, it would fail with a result code of 1.*

The same rationale applies to this test as to the last one. The first time we should be successful at creating the new directory, the second attempt should fail. We're primarily concerned here with the business of inspecting result codes from a call to the `system()` function. In our more advanced programs, we can use techniques that will yield additional information about why an operation may have failed. We'll see more of that later.

f) `/badparent/newdir`

> *Answer: This should have failed with a result code of 1.*

Of course this could have succeeded, but only if you already have a directory called `/badparent` on your system. (If you do, don't bother trying to explain why.) In Chapter 6, "Tests and Branching," you'll learn how to check for the existence of a directory before you attempt to use it for something.

g) `/etc/newdirectory`

Answer:This fails with a result code of 1 on a UNIX system.

It wouldn't fail if you're testing the program as the root user, but you're far too wise for that. Aren't you? On an MS-DOS system, there probably isn't a `/etc` directory, so it would also fail. You could create such a directory and set the attributes to be read-only if you want to test this. (Your system documentation for the MKDIR and ATTRIB programs will explain how to do it.)

2.2.3 ANSWERS

a) Write a program (`identity.pl`) that stores the value for the current working directory in a variable called `$work` and the value for the system name in `$hname`. Print those values out in a message.

Answer:Your program may differ from this one, but it should run with roughly the same results.

IDENTITY.PL
```
1  #!/usr/bin/perl
2
3  chomp ($work = `pwd`); # use CD for MS-DOS
4  chomp ($hname = `uname -n`); # use VER for MS-DOS
5
6  print "My system name is $hname.\n";
7  print "My current directory is $work.\n";
```

If you forgot to put the *chomp()* command in, you already know what effect that has. If you did this right the very first time, then make a copy of your program and remove the *chomp()* command to see how that changes the result. It's very important to see what things look like when they go wrong. (So don't simply *visualize* the results; do this.)

b) Write a program (`dinfo.pl`) that stores information about files in the current directory in a variable called `$files`. Print that variable as part of a message.

Answer:Your program may be slightly different, but it should work like this one:

DINFO.PL

```
1  #!/usr/bin/perl
2  $files = `ls -l`; # use DIR for MS-DOS
3  print "File info for current directory:\n$files";
```

This program demonstrates that you can trap many lines of output in a simple variable. In Chapter 3, "Scalar Variables," we'll see how to manipulate information that can be gathered this way.

LAB 2.2   REVIEW QUESTIONS

1) Which of these reads a line of input from the console keyboard?
    a) _____ $input = read(KBD);
    b) _____ $input = <KEYBOARD>;
    c) _____ $input = <STDIN>;
    d) _____ $input = readln();

2) Which of these functions strips the trailing newline character from a line?
    a) _____ gobble();
    b) _____ nibble();
    c) _____ chomp();
    d) _____ tickle();

3) Which of these launches an external program on the system?
    a) _____ command("pgm -options");
    b) _____ execute("pgm -options");
    c) _____ spawn("pgm -options");
    d) _____ system("pgm -options");

4) Which of these runs an external program and "captures" the output?
    a) _____ $result = command("pgm -options");
    b) _____ $result = execute <command -options;
    c) _____ $result = `pgm -options`;
    d) _____ system("pgm -options", capture);

LAB 2.3

READING QUICKLY FROM A FILE

LAB OBJECTIVES

After this lab, you will be able to:

✓ Read from Files Named on the Command Line

✓ Read from a Single Named File

✓ Print Lengthy Messages

In this Lab, you'll learn how to read data from a file (or files) named on the command line into your program. This is a common requirement of a Perl program, and the structure of Perl allows us to easily accomplish this task. You'll also see how your program can read from one specific named file, whether the name is coded into the program or typed in by the program operator using techniques we've already seen.

And to round out the Lab, we'll look at two techniques for printing lengthy messages without having to employ several print() statements to do the job.

We begin by looking at a technique that you can use to read data from each of the files named on the command line. If your program can do this, it has the flexibility to be reused many times simply by changing the way that the operator starts the program.

■ FOR EXAMPLE

You might want to run a program with a command line that looks like this:

```
$ findbob.pl file1.txt file2.txt file3.txt
```

Or you might want your program command line to look something like:

```
$ countbob.pl story1 story2 story3
```

READ DATA FROM COMMAND-LINE FILES

To read from the files named on the command line, you need to use something that Perl programmers often call the "diamond operator." It consists of the less-than sign followed immediately by the greater-than sign (like this: <>). Where it appears, it acts a little bit like the phrase <STDIN> that we used in some of our earlier programs. The difference is that it reads lines of input from the files named on the command line instead of from the keyboard. (If there are no files named on the command line, the diamond operator reads from the keyboard just like <STDIN>.)

Here is a simple program that reads the first three lines from a file named on the command line:

THREELINES.PL
```
1   #!/usr/bin/perl
2   $l = <>;
3   print "Line one: $l";
4   $l = <>;
5   print "Line two: $l";
6   $l =<>;
7   print "Line three: $l";
```

When you run this program, don't forget to put the name of a file on the command line or else the diamond operator in *lines 2, 4,* and *6* will try to read from the keyboard. If you make this mistake, you'll have to type in three lines for the program to read. Here's a sample program run:

```
$ threelines.pl names.txt

Line one: Phil Greenbelt,MD

Line two: Bill Washington,DC

Line three: Mike San Antonio,TX
```

READ LINES UNTIL DONE

The program we just saw works as long as the input file has at least three lines, and even then it prints only the first three lines of the file. What we'd probably rather do is have our program read lines of input until they have all been read.

In fact, if you remember what we did in Chapter 1, "Getting Started," you will find this next technique familiar. In the first chapter, we used the `perl -n` option to cause our program to read each line and execute our instructions on each line.

We can do this in our program (without demanding that the program operator remember to use a specific option when the program is run) by putting the following construct in our code:

```
while ($ln = <>) {
    # some instruction(s), $ln is the input line
}
```

This has essentially the same effect as if we had run our program with the `perl -n` option. Before we look at the next program, you might want to know that there's a special Perl variable that indicates the current input line number. That variable is called `$.` and we'll use it in the next example to number the lines as we print them.

COUNTLINES.PL
```
1   #!/usr/bin/perl
2   while ($ln = <>) {
3       print "Line $.: $ln";
4   }
```

This program does more than simply count the lines in our input files (as the name suggests). It actually prints the lines with line numbers. Here's what the program run looks like:

```
$ countlines.pl names.txt
Line 1: Phil Greenbelt,MD
Line 2: Bill Washington,DC
Line 3: Mike San Antonio,TX
Line 4: Larry Sebastopol,CA
Line 5: Tom Mountain View,CA
```

Now that's progress! Just one more thing before we let the diamond operator rest.

PRINT ONLY MATCHING LINES

There are some side effects of using the diamond operator (and the `print()` statement, for that matter). We can use them to make our program a little more streamlined. Perl has a default variable (called $_, although you should seldom see it explicitly used) that holds the result of a read operation when we don't designate a variable to do the work. This default variable happens to be what the `print()` statement will print if you don't specify something explicitly. (We'll explore the default variable in detail in Chapter 3, "Scalar Variables.")

If we use the diamond operator without designating a variable to hold input, the data will be stored in $_. And if we call the `print()` function without giving it an argument, it prints the content of the default variable. (Great name for it, isn't it?) This makes it easy to have your program behave just as if you had run it with `perl -p`.

```
while (<>) {
    print;
}
```

That explains a bit why the next program works. The rest of the story is something that we'll take up again in Chapter 6, "Tests and Branching."

We want a program here that will read each line from the named files and print only the lines that contain a particular string or phrase. Here's the program:

FINDBOB.PL

```
1  #!/usr/bin/perl
2  # program looks for lines that contain bob
3  while (<>) {
4      /bob/ && print;
5  }
```

We can run this program on its own source code to confirm that it works. If it is correct, it should print out *lines 2* and *4*. Let's look at a program run:

```
$ findbob.pl findbob.pl
# program looks for lines that contain bob
    /bob/ && print;
```

That looks like a success to me.

READ FROM A SPECIFIC FILE

There will be times when it's more convenient to read information from a specific file that we can define at program design time. For instance, if you know that your program will need to read the contents of motd.txt, it would be cumbersome to require the program operator to remember to type the name of that file on the command line. Your program can be smart enough to take care of this without human intervention.

To read from a file, you need to perform three steps:

1. Open the file—provide a "filehandle" and the name of the file to be opened.
2. Read from the file—do this the same way you read from STDIN. Simply surround the filehandle name with angle brackets (<>).
3. Close the file when you are finished.

■ *FOR EXAMPLE*

Here's what it looks like when you don't need to do anything special:

```
open INPUT, "motd.txt";
$line = <INPUT>;
close INPUT;
```

This opens the named file, reads a line of input, and then closes the file. We'll explore this technique in much greater detail when we get to Chapter 8, "Files and I/O." For now, however, this will enable us to write some simple programs.

Let's look at one that can print the content of a message stored in an external file. We'll start with a small message that looks like this:

MOTD.TXT
```
All system users are directed to give blood
in recompense for excessive CPU and disk usage.
Emergency contact information must be on file with
System Adminstrator, Nurse Ratchett prior to giving
blood.  Have a nice day!
```

Rather than code this message into the program, we want to place it in an external file where it can be changed without alteration to our program.

ANNOUNCE.PL
```
1   #!/usr/bin/perl
2   open IN, "motd.txt";
3   while (<IN>) {
4       print;
5   }
6   close IN;
```

This program will print the contents of the `motd.txt` file whenever it runs. Now, let's look at another example. This one prints only the lines that contain the word "bob".

COUNTBOBS.PL
```
1   #!/usr/bin/perl
2   open IN, "findbob.pl";
3   while (<IN>) {
```

```
4       /bob/ && print;
5   }
```

This program opens a file that we know contains some instances of the name "bob" and prints only those lines that contain the word.

PRINTING LENGTHY MESSAGES

Sometimes it makes sense to put lengthy messages into a file that can be changed any time without altering the program. Other times, the message that the program prints should logically be part of the program. When the message is tightly linked to the purpose of the program, then it makes sense to embed messages right into the source code.

On the other hand, it isn't much fun to maintain a message that consists of a long series of `print()` statements that display quote strings.

■ *FOR EXAMPLE*

Consider the following:

```
print "All system users are directed to give blood";
print "in recompense for excessive CPU and disk usage.";
print "Emergency contact information must be on ";
print " file with System Adminstrator, Nurse ";
print " Ratchett prior to giving blood.";
print "Have a nice day!";
```

As long as you never have to change that message, everything should be okay. But if you decide to add a word in the middle, reformatting all of the text will be a painful task.

Fortunately, Perl gives us two ways to print a message that spans several lines. The easiest way is simply to use a multi-line quoted string.

For instance, we could print our message from the last example this way:

```
print "All system users are directed to give blood
in recompense for excessive CPU and disk usage.
Emergency contact information must be on file with
System Adminstrator, Nurse Ratchett prior to giving
blood.  Have a nice day!";
```

We've seen this technique before and it works great for most occasions. You do have to be careful, however, to close your quoted string. Failure to do this could result in the entire remainder of the program being interpreted as a simple text string.

Another problem that you might encounter is that your message may include literal quote marks as part of the intended content. Perl provides a way to print information in a fashion similar to what we did to print from a file earlier, but with a message that is embedded "here" in the script. It's done like this:

**LAB
2.3**

PRINTHERE.PL

```
1    #!/usr/bin/perl
2    print << "EOM";
3    <head><body background="/images/paper.jpg">
4    All system users are directed to give blood
5    in recompense for excessive CPU and disk usage.
6    Emergency contact information must be on file with
7    System Adminstrator, Nurse Ratchett prior to giving
8    blood.  Have a nice day!</body></head>
9    EOM
```

This program does a much better job of giving us a message that can be easily reformatted if the need arises. Everything between *lines 3* and *7* will be printed verbatim. The key is in *line 2* where the << symbols form something we call the "here document." They indicate to Perl that input should come from "here", as if it were being supplied by an external file.

The quoted string "EOM" is an arbitrary marker that you choose, knowing that it will not appear in the input text. Where that token appears on a line by itself, Perl knows that the input stream is finished.

Let's put these techniques to work in some experiments.

LAB 2.3 EXERCISES

2.3.1 READ FROM FILES NAMED ON THE COMMAND LINE

In the discussion, we saw a program called `countlines.pl` that could read from a program named on the command line. The example showed the program run with one file named on the command line.

a) Run the `countlines.pl` program with three files named on the command line. Does the line numbering reset when the second file begins to print?

_____

_____

b) Run the `countlines.pl` program with no files named on the command line. What happens? If you type in a line of text and hit the Enter key, what happens then? How do you get out of this program?

_____

_____

2.3.2 READ FROM A SINGLE NAMED FILE

In the discussion, we saw how to open a named file when the name is known at program design time. The example program used a literal filename, but there's no reason that name couldn't have been stored in a variable. For instance, it is perfectly reasonable to expect something like this:

```
$nm = 'names.txt';
open IN, "$nm";
```

a) Using this knowledge, write a short program (openany.pl) that prompts the user for a filename and then opens the named file for reading.

_____

_____

b) Extend openany.pl to create a new program (openany2.pl) that also prompts the user for a search string and then prints only lines that contain the string.

_____

_____

2.3.3 PRINTING LENGTHY MESSAGES

Uncle Larry had run his newstory2.pl *program so many times that his fingers felt like they were about to drop off from typing in the answers at each of the prompts. To improve the program, he decided that it would be useful to have the program read the information from a text file. Each response would be on a line by itself.*

He began to rewrite newstory2.pl *to create a new program he called* filestory.pl. *It would read lines from a file to simulate the user answers. Each line in the file will contain the answer to exactly one of our original questions. Here's an example of a legal input file:*

FILESTORY.TXT
```
Patent Attorney
Hong Kong
Software Counterfeiter
Call Center Manager
Cuisinart
Subpoena
```

a) Write your own `filestory.pl`. It should behave just like Larry's. When you print the story, use the "here document" feature to make the story easier to modify.

LAB 2.3 EXERCISE ANSWERS

2.3.1 ANSWERS

a) Run the `countlines.pl` program with three files named on the command line. Does the line numbering reset when the second file begins to print?

Answer: No. Whenever we use the diamond operator, the line numbering remains continuous. This can turn out to be handy for concatenating files into a single numbered set.

b) Run the `countlines.pl` program with no files named on the command line. What happens? If you type in a line of text and hit the Enter key, what happens then? How do you get out of this program?

Answer: If you do this, then the diamond operator expects to read from STDIN. This means that you'll have to type in some lines of information.

As you finish entering each line, you will see that the program reads the line and then prints the line with the associated line number information. To make the program end, you'll have to press the end-of-file key. (Ctrl-D on a UNIX system; Ctrl-Z on an MS-DOS system.)

2.3.2 ANSWERS

**LAB
2.3**

a) Write a short program (`openany.pl`) that prompts the user for a
filename and then opens the named file for reading.

*Answer: Here is a program that meets these requirements. Your program may differ
somewhat. Run this one and be sure that your program acts the same way.*

OPENANY.PL
```
I   #!/usr/bin/perl
2   print "Enter the name of a file: ";
3   chomp ($nm = <STDIN>);
4   open IN, "$nm";
5   while (<IN>) {
6       print;
7   }
```

From this we can see that the second argument to the `open()` function
may be a variable that holds the name of a file.

b) Extend `openany.pl` to create a new program (`openany2.pl`)
that also prompts the user for a search string and then prints only lines
that contain the string.

*Answer: As long as your program behaves as this one does, it doesn't necessarily have
to look like this:*

OPENANY2.PL
```
I   #!/usr/bin/perl
2   print "Enter the name of a file: ";
3   chomp ($nm = <STDIN>);
4   print "Enter a search string: ";
5   chomp ($ss = <STDIN>);
6   open IN, "$nm";
7   while (<IN>) {
8       /$ss/ && print;
9   }
```

This program required a little bit of extrapolation and a leap of faith. We
had seen programs that could conditionally print a line that contained a

static pattern, but it was not necessarily clear that we could search for a variable. If you had trouble with this Exercise, don't worry. It was here to see if you'd take that great leap. In Chapter 6, "Tests and Branching," we will take a longer look at pattern matching and see how to do a more precise job of conditional printing.

2.3.3 ANSWERS

a) Write your own `filestory.pl`. It should behave just like Larry's . When you print the story, use the "here document" feature to make the story easier to modify.

   Answer: Here is one way that the program can be written. Yours may be different, but it should probably be similar.

FILESTORY.PL
```
 1  #!/usr/bin/perl
 2  open IN, "filestory.txt";
 3  chomp ($CREATURE = <IN>);
 4  chomp ($KINGDOM = <IN>);
 5  chomp ($MONSTER = <IN>);
 6  chomp ($PROFESSION = <IN>);
 7  chomp ($KITCHEN_UTENSIL = <IN>);
 8  chomp ($TOOL = <IN>);
 9  close IN;
10
11  print << "EndOfStory";
12  Once upon a time, a friendly $CREATURE
13  went on a vacation to far away $KINGDOM.
14  While he was there, he saw an evil $MONSTER
15  attacking a nice $PROFESSION with his giant
16  $KITCHEN_UTENSIL.  He beat the $MONSTER
17  mercilessly about the head and shoulders with his trusty
18  $TOOL.  Soon the $MONSTER apologized to
19  the $PROFESSION and rode away with a promise to
20  be nice from now on.  --The End--
21  EndOfStory
```

Now the program can be used many times and the story will be different as long as the contents of the input file are changed. For extra credit, see if you can fix the program so that the name of the input file can be specified on the command line.

A solution will be provided on the companion website, located at:

`http://www.phptr.com/phptrinteractive/`

LAB 2.3 REVIEW QUESTIONS

1) Which of the following is used to read lines from a file named as an argument on the command line?
   a) _____ `while ($in = <ARG>){`
   b) _____ `while ($in = <$ARGV[0]>) {`
   c) _____ `while ($in = <>) {`
   d) _____ `while (chomp($in = <IN>)) {`

2) Which of the following opens a file called "names.txt" for reading?
   a) _____ `open ">names.txt" || die "failed";`
   b) _____ `open IN, ">names.txt" || die "failed";`
   c) _____ `open IN, "names.txt";`
   d) _____ `open IN "names.txt" || die "failed";`

3) Which of the following prints only lines from an input file that contain the word "peaches"?
   a) _____ `while (<IN>){ /peaches/ && print }`
   b) _____ `print while (<IN>) == "peaches";`
   c) _____ `while (<IN> == "peaches") {print;}`
   d) _____ `while (chomp(<IN>) == "peaches")`
   `{print;}`

4) Which of the following is the correct way to employ the "here document"?
   a) _____ `print "HERE" {`
   b) _____ `print "<<HERE";`
   c) _____ `print "<<EOM"`
   d) _____ `print <<"EOM";`

CHAPTER 2

TEST YOUR THINKING

Using a combination of the techniques that you saw in this chapter, you can create a program that searches for text in file named by the program operator.

1)   Write a program that searches for text by performing the following steps:

    a) Run a system command to display a list of files in the current directory.

    b) Display a prompt that asks for a filename.

    c) Open the named file, exit if there is an error.

    d) Display a prompt that asks for a target text string.

    e) Read all the lines of the named input file, printing each line that contains the target string.

If you want to make your program more flexible, you can allow the program operator to supply a list of filenames separated by spaces. Your program can search for the target string in all of the named files by "stuffing" that list into the space reserved for the command-line arguments and then reading from the files with the "diamond operator". Here's some code that would set this up:

```
print "Enter a list of file names separated by spaces.\n";
print "For example: file1.txt file2.html file3.readme: ";
@ARGV = split /\s+/, <STDIN>;
while (<>) {
    # process the input lines
}
```

2)   Modify your program to use this approach and give it a try. (Remember that we'll be talking about these techniques in much greater detail later, but whatever you learn from doing this now, you can begin to use right away.)

CHAPTER 3

VARIABLES: LARGE AND SMALL

<table>
<tr><td colspan="2" align="center">**CHAPTER OBJECTIVES**</td></tr>
<tr><td colspan="2">In this chapter, you will learn about:</td></tr>
<tr><td>✓ Identifier Names and Scalar Variables</td><td>Page 84</td></tr>
<tr><td>✓ Simple Operators</td><td>Page 98</td></tr>
<tr><td>✓ Scalars and Context</td><td>Page 111</td></tr>
<tr><td>✓ Special Scalar Variables</td><td>Page 122</td></tr>
</table>

Variables allow your program to store useful information. They can serve as a way to declare a value that is used throughout the program. They can allow your program to gather information from some outside source and remember that information. They can serve as placeholders when you conduct repetitive processes, each time doing something a little differently, depending upon the information contained in the variable.

As an example, imagine that your program has asked the operator for the name of a file. A variable can be created to hold the answer. That variable can be referenced later when it is time to open the file, delete it, or write information into it.

A variable can range from a simple slot in memory designated to hold a number or a message to a large block of memory that can hold the entire contents of a file. Variables that hold simple information are called *scalar variables*. A table of scalar values that we might reference by index number or position within the table is called an *array*. A table can also hold information that is referenced by some arbitrary name, or key. We call this type of table an associative array or, more properly, a *hash*.

L A B   3.1

IDENTIFIER NAMES AND SCALAR VARIABLES

LAB OBJECTIVES

After this Lab, you will be able to:

✓ Declare and Initialize Scalar Variables

✓ Write a Short Program Using Variables

As you write your program, you will need to create variables to store information. That information could be a number or a text string.   In this Lab, you'll see how to form a legal variable name, how to assign information to a variable, and how to print the value stored inside one.

To create a variable, we must give it a legal identifier (that is, a name). An identifier is simply a name that conforms with certain rules. Those rules are:

- Identifiers must begin with a letter.
- The initial letter may be followed by any number of letters, digits, or underscore characters.
- When an identifier is going to be used for a scalar variable (or an array or hash), it will not conflict with any reserved words because it will always have a prefix (such as $, @, or %).
- Certain types of identifiers will not be used with prefixes (labels, filehandles, and sometimes function names) and

they may avoid conflict with reserved words by using mixed case or strictly upper case.
- Case is significant (that is, *logfile*, *LogFile*, and *Logfile* are all different from one another).

■ FOR EXAMPLE

The following are legal identifiers:

filename	Filename	FileName
Sally	sally1	sally225
LOG	LOG1	log_1
user0	username	Username

The Whole Truth

The rules for constructing identifier names are more complicated than what I've just described. Some of you will insist on knowing the entire truth, so here it is.

The Perl language specification allows identifier names to begin with a digit, but the entire name must then consist only of digits. An identifier may begin with an underscore, and may then contain letters, digits, or more underscores after that. An identifier may begin with something other than a letter, digit, or underscore, but then must be only one character in length. Save yourself trouble. Stick with letters and digits. That way, you won't choose a name that conflicts with something important defined in the system.

CONTENTS OF A SCALAR VARIABLE

A scalar value can be a number or a text string. Numbers may be represented with or without quotes. When a variable that stores a number is seen in a *numeric context*, the value will be treated as a number. By this, I mean that if you store the value 101 in a variable (say, $amount), when you add it to the number 3, you will get 104. On the other hand, if you append the string " Dalmations" to the value, you will end up with a string that contains "101 Dalmations".

■ *FOR EXAMPLE*

```
$amount = 101;
$amount = "101"; # does the same thing
$quantity = 1;
$remaining = $amount - $quantity; # numeric context: subtraction
$title = $amount . " Tin Soldier"; # string context: append opera-
tion
```

Text strings should always be presented with quotes. You might get away with using a text string that is not embedded in quotes, but it will be because you're lucky, not because you're practicing sound programming techniques. If your programs depend upon luck, you're a witch doctor, not an engineer.

The issues related to context are explored in more detail later in the lesson.

BRINGING A SCALAR VARIABLE TO LIFE

A variable comes into existence in Perl the first time it is mentioned. It need not be formally declared, although you may do so. Let's take a look at how variables might be created, and filled with information.

■ *FOR EXAMPLE*

```
$freezing = 32;
$boiling = "212";
$username = "Sally";
($d1temp, $d2temp, $d3temp) = (78, 85, 82);
$liquidRange = $boiling - $freezing;
```

In this example, the number 32 is stored in a variable named $freezing. The number 212 is stored in $boiling, and the text string "Sally" is stored in $username. The three variables ($d1temp, $d2temp, and $d3temp) are initialized to the values from the subsequent list. The variable $liquidRange is created to store the result of the expression subtracting $freezing from $boiling.

QUOTED STRINGS

Because I've raised this issue, it seems only fair to tell you some things about the different types of quotes. You've already seen code that uses *double quotes*. Within double quotes, spaces, newlines, and tabs will be considered part of the string. In addition, a special set of escape sequences is available within double quotes. These include:

\t	tab	\n	newline
\r	return	\f	form feed
\v	vertical tab	\a	alarm (bell)
\e	escape	\033	octal char
\x1b	hex char	\c[	control char
\l	lowercase next char	\u	uppercase next char
\L	lowercase until \E	\U	uppercase until \E
\E	end case modification		

Any variable references within double quotes will be *interpolated* (that is, the value held in the variable will be substituted where the variable name appears). To suppress this behavior, it is possible to precede the variable reference with a \ character. (For example, if you want to literally print $user, you would code `print "\$user";`)

An alternative way of using double quotes is an operator that looks like this:

```
qq{This is a quoted string that supports $variable interpolation.}
```

The curly braces used to delimit the quoted string are an arbitrary (but commonly used) choice. After the `qq` sequence, you may use any delimiter you like.

■ *FOR EXAMPLE*

```
qq/This is a quoted string/;
qq(There are $count users online.);
qq{It's handy when you have literal "quoted passages" within the text}
qq|Any "delimiter" may be used.|;
```

Another useful quoting mechanism is provided by *'single quotes'*. Within single quotes, variables are not interpolated. Ordinary quotation marks will be preserved instead of interpreted. In fact, a rule that you might remember that helps explain single quotes is this:

Inside a single quoted string, everything is treated literally except another instance of the single quote.

As with the double-quoted string, there is an alternative quoting mechanism that you might find handy from time to time. It looks very similar to the preceding examples, except that the operator is a single q instead of double.

■ FOR EXAMPLE

```
q{This is a single-quoted string};
q|Special $symbols will be used literally|;
q(And the 'rules' remain the same);
```

LAB 3.1 EXERCISES

3.1.1 DECLARE AND INITIALIZE SCALAR VARIABLES

Examine the following list of variable names:

$name	$completed%	$1value
$value1	$name_100	$100name
$%completed	$last-name	$value

a) Which of these are legal names for a scalar variable?

_____

_____

b) List each of the illegal names, and give a reason for each being illegal.

_____

_____

c) Write the code that will declare a variable called `score` and initialize it to 0.

_____

_____

d) Write the code that declares a variable called `player1` and initialize it to the value `Chili Palmer`.

_____

_____

Look at the code in the following lines and predict what will be printed. Assume that $boiling and $freezing have been set to 212 and 32 as in the previous examples. Test the code and confirm your conclusion

e) `print qq{Boiling temperature in Fahrenheit: $boiling\n};`

_____

_____

f) `print q{Freezing temperature in Fahrenheit: $freezing\n};`

_____

_____

g) `print qq{Liquid range for water: $boiling - $freezing\n];`

_____

_____

h) `print q{Range: $boiling - $freezing:},$boiling-$freezing,"\n";`

_____

_____

Read the following program, then run it and answer the question that follows.

vars1.pl
```
1   #!/usr/bin/perl
2
3   $num1, $num2, $num3;
4   $num1 = 2;
5   $num2 = 4;
6   $num3 = 8;
7
8   ($n4, $n5, $n6) = (16, 32, 64);
9
10  print '$num1 is: ', $num1, "\n";
11  print '$num2 is: ', $num2, "\n";
12  print "\$num3 is: $num3\n";
13
14  printf "%8s %8s %8s\n", '$n4', '$n5', '$n6';
15  printf "%8d %8d %8d\n", $n4, $n5, $n6;
```

i) What output do we get from `vars1.pl`?

_____

_____

3.1.2 WRITE A SHORT PROGRAM USING VARIABLES

You're ready now to write a program that uses variables. At first, we'll write a short program that creates and initializes variables, then prints them. After that, we'll get information from the program user and put that information into a variable, then print it.

HARDCODE THE VARIABLE VALUES

Coach Randal reflected on his career. He'd gone into coaching for the thrill of game day. He loved that feeling he got when the lights came on, when the team ran out *onto the field, resplendent in their uniforms, and the crowd roared. Nobody had ever told him about the other side of the business. Somebody had to pay the bills to get those lights to come on. Someone had to make arrangements for those uniforms and it cost money to get the word out to the crowd so that they'd know where to go and roar.*

Just now, he was thinking about the problems he'd faced keeping track of team sponsors and the amounts they'd pledged to contribute to help pay for things that keep a squad on the field. Uncle Larry had told Joe that he could write a couple of programs in Perl to handle the details. "Just think through all the steps that it takes to solve the problem, then write a program to perform those steps," Larry has said, "Then you can go back to figuring out how to avoid turning the ball over so much."

See if you can write a simple program that will solve at least some of Coach Randal's problem.

> **a)** Create a simple program that establishes variables for three sponsors, and variables to hold phone numbers for each of them. The program should declare and initialize variables for each sponsor, and for each phone number. Print each of the variable names and their values. The following table gives you some sample values.

Sponsor	Phone Number
Bob's ACME Hardware	650-555-3939
Quick Pak Grocery	408-555-9393
Honest Al's Auto Insurance	650-555-3171

> **b)** Write a program that takes the names and phone numbers of three sponsors from the console keyboard and stores them in vari-

ables. At the end, the program should print out the sponsor names and their phone numbers.

LAB 3.1 EXERCISE ANSWERS

3.1.1 ANSWERS

Look at the list of variable names presented.

a) Which of these are legal names for a scalar variable?

Answer: The legal variable names are as follows:

`$value`	`$name_100`
`$name`	`$value1`

b) List each of the illegal names and give a reason for each being illegal.

Answer: The illegal names are as follows:

`$completed%`	- Contains a % symbol in the name.
`$1value`	- Begins with a digit, contains non-digit characters.
`$100name`	- Same as above.
`$%completed`	- Contains % symbol in the name.
`$last-name`	- Contains a hyphen in the name.

c) Write the code that will declare a variable called `score` and initialize it to 0.

Answer: This instruction does the trick:
```
$score = 0;
```

Notice that it is not necessary to embed the value in quotes. When we refer to numeric literals, we can present them this way. If, on the other hand, you put quote marks around the value, Perl will interpret the value the same way. It's safe to use quote marks if you want to, and it's safe in this case to leave them off.

d) Write the code that declares a variable called `player1` and initialize it to the value `Chili Palmer`.

Answer:This code is what we need:
```
$player1 = "Chili Palmer";
```

It is imperative that we put quote marks around our value in this case. The value consists of a string that includes spaces. And if there were no spaces in the value, we would still want to surround it with quotes for clarity.

Look at the code in the following lines and predict what will be printed. Assume that `$boiling` and `$freezing` have been set to 212 and 32, as in the previous examples. Test the code and confirm your conclusion.

e) `print qq{Boiling temperature in Fahrenheit: $boiling\n};`

Answer: Here's what happens when this instruction runs:
Boiling temperature in Fahrenheit: 212

Variables are interpolated when they appear inside double quotes, or inside strings protected by the `qq{}` construct.

f) `print q{Freezing temperature in Fahrenheit: $freezing\n};`

Answer:This is what you get from this one:
Freezing temperature in Fahrenheit: $freezing\n

Neither the variable nor the special escape character for a newline (\n) can be interpreted inside a single quote or the `q{}` operator. Usually that's how we want it anyway. This style of quote is helpful to keep things from being misinterpreted. (Too bad there's nothing like it in natural language to help us with interpersonal communications.)

g) `print qq{Liquid range for water: $boiling - $freezing\n};`

Answer:This instruction prints:
```
Liquid range for water: 212 -32
```

The variables are interpolated inside this construct (as they would be for a double quoted string), but the expression that includes the subtraction operator cannot be interpreted. Our next example does the job correctly.

h) `print q{Range: $boiling - $freezing:},$boiling-`
`    $freezing,"\n";`

Answer: This code will produce:
Range: $boiling - $freezing:180

This is more like what we're trying to do. Notice that we probably want to insert a trailing space in our literal line if we want to see some separation between the string and the value. This is one of those things that you will usually tweak during the development cycle after you've seen how your program runs.

i) What output do you get from the `vars1.pl` program?

Answer: You should see the following:
```
$num1 is: 2
$num2 is: 4
$num3 is: 8


    $n4       $n5       $n6
    16        32        64
```

Not a terribly interesting program, and the output isn't that exciting either. But you can see from this how to write your own programs to use variables. (Please choose better names for your variables.)

Perhaps the most interesting part of this program is the last couple of lines that use `printf()` to produce output. This function is very much like `print()` with one major exception. The string to be printed may contain format fields. Those fields must be filled by expressions named later in the argument list to `printf()`. For instance, in *line 10* you can see a field specified as `%8s`. This means that eight positions will be preserved in the output to hold *string* data. In *line 11*, you see a field specified as %8d, which means that eight spaces will be held in reserve to represent a *decimal integer*.

This example shows you a little bit of what you can do with the function; we'll discuss it in more detail as we find need for it.

3.1.2 ANSWERS

a) Create a simple program that establishes variables for three sponsors, and variables to hold phone numbers for each of them. The program should declare and initialize variables for each sponsor, for each phone number. Print each of the variable names and their values.

Answer: There are many ways this program could be written. Here is one working example:

sponsor1.pl

```
1   #!/usr/bin/perl
2
3   $s1 = "Bob's ACME Hardware";
4   $s2 = "Quick Pack Grocery";
5   $s3 = "Honest Al's Auto Insurance";
6   $s1p = "650-555-3939";
7   $s2p = "408-555-9393";
8   $s3p = "650-555-3171";
9   print "\$s1: $s1 \t \$s1p: $s1p\n";
10  print "\$s2: $s2 \t \$s2p: $s2p\n";
11  print "\$s3: $s3 \t \$s3p: $s3p\n";
```

 By the way, don't worry just yet if the lines of your report don't line up. We'll deal with that later.

b) Write a program that takes the names and phone numbers of three sponsors from the console keyboard and stores them in variables. At the end, the program should print out the sponsor names and their phone numbers.

Answer: There are several ways to write this program. Here is one that fulfills the requirements:

sponsor2.pl

```perl
1   #!/usr/bin/perl
2
3   print "Please enter the name of a sponsor: ";
4   $s1 = <STDIN>;
5   chomp $s1;
6   print "Please enter the phone number for $s1: ";
7   $s1p = <STDIN>;
8   chomp $s1p;
9
10  print "Please enter the name of a sponsor: ";
11  $s2 = <STDIN>;
12  chomp $s2;
13  print "Please enter the phone number for $s2: ";
14  $s2p = <STDIN>;
15  chomp $s2p;
16
17  print "Please enter the name of a sponsor: ";
18  chomp ($s3 = <STDIN>);
19  print "Please enter the phone number for $s3: ";
20  chomp ($s3p = <STDIN>);
21
22  print "Sponsor: $s1 \t Phone: $s1p\n";
23  print "Sponsor: $s2 \t Phone: $s2p\n";
24  print "Sponsor: $s3 \t Phone: $s3p\n";
```

This program looks a lot like the one we discussed in the Exercise text. Note, however, that in *lines 18-20*, the chomp() is conducted directly on the read operation. This is permissible and actually quite common. If you want to do it that way, be sure not to make the mistake of saying:

```perl
$s3p = chomp (<STDIN>); # wrong!
```

 Remember that chomp() returns a count of the number of characters removed from the string. In this case, then, $s3p would be assigned the number 1.

LAB 3.1 SELF-REVIEW QUESTIONS

In order to test your progress, you should be able to answer the following questions.

1) A scalar variable can hold which of the following?
   a) _____ Only numeric information
   b) _____ Any numeric or string information
   c) _____ Up to 12 pounds of meat or grain
   d) _____ Only string information

2) A scalar variable name is immediately preceded by which of the following?
   a) _____ Any whitespace character
   b) _____ A % sign
   c) _____ A marching brass corps
   d) _____ A $ sign

3) Which of the following variable names is legal?
   a) _____ $1var
   b) _____ $1_var
   c) _____ $profit$
   d) _____ $v1alue

4) When string information is to be stored in a scalar variable, it should be enclosed in quotes.
   a) _____ True
   b) _____ False

A program contains these two instructions:
```
$name = "bob\n";
$end = chomp ($name);
```

5) Which of the following is true?
   a) _____ $name is "bob", $end is "\n"
   b) _____ $name is "bob\n", $end is "1"
   c) _____ $name is "bob", $end is "1"
   d) _____ $name is "Mick", $end is "near"

Quiz answers appear in Appendix A, Section 3.1.

L A B   3.2

SIMPLE OPERATORS

LAB OBJECTIVES

After this Lab you will be able to:

✓ Predict the Behavior of Simple Operators

✓ Write a Simple Program That Does Calculations

Operators are the tools that allow us to conduct arithmetic computations, string manipulations, value comparisons, and file test operations. The list of operators available in Perl is large. We will focus here on only those operators that deal with simple arithmetic and string computations. The others will be relevant at other spots in our journey and we'll examine them at that time.

ARITHMETIC (AND TWO OTHER) OPERATORS

The list of arithmetic operators used in Perl is not particularly daunting. Study Table 3.1 for a few moments to understand them best.

Table 3.1 Perl Arithmetic Operators

Operator	Operation	Example
=	assignment	`$value = 12; # $value gets 12`
+	addition	`$v1 = 5 + $value; # $v1 gets 17`
–	subtraction	`$v2 = 37 – $v1; # $v2 gets 20`
*	multiplication	`$v3 = $v2 * 10; # $v3 gets 200`

Operator	Operation	Example
/	division	`$v4 = $v3 / 8; # $v4 gets 25`
%	modulus	`$v5 = $v3 % 7; # $v5 gets 4`
		`$v6 = 32 % 10; # $v6 gets 2`
.	concatenation	`$msg = "w" . $v5 . " form";`
		`# $msg gets "w4 form"`
x	replication	`$bar = "-=" x 5;`
		`# $bar gets "-=-=-=-=-="`
**	exponentiation	`$v7 = $v5 ** 2; # $v7 becomes 16`
++	increment	`$v6++; # $v6 becomes 3`
--	decrement	`$v7--; # $v7 becomes 15`

**LAB
3.2**

You will certainly recall the effect of addition, subtraction, multiplication, and division. You may want to be reminded that modulus returns the remainder from integer division between the two operands. It can be useful when we want to ensure that a value remains within a bounded range.

■ FOR EXAMPLE

Imagine that you want a value that is guaranteed to fall between 0 and 9. It is easy to accomplish this with the modulus operator.

```
$v1 = $somevalue % 10; # $v1 is certainly between 0 and 9
$noteven = $v1 %  2; # $noteven will be 1 if $v1 is an odd number
```

The increment and decrement operators are what we call *unary operators*. That is, they require only one operand. Either of these operators may appear before or after its operand. If the operator appears first, the operand is altered (incremented or decremented) before it is used in any larger expression in which it appears. If the operator appears after the operand, the value of the operand is used in the larger expression, and then altered.

■ FOR EXAMPLE

```
$v1 = 10;
$v2 = 5 + $v1++; # $v2 gets 15, $v1 becomes 11 afterward
$v2++; # $v2 becomes 16, same as ++$v2;
$v3 = ++$v2 + $v1++; # $v3 gets 28, $v2 becomes 17, $v1 becomes 12
```

When the increment operator is used in a statement by itself (as in our third example here), it does not matter whether the operator is before or after the operand.

COMBINED ASSIGNMENT OPERATORS

Each of the simple arithmetic operators is augmented by a *combined assignment operator.*

■ FOR EXAMPLE

To see how these work, imagine that you want to accomplish the following effect:

```
$value = $value + 10;
```

With the combined assignment operator for addition, we can shorten this phrase to:

```
$value =+ 10;
```

Table 3.2 shows a list of these operators.

Table 3.2 Combined Assignment Operators

Operator	Description	Example
+=	assignment with addition	$val = 100; $val += 44; # $val gets 144
-=	assignment with subtraction	$val -= 16; # $val gets 128
*=	assignment with multiplication	$val *= 2; # $val gets 256
/=	assignment with division	$val /= 16; # $val gets 16
%=	assignment with modulus	$val %= 12; # $val gets 4

Operator	Description	Example
. =	assignment with string append	$val .= ".0" # $val gets 4.0
**=	assignment with exponentiation	$val **= 4; # $val gets 256

These operators are primarily useful to help make your code more concise. Usually that's a good thing. Just remember that brevity of code is a dual-edged sword; it should be wielded wisely to avoid bloodshed. Consider:

```
$a = 10; $b = 10; $c = 5; $d = 7;
$a+=++$b-$c---++$d;
```

That second statement is a legal Perl instruction, but would you want to try to figure it out when you're in a hurry to make a deadline for modifications to the program in which it appears?

If that's not enough incentive, remember that the maintenance programmer who has to work on your code will most likely be you, six months after you've written the first draft of the program. (By the way, if you guessed 8 for the phrase above, you were right. If you guessed something else—well, who could blame you?)

PRECEDENCE OF OPERATORS

The order in which operators are evaluated affects the value of an expression. For instance, you might be able to predict the result of

```
2 + 4 * 5
```

if you recall high school algebra. (If you thought it should be 22 rather than 30, you remember correctly.)

You may even accurately recall that

```
3 * 2 ** 3
```

turns out to be 24 rather than 216. Effectively, we might have said

```
3 * (2 ** 3)
```

to get the same result. The good news for Perl programmers is that the rules you learned in algebra still apply. (C and Java programmers will be happy to find that the rules for operators from those languages also apply in Perl.)

A chart illustrating the order of precedence among operators seems to be an obligatory part of any programmer's text. I certainly don't want to disappoint you. Before I present that table, however, please consider this old saw often uttered by experienced programmers:

Multiplication and division come before addition and subtraction. Everything else should be enclosed in parentheses.

This is good advice for readable code.

Oh, that table I promised.

Table 3.3 Operator Precedence

Operator	Associativity
++ --	None
**	Right to Left
* / %	Left to Right
+ -	Left to Right
= += -= *= /= %/ **=	Right to Left

Order of precedence from highest to lowest is shown here for the operators we've considered thus far. The operators at the top of the list have the highest precedence.

Associativity helps to "break the tie" when several operators with the same precedence appear in an expression.

■ *FOR EXAMPLE*

If we have the phrase

```
5 * 3 % 10
```

we might not be sure if we should first multiply 5 by 3 or get the remainder of division of 3 by 10. Both the multiplication and modulus operators have the same precedence. Because we are told that associativity of both operators is left to right, we can count on the fact that the multiplication takes place first.

Similarly, if we aren't sure how to evaluate

```
5 ** 3 ** 2
```

we can consult our table to learn that exponentiation is associative from right to left. This means that we'd take the square of three and, with that result (9), raise 5 to the 9th power.

Sometimes you may not be sure and the reference table isn't handy. This is why we use parentheses! If you use them where they are not necessary, nothing bad will happen.

LAB 3.2 EXERCISES

3.2.1 PREDICT THE BEHAVIOR OF SIMPLE OPERATORS

Predict the value of the following expressions (results should be cumulative):

a) `$val = 5 * 7 + 3 * 3;`

_____

_____

b) `$val += 10 ** 2;`

_____

_____

c) `$val /= 42 % 15;`

_____

_____

3.2.2 WRITE A SIMPLE PROGRAM THAT DOES CALCULATIONS

Coach Randal listened to the phone ring at the distant end of the connection. "I hope Uncle Larry is home today. I could use the advice," he thought. After a moment, a brisk voice replaced the ringing. "This had better be good. My tea kettle is about to boil."

Randal explained the reason for his call. "Sorry to bother you, Larry. It's just that I'm working on this Perl program and I could use your help." Larry's tone changed. "Oh, it's you, Randal. You're always welcome to call. Just what is the trouble, me lad?" Joe described the prototype program he was trying to write. He wanted to store sponsor information in a set of variables, and then record changes to one of the values. The information he wanted to store was the sponsor name, phone number, and the amount of each sponsor's pledge. He then wanted to prompt a user, accept an input amount, and modify the sponsor pledge by that amount.

Larry brightened. "This is a good start. What I want you to do now is take the problem a little bit at a time. You've already written a program that stores some of that information in a set of variables. Modifying that to include a pledge amount is fairly trivial. But rather than writing this prototype to use pledge amounts that you hardcode into the opening phrases of your program, I'd like you to learn about generating random numbers. (Actually, they're pseudo-random, but it's far too close to dinner to quibble over something like that.)

"You can use this phrase to get a random number:

```
$number = rand(99999);
```

The number you get will be between 0 and 99999. It will be a fractional number, and you'll want to take only the integer part of that. So you can write:

```
int ($number);
```

to round the value off to a whole number. Now if you divide that number by 100, you'll have some dollar amount between 0 and 1000 dollars. If you initialize your data this way, you'll know something new when you're done. Just remember, build your program in small steps, don't try to tackle the whole job at once. And when you get the data from the program user, don't forget to `chomp()`*."*

**LAB
3.2**

Randal thought about this advice and it all made sense to him. "Thanks, Larry. I think I can tackle this prototype now." Larry cheerily replied, "Oh, speaking of tackling, I was at your last game and there's some other advice I wanted to give you—oh darn. The kettle is boiling, gotta go!" The line went dead and Randal breathed a loud sigh of relief. He turned to his keyboard to start the new program.

> **a)** For each of the sponsors created in `sponsor1.pl`, initialize variables with the sponsor name and phone number. Generate a random number between 1.00 and 999.00 to represent the amount pledged by the sponsor. Print a report that shows the initial state of this data set.   Now prompt the user once for each sponsor to enter a numeric value. Subtract the value from the pledge amount and at the end, print the report again, showing the new amounts.

Here is a rough example of what the report should look like:

```
Sponsor      Amount      Phone
Bob's ACME   $ 129.39    650-555-3939
Quick Pak    $ 873.89    408-555-9393
Honest Al    $ 217.15    650-555-3171
```

LAB 3.2 EXERCISE ANSWERS

3.2.1 ANSWERS

Predict the value of the following expressions (results should be cumulative):

a) `$val = 5 * 7 + 3 * 3;`

Answer: 44. As you probably expected, the multiplications are conducted first: (5*7) + (3*3) is really 35+9 which is, of course, 44.

b) `$val += 10 ** 2;`

Answer: 144. Because `$val` *began as 44, when it is added to "ten squared," the total value becomes 144.*

c) `$val /= 42 % 15;`

Answer: 12. The result of 42% 15 is 12. When 144 is divided by that value, it becomes 12.

3.2.2 ANSWERS

a) For each of the sponsors created in `sponsor1.pl`, initialize variables with the company name and phone number. Generate a random number between 1.00 and 999.00 to represent the amount pledged by the sponsor. Print a report that shows the initial state of this data set. Now prompt the user once for each sponsor to enter a numeric value. Subtract the value from the pledge amount and at the end, print the report again, showing the new amounts.

Answer: There are many ways this program could be written. Here is one working example:

sponsor3.pl

```
1  #!/usr/bin/perl
2
3  $s1 = "Bob's ACME Hardware";
4  $s1p = "650-555-3939";
5  $s1amt = int (rand 99999) / 100;
```

LAB
3.2

```
 6
 7   $s2 = "Quick Pack Grocery";
 8   $s2p = "408-555-9393";
 9   $s2amt = int (rand 99999) / 100;
10
11   $s3 = "Honest Al's Auto Insurance";
12   $s3p = "650-555-3171";
13   $s3amt = int (rand 99999) / 100;
14
15   # formatted report
16   printf "%-38s  \$ %7s  %14s\n", "Sponsor", "Pledge", "Phone";
17   printf "%-38s  \$ %7.2f  %14s\n", $s1, $s1amt, $s1p;
18   printf "%-38s  \$ %7.2f  %14s\n", $s2, $s2amt, $s2p;
19   printf "%-38s  \$ %7.2f  %14s\n", $s3, $s3amt, $s3p;
20
21   # process the checks
22   print "\n\nPlease enter amount paid by $s1: ";
23   chomp ($chg = <STDIN>);
24   $s1amt -= $chg;
25
26   print "\n\nPlease enter amount paid by $s2: ";
27   chomp ($chg = <STDIN>);
28   $s2amt -= $chg;
29
30   print "\n\nPlease enter amount paid by $s3: ";
31   chomp ($chg = <STDIN>);
32   $s3amt -= $chg;
33
34   # another formatted report
35   printf "%-38s  \$ %7s  %14s\n", "Sponsor", "Pledge", "Phone";
36   printf "%-38s  \$ %7.2f  %14s\n", $s1, $s1amt, $s1p;
37   printf "%-38s  \$ %7.2f  %14s\n", $s2, $s2amt, $s2p;
38   printf "%-38s  \$ %7.2f  %14s\n", $s3, $s3amt, $s3p;
```

Our first stop as we attempt to understand this program should be at *line
5*. This instruction is fairly dense. The random number function (rand())
returns a number, the int() function rounds it off to create a whole
number, and then that number is divided by 100. It would certainly have
been permissible (and possibly more readily read), to say:

```
$r = rand(99999);
$wr = int ($r);
$c1amt = $wr / 100;
```

If you wrote your program that way, it's probably a good thing. If you have written your code to look like *line 5*, remember that sometimes a complex instruction like this doesn't work out the first time. The best thing you can do then is separate the instruction into its individual parts. That will allow you to see what's going on, one step at a time. You can compress it back into one line when you get it working perfectly.

In *lines 16-19*, we see use of `printf()` to get formatted output. Pay particular attention to *line 16* where `printf()` takes three format fields (`%-38s`, `%7s`, and `%14s`) and fills them with literal strings. Normally, we fill the format fields with the contents of variables, but there's nothing that stops you from providing a literal to fill a particular field if you want the value of the literal to be displayed in an exact manner.

A brief word about `printf()` is in order here. You'll want to use this function when you need a particular formatting for your output. As you saw in our examples, there should be several arguments to this function. The first is a string that defines the formatting. The number of additional arguments is driven by the number of formatting fields in the string.

There are two types of formatting fields about which we'll concern ourselves for now. Those are "`%d`" and "`%s`", which stand, respectively, for "decimal integer" and "string" values. A number can appear between the `%` sign and the field type identifier to indicate how many spaces should be reserved for the value. When you supply a negative number, it switches the alignment of the data in the field. (Numeric information is naturally right-aligned for instance, but if you use a negative field width, the information will be left-aligned.)

For each formatting field in the format string, there should be one additional argument that supplies the actual value that belongs in the field. As you saw in this example, it can be a variable or a literal value. It might even be an expression that yields the type of data that belongs in the field. We'll see more of `printf()` as we look at more code.

LAB 3.2 SELF-REVIEW QUESTIONS

In order to test your progress, you should be able to answer the following questions.

You have the following program instructions:

```
$factor = 10;
$power = 3;
$pf = $factor ** $power;
```

1)   Which of the following is the value stored in $pf ?

a) _____ 100

b) _____ 1000

c) _____ 30

d) _____ too large to print

You have the following program instructions:

```
$remainder = 16 % 3; print ++$remainder;
```

2)   What will be printed?

a) _____ 2

b) _____ 6

c) _____ the complete works of Emerson

d) _____ 5

You have the following program instructions:

```
$v1 = 10; $v2 = 3; $v3 = 5;
print $v1 * $v2 / $v3;
```

3)   What will be printed?

a) _____ 2

b) _____ 6

c) _____ 11

d) _____ 5

You have the following program instructions:

```
$v1 = 8; $v2 = 13; $v3 = 4;
print $v1 -=  --$v2 / $v3;
```

4) What will be printed?
   a) _____ 2
   b) _____ 6
   c) _____ 11
   d) _____ 5

You have the following program instructions:

```
$v1 = 8; $v2 = 16; $v3 = 4;
printf "v1: %d v2: %d v3: %d", ($v1 /=  $v2++ / $v3), $v2, $v3--;
```

5) What will be printed?
   a) _____ v1: 2 v2: 15 v3: 3
   b) _____ v1: 2 v2: 17 v3: 4
   c) _____ the complete works of Asimov
   d) _____ v1: 3 v2: 17 v3: 5

Quiz answers appear in Appendix A, Section 3.2.

L A B   3.3

SCALARS AND CONTEXT

LAB OBJECTIVES

After this Lab, you will be able to:

✓ Test Variable Context in a Short Program

✓ Use Perl's Early Warning Mode

When data is stored in a scalar variable, it may be interpreted as a number or as a text string. The decision about which interpretation is appropriate is made at the time that the value is used. That determination is based upon the *context* in which the variable appears. In this Lab, we'll look at some examples that illustrate how variables behave in various contexts.

We might want our Perl program to run with extra warnings turned on so that we can be alerted when something doesn't look right. This is helpful during the development cycle and you might want to do this by habit whenever you're writing a program. We'll look at how to use the warning mode to ask for extra messages when things are technically legal but might represent flaws in our logic.

When you program in Perl, most things you might try will work if they are logical. (I mean *logical* here in the loose lexicographic sense, not the narrow mathematical sense.)   This freedom and power can sometimes seem nearly magical but it's not really so at all.

Think about how words work in English. If I utter the word "there," you will hear a sound and know what the word means. That is, you know what it means *if* you hear me say it in a sentence. If I say only that word without any surrounding contextual clues, you might spell it "there" or "their" or perhaps "they're." Your brain takes the sound, stores it, and decides what it means when the surrounding context becomes clear.

Perl works much the same way. When you store the characters 8, 0, and 0 in a variable, it simply holds those characters and interprets them when the variable is put into some larger meaningful phrase.

ARITHMETIC CONTEXT

If the variable appears in some sort of numeric calculation, we might say that it appears in an *arithmetic context*. This will cause its content to be interpreted as a number. As long as the variable contains some value that represents an actual number, the interpretation will be reasonable. If the value is a string that clearly is not a number, the variable will appear to contain the value 0.

If the value begins with some digits (or something else that looks like a legitimate number), the value will appear to be a number represented by the part of the string that is legal. This is the most troubling case because the results are somewhat unpredictable.

STRING CONTEXT

If the variable appears in some sort of operation that manipulates a string, then we might say that it appears in a *string context*. This would include an expression that uses string concatenation, string replication, or using the variable as an argument to a function that expects a string; print() is an example of such a function.

■ FOR EXAMPLE

context1.pl

```
1   #!/usr/bin/perl
2   $v1 = 100;
3   $v2 = 80;
4   $r1 = $v1 + $v2; print "$r1 \n"; # prints 180
5   $r2 = $v1 . $v2; print "$r2 \n"; # prints 10080
6
7   $name = bob;
8   $r3 = $v1 + $name; print "$r3 \n"; # prints 100
```

```
 9  $r4 = $v1 . $name; print "$r4 \n"; # prints 100bob
10
11  $number = "800-555-1212"; # quotes are necessary here
12  $r5 = $v1 . $number; print "$r5 \n"; # prints 100800-555-1212
13  $r6 = $v1 + $number; print "$r6 \n"; # prints 900
```

In *line 11,* the comments tell us that quotes are necessary around this number. Take a moment to look at the line again and try to guess why this is true.

If you guessed that we don't want Perl to interpret the value as an equation ("800 minus 555 minus 1212"), then you were right.

LAB 3.3 EXERCISES

3.3.1 TEST VARIABLE CONTEXT IN A SHORT PROGRAM

a) Write a program in which you place each of the following values into a variable and then print the value both in a numeric and a string context to observe the results:

99,999,999
999999999999
3.14159
9.999999999999999999e+18
05551212
0x551212
0x55FF1212
0x55FFGG22
08675309

3.3.2 USE PERL'S EARLY WARNING MODE

Because Perl allows just about anything that is logical to be legal, sometimes things can happen that aren't exactly what we intend. To prevent some of these more venial errors from sneaking past us, Perl offers a higher level of care by allowing us to request warning messages when things look funny even though they might be technically legal. Do this by using the -w option to Perl.

It is a good idea to use this option whenever your program is being built. You can turn it off later when you are through, although your program will be so good that there wouldn't ever be any error messages when the job is finished, right?

PERL'S EARLY WARNING SYSTEM

When you want to request extra warning messages, use the switch. When you do this, Perl will still execute your script as requested, but the interpreter will emit warning messages when something doesn't look right. Let's take a look at the difference between running the example code with and without the warning feature.

First, run the `context1.pl` program without warnings:

```
$ perl context1.pl
```

You'll see something like this:

```
180
10080
100
100bob
100800-555-1212
900
```

Run `context1.pl` as:

```
$ perl -w context1.pl
```

a) What lines of output are new when you run the program this way?

_____

_____

b) Perl complains that "800-555-1212" is not numeric. When it was used as a number, what value was given to it?

_____

_____

You might recall from Chapter 1, "Getting Started with Perl," that you can use a command line like

```
perl -we '$val = 100; print $val;'
```

LAB
3.3

to test code when you aren't entirely sure about how it will work. When you do this, you'll get a result right away and you can integrate the result into whatever program you're working on. Don't forget this when you move on to more complicated tasks with Perl.

Use `perl -w` to test each of the following phrases:

c) `$val += 100; print $val;`

_____

_____

d) `$val += 100;`

_____

_____

e) `$val += 100; print $Val;`

_____

_____

f) `$val = 0777; print $val;`

_____

_____

g) `$val = 0779; print $val;`

The Whole Truth

If you want to include quoted strings in your one-line tests, you should use the `qq{string}` mechanism. Regular double quotes sometimes confuse the shell. Many shells strip them from the Perl instruction before the interpreter ever gets to see your code.

For example, if you wanted to write a one-liner that said:

```
perl -e '$val="Perl script appears here"; print "$val \n"'
```

the interpreter would not get to see the double quotes. They would be gone before the Perl command is invoked. That would make the first instruction invalid. The first part of the instruction would still be valid: (`$val=Perl`). It's just that the remaining part of that instruction (`script appears here`) will look like random extra information. (Also recall that on the Win32 platform, you have only the double quotes to work with anyway.)

So your test line should look like this:

```
perl -we '$val=qq{Perl script appears here}; print qq{$val \n};'
```

You should probably try to use double quotes first and see if that works from your shell's command line. If that fails, substitute the `qq{}` operator.

LAB 3.3 EXERCISE ANSWERS

3.3.1 ANSWERS

a) Write a program in which you place each of the given values into a variable and then print the value both in a numeric and a string context to observe the results.

Answer: Here's a program that does the trick:

context2.pl
```
1  #!/usr/bin/perl
2
```

```
 3  $v = "99,999,999";
 4  print "string: $v \t";
 5  print "numeric: ", $v+0, "\n";
 6
 7  $v = "999999999999";
 8  print "string: $v \t";
 9  print "numeric: ", $v+0, "\n";
10
11  $v = "3.14159";
12  print "string: $v \t";
13  print "numeric: ", $v+0, "\n";
14
15  $v = "9.999999999999999999e+18";
16  print "string: $v \t";
17  print "numeric: ", $v+0, "\n";
18
19  $v = "05551212";
20  print "string: $v \t";
21  print "numeric: ", $v+0, "\n";
22
23  $v = "0x551212";
24  print "string: $v \t";
25  print "numeric: ", $v+0, "\n";
26
27  $v = "0x55FF1212";
28  print "string: $v \t";
29  print "numeric: ", $v+0, "\n";
30
31  $v = "0x55FFGG22";
32  print "string: $v \t";
33  print "numeric: ", $v+0, "\n";
34
35  $v = "08675309";
36  print "string: $v \t";
37  print "numeric: ", $v+0, "\n";
```

LAB
3.3

Here's what happens when you run that program:

```
$ context2.pl
string: 99,999,999                     numeric: 99
string: 999999999999                   numeric: 999999999999
string: 3.14159                        numeric: 3.14159
string: 9.999999999999999999e+18       numeric: 1e+19
```

```
string: 05551212            numeric: 5551212
string: 0x551212            numeric: 0
string: 0x55FF1212          numeric: 0
string: 0x55FFGG22          numeric: 0
string: 08675309            numeric: 8675309
```

**LAB
3.3**

There were a few surprises here. The number "99,999,999" became simply "99" because the comma is not part of a legal specification for a numeric literal value in Perl. Programmers familiar with C might have been surprised to learn that the number "0x5551212" became simply "0" again because the "x" character cannot be used in part of a numeric literal.

Keep the lessons of this program in mind as you work with numeric values in your program.

3.3.2 ANSWERS

Run `context1.pl` with the `-w` option to Perl and answer the questions that follow below.

a) What lines of output are new when you run the program this way?

Answer: Here are our results from the program. The warning messages (and the operator input, as always) are shown in bold.

```
$ perl -w context1.pl
Unquoted  string  "bob"  may  clash  with  future  reserved  word  at
context1.pl line 7
180
10080
Argument "bob" isn't numeric in add at context1.pl line 8
100
100bob
100800-555-1212
Argument "800-555-1212" isn't numeric in add at context1.pl line 13
900
```

b) Perl complains that "800-555-1212" is not numeric. When it was used as a number, what value was given to it?

Answer: Perl uses the leading digits from the string. That makes this "number" look like 800.

The phrases in Figure 3.1 shows how the expressions following will behave with `perl -w:`.

```
MS-DOS Prompt
C:\>perl -we "$val=100;print $val"
100
C:\>perl -we "$val=100"
Name "main::val" used only once: possible typo at -e line 1.

C:\>perl -we "$val=100;print $Val"
Name "main::Val" used only once: possible typo at -e line 1.
Name "main::val" used only once: possible typo at -e line 1.
Use of uninitialized value at -e line 1.

C:\>perl -we "$val=0777;print $val"
511
C:\>perl -we "$val=0779;print $val"
Illegal octal digit at -e line 1, at end of line
Execution of -e aborted due to compilation errors.

C:\>
```

Figure 3.1 ■ Perl's Early Warning System

c) `$val += 100; print $val;`

Answer: No problem here. These two instructions are entirely legal and they generate no warning message.

d) `$val += 100;`

Answer: Because the variable appears only once, Perl complains. It is possible that we meant to use the variable later, but misspelled the name when we tried to reference it.

e) `$val += 100; print $Val;`

Answer: This example is even clearer. We do indeed intend to use the variable, but we have mistyped the name.

f) `$val = 0777; print $val;`

Answer: No problem with this one.

g) `$val = 0779; print $val;`

Answer: The numeric literal is not a legal octal number. We got away with this in our last Exercise because we placed the number in quotes. It looked like a string to Perl, so the value was accepted. Just remember that if a numeric literal begins with a 0, then the number is supposed to be octal. The number "9" is not an octal digit, of course.

LAB 3.3 SELF-REVIEW QUESTIONS

In order to test your progress, you should be able to answer the following questions.

You have the following program instructions:

```
$factor = 10;
$power = "bob";
$pf = $factor ** $power;
```

1) Which of the following is the value stored in `$pf` ?
    a) _____ 100
    b) _____ 1
    c) _____ 0
    d) _____ too small to print

You have the following program instructions:

```
$v1 = 16; $v2 = 3;
$r1 = $v1 + $v2; $r2 = $v1 . $v2;
```

2) Which of the following is true?
    a) _____ $r1 is 163, $r2 is 19
    b) _____ $r1 is 19, $r2 is 163
    c) _____ $r1 is the complete works of Eric Idle
    d) _____ $r1 is 193, $r2 is 16

You have the following program instructions:

```
$v1 = 8; $v2 = "bob"; $v3 = $v1 . $v2;
printf "%6s %6d", $v3, $v3;
```

3) What of the following will be printed?

    a) _____ 8bob   80

    b) _____ 8   80

    c) _____ the Detroit Yellow Pages

    d) _____ 8bob   8

4) Which of the following options tells Perl to emit extra warning messages?

    a) _____ `perl`

    b) _____ `perl -w`

    c) _____ `perl --debug`

    d) _____ `perl`

Quiz answers appear in Appendix A, Section 3.3.

**LAB
3.3**

LAB 3.4

SPECIAL SCALAR VARIABLES

LAB OBJECTIVES

After this Lab, you will be able to:

✓ Analyze a Program That Uses Special Variables

✓ Track Error Messages

Some programmers believe that every punctuation character in the English language is a special variable in Perl. It would be hard to argue with the folks who hold this opinion. There are many special variables predefined in the language.

Most of them are identified by names that look like punctuation. For instance $!, $=, $^, and $~ all have special meanings. And that's just a tiny sampling! We won't present the entire gallery here. If we did, we'd never get on to the more interesting topics.

Let's just look at the "top five" special scalar variables in Perl. There are two things to consider before you study Table 3.4. First, this is not a comprehensive list of special variables. And understanding even these is not vital right now. Just look them over and try the experiments that follow so that you'll be able to use the variables when they serve your purpose.

Table 3.4 Some Special Perl Scalar Variables

Variable	Meaning	Explanation
$_	default input pattern	This is the default pattern during file read operations. Many Perl functions operate on this variable if no other value is supplied. Most times when this variable is used, we do not see it.
$0	name of this script	This contains the name of the current program. Useful in error messages among other things.
$$	current process id	The most common use of this information is to create unique temporary filenames. It could be helpful in other ways, as we'll see later.
$!	current error string	When an error condition occurs, this variable contains some explanatory information.
$?	last exit status	This contains the exit status of the last system command, subprocess, or pipe operation.

LAB 3.4

We'll look at the default input pattern variable in some depth later. It is included here because it might very well be the very most common of Perl special variables.

We can inspect the value of $0 and $$ at any time. Our program will always have a notion of these values.

The variable $0 allows our program to be aware of its context. It contains the name of our program. Whenever the program needs to write a log file message or an error message, it is considered polite to include the program identity. Hardcoding the program name into the error message is one option, but a shortsighted one. I might decide to call my program vincent_vars.pl today and later in the development cycle, I might decide to call it universal_vars.pl. At that time it would be nice if I didn't have to go through all of my source code doing a search-and-replace operation. If I always say $0, I'll always have the correct program name.

■ FOR EXAMPLE

```
# hardcoded log message -- not preferred
print "vincent_vars.pl: Illegal attempt to pirouette.\n";
# variable program name -- much better
print "$0: Illegal maneuver at center stage.\n";
```

There's another issue that you should consider when you want to emit an error or log message. It is considered proper to send error messages out in a way that is different from regular program output. The easiest way to demonstrate this is just to show you an example:

```
print STDERR "$0: Found a problem - $! \n";
```

When the first argument to the `print()` function is a filehandle, the output goes to that destination instead of the default standard output. The STDERR filehandle is open when your program starts, so you may write to it at any time. (What's a filehandle? We'll discuss it in Chapter 9, "Files: Outside and In," but you can certainly know the broad definition here. A filehandle is a variable that allows your program to access files, pipes, sockets, and other I/O devices.)

As our programs evolve, we'll have ample opportunity to write error and logging messages, and the format you've just seen is the way that it should be done.

In order to force an error so that we could see an error string (stored in $!), we could attempt to print to a non-existent filehandle. Here's an example of how that might look:

```
print IMAGINARY "this output will never appear.\n";
print STDERR "$0: print failed.  It said: $!";
```

In order to see the exit status of an external program, we can use the Perl `system()` function. We saw this briefly in Chapter 2, "The Nickel Tour." When we run a program this way, the program is run in a subshell and its return code is given to us (or our Perl program) in the $? variable.

Let's see a program that uses most of these variables.

LAB 3.4 EXERCISES

3.4.1 ANALYZE A PROGRAM THAT USES SPECIAL VARIABLES

Run this program and observe the results.

svars.pl

```
1   #!/usr/bin/perl
2   print "Hello, my name is: $0\n";
3   print "My process id is: $$\n";
4
5   # run an external command
6   system "date"; # use "mem" for MS-DOS prompt
7   print "Date command yielded $?\n";
8
9   # run a command that should fail
10  system "tail somebogusfilename"; # use "type bogusfile" for MS-DOS
11  print "tail command yielded $?\n";
12
13  print BOGUSFILEHANDLE "important information\n";
14  print "Writing to bogus filehandle; Error string is set to [$!]\n";
```

a) In line 3, when the program name is printed, does it show the fully qualified pathname of your script?

_____

_____

b) If you run the program by specifying the full path on the command line (like `/home/myfiles/src/svars.pl`), does the printed program name include full path information?

_____

_____

c) After the `date(1)` command runs successfully, what is the result code?

_____

_____

d) After the `tail(1)` command fails, what is the result code?

_____

_____

e) When the error string prints, is there evidence of an invisible character?

3.4.2 CREATE STANDARDIZED ERROR MESSAGES

Here's a program that produces regular output and error message output:

emessage.pl

```
1  #!/usr/bin/perl
2  print "This is regular program output\n";
3  print STDERR "$0: Error - This is simulated error output!\n";
4  print "The program is designed to produce two lines of output\n";
```

Run this program and observe the output.

a) Where does the standard output go? Where does the error message go?

_____

_____

Run the program as follows:

```
$ emessage.pl >junkfile
```

b) Where does the error message go? What happened to the standard output?

_____

_____

LAB 3.4 EXERCISE ANSWERS

3.4.1 ANSWERS

Run the given program and observe result.

a) In line 1, when the program name is printed, does it show the fully qualified pathname of your script?

Answer: The program basename is all you should see at this point.

That is to say, if the fully qualified pathname is `/home/myfiles/src/perl/svars.pl`, you would see only `svars.pl` when you run this program. (You might see `"./svars.pl"` instead, depending upon your shell and operating system.)

b) If you run the program by specifying the full path on the command line (like `/home/myfiles/src/svars.pl`), does the printed program name include full path information?

Answer: This time we should see the full path to the program.

c) After the `date(1)` command runs successfully, what is the result code?

Answer: Because the command succeeds, we see an exit code of 0.

This is standard and you should design your own programs to return a 0 when everything goes okay.

d) After the `tail(1)` command fails, what is the result code?

Answer: The result code is non-zero.

Usually it will simply be 1, but it could have been anything. The philosophy here is that when things go right, that's a simple result. When things go wrong, there could be any number of reasons. The non-zero exit codes can be used to provide some information about what went awry.

e) When the error string prints, is there evidence of an invisible character?

Answer: Because we embedded our variable in square brackets, we can see that the variable contents include a newline character.   (On some systems, the error message may not include a newline character. On most standard UNIX systems and on Win32 platforms, however, you will see that the error string includes a newline.)

This is a strong habit, and any time you are printing out the contents of a variable, you should embed the variable in some sort of delimiters that will help us to see what would otherwise be invisible content.

3.4.2 ANSWERS

Run the given program and observe the output.

a) Where does the standard output go? Where does the error message go?

Answer: Both the standard information and the error message will go to the console screen if we run the program in a traditional way.

Run the program as follows:
```
pgm.pl >junkfile.
```

b) Where does the error message go? What happens to the standard output?

Answer: This time, the error messages still go to the terminal screen, but the standard output is sent to the file named on the command line.

LAB 3.4 SELF-REVIEW QUESTIONS

1) The $0 special variable refers to which of the following?
    a) _____The first argument on the command line
    b) _____The name of the current program
    c) _____The cost of a Japanese fighter aircraft
    d) _____The line separator character

2) After running an external program with the `system()` function, the indicator that reports the success of the program is found in which of the following?
    a) _____$!
    b) _____$$
    c) _____$?
    d) _____$&

3) Which of the following demonstrates the correct way to format an error or debugging message?
    a) _____ `print "$ARGV[0]: error occurred\n";`
    b) _____ `print STDERR "$$: error occurred\n";`
    c) _____ `print STDERR "$0: error occurred\n";`
    d) _____ `print "pgm.pl: error occurred\n";`

C H A P T E R 3

TEST YOUR THINKING

1) To create names for our variables, we had to follow the rules for creating a legal identifier in Perl. What are those rules?

2) A variable can hold numeric information or it can hold string information. How can you declare which type of data a variable is going to hold?

3) You might readily recall that the + sign is used to add two numeric values together. Which operator is used to add two string values together (or concatenate them)?

4) We have a variable called $guess that contains some unknown number,. We want $guess to be a number in the range 15 through 50 (inclusive). Write the instruction that will ensure that $guess is set to a value in the appropriate range.

5) From what we've seen in the first three chapters, it should be possible to write the following program: Read two values from the command line, and save the first as a target pattern, the second as a filename. Open the named file and print each line that contains the target pattern.

C H A P T E R 4

ARRAYS
AND LISTS

CHAPTER OBJECTIVES

In this chapter, you will learn about:

Scalar variables provide a simple way to hold information, but sometimes you need more. When you want to hold a collection of related information that can be indexed by number in Perl, you use a data structure called an array.

Sometimes you want to represent a collection of data on an ad hoc basis. You don't need to keep the collection around for very long, but you do need to represent it temporarily as an indexed set of data. For this purpose, you can use a Perl structure called a *list*.

In this lesson, you'll see how to use each of these data types. You'll learn how to create, access, and manipulate each of them to give your programs flexibility and power.

L A B   4.1

USING ARRAYS
AND LISTS

LAB OBJECTIVES

After this Lab, you will be able to:

✓ Create a List and an Array

✓ Use an Array

✓ Declare, Initialize, and Access an Array

We've seen that a scalar variable holds one piece of information. An array can hold many pieces of information "glued" together under one name. Sometimes this turns out to be a big advantage.

In this Lab, we'll look at how an array might be created, populated, and referenced with fairly simple instructions. We'll also see an example of how we might decide whether to use an array or a set of scalar variables.

LISTS AND ARRAYS

While speaking and reading about Perl, we encounter the terms *list* and *array* frequently; it seems almost as if they are interchangeable. Perhaps the best way to think about it is this:

A list is a collection of scalar values.

You create a list by enclosing a comma-separated group of values in parentheses. The values can be numeric literals, strings, or scalar variables.

■ FOR EXAMPLE

Here are some examples of lists. The last example illustrates some code that would create the list shown in Figure 4.1.

```
(100, 101, 102, 103, 104)
("bob", "carol", "ted", "alice")
($cust1, $cust2, $cust4)
("ACME Corp.", "800-555-9696", "45129.39")
```

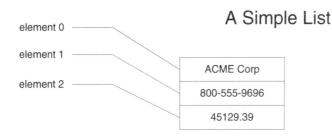

Figure 4.1 ■ A list is a collection of scalar values.

When you specify a list, you might find it useful to use the *range operator*(..). Instead of having to list every value between 100 and 104 (as we did in the previous example), or every letter between a and j, you can specify a range as `100..104` or `a..j` to get the same result.

Obviously, a range operator may be used only when you refer to a group of items that is comprised of sequential values. What may not be immediately obvious is that you can use a range operator to specify a sequence of floating point numbers as long as the members of the sequence are separated by exactly one.

■ FOR EXAMPLE

Here are some lists specified with the use of the range operator. Take particular note of the third example where we mix ordinary individual values and ranges. Also see the fourth example where we generate a range of floating point numbers.

```
(100..104) # same group as last example
(L..S) # Best part of the encyclopedia
(4, 6, 8..10, 12, 14..16) # first few non-prime numbers
(1.5..4.8) # gives (1.5, 2.5, 3.5, 4.5)
```

An array is simply a variable that holds a list.

An array name is formed in a special way, as we shall see. Arrays and lists are nearly interchangable. Whenever we are expected to provide a list, we could provide the name of an array instead. And when a function is designed to return a list, we can store that return value in an array variable.

CREATING AN ARRAY

If you know how to form a list, you know how to populate an array.

Names for arrays are formed by using the normal rules for identifiers. The first character in the name of an array will be @. You can initialize an array by filling it with a list.

■ FOR EXAMPLE

This code will create the array that is illustrated in Figure 4-2.

```
@tbl = (100, 200, 300, 400);
```

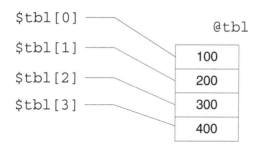

Figure 4.2 ■ An array is a variable that holds a list.

To refer to a particular array element, use the array name followed by an index number in square brackets. The first element in the array has index number 0. Because an *individual element* of an array is still a scalar value, its name begins with the $ character.

You can also create an array simply by assigning a value to one of its elements.

■ FOR EXAMPLE

```
print $tbl[2]; # prints the number 300
$newtbl[0] = 700; # creates another array @newtbl with one element
```

You can simply name an array in a print statement if you want to see its contents. When an array is named inside a quoted string, its contents are displayed with spaces to delimit the elements. When it is named outside a quoted string, the contents are presented with no delimiting characters.

LAB 4.1 EXERCISES

4.1.1 CREATE A LIST AND AN ARRAY

By itself, a list may not be very useful. But when used in conjunction with Perl functions that operate on a list, things get a little more interesting. To demonstrate this, we'll use the simple function `sort()`. This function expects you to provide a list as input, and it will return a sorted version of that same list. Let's take a look at it in action.

Major Ellie was disgusted. Her promotion to program director had changed her concerns from valve pressure, axis alignments, and burn times to program deadlines, budgetary goals, and vendor deliverable dates. "But a job is a job," she thought. To make the best of it, she decided to use Perl to track some of the numbers she would need to watch. In order to understand how lists work, she started by writing this program.

```
        SLIST.PL
1   #!/usr/bin/perl
2   $project1 = "Progress";
3   $project2 = "Apollo";
4   $project3 = "Gemini";
5   print ($project1, $project2, $project3); print "\n";
6   print sort ($project1, $project2, $project3); print "\n";
```

Run her code and observe the output.

a) How are the elements of the list formatted with respect to spacing?

_____

_____

b) Does the second printout (*line 6*) appear to sort the elements properly?

_____

_____

Ellie thought this looked promising. She showed the little program to Uncle Larry, who told her that there was an even "cleaner" way to specify a list. "If you use the qw{} *operator," he said, "you can create lists in a way that will be more readable." He wrote for a moment, and then showed her a program that demonstrated the difference.*

Run his program and observe the output.

QWLIST.PL
```
1 #!/usr/ bin/perl
2 # print a list
3 print ("Houston", "Miami", "Huntsville", "Minsk"); print "\n";
4 # this should do the same thing
5 print qw{Houston Miami Huntsville Minsk}; print "\n";
6 # what if I leave in the quote marks?
7 print qw{"Houston", "Miami", "Huntsville", "Minsk"}; print "\n";
8 # can I mix them up?
9 print qw{Ames, Johnson}, ("Jet Propulsion Labs", "Andrews", "\n");
```

c) Larry seems to expect *lines 3* and *5* to produce the same output. Do you agree?

_____

_____

d) What happened when Larry left in the quotes and commas (*line 7*)?

_____

_____

e) In *line 9*, he tried to mix lists built in different ways; did that work?

_____

_____

4.1.2 USE AN ARRAY

The output from the programs in Exercise 4.1.1 is not exactly pretty or useful. It did prove that our list is being seen and processed by the `sort` function. When we take a list and give it a name (that is, when we turn it into an array), we find that the list becomes more useful.

Coach Randall thought about his fundraising data and decided that it might be possible to use an array to represent the information about his team sponsors. "Before I try to do that," he thought, "I should experiment a little bit to be sure that an array is the thing that I need." He wrote the following program to get a handle on the behavior of arrays.

Run his program and observe the result.

ARRAYPRINT.PL
```
1 @t1 = (2, 4, 8, 16, 32, 64, 128, 256);
2 print "table 1: [", @t1, "]\n";
3 print "table 1 again: [", "@t1", "]\n";
4 print "table 1 in numeric context: [", @t1+0, "]\n";
5 print "If I forget that it's an array: [$t]\n";
```

After seeing the output from `arrayprint.pl`, answer the following questions:

a) Is it possible to differentiate the elements of the array when it is printed in *line 2*?

_____

_____

b) How does the second print statement (*line 3*) change things to make the content more readable?

_____

_____

c) Rewrite *line 3* to eliminate the unnecessary commas and quote marks.

_____

_____

d) When the array name is used as an operand in a numeric expression (*line 4*), what value does it appear to represent?

_____

_____

e) Write a simple two-line program that can test your conclusion (that is, create an array, and then put its name in a simple equation to see what number it appears to be).

_____

_____

USE AN ARRAY TO STORE RELATED DATA

Now we should be able to take our sponsor data from Chapter 3 and store it easily into an array. Figure 4.3 shows how we might want the data to be arranged. Each sponsor will be represented by an array. The individual elements of the array represent the information about each sponsor.

Figure 4.3 ■ Three arrays can hold the information that took nine variable names before.

Run this program and observe the result.

SPONSOR.PL
```
 1   $name = "ACME Corp";
 2   $phone = "800-555-9966";
 3   $amt = int (rand 9999999) / 100;
 4   @c1 = ($name, $phone, $amt);
 5   print "Sponsor 1 info: @c1\n";
 6
 7   $name = "ABC Inc";
 8   $phone = "888-555-2245";
 9   $amt = int (rand 9999999) / 100;
10   @c2 = ($name, $phone, $amt);
11   print "Sponsor 2 info: @c2\n";
12
13   $name = "IBM Corp";$phone = "800-425-9000";
14   $amt = int (rand 9999999) / 100;
15   @c3 = ($name, $phone, $amt);
16   print "Sponsor 3 info: @c3\n";
```

f) How could the information for sponsor 1 have been stored in @c1 without the use of the intermediate variables $name, $phone, and $amt?

_____

_____

g) What code would you use to print out just the phone number for sponsor 3?

_____

_____

Rewrite *line 14* from the program to look like this:

```
@c3 = qw{$name $phone $amt};
```

h) Does the outcome change at all?

_____

_____

4.1.3 USING SORT ON AN ARRAY

What actually happens when you call `sort()` is that the data in the list is compared using the ASCII values of the elements. (Some of us call this sorting criteria ASCIIbetical sorting.) It is as if each two elements of the array are evaluated according to the following formula:

```
if $item1 comes before $item2, return
if $item1 is the same as $item2, return 0
if $item1 comes after $item2, return 1
```

The result from this operation is used to order the data in the list. To state it in terms of Perl syntax:

```
$item1 cmp $item2;
```

**LAB
4.1**

Major Ellie knew that there would be some sorting involved in the new job: sorting pri-orities, sorting expense items, sorting target dates, and sometimes even sorting per-sonnel. To understand how Perl normally conducts sort operations, she decided to observe the behavior of the cmp operator.

Run her program and observe the result:

COMPARE.PL

```
1  @wlist = qw{Gagarin Armstrong Aldrin Collins};
2  $, = " "; # put a space between list elements
3
4  print "word1: $wlist[0]\n";
5  print "word2: $wlist[1]\n";
6  print qq{Compare "word1 cmp word2": },$wlist[0] cmp $wlist[1], "\n";
7
8  print "word3: $wlist[2]\n";
9  print "word4: $wlist[3]\n";
10 print qq{Compare "word3 cmp word4": },$wlist[2] cmp $wlist[3], "\n";
11
12 print qq{Compare "word3 cmp word3": },$wlist[2] cmp $wlist[2], "\n";
13
```

a) What benefit is there to using the `qq{}` quoting operator in the print lines?

_____

_____

b) The `cmp` operator can return one of three results. Which of the three results indicates that the items being compared should be reversed in order?

_____

_____

This approach to comparison works just fine as long as you want to sort string data. But if you want to sort numeric data, things behave differently.

Ellie modified her program to observe the effects of sorting numeric information. If she had a list of numbers like "10, 20, 30, 108", she wanted to be sure that the number 20 would come before the number 108.

Read her program carefully before running it. Try to anticipate the program's output.

COMPARE2.PL

```
1   #!/usr/bin/perl
2   $, = " "; # put a space between list elements
3
4   $word1 = 20; print '$word1 is: ', $word1, "\n";
5   $word2 = 108; print '$word2 is: ', $word2, "\n";
6   print qq{Compare "word1 cmp word2": }, $word1 cmp $word2, "\n";
7   print "When sorted: ", sort ($word1, $word2), "\n";
8
9   @numlist = qw{2 10 20 30 107 108 219 1143};
10  $word1 = $numlist[0]; print '$word1 is: ', $word1, "\n";
11  $word2 = $numlist[1]; print '$word2 is: ', $word2, "\n";
12  print qq{Compare "word1 cmp word2": }, $word1 cmp $word2, "\n";
13  print "Entire list in raw form:\n", @numlist, "\n";
14  print "Entire list sorted:\n", (sort @numlist), "\n";
```

> **c)** With the result from the comparison operation in *line 6*, might we expect the numbers to be reversed when sorted?
>
> _____
>
> _____
>
> **d)** In *line 10*, a single quote is used to prevent the literal word $word1 from being interpolated as a variable. How could *lines 6* and *12* be rewritten to allow them to say, literally, $word1 cmp $word2 rather than the approximation that is used?
>
> _____
>
> _____

Clearly, the cmp operator will not help us when we want to do a numerical sort, but there is an operator that can do the job. The <=> operator does for numbers what `cmp` does for strings. Let's watch as Ellie modifies her program to use this approach.

Ellie heard a knock at the door. It was Coach Randal, dropping by for a break after late practice. Ellie explained what she was working on and Coach Randal became animated as he said, "Yes, that's it! You're on the right path. Now change the way you call the `sort()` *function so that the first argument is a program block. The block should act as if there are two items to compare,* `$a` *and* `$b`. *Have the block return a value of* `-1`, `0`, *or* `1`, *depending upon whether the items are in correct order, equal, or reverse order."*

Joe went to the whiteboard and drew a phrase:

```
sort {$a cmp $b} @list;
```

"This is how `sort()` *works by default. You can supply your own code block to alter the behavior of* `sort()`."

"I don't get it," Ellie complained. "Where do `$a` *and* `$b` *come from? And what do you mean by 'have the block return' ?"*

"Good questions," Randal replied. "It's not entirely clear from what you see here. Try to think about it like this. You start with a list or an array. When you pass it to `sort()`, *two of the elements in the list are compared. Under ordinary circumstances, the items are compared in the way you see here." He waved at the whiteboard for emphasis. "One of the items is temporarily assigned to* `$a` *and the other one to* `$b`. *If the order of the two elements is irrelevant, then the block should return the value 0. If the value in* `$a` *should be placed after the value for* `$b` *in a sorted list, then your block should return 1."*

Ellie opened her mouth to object, but Randal continued before she could say anything. "A block 'returns' the value produced by the last statement. In this example, there is only one statement, and it returns exactly the range of values we need."

"That wasn't what I was going to ask," Ellie smiled. "I sort of got that from your example. What I was going to ask is whether the block can be complicated and have several statements. Or could it be an entire function in itself?"

Randal beamed. "You can put whatever you like in that block, as long as the last statement resolves to one of the three values we need to see.

"I can see that you're itching to write a program to test this out. I have to get this stuff back to the equipment room, so I'll come back later and we can talk about this some more."

"Thanks." Ellie was already starting to get that distant look in her eyes. But not distant enough. "By the way, are you going to keep starting that tall red-headed kid with the butterfingers at split end?"

"Uhhm," Randal frowned in spite of himself. "I'll talk to you later, Ellie." He slipped out of the door before he could see her break into a grin.

Here is the program that Ellie wrote. Read it carefully and then run it to see what happens.

COMPARE3.PL

```
1   #!/usr/bin/perl
2   $, = " "; # put a space between list elements
3
4   $word1 = 20; print '$word1 is: ', $word1, "\n";
5   $word2 = 108; print '$word2 is: ', $word2, "\n";
6   print q{Compare "$word1 <=> $word2": }, $word1 <=> $word2, "\n";
7   print "When sorted: ",  sort {$a <=> $b} ($word1, $word2);
8   print "\n";
9
10  # I had better randomize these a bit
11  @numlist = qw{108 2 20 107 10 219 30 1143};
12  print "Entire list in raw form:\n", @numlist, "\n";
13  print "Entire list sorted:\n", (sort {$a <=> $b} @numlist);
14  print "\n";
```

e) When calling `sort()` in *line 7*, is there a comma after the comparison block?

_____

_____

f) Alter the program by putting a comma after the comparison block and tell what happens when you run it.

_____

_____

LAB 4.1 EXERCISE ANSWERS

4.1.1 ANSWERS

Run the `slist.pl` program and observe the output.

a) How are the elements of the list formatted with respect to spacing?

Answer: There is no space between elements when they are printed this way.

Whenever a list (or later, an array) is printed outside of double quotes, the elements are crammed together this way. Later in this Lab you'll learn three ways to deal with this, if it bothers you.

b) Does the second printout (*line 6*) appear to sort the elements properly?

Answer: The short answer is probably, "Well, yeah." But no Perl programmer worthy of their salsa would let a question like this go by without asking, "What do you mean by sorting the elements properly?" You'll learn later in the lab about sorting in ASCII order (which is what happened here), as well as other ways you might want to sort things.

Wherever a list is expected, you can use an array, and whenever you have an array, you can fill it with a list. Such a situation is usually known as an array context. You saw this earlier when we passed a list to the `sort()` function in the `slist.pl` program.

What may not have been as easy to see is that `sort()` returns a list as well. Let's take a closer look at what really happens.

Here's a modified version of the program:

SLIST2.PL

```
1  #!/usr/bin/perl
2  $project1 = "Progress";
3  $project2 = "Apollo";
4  $project3 = "Gemini";
5
6  @rawlist = ($project1, $project2, $project3);
7  print "Raw list: @rawlist\n";
8
9  @cookedlist = sort @rawlist;
10 print "Sorted list: @cookedlist\n";
```

Here's how it runs:

```
$ slist2.pl

Raw list: Progress Apollo Gemini

Sorted list: Apollo Gemini  Progress
```

In *line 8*, you can see that the list returned by `sort()` is placed in an array (`@cookedlist`). Because we keep the data in an array, we may display it more conveniently. Our original program crammed all of the elements together into one conglomerate string. With an array in hand, we can place it into a printing context (a quoted string in this case) that allows us to see the elements separated by spaces.

Run the `qwlist.pl` program and observe the output.

c) Larry seems to expect *lines 3* and *5* to produce the same output. Do you agree?

Answer: It's always a good idea to agree with Larry. In this case, it also happens to be the correct answer.

Use of the `qw{}` operator to quote a list is not only convenient, it will be done by so many other Perl programmers that you might as well get used to reading it, even if you don't use it yourself.

d) What happened when Larry left in the quotes and commas?

Answer: The quotes and commas became part of the data when included in this way.

In this example, we see proof that although many times Perl allows you to get Pretty Much What You Might Expect (*PMWYME*), there are limits. Sometimes Perl just has to do what you say instead of what you mean.

e) In *line 9*, Larry tried to mix lists built in different ways; did that work?

Answer: *Mixing a list by forming part with the* qw{} *operator, and part with a traditional parenthesized list is allowable.*

Use the approach to specifying a list that suits your purpose at a given moment. Note that Larry might have tried to create the list like this:

```
@list = qw{Ames Dryden Jet Propulsion Labs};
```

The list would consist of five elements rather than the three that are probably intended. (We know, of course, that the name "Jet Propulsion Labs" refers to one place, not three.) If he'd decided to be clever, he might have tried:

```
@list = qw{Ames Dryden "Jet Propulsion Labs"};
```

There would still be five list elements, only now two of them would also be burdened with dangling quote marks. Sometimes it just doesn't pay to be clever.

4.1.2 ANSWERS

After seeing the output from `arrayprint.pl`, answer the following questions:

a) Is it possible to differentiate the elements of the array when the program prints it in line 3?

Answer: *Not really.*

You would have to know what the data was originally in order to differentiate the individual elements from this printout.

b) How does the second print statement (*line 4*) change things to make the content more readable?

Answer: Because we placed the name of the array inside a quoted string, the print statement puts a space between each of the elements.

This still isn't the best way to print the contents of an array, but it's a quick solution when you're in a hurry to see diagnostic information as you build your program.

The Whole Truth

If you print an array by enclosing it within a quoted string, you will see the elements separated with spaces. Normally, when you print a list or array without enclosing it in quotes, the elements are not separated by anything. They're all jammed together like sorority sisters headed for the beach in a Yugo. But there is a Perl variable ($,), which may be set to indicate a character that should be printed between elements of a list. Don't worry too much about memorizing this fact, but if it turns out to be handy for you, use it to make your output more easily read. You'll see it used in some examples later in this chapter.

---

c) Rewrite *line 4* to eliminate the unnecessary commas and quote marks.

Answer: Here's one way to do the job.
```
print "table 1 again: [@t1]\n";
```

I hope you didn't work too hard on that. It was a simple matter of deleting the commas and quote marks from the middle of the print statement. It works because the double quotes allow us to include variables for interpolation.

d) When the array name is used as an operand in a numeric expression, what value does it appear to represent?

Answer: It seems from our experiment that placing the array name in a numeric context causes it to be interpreted as a number equal to the number of elements it contains.

Taking advantage of this fact is not always a good idea. If you do it by design, it can be a shortcut; but if you do it by accident, it could take you over "the scenic route through the County of Debugging." Here's some code that might show you a little bit about what to expect:

ACONTEXT.PL

```
1  @t = qw{one two three};
2  print "array is: [@t]\n";
3
4  # put @t in a scalar context
5  $n1 = @t;
6  print "n1 (\@t assigned to a scalar): [$n1]\n";
7
8  # use the scalar() function
9  $n2 = scalar(@t);
10 print "n2 (\@t passed to scalar() function): [$n2]\n";
11
12 # let's try that special array variable
13 $n3 = $#t;
14 print qq{n3 (\@t evaluated with "dollar-pound"): [$n3]\n};
```

Wait a minute, what's that last example in *lines 12-14*? Well, it turns out that every array has a special array variable called $#arrayname. While the array name in a scalar context resolves to the number of elements in the array, the variable $#arrayname tells us the highest numbered element in use. Figure 4.4 illustrates three different ways to refer to the length of an array.

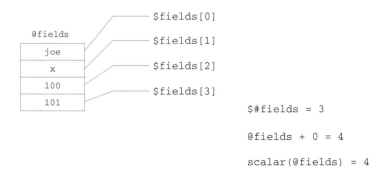

Figure 4.4 ■ There are three ways to implicitly determine the length of an array.

e) Write a simple two-line program that can test your conclusion.

Answer: Well, the program we saw in the last answer would do the trick, but it's not simple or two lines long. Here's an example of two that are:
```
@array = qw{one two three};
print (@array * 2), "\n"; # should print 6 because 3x2=6


# or
@array = qw{Babe Roger Hank Mark Sammy};
print (@array**2), "\n"; # should print 25 that's 5 squared
```
After running `sponsor.pl`, answer the following questions:

f) How could the information for sponsor 1 have been stored in `@c1` without the use of the intermediate variables `$name`, `$phone`, and `$amt`?

Answer: Well, let's see. The first two elements are literal strings, so we could start the array by initializing it with:
```
@c1 = ("ACME Corp", "800-555-9966");
```
The last element is a little bit more problematic because it has to be calculated. But as long as we don't mind using a second program instruction (which would still put us two statements and three intermediate variables ahead of our original approach), we could say:
```
$c1[2] = int (rand 9999999) / 100;
```

g) What code would you use to print out just the phone number for sponsor 3?

Answer: Printing just one element of an array is simple if we know how to specify that element. Here's a line of code that does the trick:
```
print "Sponsor 3 phone number: $c3[1]\n";
```
Rewrite *line 15* from the program to look like this:
```
@c3 = qw{$name $phone $amt};
```

h) Does the outcome change at all?

Answer: Yes! If you use the `qw{}` operator, the elements that are listed inside should be literal values. It isn't the right way to specify a list every time (as we can see here), but it can be useful in many cases.

4.1.3 ANSWERS

a) What benefit is there to using the `qq{}` quoting operator in the print lines of `compare.pl`?

Answer: The quoted strings contain literal quotation marks themselves. Our choices are to use the backslash to escape the embedded quote marks, or use the special quoting operator as we did. The result is easier to read.

b) The `cmp` operator can return one of three results. Which of the three results indicates that the items being compared should be reversed in order?

Answer: If it returns 1, there is no doubt that the items are in reverse order. If a 0 is returned, the items may be reversed with no effect because they are equivalent. When a -1 is returned, we know that the items are already in their preferred order.

c) With the result from the comparison operation in *line 5*, might we expect the numbers to be reversed when sorted?

Answer: Yes, they will be reversed.

Line 5 compares the two values exactly as the `sort()` function does by default. Because the two values are compared as words might be from the dictionary, the first character is the only important consideration. If the first characters are equivalent, then the second character is examined, and so forth. This means that `108` would come before `20`.

d) In *line 10*, a single quote is used to prevent the literal word `$word1` from being interpolated as a variable. How could *lines 6* and *12* be rewritten to allow them to say, literally, `$word1 cmp $word2` rather than the approximation that is used?

Answer: Originally, line 6 reads:

```
print qq{Compare "word1 cmp word2": }, $word1 cmp $word2, "\n";
```

Another way to write it so that the output is more precise:

```
print q{Compare "$word1 cmp $word2": }, $word cmp $word2, "\n";
```

By using the single quote equivalent of the quoting operator, the variable names may be used literally in the string without interpolation.

e) When calling `sort()` in *line 7* of `compare3.pl`, is there a comma after the comparison block?

Answer: Well, no, there isn't.

It wasn't a trick question, just a chance to point out that sometimes the first argument to a function might be presented without a comma to separate it from the following arguments. You'll see this later with the print statement.

f) Alter the program by putting a comma after the comparison block and tell what happens when you run it.

Answer: Now this one was a trick question. The program fails to run when you put a comma after the comparison block. Now that you've done that, you know what it looks like and if you do it by accident some time, you'll know what the problem is, right?

Major Ellie finished her sorting program and called Coach Randal to thank him for the help. "I can see how to sort things numerically, but this 'program block' thing is still a little unclear. When we talked about it before, you said that we could do any kind of comparison we want to do in this block."

"Yes," Randal replied, "you can do some interesting things. If you wanted to take a list of filenames and compare them on the basis of size or timestamps, that's easy to do. But the example I was thinking of comes from the late 20th century. In those days, the top college football teams were ranked according to a complex formula. Their win-loss record was factored in along with the relative strength of the teams they'd played, and the margin of victory when they won, and a host of other things that might help determine which team was better.

"No one knows exactly why it was done this way, but it would provide an interesting Perl programming exercise." Randal paused on the line for a moment. "Maybe that WAS the reason they did it that way." Ellie smiled to herself. "But in any case," Randal continued, "we could have written a pro-

gram that calls the `sort()` *by providing a program block to would look up the relevant factors and at the end, emit the correct value."*

"Of course, you may also find other uses for the numeric comparison operator I showed you. (Remember <=>*) You'll like the 'street name' for that operator. Many Perl programmers call it 'the spaceship operator'. I think you can see why."*

LAB 4.1 SELF-REVIEW QUESTIONS

In order to test your progress, you should be able to answer the following questions.

1) In Perl, a list contains which of the following?
   a) _____ only numeric information
   b) _____ a collection of scalar values
   c) _____ phone numbers of people I have to call
   d) _____ only string information

2) An array in Perl contains which of the following?
   a) _____ a list
   b) _____ parentheses, values, and commas
   c) _____ a colon-separated list of numbers
   d) _____ enough solar panels to illuminate Reno

3) The name of an array in Perl is preceded by which of the following?
   a) _____ a three minute warning tone
   b) _____ the declaration "array"
   c) _____ the @ symbol
   d) _____ the & symbol

4) Which of the following legally defines an array?
   i) `@a = ("Mercury", "Venus", "Earth", and "Mars");`
   ii) `@a = ("Mercury", "Venus", "Earth", "Mars");`
   iii) `@a = qw{Mercury", "Venus", "Earth", and "Mars"};`
   iv) `@a = qw{Mercury Venus Earth Mars};`
   v) `@a = array(Mercury Venus Earth Mars);`

a) _____ ii, iii, and iv
b) _____ ii and iv
c) _____ All of them
d) _____ i, ii, and iv

A program contains these two instructions:

```
@tbl = qw{Io Callisto Europa};
print "$tbl[2]\n";
```

5) What will be printed?
a) _____ Callisto
b) _____ Europa
c) _____ nothing, the second line is ill-formed
d) _____ a topographical map of the Great Red Spot

Quiz answers appear in Appendix A, Section 4.1.

L A B   4.2

LAB
4.2

TRAVERSING AN ARRAY OR LIST

LAB OBJECTIVES

After this lab, you will be able to:

✓ Traverse an Array

✓ Traverse a List

✓ Reverse the Order of Elements in an Array

Now that you can store data in an array, one of the logical things you might want to do is to print out the elements in an orderly fashion. You learned earlier that you can print the array contents by using its name, but the result is not easy to use. In this Lab, you'll see how you can easily write a routine that will take each element in an array and present them to us one at a time.

You might expect that you could use the same approach to make your way through each of the items in a list. If that's what you guessed, you're right. You'll see in this Lab how to traverse a list as easily as an array.

As a practical demonstration of this technique, you'll wrap up this Lab by reversing the order of elements in an array. You'll see two ways to get the job done, proving once again that in Perl, There's More Than One Way To Do It (TMTOWTDI).

TRAVERSE AN ARRAY

If you want to go through an array, dealing with each element as you encounter it, you can simply use a `foreach()` loop.   A loop is a block of code that is designed to repeat some number of times. You will study several types of loops in Chapter 8, "Loops and other Repetitive Experiences," but you can easily see here how this particular loop helps with an array.

To create a `foreach()` loop, you provide a variable that will be used to hold the values from the array, one element at a time.

■ FOR EXAMPLE

This simple program demonstrates a `foreach()` loop.

TRAVERSE.PL
```
1  #!/usr/bin/perl
2  @table = (100, 200, 300, 400);
3  foreach $item (@table) {
4      print "the value is now ", 1000 + $item, "\n";
5  }
```

The first time through this loop, `$item` is set to 100. The second time, it's set to 200, and so forth, until there is no more data in the array. Here's what happens when our program runs.

```
$ traverse.pl
the value is now: 1100
the value is now: 1200
the value is now: 1300
the value is now: 1400
```

That seems to work okay. We'll see it again in a little bit. Right now I want to tell you about a function that you might find handy when you need to manipulate strings and arrays. It's called `split()` and it does About What You Might Expect (AYME). This function should be given two arguments. The `split()` function takes the scalar value in the second argument and splits it into a list using the character in the first argument as a field separator.

■ *FOR EXAMPLE*

Perhaps the best way to demonstrate it would be to show you this short program:

PWSPLIT1.PL
```perl
#!/usr/bin/perl
$record = "joe:x:100:101:Coach Joe:/users/joe:/bin/bash";
@fields = split (':', $record);
print "Login name is: -> $fields[0] <-\n";
print "Real name is: -> $fields[4] <-\n";
```

You may recognize our data record as a traditional UNIX `passwd` file entry. We use `split()` to turn the line into an array called `@fields`. In case you haven't seen a `passwd` file entry in a while, let me remind you that the first field is the login name and the fifth field has the user's real name.

Figure 4.5 ■ The `split()` **function turns a string into a list or array.**

TRAVERSE THE ELEMENTS OF A LIST

Because we can use a loop to traverse an array, you might imagine that you could use the same technique to process each of the items in a list. If you imagined this, then you would be right. (That happens a lot with Perl.) If you look closely, you can see that what actually happens is that the `foreach()` loop expects a variable followed by a list. In our last Exercises, we supplied an array and that served to fulfill the requirement for a list.

■ FOR EXAMPLE

Both of the following code fragments should have the same effect:

```
foreach $item ("bob", "carol", "ted", "alice") {
   print "The next Saturday, I went with $item\n";
}

@names = qw{bob carol ted alice};
foreach $item (@names) {
   print " The next Saturday, I went with $item\n";
}
```

The reason this is important is that we sometimes want to traverse a list that consists of a logical range of things. For instance, we might want to do something for each of the numbers from 1 through 20. We might want to do something for each letter from j through w. The Perl range operator helps us easily form a list that represents ranges, and the `foreach()` loop helps us traverse such a list.

■ FOR EXAMPLE

We could write a loop that uses each of the letters from l through z as simply as this:

```
foreach $letter (l..z) {
   print "Next letter is: :$letter:\n";
}
```

Or we could print the squares of all numbers up to 25:

```
foreach $value (0..25) {
   print "The square of $value is [",$value**2,"]\n";
}
```

REVERSE THE ELEMENTS IN AN ARRAY

There are a couple of the ways we might go about reversing the order of elements in an array. The most straightforward way we might try, using only the facts we've learned here so far, would follow these steps.

- Set an index ($idx_old) to point at the end of the original array.
- Fill a new array by putting the next element from the original array into the new array at the position marked by $idx_old.
- Decrement $idx_old.

By the time we get to the last element of the original array, we should be populating the first position in the new array. Here's a program that can do it.

AREVERSE.PL

```
1  #!/usr/bin/perl
2  @original = qw{Hollowed out, clay makes a pot.
3     Where the pot is not is where it is useful.};
4  $idx = $#original;
5
6  # just to be sure, let's look at the original array
7  foreach $w (@original) { print "$w "; } print "\n";
8
9  @backward = ();
10 foreach $element (@original) {
11    $backward[$idx] = $element;
12    $idx = $idx - 1;
13 }
14
15 # and now, reversed...
16 foreach $w (@backward) { print "$w "; } print "\n";
```

There are a couple of things that this program does differently from the programs we've seen so far. For instance, in *line 4*, we set $idx equal to the highest index in use in the array @original. You might also have said:

```
$idx = @original
```

You will also see that the entire array traversal loop is written on *line 7*. This is an example of a case where it is logical and convenient to place several instructions on one line. In general, we should stick with the venerable old law, *"one command, one line."* If for no other reason, this helps a lot when we use a debugger. But in this case, the transient nature of the program (we intend to run it only to explore a concept) and the fairly trivial nature of the loop we've written make it okay to jam things together this way.

There are several ways to improve this program. For instance, when we write the `foreach()` loop, we can omit the name of the utility variable; the default variable, (`$_`) will be used instead. If we take advantage of this, we can rely upon the fact that the `print` statement also uses the default variable. That makes *line 7* look like this:

```
foreach (@original) {print} print "\n";
```

Is that an improvement? You have to decide this for yourself. It's more concise, and when you're conversant with Perl, you may find it to be entirely readable. On the other hand, be sure to remember that *code you write today is code you may have to maintain next month*. Brevity is not always the highest form of elegance (in spite of what many Perl programmers will inflict upon you).

Another improvement that might be made (again in the name of brevity) would be to use the increment operator for the work we do in *line 12*. We can increment a variable just after we use it; that would allow us to eliminate *line 12* completely. We would just change *line 11* to look like:

```
$backward[$idx--] = $element;
```

Run the `areverse.pl` program now to see how it works. We'll look at a version that incorporates these changes when we do Lab Exercise 4.2.3.

LAB 4.2 EXERCISES

4.2.1 TRAVERSE AN ARRAY

Read this program and then see if it behaves as you expect.

PWSPLIT2.PL

```
1   #!/usr/bin/perl
2   $record = "joe:x:100:101:Coach Joe:/users/joe:/bin/bash";
3
4   ($name, $pw, $uid, $gid, $gcos) = split (':', $record);
5   print "Login name is: -> $name <-\n";
6   print "Real name is: -> $gcos <-\n";
7
8   # let's try something new, list slicing
9   ($name2, $gcos2) = (split (':', $record))[0,4];
10  print "Login name is: -> $name2 <-\n";
11  print "Real name is: -> $gcos2 <-\n";
12
13  # let's get the data on the fly...inside the print statement
14  $, = "\t"; # separate list items with a tab when we print a list
15  print "Logname\tIRLname\n"; # headers, separated by a tab
16  print ((split ':', $record)[0,4]);
17  print "\n";
```

a) In *line 4,* split() breaks the string into a list with seven entries. We use only five of those. Were the two extra fields discarded or were they assigned to the last entry in our ad hoc list on the left side of the assignment operator?

_____

_____

b) In *line 9,* the program takes advantage of "list slicing" notation to say, in essence, *take the list produced by* split() *and give us the first and fifth elements.* What would be assigned to $gcos2 if we changed the line to look like:

```
($name2, $gcos2) = (split (':', $record))[0..4];
```

_____

_____

c) Looking carefully at *line 16*, it appears that when we call the `split()` function, it is not necessary to enclose the arguments in parentheses. Did this change the outcome of the split operation?

_____

_____

Major Ellie was beginning to see the light. Lists and arrays could turn out to be a big help as she wrote tools to help with her administrative drudgery. "There's no sense in turning to that drudgery just yet," she mused. Before digging in to write the actual programs she needed, Ellie decided to crystallize her understanding by writing a program that manipulated data she found more interesting.

"I'll populate an array with colon-separated pairs that represent planets' names and their distances from the sun. Then I can retrieve and print the elements one by one to produce an interesting report."

Here's the program that Ellie wrote first to get started. (She used Coach Randal's 8th Rule of Victory: "Don't try to do too much at one time.") Use this program as a foundation for your own version of the program Ellie wants.

PLANET2.PL
```
1   #!/usr/bin/perl
2   # data in the array is planet name, followed by mean distance
3   # from sun in millions of kilometers
4   #
5   $au = 149.6;
6   @ptable = qw{
7       Mercury:57.9 Venus:108.2 Earth:149.6
8       Mars:227.9 Jupiter:778.3 Saturn:1427
9       Uranus:2870 Neptune:4497 Pluto:5900
10  };
11
12  foreach $p (@ptable) {
13      print "Distance from sun for planet $p million km\n";
14  }
```

d) Using the `planet2.pl` program as a basis, write a new program that prints out a neat report that looks like this:

```
$ planet3.pl
    Planet    Distance from Sun       Distance in AU

                 (Million KM)

  ----------   ------------------    ------------------

    Mercury               57.9       0.387032085561497

      Venus              108.2       0.723262032085562

      Earth              149.6                       1

       Mars              227.9        1.52339572192513

    Jupiter              778.3        5.20254010695187

     Saturn               1427        9.53877005347594

     Uranus               2870        19.1844919786096

    Neptune               4497        30.0601604278075

      Pluto               5900        39.4385026737968
```

4.2.2 TRAVERSE THE ELEMENTS OF A LIST

a) Write a `foreach()` loop that iterates across the range of the letters from a through z. For each letter, print out a string that has the form:

```
Letter # x in the alphabet is y.
```

The value for `x` should be a sequence number, the value for `y` should be the identity of the current letter.

When you are finished, your output should look something like this:

```
$ ordinal.pl
Letter #1 is: a
Letter #2 is: b
Letter #3 is: c
Letter #4 is: d
...
Letter #26 is: z
```

Major Ellie was starting to get excited by Perl. (Yes, Space Service personnel did have abysmal personal lives.) She looked at her pilot roster and thought about how she could easily cut email orders to everyone on the roster with a simple program.

She began by building an array that contained the last names of all her pilots.

```
@pilots = qw{Ray Cunningham Tombs Rickenbacher Richthofen};
```

Now for the orders. Each pilot was required to respond to a standard set of orders that directed them to their destination. Ellie decided that she could provide the destination from the command line. The program would then need to produce an identical email message for each of the pilots. She would run the program like this:

```
$ routing.pl Ganymede
```

The program should then produce a message for each one that looked like:

```
Attn: Captain Ray
From: Major Ellie, Logistics Program Director
Your orders are as follows: Proceed from your current
location to rendezvous with outposts at Ganymede.
Best of luck, pilot safely!
```

This doesn't seem like such a difficult task. Let's see if you can do it as well as Ellie.

b) Write a program that reads a destination name from the command line. Using the array of pilot names, print a message for each one.

_____

_____

4.2.3 REVERSE THE ORDER OF DATA IN AN ARRAY

Earlier, we looked at a program that demonstrated one way to reverse the elements of an array (areverse.pl). We also talked about some changes that could improve the program.

Take a look at the revised program and decide whether you think we've improved it or not. In either case, answer the questions that follow.

A2REVERSE.PL

```
 1  #!/usr/bin/perl
 2  @original = qw{Hollowed out, clay makes a pot.
 3     Where the pot is not is where it is useful.};
 4  $idx = $#original;
 5
 6  # just to be sure, let's look at the original array
 7  foreach (@original) { print } print "\n";
 8
 9  @backward = ();
10  foreach $element (@original) {
11      $backward[$idx--] = $element;
12  }
13
14  # and now, reversed...
15  foreach (@backward) { print } print "\n";
```

a) By using the default variable in the `foreach()` loops and implicitly in the `print` statements, what difference do we see in this program's output from that of `areverse.pl`?

_____

_____

b) Try filling the special variable, ($,), with a space to see if that will fix the problem.

_____

_____

USE THE reverse() FUNCTION

We can reverse the elements of an array with a simple function. Run the following code and see what happens.

INNER.PL
```
1  #!/usr/bin/perl
2  @inner = qw{Mercury Venus Earth Mars};
3  foreach $p (reverse @inner) {
4    print "$p\n";
5  }
```

c) What is the first element of the list printed?

_____

_____

d) What element will be printed first if we change the foreach() loop as follows?
```
foreach $p (reverse sort @inner) {
```

_____

_____

e) Can you code this so that the array @inner will not be necessary?

_____

_____

LAB 4.2 EXERCISE ANSWERS

4.2.1 ANSWERS

a) In *line 2,* `split()` breaks the string into a list with seven entries. We use only five of those. Were the two extra fields discarded or were they assigned to the last entry in our ad hoc list on the left side of the assignment operator?

Answer: The information was discarded.

If you take a large list and assign its elements to a small list, the small list will be populated until it is full, and then the assignment operation stops. Excess information is ignored.

b) In *line 9,* the program takes advantage of "list slicing" notation to say in essence, *take the list produced by* `split()` *and give us the first and fifth elements.* What would be assigned to `$gcos2` if we changed the line to look like:

```
($name2, $gcos2) = (split (':', $record))[0..4];
```

Answer: If you change the line to look like this, `$name2` would still be assigned the first field from the input string as before, but the `$gcos2` field would be assigned the value of the second input field (in this case, "x").

The combination of "list slicing" and the range operator produces a list with five elements, and we are set up here to assign two of those elements to named variables. Let's go through that again real slow.

The `split()` function produces a list consisting of seven elements from the original string. The "list slice" we take from that grabs elements 0 through 4; it produces a list consisting of five elements. The assignment operation feeds a list that consists of two variables. So the first two values from our list are used to populate the variables.

c) Looking carefully at *line 16,* it appears that when we call the `split()` function, it is not necessary to enclose the arguments in parentheses. Did this change the outcome of the split operation?

Answer: There is no change that we can detect.

You can call most Perl functions without encasing the arguments in parentheses. This illustrates Perl's "free-range approach" to syntax. You can say:

```
print ("this string is followed by: ", $idx+1, " which is a number");
```

Or you can say:

```
print "this string is followed by: ", $idx+1, " which is a number";
```

LAB
4.2

d) Using the `planet2.pl` program as a basis, write a new program that prints out a neat report that looks like the printout in the Exercise.

Answer: Some latitude is left in the program specification, so your program may look very different from this one:

PLANET3.PL

```
1    #!/usr/bin/perl
2
3    # data in the array is planet name, followed by mean distance
4    # from sun in millions of kilometers
5    #
6
7    $au = 149.6;
8    @ptable = qw{
9       Mercury:57.9 Venus:108.2 Earth:149.6
10      Mars:227.9 Jupiter:778.3 Saturn:1427
11      Uranus:2870 Neptune:4497 Pluto:5900
12   };
13
14   # report header
15   printf "%10s  %18s  %18s\n",
16      "Planet", "Distance from Sun", "Distance in AU";
17   printf "%10s  %18s  %18s\n", "", "(Million KM)", "";
18   printf "%10s  %18s  %18s\n", "-"x10, "-"x18, "-"x18;
19
20   # report body
21   foreach $record (@ptable) {
22      ($p, $d) = split ':', $record;
23      printf "%10s  %18s  %18s\n", $p, $d, $d/$au;
24   }
```

Your program may have taken a very different approach to producing output from that taken in *lines 15-18*. If so, take a careful look at what

you see here; you'll probably be able to use this technique again somewhere else. Note that all three program instructions use the same format
string. This makes it easy to get uniform output. In fact, when it is time
to print the body of this little report, the format string is still identical.

We'll explore another method for creating output when we get to Chapter
11, "Ends and Odds." Until then, you can get a lot of mileage from the
`printf()` function.

4.2.2 ANSWERS

a) Write a `foreach()` loop that iterates across the range of the letters
from a through z. For each letter, print out a string that has the form:
Letter # x in the alphabet is y.

Answer: Your program might look like this:

ORDINAL.PL
```
1  #!/usr/bin/pl
2  # ordinal.pl
3  $idx = 1;
4  foreach $letter (a..z) {
5     print "Letter #",$idx++," is: $letter\n";
6  }
```

Not much to this one. We set up an index variable to keep track of our
position in the sequence. We set up a `foreach()` loop that uses each of
the letters from a through z. Each time through the loop, we print the letter and the index variable, incrementing the index variable to prepare it
for the next iteration of the loop.

b) Write a program that reads a destination name from the command
line. Using the array of pilot names, print a message for each one.

Answer: Here is one program that meets the spec; yours may look very different.

ROUTING.PL
```
1  #!/usr/bin/perl
2  $destination = shift;
3  @staff = qw{Ray Cunningham Tombs Rickenbacher Richthofen};
4  foreach $pilot (@staff) {
```

```
5      print "
6  Attn: Captain $pilot:
7  From: Major Ellie, Logistics Program Director
8
9  Your orders are as follows: Proceed from your current
10 location to rendezvous with outposts at $destination.
11
12 Best of luck, pilot safely!
13 ";
14 print "------ cut here -----------\n"
15 }
```

This program sets up the array in *line 4*. Then in *lines 5-12*, it prints a message that includes variables for pilot and destination. At the end of each message, a delimiter line is printed to show visually where each of the messages ends. In real life, the messages would probably be sent to email. We'll see how to do such a thing in Chapter 9, "Files: Outside and In."

4.2.3 ANSWERS

Take a look at our program with these changes incorporated and decide whether you think we've improved it or not. In either case, answer the questions that follow.

a) By using the default variable in the `foreach()` loops and implicitly in the `print` statements, what difference do we see in this program's output from that of `areverse.pl`?

Answer: The print statements allow the words to run together in one long mish-mash. Unfortunately, in the quest for brevity, the use of the implied default variable doesn't allow us a chance to introduce a space between words as we did in the first example.

b) Try filling the special variable, ($,), with a space to see if that will fix the problem.

Answer: It doesn't change the result.

The $, special variable applies only when we print an entire array or list at one time. In this program, we are printing one scalar value at a time.

One way to fix this problem is to print the default variable explicitly and introduce a space afterward. It's still better than the first program if we do this, because we don't have to use a transient temporary variable, but it makes our program instruction more like the original:

```
foreach (@original) { print "$_ "} print "\n";
```

Run the `inner.pl` program and see what happens.

c) What is the first element of the list printed?

Answer: The first element printed is Mars.

The reverse function simply takes a list and returns a list that consists of the list elements in reverse order.

d) What element will be printed first if we change the `foreach` line to read:

```
foreach $p (reverse sort @inner) {
```

Answer: The first element printed would be Venus.

In this case, the elements are first sorted, and then they are reversed. After sorting, Venus would be at the end of the list, and the reversal would make it first.

e) Can you code this so that the array `@inner` will not be necessary?

Answer: Something tells me that many of you will simply say, "Yes, I can." So let me ask those of you, "How would you code this to eliminate `@inner`?" The rest of you may have already answered:

```
foreach $p (reverse qw{Mercury Venus Earth Mars}) {print "$p\n";}
```

Perhaps you said:

```
foreach $p (reverse ("Mercury", "Venus", "Earth", "Mars")){
    print "$p\n";
}
```

LAB 4.2 SELF-REVIEW QUESTIONS

In order to test your progress, you should be able to answer the following questions.

1) Which of the following iterates through an array called `@animals`, printing each value?

   a) _____ `foreach @beast (@animals) {print @beast, '\n';}`

   b) _____ `foreach $beast {@animals} (print $beast, '\n';)`

   c) _____ `foreach $beast (@animals) {print $beast, '\n';}`

   d) _____ `call @Noah; get $inventory or smite($angrily);`

2) Which of the following functions breaks a string into an array or list?

   a) _____ `break();`

   b) _____ `split();`

   c) _____ `separate();`

   d) _____ just give it to Manny

3) To put the items from a list in order, you use the function:

   a) _____ `assemble();`

   b) _____ `order();`

   c) _____ `sort();`

   d) _____ `organize();`

4) To put the items from a list in opposite order, you would use:

   a) _____ a common meat tenderizer

   b) _____ `reverse();`

   c) _____ `invert();`

   d) _____ `swap();`

A program contains these two instructions:

```
@tbl = sort qw{Io Callisto Europa};
foreach (@tbl) {
```

5) Inside the body of the `foreach()` loop, what variable will refer to the individual element currently under consideration?

   a) _____ `$this`

   b) _____ `$current`

   c) _____ `$_`

   d) _____ `$a`

Quiz answers appear in Appendix A, Section 4.2.

L A B 4.3

FUNCTIONS THAT OPERATE ON ARRAYS

LAB OBJECTIVES

After this Lab, you will be able to:

✓ Use an Array as a Stack

✓ Use an Array as a Queue

✓ Splice Things; Arrays and Strings

Perl offers many functions that are designed to operate on an array or a list. We've already looked together at two of those functions.

The functions we'll examine first in this Lab allow you to treat an array as a stack or a queue. With a combination of these functions, you could create a traditional stack, a queue, or a super-queue that allows you to insert and remove items from the middle.

We will wrap this Lab up by learning about a function that can turn an array into a string in almost a mirror image of the way that split() breaks a string up into an array.

WHAT IS A STACK?

Our first job will be to see how we can use an array as a stack. The key to this is a pair of functions, push() and pop(). If you've ever worked with a stack before, these functions will behave as you probably expect. But just to be sure, let's take a detailed look.

A stack is a data storage unit that has new information added at the end. When information is removed, it is taken from the same end. One simile often used to illustrate the concept is that of a cafeteria tray dispenser. When fresh trays are brought by the scullery, they are added to the top which push down the trays that are already in place. When trays are taken by arriving diners, they are removed from the top as well. The newest trays will be the first ones taken.

In our examples, we implement a stack by adding new data to the bottom. The key concept is simply that data will be taken from the same end of the storage unit as it is added. Or more importantly, the last information in is the first information out.

In Perl, we place information into our "stack" with the `push()` function. This adds the value to the end of the array that we name. Information is removed with the `pop()` function. This function removes the last element of the array and returns it to the calling program.

Figure 4.6 illustrates one way we might visualize this process.

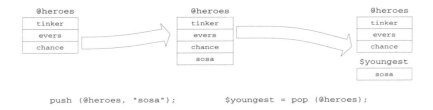

```
push (@heroes, "sosa");        $youngest = pop (@heroes);
```

Figure 4.6 ■ A stack has information added at the end, and taken from the same end.

WHAT IS A QUEUE?

Another common use for an array is for the implementation of a queue. Perl provides two functions that make it easy to use an array as a queue. Those functions are `push()` and `shift()`.

A queue is a data storage unit that holds information by placing new items at the end, and taking items out from the beginning. In a sense, each item in the queue must wait its turn before being taken out to be used. Look at Figure 4.7 for an illustration of how the data is treated in a queue.

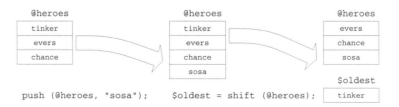

Figure 4.7 ■ A queue has information added at the end, and taken from the beginning.

A VERY SPECIAL PERL ARRAY

Any time your Perl program begins, one array is automatically defined for your use. It is the array that holds the value of any command-line arguments. It is called @ARGV and everything you already know about arrays can be applied to this one.

To see it in action, imagine that you have a program that you want to run like this from the command line:

$ args.pl -f logfile.txt -v -u bob

For your program to read the command-line arguments, it might look like this:

ARGS.PL
```
1  #!/usr/bin/perl
2  $count = 1;
3  foreach $arg (@ARGV) {
4      print $count++, ". $arg\n";
5  }
```

The program run would look like this:

```
$ args.pl -f logfile.txt -v -u bob
1. -f
2. filename
3. -v
4. -u
5. bob
```

Now, let's treat @ARGV as a stack. If we use the pop() function to retrieve the arguments, it should give them to us in reverse order. The only new thing we need to know is how to loop through an array using pop(). As always with Perl, there are many ways. One is to use a phrase like this:

```
while ($arg = pop @ARGV) {
    # do something useful
}
```

The first time that the pop() function finds @ARGV to be empty, the loop will end. That should be exactly what we need.

ARRAYS INTO STRINGS

It is easy to turn an array into a string. The join() function works as almost a mirror image of split(). You supply a delimiter character and the array (or list) to be joined. The function returns a string constructed from the elements in the array.

■ FOR EXAMPLE

This program takes a small array and converts it to a string.

JOIN1.PL
```
1   #!/usr/bin/perl
2   @innerdata = qw{
3       Mercury 57.9 4880
4       Venus 108.2 12100
5       Earth 149.6 12756
```

```
 6      Mars 227.9 6794
 7   };
 8
 9   $allplanets = join ":", @innerdata;
10
11   print "Here comes the whole array...\n";
12   foreach (@innerdata) {print} print "\n";
13
14   print "Now here comes the array as a string...\n";
15   print "$allplanets\n";
```

When the program runs, it looks like this:

```
$ join1.pl

Here comes the whole array...

Mercury57.94880Venus108.212100Earth149.612756Mars227.96794

Now here comes the array as a string...

Mercury:57.9:4880:Venus:108.2:12100:Earth:149.6:12756:Mars:227.9:6794
```

So we can turn a formatted string into an array, and an array into a formatted string. In versions of Perl prior to 5.0, this was how we could represent data in two dimensions. Although our arrays could only hold scalar data in a one-dimensional list, we could patch data together into a string to fake a second dimension.

Even with the addition of multidimensioned storage in Perl 5, we can still utilize this technique to good effect. Look at the sample data in the join1.pl program. The first element in the array is a planet name. The second element is the planet's mean distance from the sun in millions of kilometers. The third element is the planet's diameter in kilometers. The next element is the name of another planet a,nd from there the sequence of data repeats.

If we patch the elements together into strings that represent groups of three facts, each string would represent the information about just one planet. We could then store those strings in an array.

LAB 4.3 EXERCISES

4.3.1 USE AN ARRAY AS A STACK

Read this simple program and then run it to see if it behaves as you imagine it should.

STACK1.PL

```
1   #!/usr/bin/perl
2   @heroes = qw{tinker evers chance};
3   print "size of \@heroes: ",scalar(@heroes)," ";# print array size
4   print "highest index: $#heroes  ";# print highest index
5   print "last element: $heroes[$#heroes]\n\n";
6
7   push (@heroes, "sosa");
8   print "size of \@heroes: ",scalar(@heroes)," ";# print array size
9   print "highest index: $#heroes  ";# print highest index
10  print "last element: $heroes[$#heroes]\n\n";
11
12  $youngest = pop @heroes;
13  print "popped the word [$youngest] from \@heroes\n";
14  print "size of \@heroes: ",scalar(@heroes)," ";# print array size
15  print "highest index: $#heroes  ";# print highest index
16  print "last element: $heroes[$#heroes]\n\n";
```

In the first four lines, we set up a simple array and check on some of its statistics. In *line 7*, we use `push()` to add a new element to the array, then we check the statistics to be sure that we get what we expected. In *line 12*, we take an element from the end of the array and assign it to `$youngest`. Again, we print the statistics to be sure that everything works the way we understand that it should.

> **a)** In *lines 3-5* of `stack1.pl`, we printed out some information that contained statistics about the array. Write a simple `foreach()` loop that would print the array elements in a readable fashion.

_____

_____

b) Rewrite *lines 13-16* as one print statement, and include a loop to emit the entire contents of the @heroes array.

_____

_____

Coach Randal needed a system for assigning players to various roles during practice. He wanted to come up with a system that rewarded the players who showed hustle. Each practice started with conditioning and Randal believed that the players who finished their laps first should get a little bit longer time to rest before they continued practice.

He decided that by using a stack to keep track of their names, the players who clocked in first after finishing their run would be the last to be called for the next drill. To simulate this, he wrote the following program.

NEXTDRILL.PL
```
 1  #!/usr/bin/perl
 2  @players = qw{bob wayne ellen sylvia phil};
 3
 4  $order = 1;
 5  print "Players finished in this order:\n";
 6  foreach $p (@players) {
 7      print $order++, ": $p\n";
 8      push @drill, $p;
 9  }
10  print "\n";
11
12  $order = 1;
13  print qq{Call them for "fire lifts" in this order:\n};
14  foreach (@players) {
15      $next = pop @drill;
16      print $order++, ": $next\n";
17  }
```

In *lines 3-11* you can see that Joe simulated a group of players finishing their runs in a specific order. In *line 8* each player is added to an array called @drill, which will serve as the stack. In the loop that begins on *line 11*, each player is popped from the stack in reverse order.

c) You may notice that in *line 14* of `nextdrill.pl`, the loop is keyed to `@players`. What would happen if the loop simply printed the contents of `@drill` in order instead?

_____

_____

Perl provides an `unshift()` function that adds things to an array at element 0. The existing elements are "pushed down" to make room for the new element. This function could be used to make Coach Randal's experiment a little bit less contrived. The function works just like `push()`, it just adds the data at the opposite end of the array.

```
unshift (@heroes, "sosa");
```

d) Rewrite `nextdrill.pl` so that it uses `unshift()` to put information into the stack. Then rewrite the `foreach` loop at *line 14* to traverse `@drill`.

_____

_____

4.3.2 USE AN ARRAY AS A QUEUE

To implement a queue in Perl, we use `push()` to put data into the array and `shift()` to take the data out. The following program implements and tests a queue. Read it completely and then run it to see what happens.

QUEUE1.PL

```perl
1   #!/usr/bin/perl
2   @heroes = qw{tinker evers chance};
3   print "size: ", scalar(@heroes), "\n";
4   foreach (@heroes) { print "$_ " } print "\n";
5
6   push (@heroes, "sosa");
7   print "size: ", scalar(@heroes), "\n";
8   foreach (@heroes) { print "$_ " } print "\n";
9
```

```
10 $oldest = shift @heroes;
11 print "shifted the word [$oldest] from \@heroes\n";
12 print "size: ", scalar(@heroes), "\n";
13 foreach (@heroes) { print "$_ " } print "\n";
```

Just like `stack1.pl`, we start by populating an array and then inspect it by printing some of its statistics as well as its contents. We push some data onto the end, just as before. In *line 10*, we remove some data from the array by using the `shift()` function. We expect the data to come from the beginning of the array and our inspection in *lines 11-13* should bear this out.

Let's see what we could do with a queue. Better yet, let's look in on Coach Randal and see what he's found to do with this data structure.

Coach Randal thought he might be the world's greatest anti-egalitarian. He did not believe that all players were created equal. Some showed more enthusiasm and those he favored. Promptness was a sign of enthusiasm, in Randal's opinion. To reward prompt arrival at practice, Coach Randal liked to keep a batting practice list based upon the order in which the players showed up each day. If you showed up early, you got to bat early, and maybe take a second turn later in the day if time allowed.

Again, Coach Randal wrote a simulation to test the concept. Read through it and see if you can find two flaws in his program.

BATTING.PL

```
 1  #!/usr/bin/perl
 2  @players = qw{bob wayne ellen sylvia phil};
 3
 4  foreach $p (@players) {
 5      print "$p just arrived, adding to batters' list\n";
 6      push @batters, $player;
 7  }
 8
 9  foreach $batter (0..$#players) {
10      $next = shift @batters;
11      print "Time for $next to bat/n";
12  }
```

a) There are two bugs in the `batting.pl` program. What are they?

_____

_____

b) Rewrite the program to fix the problems.

_____

**LAB
4.3**

_____

c) Would *line 9* work if it were rewritten as:

```
foreach $batter (1..scalar(@players)) {
```

_____

_____

d) Using the command-line arguments array (`@ARGV`) and the loop demonstrated in the Lab discussion, write a program that prints the arguments in reverse order from their appearance on the program command line.

_____

_____

4.3.3 SPLICING THINGS; ARRAYS AND STRINGS

In the Lab discussion, we saw how to use the `join()` function to turn an array into a string. Let's look in on Ellie to see how she's using this approach.

Major Ellie was looking for a way to model information about the planets of the inner solar system. She knew she could keep everything in a simple array, but she thought there was probably a better way. She talked to Uncle Larry about the `join()` function and wrote the following program to test its behavior.

Read Ellie's program carefully, then run it and see if it does what you expected it to do.

JOINBY3.PL

```perl
1   #!/usr/bin/perl
2   @innerdata = qw{
3       Mercury 57.9 4880
4       Venus 108.2 12100
5       Earth 149.6 12756
6       Mars 227.9 6794
7   };
8
9   print "Here comes the whole array...\n";
10  foreach (@innerdata) {print "$_\n"} print "\n";
11
12  while ($planet = shift @innerdata) {
13      $odistance = shift @innerdata;# we trust there's enough data
14      $diameter = shift @innerdata;
15      $planetstats = join ":", ($planet, $odistance, $diameter);
16      push @ptable, $planetstats;
17  }
18
19  print "Here comes the consolidated table...\n";
20  foreach (@ptable) { print "$_\n"; } print "\n";
```

a) In *line 15* the program pastes together three scalar values into one string. On the second iteration, what should $planetstats look like, after *line 15* is executed?

_____

_____

b) How might the program be rewritten so that the planets could be sorted according to orbital distance?

Hint: This is moderately difficult and will require some thought. If you get stuck, read just the first paragraph of the answer and try again. You have learned enough to solve this.

SURGERY ON ARRAYS WITH `splice()`

One of the more awkward features of the last program (`joinby3.pl`) was the way that three values had to be shifted from the array in separate statements. It would have been more useful to have all three elements presented to us as a list. This is one of the things that the multi-talented `splice()` function can do for us.

The complete specification for the function tells us to provide four arguments. They might be stated like this:

```
splice (ARRAY, OFFSET, LENGTH, LIST)
```

They are the original array, the offset from the beginning of the array, the number of elements from the array that will be removed, and a list of elements that should replace the original elements. The `splice()` function returns a list that consists of the elements that have been removed from the original array.

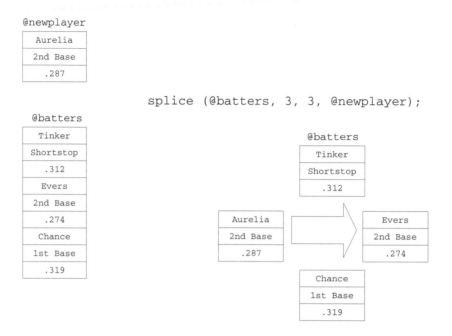

Figure 4.8 ■ `splice()` **can replace information in an array.**

The trick to using this function is that you don't actually have to provide all of the parameters. The list you provide in the last parameter is optional if you don't want to add anything new to the array. This means that we could use it to return (and remove from the array) the first three elements. To accomplish this, you might write:

```
@nextbatter = splice (@batters, 0, 3);
```

Or you might say:

```
($name, $position, $average) = splice (@batters, 0, 3);
```

The third parameter to `splice()` is also optional. If you don't provide a run length for the operation, `splice()` interprets this to mean that you want to affect all of the elements through the end of the array. So to return and remove the last three elements of the array from Figure 4.8 above, you might say:

```
($n, $p, $a) = splice (@batters, 6);
```

Or if we aren't sure of the exact length of `@batters` (which is the more common case):

```
($n, $p, $a) = splice (@batters, $#batters-2);
```

Although the name of the function implies that we'll be patching information into an array, you can see that it has several other uses as well.

Ellie looked at her solar system program and knew that `splice()` *would help make it more elegant. All she needed to do now was to rewrite it so that in each iteration of the main program loop she would retrieve three elements from the array and place them together in a string that could be pushed into the target array.*

LAB 4.3

In order to complete the program, she needed a way to control the `while()` *loop. Rather than dig through documentation to see if it was legal, she decided to try an experiment to determine the legality of the following phrase:*

```
while (scalar(@inner) > 0) {print "something"}
```

"If that works," she thought, "I can trim this little program down to just the necessary parts." And that is the goal of any good Perl programmer.

> **c)** Write a three- or four-line program to test Ellie's assumption about the "greater-than" operator.

_____

_____

_____

_____

> **d)** Rewrite the `joinby3.pl` program to use `splice` instead of three `shift()` statements.

_____

_____

LAB 4.3 EXERCISE ANSWERS

4.3.1 ANSWERS

a) In *lines 3-5* of `stack1.pl`, we printed out some information that contained statistics about the array. Write a simple `foreach()` loop that would print the array elements in a readable fashion.

Answer: One easy way to do it would be like this:
```
foreach (@heroes) {print "$_ "} print "\n";
```

Or you could probably compress the intent of lines 3-5 into these two lines:
```
foreach (@heroes){print "$_ "}
print "Array size: ", scalar(@heroes), "\n";
```

b) Rewrite *lines 13-16* as one print statement, and include a loop to emit the entire contents of the `@heroes` array.

Answer: The second answer to Question a certainly meets the spirit of this question. But to meet the specification exactly, we could write:
```
print "
    popped the word [$youngest] from \@heroes
    size of \@heroes: ",scalar(@heroes),"
    highest index: $#heroes
    last element: $heroes[$#heroes]\n\n";
```

c) You may notice that in *line 14* of `nextdrill.pl`, the loop is keyed to `@players`. What would happen if the loop simply printed the contents of `@drill` in order instead?

Answer: If you simply set up a `foreach` loop on `@drill`, the elements will print exactly in the order they are added. That would make our storage unit a queue rather than a stack. If you set up the `foreach` loop on `@drill` and then `pop()` each element so that you can print it, the elements will come out in the intended order, but somewhere around halfway through the array you will `pop()` the element that should provide the next iteration of our loop and the whole process would stop.

We iterate over `@players` because it has exactly the right number of elements, and we will not accidentally exhaust it as we `pop()` elements for printing. This entire approach is somewhat contrived. Until we learn more about other types of loops, we're forced to bend over a little bit backward to get the behavior we want. On the other hand, you can see from this that Perl allows us to do many things even if we know only a little bit of the language.

I also need to explain to you why we're taking data out of one array and putting it pretty much in the same order into another array. The idea here is to show you how you would use a stack (and later a queue). The second array serves that purpose and the first array is simply a place where data can be found. You might as well find the data in a file, from the command line, or in a pipeline that comes from another program. We'll see more of that as we continue our exploration of Perl.

LAB 4.3

d) Rewrite `nextdrill.pl` so that it uses `unshift()` to put information into the stack. Then rewrite the `foreach` loop at *line 14* to traverse `@drill`.

Answer: This program shows one way to do the job.

NEXTDRILL2.PL

```
 1  #!/usr/bin/perl
 2  @players = qw{bob wayne ellen sylvia phil};
 3
 4  $order = 1;
 5  print "Players finished in this order:\n";
 6  foreach $p (@players) {
 7      print $order++, ": $p\n";
 8      unshift @drill, $p;
 9  }
10  print "\n";
11
12  $order = 1;
13  print qq{Call them for "fire lifts" in this order:\n};
14  foreach $p (@drill) {
15      print $order++, ": $p\n";
16  }
```

Look at how this simplifies the program. In *line 8*, we add the players to the stack with `unshift()` and each new player becomes element 0 momentarily until another one comes along. To bring them out of the stack then, we could use `shift()` but it turns out to be easier to simply run a loop that starts at element 0 and works its way through the players (see *line 14*).

4.3.2 ANSWERS

a)   There are two bugs in the `batting.pl` program. What are they?

Answer: In line 6, instead of pushing $p onto the queue, the program pushes an uninitialized variable, $player. And the print statement in line 11 prints a forward slash and the letter n rather than the newline character that is intended.

Not every bug is as easy to spot as these. But many have the additional danger, as these do, of being perfectly legal code. Run the *batting.pl* program with *perl -w* to see if at least one of the bugs is highlighted in a warning message.

b)   Rewrite the program to fix the problems.

Answer: If you ran perl -w *to see the errors in the first program, you might have written the corrected program like this:*

BATTING2.PL
```perl
1   #!/usr/bin/perl
2   @players = qw{bob wayne ellen sylvia phil};
3
4   foreach $p (@players) {
5       print "$p just arrived, adding to batters' list\n";
6       push @batters, $p; # got that fixed
7   }
8
9   foreach (0..$#players) {
10      $next = shift @batters;
11      print "Time for $next to bat\n"; # use a real newline
12  }
```

One of the warning messages reports that the utility variable, $batters, used in the `foreach` loop at *line 9* is never put to use anywhere. In fact, the loop in *line 9* is set up to ensure that we print out only as many lines as there are elements in the @batters array. So we could have used the default variable instead of $batters in that loop with no problem.

c) Would *line 9* still work if it were rewritten as:

```
foreach $batter (1..scalar(@players)) {
```

Answer: Yes. Again, the main reason for this loop is to make sure that we continue only as long as there are elements in the array. The range "0 through `myarray_highest_index`*" is similar to the range "1 through* `myarray_number_of_elements`*".*

d) Using the command-line arguments array (`@ARGV`) and the loop demonstrated here, write a program that prints the arguments in reverse order from their appearance on the program command line.

Answer: There are several ways (as always) you could write this program, but you might have written something like this:

ARGSTACK.PL

```
1  #!/usr/bin/perl
2  while ($a = pop @ARGV) {
3     print "last argument is $a\n";
4  }
```

**LAB
4.3**

4.3.3 ANSWERS

a) In *line 12*, the `joinby3.pl` program pastes together three scalar values into one string. On the second iteration of the loop, what should `$planetstats` look like, after *line 12* is executed?

Answer: Given the data as it was presented, the result of this operation should yield the following on the second iteration:
```
Venus:108.2:12100
```

b) How might the program be rewritten so that the planets could be sorted according to orbital distance?

Answer: The key to solving this problem would first be to realize that the elements can be combined in any order to form our composite string. The second part is more difficult because we cannot be satisfied here with a simple dictionary sort. The values we need to sort are real numbers and will have to be compared numerically. We'll have to write an evaluation block for the `sort` *function that can separate the data elements and compare the numeric parts to determine whether any given pair of elements should be swapped.*

> *So imagine that we decide to combine the elements in the order* orbit, name, diameter *for our composite string.*

Here is an example of the block that would make it possible to sort them by orbit. Remember that in an evaluation block of this type, we have an implicit $a and $b; they represent the pair of elements currently being evaluated during the sort operation.

**LAB
4.3**

```
{
    ($o1, $p, $d) = split ":", $a;
    ($o2, $p, $d) = split ":", $b;
    return $o1 <=> $o2;
}
```

Now this works great, but there's some waste involved. Notice that when we split the first element, we store the planet name and diameter in $p and $d respectively. When we split the second element, we reuse those variables. The truth is that we don't need them at all. We only care about extracting the orbital distance information from each of the elements and then comparing those numbers.

We could rewrite our block as:

```
{
    ($o1) = split ":", $a;
    ($o2) = split ":", $b;
    return $o1 <=> $o2;
}
```

That's an improvement. It works because we know that split() provides a list. When we assign a large list to a smaller one, the elements we don't need are ignored. (By the way, for extra credit, try to guess what happens when you omit the parentheses around $o1 in the block above.)

Another way we might write our first statement would be:

```
$o1 = (split ":", $a)[0]
```

This says in effect, "Take the first element of the list produced by the split operation and assign it to $o1." Well, the only reason we needed $o1 in the first place was to hold the orbital distance information, but the expression we've just created does exactly that. So we can write our evaluation block as:

```
{(split ":", $a)[0] <=> (split ":", $b)[0]}
```

Now that's the spirit of Perl! Until you're fairly experienced, you may want to code it the way we did in our first try. But after some time, you'll begin to appreciate this last approach. Here's the program:

ORBITSORT.PL

LAB
4.3

```
 1  #!/usr/bin/perl
 2
 3  @innerdata = qw{
 4      Venus 108.2 12100
 5      Mars 227.9 6794
 6      Earth 149.6 12756
 7      Mercury 57.9 4880
 8  };
 9
10  while ($planet = shift @innerdata) {
11      $odistance = shift @innerdata;
12      $diameter = shift @innerdata;
13      $planetstats = join ":", ($odistance, $planet, $diameter);
14      push @ptable, $planetstats;
15  }
16
17  print "Here comes the consolidated table...\n";
18  foreach (@ptable) { print "$_\n"; } print "\n";
19
20  $, = "\n"; # each element on a new line
21  print "Here comes the sorted table...\n";
22  print sort { (split ":", $a)[0] <=> (split ":", $b)[0] } @ptable;
23  print "\n";
24
25  print "Bonus: sorted by diameter...\n";
26  print sort { (split ":", $a)[2] <=> (split ":", $b)[2] } @ptable;
27  print "\n";
```

If your program is longer, but easier to read, you've probably written a better program. The most important thing is that you understand how to combine array elements, split a string apart, and provide an evaluation block to the sort() function. If you can do those things, the program you wrote is a good one.

Ellie decided to try an experiment to determine the legality of the following phrase:

```
while (scalar(@inner) > 0) {print "something"}
```

c) Write a three- or four-line program to test Ellie's assumption about the "greater-than" operator.

Answer: Here's one program that will serve.

**LAB
4.3**

ENOUGH.PL
```
1   #!/usr/bin/perl
2
3   @inner = qw{Mercury Venus Earth Mars};
4   while (scalar(@inner) > 0) {
5       print scalar(@inner), " elements remain.  ",
6           shift @inner, " is at the top of the list.\n";
7   }
```

Yours may be simpler. It should simply prove that this sort of loop will terminate when the elements of the array are exhausted.

d) Rewrite the `joinby3.pl` program to use `splice` instead of three `shift()` statements.

Answer: The key to this will be the main program loop. You might have tightened it up by writing a loop that looks like this:

```
while (scalar(@innerdata) > 0) {
    @pdata = splice (@innerdata, 0, 3);
    $planetstats = join ":", @pdata;
    push @ptable, $planetstats;
}
```

Or you might have compressed that operation to eliminate the temporary array `@pdata`.

```
while (scalar(@innerdata) > 0) {
    $planetstats = join ":", splice (@innerdata, 0, 3);
    push @ptable, $planetstats;
}
```

Or you might have been truly ambitious and tried to compress the whole thing down to one line:

```
while (scalar(@innerdata) > 0) {
    push @ptable, join ":", splice (@innerdata, 0, 3);
}
```

But if you went that far, you're begging for punishment, and you'll get it when it's time to debug or maintain your code. This approach will work as long as all of your assumptions are accurate and you've been very careful with your syntax. If you're confident, go ahead and code it like this.

Here's the whole program with the simpler form of the loop in place:

JOINBYGROUP.PL

LAB
4.3

```perl
 1  #!/usr/bin/perl
 2
 3  @innerdata = qw{
 4     Mercury 57.9 4880
 5     Venus 108.2 12100
 6     Earth 149.6 12756
 7     Mars 227.9 6794
 8  };
 9
10  print "Here comes the whole array...\n";
11  foreach (@innerdata) {print "$_\n"} print "\n";
12
13  while (scalar(@innerdata) > 0) {
14     @pdata = splice (@innerdata, 0, 3);
15     $planetstats = join ":", @pdata;
16     push @ptable, $planetstats;
17  }
18
19  print "Here comes the consolidated table...\n";
20  foreach (@ptable) { print "$_\n"; } print "\n";
21
```

This program meets the design specification and it does what we need it to do. And *that* is the definition of a good program.

LAB 4.3 SELF-REVIEW QUESTIONS

In order to test your progress, you should be able to answer the following questions.

1) Where does the `push()` function send a scalar value?
a) _____to the beginning of the array named in the first argument
b) _____to the end of the array named in the first argument
c) _____over the data event horizon, never again to be seen
d) _____to the function named in the first argument

2) Which of the following does the `pop()` function return?
a) _____the first element of an array
b) _____the last element of an array
c) _____the number of elements in an array
d) _____to Capistrano every year around the second week of April

3) A queue is a data storage unit that is which of the following?
a) _____has elements added at the end, and removed from the beginning
b) _____has elements added and removed from the end
c) _____holds all the knowledge of the universe, but uses it irresponsibly
d) _____has elements added according to their priority

4) The `unshift()` function changes an array by doing which of the following?
a) _____removing the first element
b) _____adding a new element at the beginning
c) _____adding a new element at the end
d) _____replacing wallpaper with sponge-painted stucco and updating all plumbing fixtures

5) Which of the following will add three new elements to `@table` without displacing any?
a) _____ `insert (@table, qw{one two three}, 3, 0,);`
b) _____ `splice (@table, 0, 3, qw{one two three});`
c) _____ `splice (@table, 3, 0, qw{one two three});`
d) _____ `insert (@table, 3, 0, qw{one two three});`

Quiz answers appear in Appendix A, Section 4.3.

CHAPTER 4

TEST YOUR THINKING

1) Think about the two ways that you can fully initialize an array. Which is more convenient?

2) Under what circumstances would you be unable to use the more convenient approach to initializing an array?

In Chapter 2, "The Nickel Tour," we saw how to read lines of information from a file.

```
open IN, "datafile.txt" || die "couldn't open file";
while ($line = <IN>) {
    # do something
}
```

3) Write a program that opens a file named on the command line. It should read the lines of data and store each of them in an array to be printed out later. Close the file, and then print out the contents of the array.

4) Modify the program written in the last question. This time inspect each line of input data and store the line only if it matches the pattern provided as the second command-line argument. Since the presence of the second argument is critical, you can use the following line of code to check for it. (Put this line at the beginning of your program.)

```
defined $ARGV[1] || die "usage: $0 file pattern";
```

5) Write one last version of your program to expect the pattern to be in the first command-line argument. Following that can be any number of file names. When an input line matches the pattern, you'll need to store that line along with the filename and line number. Use the techniques you learned in this chapter to embed all of that information into one array entry.

Be sure to visit the website for a look at the various solutions to this project. There are some handy tricks you might want to know.

C H A P T E R 5

HASHES: OUR THINGS SHOULD HAVE NAMES

CHAPTER OBJECTIVES

In this chapter, you will learn about:

You've seen how scalar variables can be used to represent data in your Perl programs. You've seen how arrays can represent collections of data. In Chapter 4, "Arrays and Lists," you might have decided that if those are the only tools we have, things can get awkward at times. Fortunately, we have hashes to serve where a simple scalar variable or an array will not do. A hash can simplify many programming problems. In fact, hashes are so easy to use and so powerful that most Perl programmers use them in almost every program.

Simply stated, a hash is a collection of scalar values that are indexed by name. A hash is like an array that uses names instead of numbers. You may also see hashes referred to as *associative arrays*. That is simply an older, less concise term for the same thing.

You'll see in this chapter how to create and use them.

L A B   5.1

CREATING AND ACCESSING A HASH

LAB OBJECTIVES

After this Lab, you will be able to:

✓ Fully Initialize a Hash

✓ Add and Remove Elements in a Hash

✓ Populate a Hash from the Contents of a File

With an array, you can represent a group of things by name, and access them by a numeric key. This is useful as far as it goes, but we can do better, and often need to. In Perl, we have a data structure called a *hash* that allows us to represent a collection of things and access them by name.

Let's ponder Old St. Nick's management problem from the opening of this chapter. Would we be able to think about Christmas Eve the same way if we had heard him exclaim, "On reindeer[0], on reindeer[1]...?" I think not. When we have a set of things, we like to have a name for the set, and a name for each of the elements, if possible.

Does this mean that once we know how to use a hash, we won't ever bother using an array? Not at all! Arrays are very important to us. They just aren't the right tool for every job.

To see what I mean, take a look at Figure 5.1. In our first Exercise, we'll see how to create and print a hash.

Figure 5.1 ■ Information that is collected together awkwardly with an array is much more logical when represented in two hashes.

CREATING A HASH

The name for a hash follows the standard rules for identifiers that we learned in Chapter 3, "Variables Large and Small." A hash name is prefixed with a % symbol to indicate that its contents consist of name and value pairs. Just as with arrays, the individual elements are still prefixed with a $ symbol to indicate that they are scalar values.

To refer to an individual element from a hash, place the key inside curly braces. If the key is being given as a literal string, it's probably best to place it in single quotes to protect it fully from expansion.

■ *FOR EXAMPLE*

Using Figure 5.1 as a model, the following names are legal:

```
%averages # name of the complete averages hash
$averages{'Tinker'} # name of a single element in that hash
```

It is also legal to use a variable as a key for a hash element. (In fact, the key can be any expression that yields a scalar value.)

```
$player = "Chance";
print $averages{$player};
```

Like an array, a hash can be initialized with any list. The difference is that each odd-numbered element from the list will be treated as a key, and each even-numbered element will be treated as a value.

■ FOR EXAMPLE

Again, using Figure 5.1, we might expect to see:

```
%averages = ('Tinker', .312, 'Evers', .274, 'Chance', .319);
```

Or you might try:

```
%averages = qw{Tinker .312 Evers .274 Chance .319};
```

Both approaches are legal and they work fine. On the other hand, there is a way to initialize a hash that works better visually. That means you'll find it easier to debug and maintain your code if you do it this way.

```
%averages = (
    'Tinker', .312,
    'Evers', .274,
    'Chance', .319
);
```

This is probably the longest-standing traditional way to initialize a hash. You can tell at a glance if there are enough elements to completely initialize. If you add elements later, you can see exactly where they should go and you can tell easily if you've added them correctly.

With the release of Perl 5, there is another way that is often used:

```
%averages = (
    'Tinker' => .312,
    'Evers' => .274,
    'Chance' => .319
);
```

The only difference is the way that the expression is phrased. This difference is what the creator of Perl calls *syntactic sugar*. The effect is identical, but you may find it more convenient, more memorable, or more elegant to do it this way. It's just another illustration of the philosophy in Perl that redundancy is not always a bad thing.

THE INCIDENTAL HASH: BUILDING AS WE GO

Now you know how to build a hash by initializing it completely with its keys and values. Most times a hash is built by accretion; we usually don't know all of the values that should be stored in a hash when we begin to use it.

We need to be able to add elements to an array when they become available. That part is easy. Like scalar variables and arrays, a hash will come into being as soon as we put one element into it, and if we add more elements later, they will simply be inserted at the appropriate place.

To add an element to a hash, we simply assign it a value. If the hash already exists, the new element will simply be added. If the hash never existed before, it will be created at that time.

```
$solsys{'Jupiter'} = '778.3:142800';
```

To remove an element from a hash, we can use the delete function:

```
delete ($solsys{'Earth'});
```

You probably already guessed this, but case and spelling of the key are vital. If you talk about `$solsys{'earth'}`, that is a very different thing from `$solsys{'Earth'}`.

We haven't talked about it explicitly yet, but you might also have imagined that if you want to print a specific element of a hash, you can say:

```
print ($solsys{'Mars'});
```

■ FOR EXAMPLE

Let's see all of this in one place (Note: These examples make most sense as an extension to the code you'll write in Exercise 5.1.1, question d. If you stop and do that Exercise now, you might get more from the examples):

```
$solsys{'Saturn'} = '1427:120660'; # add an element to our hash
delete ($solsys{'Minerva'}; # hello asteroid belt!
print "Mercury stats: ", $solsys{'Mercury'}, "\n";
print "Venus stats: $solsys{'Venus'}\n"; # no surprise here eh?
print "Mars diameter: ", (split ":", $solsys{'Mars'})[1], "\n";
```

The last line should be the only one that comes as a surprise. And even that is something that we've tried before. If you look carefully, you can see that we split the data value for the hash entry that represents Mars (split ":", $solsys{'Mars'}). We split on the : character because that is our data separator. The split() function produces a list and we simply use the list index operator ([1]) to take the second element of the list for use by the print() statement.

Now let's do a little work with some hashes to gain a better understanding of how they work.

LAB 5.1 EXERCISES

5.1.1 FULLY INITIALIZE A HASH

You've seen three different ways to initialize a hash. We'll use the last approach until a good reason comes to choose another one.

It may seem logical to you that we could print a hash by placing it in a print() statement, just as we did with an array. And the behavior will be similar to what we saw with an array. If we place the hash name outside of a quoted string, the elements will be packed together, just like what we saw with an array. If we have some value stored in $, then that value will separate the values. If we place the hash name inside a quoted string, the literal name will appear. That's important to remember.

Hash names are not interpolated inside quoted strings.

Run this program and answer the questions that follow:

FIRSTHASH.PL

```perl
1  #!/usr/bin/perl
2
3  %averages = (
4      'Tinker' => 312,
5      'Evers' => 284,
6      'Chance' => 319
7  );
8
9  print "Print hash outside our string.\n", %averages, "\n";
10 print "Print hash inside our string.\n %averages \n";
11 $, = ":";
12 print "We could set \$, to $, and ";
13 print "print hash outside the string.\n",%averages,"\n";
```

a) In *line 10*, our program attempts to print a hash inside a quoted string. What result do we see when this runs?

_____

_____

b) When the hash is printed, do the values appear, or the indexes, or both?

_____

_____

c) In the hash initialization (*lines 3-7*), the values are represented as literal decimal numbers. Any baseball fan will tell you that a batting average should look like .312 rather than 312. Change the values in the program to make each of them appear as a fractional number. Does your program still work?

_____

_____

**LAB
5.1**

Major Ellie immediately saw the value of using a hash for her Solar System model. She decided that she could key a hash with the planet names, and she could fill it with composite strings that represented the planets' statistics. Here are the statistics for the inner planets again.

Planet Name	Distance from Sun (Million km)	Diameter (km)
Mercury	57.9	4880
Venus	108.2	12100
Earth	149.6	12756
Mars	227.9	6794

d) Write a program that initializes a hash with these values. Just as we did in Chapter 4, represent the data values by separating the distance and diameter information with a : character.

e) You might visualize the hash like this:

Key	Value
Mercury	57.9:4880
Venus	108.2:12100
Earth	149.6:12756
Mars	227.9:6794

5.1.2 ADD AND REMOVE ELEMENTS IN A HASH

In Chapter 2, "The Nickel Tour," we saw how to use the output from a system command in a Perl program.

■ *FOR EXAMPLE*

If you would like to store the contents of the current directory in a variable:

```
$files = `ls`;
```

If you do this, you might have quite a bit of data in your variable, but you know how to convert it to an array with `split()` or, if you think about it a little bit, you could convert the data to a hash by splitting and choosing.

Let's see a program that does this. To understand the program, we first need to review the output of the `ls(1)` program. Here's something you might try from your shell prompt:

```
$ ls -1 /tmp
total 6938
-rw-r--r--    1 vinny    everyone         125 Feb 26  1998 DATA.TAG
-rw-r--r--    1 vinny    everyone         800 Jun 23  1994 LEO.ICO
-rwxr-xr-x    1 vinny    everyone       59904 Aug 26  1997 SETUP.EXE
-rw-r--r--    1 bob      everyone          76 Feb 26  1998 SETUP.INI
-rw-r--r--    1 vinny    everyone        2176 Jul 29 13:47 ball1.jpg
-rw-r--r--    1 root     everyone    12132580 Feb 26  1998 data1.cab
```

If your system doesn't have the `ls(1)` program, you can still run these examples. We've provided a Perl program called `fls.pl` that will simulate the output for you. If you run it with the option, it will give you simulated output that is the same every time. Even if you are running on a UNIX system and have an `ls(1)` program, you may still want to use `fls.pl` to simulate input while you are testing.

Let's use that data in a program. In order for this to work though, we'll have to dig a little more deeply into the `split()` function.

The Whole Truth

So far, we've been using a single character to split our data apart. Our data has been delimited with the colon character or the newline character and we've been able to give `split()` a simple string that contains the character we expect to use as a delimiter.

That's fine until we encounter data, as we do above, that is delimited by a series of spaces, or maybe spaces between some fields, but tabs between other fields. The `split()` function really knows how to deal with this situation as long as *we* know that the first argument should be a *regular expression*.

We'll study regular expressions in Chapter 7, "Regular Expressions," but for now you should be aware that the simplest form of a regular expression is a literal string. That's why the string `":"` has been a legal first argument to `split()`.

From this point on, when we want to use the `split()` function, we'll state the first argument as `/:/` or `/\n/` even when a simple quoted string will suffice. And to deal with the situation where data is delimited by a series of spaces or tabs, we can use the special regular expression `/\s+/`.

Look over this program, run it, and answer the questions that follow:

DIRSPLIT.PL

```
1  #!/usr/bin/perl
2
3  $info = `ls -l /tmp`; # get a directory listing
4  # $info = `perl fls.pl`
5  @infolist = split /\n/, $info; # now, it's in an array
6  shift @infolist; # get rid of that first line
7
8  foreach $line (@infolist) {
9      @details = split /\s+/, $line;
10     $perms = @details[0];
11     $owner = @details[2];
12     $size = @details[4];
13     $name = @details[8];
14
15     # perhaps we could have said...
16     #($perms, $owner, $size, $name) = @details[0,2,4,8];
17     # or better yet...
18     #($perms, $owner, $size, $name) =
19     #   (split /\s+/, $line)[0,2,4,8];
```

```
20
21    $usage{$owner} += $size;
22    $filecount{$owner}++;
23    $access{$name} = $perms;
24 }
25
26 $, = "...";
27 print "Usage hash: ", %usage, "\n";
28 print "Filecount hash: ", %filecount, "\n";
29 print "Access hash: ", %access, "\n";
```

a) In *line 21*, what exactly is going on?

_____

_____

b) What benefit would we achieve if we used the code in *lines 18* and *19*?

_____

_____

READING A PARAMETER LIST

Sometimes data is presented in a format that looks like:

NAME=value

Processing data that is in this format is easy for our Perl program. To see an example, we can use the output of the **set** command. This command emits the content of the current shell environment. Its output looks a little bit like this:

```
$ set
PATH=/usr/bin:/util:/opt/vim5:/opt/
perl5/bin

SHELL=/bin/sh

UID=500

TEMP=/tmp

TERM=xterm
```

(Note: If your system doesn't give you output like this when you use the `set` command, try using `printenv` to see if that does the trick.)

> **c)** Write a program that will take the output of the `set` command and store each line in a hash keyed to the value seen before the = sign. From our example output, we would expect to see a hash that looks like this:

Key	Value
PATH	/usr/bin/:/util:/opt/vim5:/opt/perl5/bin
SHELL	/bin/sh
UID	500
TEMP	/tmp
TERM	xterm

_____

_____

5.1.3 POPULATE A HASH FROM THE CONTENTS OF A FILE

If you solved the last Exercise question (or understood the solution proposed in the Answers section), you can see how data from an outside source can be represented in your Perl program. In fact, the task of taking configuration information of the form *NAME=VALUE* (as `set` presents it) is one that often comes up for a Perl programmer.

Here's an example configuration file we might use:

CONFIG.TXT
```
FONT=courier
SIZE=12
WIDTH=80
HEIGHT=25
```

We'll instruct our program operator to provide the configuration filename on the command line and we can read it as we did in Chapter 2, "The Nickel Tour."

READCONFIG.PL
```
1  #!/usr/bin/perl
2  while ($nextline = <>){
3     chomp $nextline;
4     ($name, $val) = split /=/, $nextline;
5     $config{$name} = $val;
6  }
7  $, = "=>";
8  print %config, "\n";
```

Run this program as we've instructed our program operator to do, and answer the following questions.

a) What does the program report as the value for width?

_____

_____

b) What happens if you forget to provide the name of the input file?

_____

_____

Instead of blindly trusting the command line to contain a filename, we can open the file explicitly and force the program to exit if no filename exists. We saw something like this in Chapter 2, "The Nickel Tour."

```
open (IN, $ARGV[0]) or die "Couldn't open file: $ARGV[0]";
```

Let's add that to our program:

FILECONFIG.PL

```
 1 #!/usr/bin/perl
 2
 3 open (IN, "config.txt") or die "Couldn't open config.txt";
 4
 5 while ($nextline = <IN>){
 6    chomp $nextline;
 7    ($name, $val) = split /=/, $nextline;
 8    $config{$name} = $val;
 9 }
10
11 $, = "=>";
12 print %config, "\n";
```

It didn't change very much at all! We simply added a call in _line 3_ that opens the file, and we changed _line 4_ slightly to read from the newly opened filehandle instead of STDIN.

Now let's see how this technique could be used in practice.

Coach Randall decided that his ballpark model program would be initialized from a file that contained information in the format ATTRIBUTE=value. Each configuration parameter would appear on a line by itself and there would be no blank lines.

To test the concept, he wanted to write a simple program that would simply read the data in, then dump it in raw format so he could be sure that file was being read correctly. To print the data, he decided to put a : character in $, so that the keys and values would be differentiated.

He wanted the data file name to be specified by the user on the command line. He imagined that the following table would help him to predict the sort of data that would be seen.

Attribute Name	Possible Values
field condition	dry, wet, moist, slippery, muddy, icy
wind direction	N, NE, E, SE, S, SW, W, NW
wind speed	30kt, 15kt, 5kt
time of day	10:00am, 2:00pm, 8:00pm
sky condition	clear, cloudy, overcast, partly sunny
lighting	bright, mixed, dim, dark

c) Write the program that Coach Randal is thinking about, and test it against two configuration files, `sept.cfg` and `dec.cfg`

SEPT.CFG
```
field condition=slippery
wind direction=NW
wind speed=25kt
sky condition=clear
```

DEC.CFG
```
field condition=icy
wind direction=N
wind speed=15kt
sky condition=overcast
```

For now it's okay if your program output is not terribly readable. We'll address that problem in Exercise 5.2.1.

_____

_____

LAB 5.1 EXERCISE ANSWERS

5.1.1 ANSWERS

a) In *line 10*, our program attempts to print a hash inside a quoted string. What result do we see when this runs?

Answer: The hash itself doesn't print. Only its name appears.

There are a couple of good ways to print a hash, but throwing the name into a quoted string is not one of those ways.

b) When the hash is printed, do the values appear, or the indexes, or both?

Answer: When printed this way, the keys and the values are both printed. You may also have noticed that the elements are printed in a seemingly arbitrary order.

Perl stores information in your hash in a way that is efficient. You cannot rely upon the order of elements in a hash, but it doesn't matter. If you want some element from a hash, you'll access it by name. When you want to access all of the elements in a particular sequence, there are methods for doing this, too. We'll see these in detail later in the chapter.

c) In the hash initialization (*lines 3-7*), the values are represented as literal decimal numbers. Any baseball fan will tell you that a batting average should look like *.312* rather than *312*. Change the values in the program to make each of them appear as a fractional number. Does your program still work?

Answer: The program still works. When the values print, however, they are represented as 0.312 rather than .312 as we would like.

This probably makes a baseball fan's teeth hurt more than our original representation. If we initialize the hash by presenting the averages in quotes, the values will be seen as strings and printed that way. So our hash should be initialized like this:

```
%averages = (
    Tinker => '.312',
    Evers => '.284',
    Chance => '.319'
);
```

d) Write a program that initializes a hash with these values. Just as we did in Chapter 4, represent the data values by separating the distance and diameter information with a : character.

Answer: As always, there are several ways that you might write this program, but this is one that mimics a common approach taken by many Perl programmers.

```
%solsys = (
    Mercury => '57.9:4880',
    Venus => '108.2:12100',
    Earth => '149.6:12756',
    Mars => '227.9:6794',
);
```

Notice that the last element of the hash is followed by a comma even though that would not be necessary. The reason for doing this is that we may want to add more elements later and we can be sure that we won't forget to add the comma at that time. Also notice that the data elements are presented in single quotes. Double quotes would suffice here, but most programmers tend to prefer the stronger single quote to prevent misinterpretation in case the data values contain special characters.

5.1.2 ANSWERS

a) In *line 21*, what exactly is going on?

Answer: We are taking the number stored in `$size` *and adding it to the value already stored in the hash* `%usage` *under the key represented by* `$owner`.

As an example, if we were processing the third line of our sample data from the Exercise, we would add the number *59904* to the element `$usage{'vinny'}`. If the element doesn't currently exist, this operation will create it. In fact, most hashes are built up this way rather than being initialized by explicit code.

If this program was a little bit difficult to understand at first, don't worry; with practice, all of this will become second nature to you. Figure 5.2 may give you an overview of what the program is trying to do.

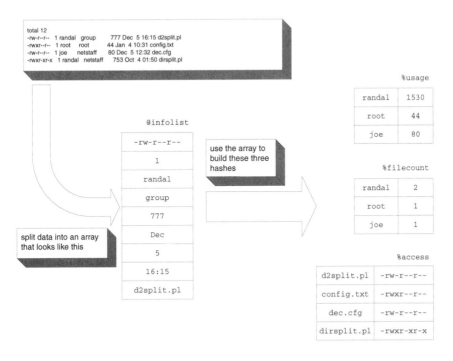

Figure 5.2 ■ From raw data to array to hash.

If you had trouble understanding the program, study this diagram and then look at the program again.

b)   What benefit would we achieve if we used the code in *lines 18* and *19?*

Answer: Of course, lines 18 and 19 are really one logical line of code. By taking this approach, we can dispense with the temporary array @details.

Let's break that line apart and see what we're really doing.

```
($perms, $owner, $size, $name) = (split /\s+/, $line)[0,2,4,8];
```

The *split()* function takes the data in *$line* and breaks it apart, using any occurrence of whitespace as a delimiter. From the resulting list, we take the first, third, fifth and ninth elements, assigning them to the variables named in the list on the left side of the assignment operator (*$perms, $owner,* and so forth). Perhaps now you can see why we spent so much time with arrays and lists in the last chapter. An operation like this is easy when you have some practice, but it may look like magic to the innocent bystander.

c)   Write a program that will take the output of the set command and store each line in a hash keyed to the value seen before the = sign.

Answer: Your program may look like this, or it could differ greatly. This is one way to write the program.

READSET.PL
```
1 #!/usr/bin/perl
2 $data = `set`;
3 #$data = `printenv`;  # Use this if set fails
4 @lines = split /\n/, $data;
5 foreach $line (@lines) {
6     ($key, $val) = split /=/, $line;
7     $env{$key} = $val;
8 }
9
10 $, = "\t";
11 print %env;
```

The output from this program is not terribly elegant. For that matter, dirsplit.pl had pretty ragged output as well. You may have wondered

why we didn't use a `foreach()` loop on this hash or the one we build in
`dirsplit.pl`. The fact is, we cannot use a `foreach()` loop directly to
iterate through a hash. We'll see how to do it in the next Lab. For now,
let's continue to focus on getting data into the hash.

5.1.3 ANSWERS

a) What does the program report as the value for width?

*Answer: If you typed in the information shown in this book or used the example file
from the companion website, the answer would be 80. The result depends upon the
data that is provided in the* `config.txt` *file. And that is the point of the whole
thing.*

b) What happens if you forget to provide the name of the input file?

*Answer: Your cursor will sit there and blink at you. In any case, nothing interesting will
happen.*

You may think the program has stopped or hung. In reality, it is waiting
to see some data on the standard input source. You can provide this by
typing in configuration information at the terminal. Simply type in lines
of the form shown in the Exercise. When you've provided enough information, type the end-of-file character. (That would be Ctrl-D if you're
working on a UNIX system. It will be Ctrl-Z if you're working on a Win32
machine. Check your system documentation if neither of those works for
you.)

c) Write the program that Coach Joe is thinking about, and test it against
two configuration files: `sept.cfg` and `dec.cfg`.

*Answer: This program should look very much like the program shown in the Exercise
text. The main difference is that the file to be opened is named as a command-line
argument. Here's one way to write it:*

FILECONFIG.PL

```
1  #!/usr/bin/perl
2
3  open (IN, $ARGV[0]) or die "Couldn't open file [$ARGV[0]]";
4
5  while ($nextline = <IN>){
6      chomp $nextline;
7      ($name, $val) = split /=/, $nextline;
```

**LAB
5.1**

```
 8    $config{$name} = $val;
 9 }
10
11 $, = ":";
12 print %config, "\n";
```

LAB 5.1 SELF-REVIEW QUESTIONS

In order to test your progress, you should be able to answer the following questions.

1) Which of the following legally initializes a hash?
   i)   %plants = {"Mercury", 100, "Venus", 200, "Earth", 300 };
   ii) %planets = ("Mercury", 100, "Venus", 200, "Earth", 300);
   iii) %planets = ("Mercury" => 100, "Venus" => 200, "Earth" => 300);
   iv) %planets = {"Mercury" => 100, "Venus" => 200, "Earth" => 300 };
   a) _____ i and iv
   b) _____ ii and iii
   c) _____ ii and iv
   d) _____ none of them

2) To print the raw values from a hash, you must do which of the following?
   a) _____ Place the hash name inside a quoted string
   b) _____ Place the hash name outside a quoted string
   c) _____ Place the hash name inside a clay pot
   d) _____ Use the special operator `qh{}` to enclose the hash name

3) When you print a hash simply by providing its name in a `print()` statement, which of the following do you get?
   a) _____ Both keys and values, printed in order by key
   b) _____ Only the keys
   c) _____ Only the values
   d) _____ Both keys and values, jumbled together, and in seemingly arbitrary order

4) To print a single entry from a hash (%tbl) with a key of "George", which of the following would you code:

    a) _____ `print '$tbl{"George"}\n';`

    b) _____ `print "$tbl[George]\n";`

    c) _____ `print "$tbl{'George'}\n";`

    d) _____ `print "%tbl{'George'}\n";`

5) To create a hash called %mail_addresses, you must do which of the following?

    a) _____ Declare it at the top of your program

    b) _____ Declare it anywhere in your program

    c) _____ Initialize it before you want to use it

    d) _____ Simply assign one element to it when you're ready

L A B 5.2

TRAVERSING A HASH

LAB OBJECTIVES

After this Lab, you will be able to:

✓ Traverse a Hash in Arbitrary Order

✓ Traverse in Order by Key or Value

✓ Use the Environment Hash

When we wanted to traverse an array, we started at the beginning and went to the end. In a hash, there's no clear definition of what constitutes the beginning or how we proceed toward the end. You might already have noticed that when we print the data in a hash, it appears to be stored in an arbitrary order.

From our perspective, this is true. The data is stored in a meaningful order, but that order is determined by Perl to achieve the most efficient storage and retrieval. So there's not a specific "beginning" or "end."

This is really okay, because we have a number of ways to traverse the hash. In this Lab, we'll start by going through the data in arbitrary order, then we'll see how we can sort the data by key, and at last by the data value itself.

We used a foreach() loop to iterate through an array, but we'll have to work a little harder to do this with a hash. The foreach() loop works only with a list or array. Each element of a hash is really two things: a key and a value. This is okay though, because we have two functions that can produce a list from a hash. The keys() function will produce a list of all the keys in a hash, and the `values()` function will generate a list of all the data values.

■ *FOR EXAMPLE*

To get a list of the keys in a hash, we could do this:

KEYCHILD.PL
```
1  #!/usr/bin/perl
2  %days = (
3      Monday => "Fair of Face",
4      Tuesday => "Full of Grace",
5      Wednesday => "Full of Woe"
6  );
7  $, = ":"; print (keys %days), "\n";
```

If we run this code, we see something like:

```
$ perl keychild.pl
Monday:Wednesday:Tuesday
```

What happened here? The `keys()` function produced a list. We can treat it exactly as if it were an array with a name. By populating the `$,` variable with a character to give us visual separation, we can get some output that is close to readable.

It turns out to be a short leap to take that list and use it to control a `foreach()` loop. Let's try it.

LAB 5.2 EXERCISES

5.2.1 TRAVERSE A HASH IN ARBITRARY ORDER

Earlier in this Lab, we took the output from the `ls(1)` command and turned that data into a hash. We'll use this approach again to see how we can traverse a hash. This time, we'll use the `fls.pl` program to get simulated input.

Run the `fls.pl` program by hand so that you can see the output it produces.

```
$ fls.pl -f
```
Now read and run the following program. Answer the questions at the end.

D2SPLIT.PL

```
 1 #!/usr/bin/perl
 2
 3 # remember, our output looks like this:
 4 # total 12
 5 # -rw-r--r--   1 root    group        44 Oct  4 10:31 config.txt
 6 # -rw-r--r--   1 randal  wheel       547 Oct  5 15:58 d2split.pl
 7 # -rw-r--r--   1 joe     netstaff     80 Oct  5 12:32 dec.cfg
 8
 9 #$info = `ls -l /tmp`; # get a live directory listing
10 $info = `perl fls.pl -f`; # use fls.pl to get simulated data
11 @infolist = split "\n", $info; # now, it's in an array
12 shift @infolist; # get rid of that first line
13
14 foreach $line (@infolist) {
15    ($owner, $size, $month) = (split /\s+/, $line)[2,4,5];
16
17    $usage{$owner} += $size;
18    $filecount{$month}++;
19 }
20
21 print "in the usage hash:\n";
22 foreach $i (keys %usage) {
23    print "key: $i\tvalue: $usage{$i}\n";
24 }
25
26 print "in the filecount hash:\n";
27 foreach $i (keys %filecount) {
28    print "key: $i\tvalue: $filecount{$i}\n";
29 }
```

a) Is *line 9* a program instruction or a comment?

_____

_____

b) How could the loops starting in *line 22* and *28* be rewritten to eliminate the use of the `$i` variable?

_____

_____

c) Add the following line at the end of the program and report what happens:

```
foreach (values %filecount){print "value: $_\n"};
```

_____

_____

Coach Randal was staring at an old javelin on his wall when the phone rang. It was Major Ellie. "Hey, Randal," Ellie began. "Do you know what event was taking place during the occasion of the first television broadcast signal from Earth strong enough to reach into space?"

"That's easy," said Randal. "It was the 1936 Olympics from Berlin." After chatting with his friend for a while longer, Randal took out an old record book with information about the Olympic Games. He built a data file that contained the names of the hosting countries or states, beginning with the first year that both summer and winter games were held (1924). His data file looked like this:

OLYMPICS.DAT
```
1924=Paris, France:Chamonix, France
1928=Amsterdam, The Netherlands:St. Moritz, Switzerland
1932=Los Angeles, California:Lake Placid, New York
1936=Berlin, Germany:Garmisch-Partenkirchen, Germany
1948=London, England:St. Moritz, Switzerland
```

To get a little bit of practice at extracting data and storing it into an array, he wrote a program that produced the following report:

```
First five "full" Olympic years...
Year: 1924
  Summer: Paris, France
  Winter: Chamonix, France
```

```
Year: 1936
   Summer: Berlin, Germany
   Winter: Garmisch-Partenkirchen, Germany
Year: 1928
   Summer: Amsterdam, The Netherlands
   Winter: St. Moritz, Switzerland
Year: 1948
   Summer: London, England
   Winter: St. Moritz, Switzerland
Year: 1932
   Summer: Los Angeles, California
   Winter: Lake Placid, New York


California hosted the Olympics 1 time.

England hosted the Olympics 1 time.

The Netherlands hosted the Olympics 1
time.

Germany hosted the Olympics 2 times.

New York hosted the Olympics 1 time.

Switzerland hosted the Olympics 2 times.

France hosted the Olympics 2 times.
```

The most important thing is to extract the data, storing it into a set of hashes. Randal's program reads the file and uses three hashes to represent the data. These tables show an example of how they are structured.

Example of %summer

Key	Value
1936	Berlin
1928	Amsterdam

Example of %winter

Key   Value

1924 Chamonix, France

1932 Lake Placid, New York

Example of %events

Key   Value

Germany 2

California 1

> **d)** Write a program that does the same. Don't get carried away with formatting; we will study that in detail later.

_____

_____

5.2.2 Traverse in Order by Key or Value

Both the `keys()` and the `values()` functions appear to present the contents of the hash in an arbitrary order. You will often want to access your information in some specific order. This is easy to do in Perl. You can simply pass the list produced by `keys()` to the `sort()` function.

■ FOR EXAMPLE

The simplest code we could use to present a sorted hash would look like this:

```
foreach $k (sort keys %myhash) {
   print "next key: $k \t value: $myhash{$k}\n";
}
```

And if we want to invert the order:

```
foreach $k (reverse sort keys %myhash) {
```

```
    print "next key: $k \t value: $myhash{$k}\n";
}
```

If you've programmed in other languages, you might be surprised at the "free range" attitude that Perl exhibits toward the use of parentheses. You may use parentheses when it adds to clarity or helps to force a particular order of execution, but you are in no way required to do so in most circumstances. On the other hand, if you wanted to parenthesize fully, you might write:

```
foreach $k (reverse (sort (keys (%myhash)))) {
```

That would be just a little bit more explicit than we need to be. You might also note that the way we stated it the first time is much closer to how we would state the instruction in English: "*Reverse the sorted list of keys from %myhash.*"

Now let's take a closer look at what these functions can do for us when we're working with a hash.

Run this code and answer the questions that follow:

PLANET4.PL

```
 1  #!/usr/bin/perl
 2
 3  # keys in the hash are planets' names, value is mean distance
 4  # from sun in kilometers
 5  #
 6
 7  $au = 149.6;
 8  %ptable = (
 9      Mercury=>57.9, Venus=>108.2, Earth=>149.6,
10      Mars=>227.9, Jupiter=>778.3, Saturn=>1427,
11      Uranus=>2870, Neptune=>4497, Pluto=>5900,
12  );
13
14  # report header, the hard way!
15  print "Planet\t\tDistance from Sun\tDistance in AU\n";
16  print "\t\t(Million KM)\n";
17  print "-"x10,"\t","-"x17,"\t","-"x9,"\n";
18
19  foreach $p (sort keys %ptable) {
20      $d = $ptable{$p};
21      print "$p\t\t$d\t\t\t", $d/$au, "\n";
22  }
```

```
23
24 # now, without sorting
25 print "\n\n";
26 foreach $p (keys %ptable) {
27     $d = $ptable{$p};
28     print "$p\t\t$d\t\t\t", $d/$au, "\n";
29 }
```

**LAB
5.2**

a) In what order are the planets the first time the list is printed?

_____

_____

b) Add a phrase to the end of the program that prints the distance values in sorted order. They don't have to be printed with the associated planet name this time, just produce a list of numbers.

_____

_____

Now let's consider what it would take to truly sort this hash by value. One simple way might be to traverse the hash in any order, taking each value and using it as the key for a new hash, and using each key as the value in that new hash.

We could just get the information from the hash by traversing a list of keys as we did previously, but this is a great chance for us to look at another way to iterate through each of the elements of a hash. The key to this approach is a function called each(). The first time we call it on a hash, the function returns a list consisting of a key and value pair. The next time we call it, another key/value pair is returned as a list. This continues until the hash is exhausted and then each() returns a value that we may interpret in Perl as false. That means we can say:

```
while (($k, $v) = each %myhash) {
    # do something with the information
}
```

So our program to sort the information by value would look like:

VSORT.PL

```
 1 #!/usr/bin/perl
 2
 3 $au = 149.6;
 4 %ptable = (
 5    Mercury=>57.9, Venus=>108.2, Earth=>149.6,
 6    Mars=>227.9, Jupiter=>778.3, Saturn=>1427,
 7    Uranus=>2870, Neptune=>4497, Pluto=>5900,
 8 );
 9
10 while (($k, $v) = each %ptable){
11    $vtable{$v} = $k;
12 }
13
14 # report header, the hard way!
15 print "Planet\t\tDistance from Sun\tDistance in AU\n";
16 print "\t\t(Million KM)\n";
17 print "-"x10,"\t","-"x17,"\t","-"x9,"\n";
18
19 foreach $d (sort {$a<=>$b} keys %vtable){
20    $p = $vtable{$d};
21    print "$p\t\t$d\t\t\t", $d/$au, "\n";
22 }
```

This is very close to the program we saw before. If you look at the code in *lines 10-12*, you'll see a loop that gets all of the data from the hash, one element at a time. Inside the loop, a new hash is created, using the data as the key and the key as the new data.

Now in *lines 19-22* we can use a loop very much like the one we used before to sort the keys and iterate over that list. Note that we use a numeric sort. It's terribly critical here because the idea is to get the planets to come out exactly in order by their orbital distance from the sun. We've already seen what would happen here if we use merely an ASCII sort.

Now it's your turn.

Major Ellie nudged her chair backward just a bit. She only half hoped that it wouldn't roll over Randal's toe. The Coach was breathing a little too closely down Ellie's neck as she coded the latest enhancement to her solar system model based on the `orbitsort.pl` *program.*

The idea is to store the information about the planets in a hash, keyed by planet name. The data in the hash would consist of distance and diameter figures separated by a : character. With the information represented this way, Ellie wanted to print one table that showed the planets in order by distance from the sun, and another table that showed the planets in order by diameter.

> **c)** Write the program that Ellie is trying to finish. Fortunately for you, Coach Randal isn't there to *help* you. Use the data provided in Table 5.1.

5.2.3 USE THE ENVIRONMENT HASH

In Exercise 5.1.2, we looked at a program that took the output of the set command and parsed it into a hash. The information we got by doing this showed us the current state of the operating system shell environment. Knowing what's in the environment can be very useful to us. We can learn things like the current user home directory ($HOME), value of the execution path ($PATH), login terminal type ($TERM), and current user id ($UID).

When we're using the shell interactively, these things may not seem terribly valuable to you because you already know what the name of your home directory or terminal type is. But a Perl program might benefit from having access to these things. Even on a machine that doesn't have a Unix shell to work with, the environment can still be useful in some ways.

THE CURRENT ENVIRONMENT HASH %ENV

We already saw how we could store the output from the set command in a string with the backtick operator. But this really isn't necessary because our programs automatically start with a hash called %ENV that holds the contents of the environment.

Accessing an environment variable is as simple as referencing the content of any hash. The $TERM value is stored in:

```
$ENV{'TERM'}
```
and the **$PATH** variable is available in:

```
$ENV{'PATH'}
```

Let's run a quick experiment to see that this hash contains about what we expect.

a) From your command prompt, run the `set` command and look at the output. Write down the values for $PATH, $SHELL, and $HOST-NAME. If your program doesn't show these variables, choose substitutes for the missing ones.

_____

_____

b) Write a short program that prints out the values for these variables by reading the `%ENV` hash.

_____

_____

LAB 5.2 EXERCISE ANSWERS

5.2.1 ANSWERS

a) Is *line 9* a program instruction or a comment?

Answer: Well, it's really both. (If you simply answered "yes" to this question, you are sentenced to three hours in a coffee house that has a climbing wall—on open-mike poetry night! On the other hand, you'll fit in well with the Perl programming community.)

It is common for programmers to include instructions that are "commented out" so that they can be used later, reviewed for reference, or just "deadened" while other testing takes place. In fact, while you're deep in your development/testing cycle, you may want to avoid deleting lines until you're sure that you won't need them later. Just comment them out until you need them or until you're sure you never will. Of course you already knew this since we talked about it in Chapter 2, "The Nickel Tour," but I wanted to be sure you were still awake.

b) How could the loops starting in *line 22* and *28* be rewritten to eliminate the use of the `$i` variable?

Answer: By using the default variable, those loops can be rewritten to look like:

```perl
foreach (keys %filecount) {
   print "key: $_\tvalue: $filecount{$_}\n";
}
```

The code isn't shorter or more elegant in any way except that there's one less variable rattling around in memory. Sometimes, every little bit helps.

c) Add the following line at the end of the program and report what happens:

```perl
foreach (values %filecount){print "value: $_\n"};
```

Answer: The values from the hash are printed as if they were in an array with an arbitrary order. In fact, we might say that the `values()` *function turns a hash into an array.*

d) See if you can write a program that produces the same report that Randal's program did.

Answer: Because of the complexity of this program and latitude offered by Perl, your program may not look very much like this at all. The most important thing is that it produces the output you want. Next important (and not much less critical) is that you have written it in a way that is logical and understandable to you. Here's what Joe wrote:

OSITE.PL

```perl
1  #!/usr/bin/perl
2
3  open (DAT, "olympics.dat") or die "Couldn't open data file.";
4
5  while ($ln = <DAT>) {
6
7  # break up the data by splitting on the = sign
8     chomp $ln;
9     ($year, $sites) = split /=/, $ln;
10
11 # build summer and winter tables by year
12     ($run, $ski) = split /:/, $sites;
13     $summer{$year} = $run;
```

```
14      $winter{$year} = $ski;
15
16 # accumulator table by country
17    foreach $season ($run, $ski) {
18        $country = (split /,/, $season)[1];
19        $events{$country}++;
20    }
21 } # finished reading file
22 close DAT;
23
24 print qq{\t\tFirst five "full" Olympic years...\n};
25 foreach $yr (keys %summer) {
26    print "Year: $yr\n",
27        "\t\tSummer: $summer{$yr}\n",
28        "\t\tWinter: $winter{$yr}\n";
29 }
30
31 print "\n";
32 foreach $host (keys %events) {
33    print "$host hosted the Olympics $events{$host}",
34        $events{$host} == 1 ? " time" : " times",
35        ".\n";
36 }
```

With the loop that begins in *line 5*, Randal takes the data from the file and splits it on the = sign. This gives two pieces, $year and $sites. The latter is a composite string made up of two data elements, the city and country or state of the summer games followed by a :, and then the city and country or state of the winter games.

This information is split into two elements ($run for the summer site, and $ski for the winter site), then each is used as the value in a hash that is keyed by year.

At last an accumulator is incremented, filling a hash that uses the country or state as a key. To get the key, the program must split the site value one last time, using the comma as a separator.

5.2.2 ANSWERS

a) In what order are the planets the first time the list is printed?

Answer: They appear to be in alphabetical order by name of planet. That would make sense because the keys are being sorted.

b) Add a phrase to the end of the program that prints the distance values in sorted order. They don't have to be printed with the associated planet name this time, just produce a list of numbers.

Answer: There are two ways you might have done this. The question doesn't specify the type of sort that should be done, so you might have done either of the following:

PLANET5.PL (EXCERPT)

```
 1 @distances = values %ptable;
 2 print "\n\n";
 3 print "an ASCIIbetical sort\n";
 4 foreach $d (sort @distances) {
 5    print "$d: ";
 6 }
 7 print "\n";
 8
 9 print "\n";
10 print "a numeric sort\n";
11 foreach $d (sort {$a<=>$b} @distances) {
12    print "$d: ";
13 }
14 print "\n";
```

In the first loop (*lines 4-6*), this code requested a simple sort in ASCIIbetical order. The second attempt (*lines 11-13*) sorts by doing a numeric comparison of the successive values. You can observe the behavior of this code by running the `planet5.pl` example program (available from the companion website).

c) Write the program that Ellie is trying to finish.

Answer: Here's one way you might have written the program:

PLANET6.PL

```
 1 #!/usr/bin/perl
 2
 3 %innerdata = (
 4    Venus => "108.2:12100",
 5    Mars => "227.9:6794",
 6    Earth => "149.6:12756",
 7    Mercury => "57.9:4880",
```

**LAB
5.2**

```
 8 );
 9
10 while (($planet, $data) = each %innerdata){
11     $c = join ":", ($data, $planet);
12     push @composite, $c;
13 }
14
15 print "Planets in order from the Sun\n";
16 foreach $rec (sort {
17         $o1 = (split /:/, $a)[0];
18         $o2 = (split /:/, $b)[0];
19         return $o1 <=> $o2;
20         } @composite) {
21     ($dist, $dia, $p) = split /:/, $rec;
22     print "\t$p:\t$dist\n";
23 }
24
25 print "Planets in order by size\n";
26 # let's use the default variable and
27 # collapse the sort evaluation block
28 foreach (sort {(split /:/, $a)[1] <=> (split /:/, $b)[1]}
29         @composite) {
30     ($dist, $dia, $p) = split /:/;
31     print "\t$p:\t$dia\n";
32 }
```

There are several interesting things about this program. First, in *lines 10-13*, the information is pulled from the hash one key/value pair at a time. That information is pasted together into a string by appending the key at the end of the data string. Then this string is pushed onto the end of an array that holds the data in the form we'll need. In essence, a record from the new array might look like this:

```
108.2:12100:Venus
```

The fun part of this program is that when it's time to sort the data, it is passed to an evaluation block that plucks out the portion that we intend to evaluate. For instance, to sort by distance from the sun, the string must be split on the : character, and the first element in the resulting list is the part that's important to us.

Look at how the evaluation block is formed in *lines 16-20*. It is broken down onto several lines to make it more readable. Each element being compared by the sort routine is broken into parts and the important part is preserved in $o1 or $o2. Those values are compared by using the "spaceship operator" and the result is returned. Be sure you understand this, because in *line 29* we combine all of that activity into one line!

The only thing different in *line 29* is the portion of the input strings that we examine and compare. You might not want to write your own code this way, but you very well may inherit a body of Perl code that does something this way. It will be good if you can read and understand it.

5.2.3 ANSWERS

a) From your command prompt, run the `set` command and look at the output. Write down the values for `$PATH`, `$SHELL` and `$HOSTNAME`. If your program doesn't show these variables, choose substitutes for the missing ones.

Answer: The values from this will vary from system to system. An MS-DOS or Win32 system may have only a couple of the values assigned. You could assign them from the same command prompt window where you'll run your Perl program in a moment.

b) Write a short program that prints out the values for these variables by reading the `%ENV` hash.

Answer: The simplest way to write the program is something like this:

ENVPRINT.PL
```
1  #!/usr/bin/perl
2  print "Environment says that \$TERM is $ENV{'TERM'}\n";
3  print "Environment says that \$HOSTNAME is $ENV{'HOSTNAME'}\n";
4  print "Environment says that \$SHELL is $ENV{'SHELL'}\n";
```

This is much easier than digging through the output of the `set` or `printenv` commands isn't it? As long as you remember how to get an element from a hash, you can always get at the values stored in the environment.

LAB 5.2 SELF-REVIEW QUESTIONS

In order to test your progress, you should be able to answer the following questions.

1) Which of these lines will iterate over a hash, processing each element?
   i) foreach $element (%htable) { *do something* };
   ii) foreach $element (keys %htable) { *do something* };
   iii) foreach $element (sort %htable) { *do something* };
   iv) foreach $element (sort values %htable) { *do something* };
   a) _____i and iv
   b) _____ii and iii
   c) _____ ii and iv
   d) _____none of them

2) Which of the following are three functions that extract the data from a hash?
   a) _____ keys(),split(),and each()
   b) _____ keys(),values(),and each()
   c) _____ slurp(),spoon(),and shovel()
   d) _____ foreach(),split(),and join()

3) How many lines will be printed by the following program?

```
%couples = (
   george => gracie,
   abbot => costello,
   johnson => boswell );
foreach $c (each %couples) {
   print "$c\n";
};
```

   a) _____ three
   b) _____ six
   c) _____ two, one for george, one for gracie
   d) _____ never

4) The following code will print the size of the hash called %names:

```
%names = ( 100 => "scooby", 200 => "tick", 300 => "jetson" );
@index = keys %names;
print "size of hash is: ", $#index + 1, "\n";
```

      a) _____ True

      b) _____ False

5) A hash may contain which of the following?

      a) _____only numeric data

      b) _____only character strings

      c) _____ oats, peas, beans, and barley

      d) _____string or numeric data

      Quiz answers appear in Appendix A, Section 5.2.

**LAB
5.2**

C H A P T E R 5

TEST YOUR THINKING

1) Take the output from the `ls(1)` command (or better yet, `fls.pl -f`) and store the information in a hash that is keyed by file ownership. Produce a report that shows each file owner and how many bytes they consume in file space.

There are many ways to extract the table of contents from a gzip-compressed tar file (a format very common on the Internet). Here is one command line that almost always works:

```
gzip -dc tarfile.tar.gz | tar tvf -
```

2) Write a program that expects the type of output that comes from this command and prints a report that analyzes it. Store the information in a hash that allows you to report based upon file ownership and file size. (If you don't have a tar file that gives you varied enough results for this project, visit the companion website and get the program simtar.pl which will give you a variety of results appropriate for testing.)

CHAPTER 6

TESTS AND BRANCHING

Without the ability to make decisions and test for the truth of various conditions, our programs will be little more than execution scripts. In this chapter, we'll see how to enable Perl programs to select among different branches of execution. We'll learn that Perl offers us a great deal of flexibility when it comes to stating the logic that controls our program.

We'll start by learning about the various forms of zero that exist in Perl. This will lead us to a definition of "true" and "false." From there, we'll see what options we have when it comes to basing an execution choice on the truth of various assertions.

L A B   6.1

TRUTH, BRANCHING, AND THE MANY FACES OF NOTHING

LAB OBJECTIVES

After this Lab, you will be able to:

✓ Conditionally Execute Simple Statements

✓ Combine Conditions

✓ Use the Logical Negation Operator

Our first job as we explore conditional execution and branching will be to define the values for "true" and "false." Once we have a clear definition of these concepts, we can have our program make decisions.

We already did a little bit of conditional execution in Chapter 1, "Getting Started," when we wrote programs that printed only certain lines. In this Lab, we'll see how that really works. In addition, we'll look at how our program can branch according to complex sets of conditions.

We must begin by looking at "nothing." In Perl, there are several values that represent nothing. One of those is the number 0 (zero). This number can be held in a scalar value, it can be inside an element of an array or a hash, or it could simply be stated literally. The string equivalent of zero is the null string. One way to state that value is to use empty quote marks: ("") Another near-equivalent to zero is the value "undefined." On occasion, this is the value that a function will return to tell us that an error occurred.

■ *FOR EXAMPLE*

Each of the following lines assigns to $val a value that we can consider to be "zero."

```
1   $val = 0;
2   $val = 6
3   $val = "";
4   $val = '';
5   $val = $variableThatIHaveNotYetCreated;
6   $val = undef;
7   undef ($val);
```

In *line 5*, $val is assigned to the value of a variable that has never been created. This will result in $val being assigned the "undefined" value. In *lines 6 and 7*, the same thing happens.

DOES THIS THING ALREADY EXIST?

You can test to see if a variable (or, more usefully, an array or hash element) has ever been created with the "defined" operator. The syntax looks like this:

```
$val = defined $variableThatIHaveNotYetCreated;
```

This has the same effect as *line 5* above in our case, but with one minor difference: In *line 5*, if $variableThatIHaveNotYetCreated actually holds some value, then $val will also be assigned that value. When we use the defined() operator, $val will either be assigned the value 1 (a non-zero, thus "true") or will itself get the value, undef.

PRONOUNCING TRUTH IN PERL

The reason that it was necessary to have this little discussion of zero is that any form of zero may be considered to be the equivalent of the value "false" when we make a test or ask a question in Perl. Any non-zero value is considered to be "true."

There are other ways to end up with a value that is "true" or "false." There are comparison operators (such as <, >=, and ==, all of which we will explore in Lab 6.3), there are test operators (to test for file characteristics, string characteristics, and other things), or we might rely upon the result returned from a function.

The Whole Truth

Is it True or False?

If you want to anticipate whether a value will be considered true or false, you can use this logic (just be aware that it only approximates what really takes place in Perl):

If the value is undefined, then it is false.

If it is an empty string, then it is false.

If it is a number, convert it to a string, and if that string is "0", then it is false.

The strange thing here is that if you have a string like "00" or "0.000," they will both evaluate to true. (On the other hand, what were you doing with those strings?)

In general, the rules are pretty logical, and if you want to be certain, you can use the comparison operators discussed in Lab 6.3.

CONDITIONAL EXECUTION

The simplest way to have your program perform conditional execution is to add a phrase at the end of a statement that names a condition that must be true (or false) in order for the statement to be executed.

■ *FOR EXAMPLE*

To give you a real-world example, consider this phrase:

```
See the barber IF you have soup in your beard.
```

It is legal (and convenient) in Perl to issue statements that work just this way. For instance:

```
print "See the barber\n" if defined $soup_in_beard;
```

Such a statement would print the message only if the variable named $soup_in_beard has been previously assigned a value. We can also reverse the sense of the condition. Again, let's look at a real-world example first:

```
Buy milk UNLESS we have at least a half-gallon.
```

We could state this in Perl (roughly) by saying:

```
print "Buy some milk.\n" unless defined $half_gallon;
```

This gives us two powerful ways to set conditions on a statement. You can use this technique to easily implement a common debugging strategy. The keys to this strategy are twofold. First, form your debugging lines in a way that makes it easy to identify and remove them from the program later, when you're ready for production. And secondly, allow the program to be run with varying "debug levels," with more information being printed as the debugging level increases. So if we have debug level 9 in effect, your program would want to print a lot of information. At debug level 1, only the most critical messages should be printed. Take a look at this program to see how you might do this yourself.

DEBUGLEVEL.PL

```
1  #!/usr/bin/perl
2  $debug = 3;
3  print "high priority\n" if 1 <= $debug;
4  print "medium priority\n" if 3 <= $debug;
5  print "minimum priority\n" if 9 <= $debug;
```

We haven't looked at this explicitly yet, but you might have guessed that <= means "less than or equal." We'll see more of this in Lab 6.3

You might find it odd that we say:

```
$1 <= $debug;
```

when it might seem more straightforward to say:

```
$debug >= 1;
```

The benefit to taking the approach shown in this example is that you can strip out all of the debugging lines when you're ready to ship your program. Any good editor (or a Perl program) can easily identify and delete any lines that end with the string "debug;".

COMBINING CONDITIONS

There will be times that you'd like to have an instruction execute only if both of two conditions are true. Or you may want to execute a certain instruction if either of two conditions is true. Perl allows us to easily combine conditions with an AND as well as an OR operator. There are actually two forms of each operator.

To create a phrase that would be true only if both of two conditions are true, you can use syntax that looks like this:

```
condition1 && condition2
```

Beginning with version 5 of Perl, you can also write your statement this way:

```
condition1 and condition2
```

■ *FOR EXAMPLE*

Suppose you want to print a simple message if both of two environment variables are defined. You might write something like:

```
print "Ready to go!\n" if
    (defined $ENV{'TERM'} && defined $ENV{'VISUAL'});
```

Or you might express it as:

```
print "Ready to go!\n" if
    (defined $ENV{'TERM'} and defined $ENV{'VISUAL'});
```

Or imagine that you want to test whether there is either a command-line argument or an environment variable for DEBUG_LEVEL. Your code might look like:

```
print "Found the stuff!\n" if
    (defined $ARGV[0] || defined $ENV{'DEBUG_LEVEL'});
```

And if you are using Perl 5 or later, you can also say:

```
print "Found the stuff!\n" if
    (defined $ARGV[0] and defined $ENV{'DEBUG_LEVEL'});
```

Note that in all four cases, the parentheses are for clarity only. You may encounter situations in which they are necessary due to the side-effects of other operations. In a situation as simple as this, they serve only to make the code less opaque.

THAT'S NOT WHAT I MEAN (LOGICAL NEGATION)

On occasion, a test will yield the opposite of the condition you want to check. For instance, you might want to take some action in the event that neither the command-line argument nor the environment variable exists.

This is where the "logical negation operator" (!) comes in handy. Use it when you can make your code more understandable, when it streamlines the logic, or when the traditional test just won't do.

■ *FOR EXAMPLE*

Let's print a message if there is no command-line argument and no environment variable for DEBUG_LEVEL. Our code might look like:

```
print "No debug info.\n" if
    (! defined $ARGV[0]) && (! defined $ENV{'DEBUG_LEVEL'});
```

This time again, the parentheses are redundant. The negation operator has a higher precedence than the logical and operator. If you forget that, though, this code will always work with the parentheses present. When you work with several programming languages, the ability to avoid relying on order of precedence is a big deal. Remember that parentheses are essentially free.

Here's a chance to try some of these things yourself.

LAB 6.1 EXERCISES

6.1.1 CONDITIONAL EXECUTION

In this Lab discussion, we looked at a program (debuglevel.pl) that shows you how to conditionally print messages depending on the value stored in a variable. Let's enhance that program just a little bit.

DEBUGLEVEL2.PL

```
1  #!/usr/bin/perl
2  $debug = shift; # get debug level from command-line
3  $debug = 3 unless $debug;
4  print "high priority failure\n" unless 1 > $debug;
5  print "medium priority failure\n" unless 3 > $debug;
6  print "minimum priority failure\n" unless 9 > $debug;
```

This program is actually almost identical to the original. A particular message should be printed if the assigned debug level (stored in $debug) is less than or equal to the importance of the message (as indicated by the literal value in the statement). The major change in this program is that we take advantage of Perl's rich collection of logical modifiers to make the code easier to read. Some people believe that

```
... unless 3 > $debug;
```
is easier to read than

```
... if ! 3 > $debug;
```
There is one minor logic flaw in the program, however. Let's see if you can find it.

> **a)** Run the `debuglevel2.pl` program using each of the following test values on the command line. Does it produce the expected result for each one?

1	3	9
2	4	10
255	-1	0

_____

_____

> **b)** Which line in the program produces the logic bug that results in the failure? How would you rewrite the line?

_____

_____

> **c)** Write an instruction that prints out the message "customized" if it detects the presence of the environment variable PERL5LIB.

_____

_____

6.1.2 COMBINE CONDITIONS

a) Write a short program (`edname.pl`) that prints a simple message (something like "editor preference detected") if either of the environment variables `EDITOR` or `VISUAL` is defined.

_____

_____

b) Write a program (`argcheck.pl`) that prints the message "ready to go" if there is a command-line argument that is a number higher than 5.

_____

_____

6.1.3 USE THE LOGICAL NEGATION OPERATOR

a) Write an instruction that prints a message if neither of the environment variables `EDITOR` nor `VISUAL` is defined.

_____

_____

Uncle Larry admired his image in the large barbershop mirror. Barber Tom had done his usual sterling job. And it was a good thing, too, because Larry was headed to a Storyteller's conference at the end of the week.

I'll have to remember to write up that limerick you told me, Tom. I've never heard a clean one before."

"It's funny you should say that," Tom replied. "People almost always say 'I have to remember...' when they're in here. It's led me to think that I might be able to do something that would help.

"I know that most folks understand that the best thing they can do is write these things in a 'To Do List.' The biggest problem is getting started. What I've been thinking of doing is offering a place to keep the lists. You see the clipboard over there? That's the first step.

"What I want to do next is to convert this old useless PC into a 'To Do List Kiosk.' I thought you might have some ideas about that."

Larry nearly beamed. "You bet! This would be an easy thing to do in Perl. I'll give you some tasks to work on while I'm on my trip and when I return we can put the things you build into a larger program that will do what you want. We'll get rid of that clipboard in no time!"

Tom needs to write a program that reads two command-line arguments and uses them to access a hash that is built into the program (think of the hash as a user database). The first argument is a key, and the second argument is a value. Print a message if the arguments do not match any pair from the built-in hash. Here's a program template that will start you off.

UC.PL

```
 1  #!/usr/bin/perl
 2  %users = (
 3      Larry => "lingo",
 4      Tom => "tonic",
 5      Ellie => "plasma",
 6      Randal => "effort",
 7      Mike => "fire",
 8  );
 9
10  # on fewer than two command-line args, either exit(1) or die()
11
12  # get the args into $user and $passwd
13
14  # if no entry for $user exists, print a message and exit
15
16  # otherwise
17  print "We're ready to go then...\n";
```

b) Write the program (`usercheck.pl`) that will be the first step in Tom's "To Do" program. Don't worry about the fact that we don't check the password in this program. We'll get to that later in the chapter. For now, just flesh out the parts as suggested by the comments in the template.

LAB 6.1 EXERCISE ANSWERS

6.1.1 ANSWERS

a) Run the `debuglevel2.pl` program using each of the test values from the list. Does it produce the expected result for each one?

Answer: The program works fine for each of the test values except the value 0. It is supposed to print any messages that represent debug levels equal to or lower than the one we set.

So if we ask for a debug level of 7, it should print any debugging messages at level 1 and level 3. That's fine, but when we use 0 as an input value, the program prints messages for high and medium priority.

This exercise gave us a chance to examine a very important issue related to your program development cycle. It is vitally important to test your program thoroughly before you pronounce it finished.

Testing is an important part of a programmer's job. The rigor with which a program is tested marks the difference between a hobbyist and a professional developer.

Typically, you should test a program with a solid cross-section of inputs that are typical of what might happen when the program is run legitimately. Then test it with as many "suspicious" values as are relevant. The numbers 0, -1, 255, -128, 127, and 65535 are all sufficiently suspicious to merit membership in the test data set.

Even if you intend to program only as a hobby, try to write your programs as if your job depended upon how well you do. Remember that the term "amateur" was once applied to the person who did a job for the love of the work.

b) Which line in the program produces the logic bug that results in the failure? How would you rewrite the line?

Answer: The problem is in line 3.

```
$debug = 3 unless $debug;
```

Here we appear to be checking to see if we successfully got a debug level from the command line. Because we take a (fairly common) shortcut with this check, if the value 0 is used, we interpret that as *false* and mistakenly assign the default debug level of 3.

Here's a replacement that would fix the problem:

```
$debug = 3 unless defined $debug;
```

c) Write an instruction that prints out the message "customized" if it detects the presence of the environment variable PERL5LIB.

Answer: This line does the trick:
```
print "customized\n" if defined $ENV{PERL5LIB}:
```

6.1.2 ANSWERS

a) Write a short program (edname.pl) that prints a simple message (something like "editor preference detected") if either of the environment variables EDITOR or VISUAL is defined.

Answer: Here's a program that does what we want.

EDNAME.PL
```
1  #!/usr/bin/perl
2  if (defined $ENV{'EDITOR'} or defined $ENV{'VISUAL'}) {
3      print "Environment defines an editor\n";
4  }
5  else {
6      print "Environment defines no editor\n";
7  }
```

The exercise didn't require it, but you'll note that this program prints a message if no editor is detected. During development, this is the sort of thing you might want to do as well. The traditional UNIX philosophy is that a program should say nothing if everything went okay. This is a sound approach for your production code.

**LAB
6.1**

During development, however, you may want to get positive confirmation that something happened, especially if it was not the thing you expected.

b) Write a program (`argcheck.pl`) that prints the message "ready to go" if there is a command-line argument and that argument is a number higher than 5.

Answer: Here's one way you might have written this program:

ARGCHECK.PL
```
1  #!/usr/bin/perl
2  print "Ready to go!\n" if
3     defined $ARGV[0] &&
4     ($debug = shift) > 5;
```

It might have been more direct in *line 4* to have compared `$ARGV[0]` directly to 5. Given the fact that this program is not trying to do anything fancy, that would probably have been the best choice.

I did want you to see, however, that you could combine an assignment operation with a comparison when it suits you. Because we parenthesize the assignment operation, it becomes an "atomic" expression. That just means that we can treat it all as one thing. The whole operation evaluates to a value equal to whatever has been assigned to `$debug` in this case.

Without the parentheses, it might have still worked just fine. It would depend upon the order of precedence between the assignment and the comparison operators. Do you feel like looking that up? If not, just reach for the parentheses.

6.1.3 ANSWERS

a) Write an instruction that prints a message if neither of the environment variables `EDITOR` nor `VISUAL` is defined.

Answer: Here's what you might put in your program when you need to do this:
```
print "no editor found\n"
   if ! (defined $ENV{EDITOR} || defined $ENV{VISUAL});
```
Here's another way you might code it:
```
print "no editor found\n"
   unless (defined $ENV{EDITOR} || defined $ENV{VISUAL});
```

There are other ways that would work. Like a natural language, Perl offers you many ways to say just about anything. This accounts for the wide variety of styles found in the Perl programming community. That's why it's so important to focus on clarity when we write our code.

b) Write the program (usercheck.pl) that will be the first step in Tom's "To Do" program.

> *Answer: This is the first step in a larger program. It doesn't need much to be added to the template. Here's what you might have done:*

USERCHECK.PL

```
 1  #!/usr/bin/perl
 2  %users = (
 3      Larry => "lingo",
 4      Tom => "tonic",
 5      Ellie => "plasma",
 6      Randal => "effort",
 7      Mike => "fire",
 8  );
 9
10  # on fewer than two command-line args, either exit(1) or die()
11  die "usage: $0 username password" unless defined $ARGV[1];
12  # get the args into $user and $passwd
13  ($user, $passwd) = @ARGV;
14
15  # if no entry for $user exists, print a message and exit
16  die "undefined user\n" unless defined $users{$user};
17
18  # otherwise
19  print "We're ready to go then...\n";
```

There are some things you might want to do to improve this program. The command-line integrity check in *line 11* is a little bit on the weak side. All it does is confirm that there are at least two arguments. You might want to confirm that there are exactly two arguments.

One thing about this program that makes me uneasy is the fact that there is a hash called "%users" and a scalar variable called "$user", which we later use to access the hash by talking about "$users{$user}". Now this is perfectly legal, but it's just begging for trouble.

**LAB
6.1**

Did you ever notice how the hero and the antagonist in a movie are typically very different in appearance? One might be blonde while the other one is dark-haired. This is no accident. Masterful directors (and casting agents, and programmers for that matter) know that if you make things visually distinct, it will be easier to differentiate them in our minds when we're busy concentrating on other more important matters.

If we choose $name instead of $user for the utility variable in this program, we'll find that we have fewer problems later. You can take my word for this now, or ignore me and learn it for yourself later, sometime in the middle of the night.

LAB 6.1 REVIEW QUESTIONS

1) A simple Perl statement can be modified with a conditional clause. Which conditional operators can be used as modifiers?

   a) _____ `if, unless, insteadof, aslongas`
   b) _____ `if, unless, insteadof`
   c) _____ `if, insteadof`
   d) _____ `if, unless`

2) Which of these is a legal way to modify a Perl statement?

   a) _____ `{print "message"} if { defined $flag };`
   b) _____ `print "message" if defined $flag;`
   c) _____ `print "message" if defined $flag;`
   d) _____ `print $msg1 insteadof $msg2;`

3) When you modify a Perl statement with a conditional, there are two parts: the action part and the conditional part. Which of the following is true concerning the use of parentheses?

   a) _____ You must enclose the action part of the statement in parentheses.
   b) _____ You may enclose the action part of the statement in parentheses.
   c) _____ You must not enclose the action part of the statement in parentheses.
   d) _____ You should always ask the price before ever using parentheses.

4) A conditional clause that tests for the truth of each of two separate conditions, would look like which of the following:

   a) _____ `print "msg" if (defined $flag & defined $f2);`
   b) _____ `print "msg" if (defined $flag && defined $f2);`
   c) _____ `print "msg" if (defined $flag || defined $f2);`
   d) _____ `print "msg" if defined $flag AND defined $f2;`

5) To execute a `print()` statement only when a variable is undefined, your code would look like:

   a) _____ `print "msg" if ! defined $flag;`
   b) _____ `print "msg" if undefined $flag;`
   c) _____ `print "msg" if NOT defined $flag;`
   d) _____ `print "msg" if not_defined $flag;`

Quiz answers appear in Appendix A, Section 6.1.

L A B   6.2

TRADITIONAL BRANCHING CONSTRUCTS

LAB OBJECTIVES

After this Lab, you will be able to:

✓ Conditionally Execute Entire Blocks of Code

✓ Use the Short-Circuit Operator

✓ Use the Conditional Operator

Sometimes the condition you have to check is a simple one, but what you'll do as a result of the test might be complex. And sometimes you want to do one thing if the test turns out to be true, something else if the test yields false. In this Lab, we'll look at how we might accomplish both of these goals. We'll also look at a of couple syntactical shortcuts. Hopefully we'll master them well enough to avoid getting lost.

CONDITIONALLY EXECUTE PROGRAM BLOCKS

We saw in the last Lab how to execute a single statement in response to the outcome of a logical test. But what do we do if we need to execute 10 statements when our test turns out to be true? We wouldn't want to have to conduct the test 10 times!

Of course, that isn't necessary. We can execute an entire block of code in response to the outcome of a test. Before we try it, a simple definition.

A "block" of code is (generally) a set of instructions encased in curly braces.

There are exceptions to this rule, but they are obscure enough that we can use this definition for a long time without ever encountering an exception. So let's go with it.

The syntax we're looking for allows us to execute a block of code in response to an expression that yields the value true. Here's the structure:

```
if (some_condition) {
    some instruction;
    another instruction;
}
```

Let's set up some tasks that we want to do if our command line has enough arguments present.

ARGDEFAULTS.PL

```
1  #!/usr/bin/perl
2  if (defined $ARGV[1]) {
3      $name = shift;
4      $task = shift;
5      printf "name: %-10s task: %-16s\n", $name, $task;
6  }
```

In this program fragment, the argument list is used only if there are enough arguments present to populate our variables (`$name` and `$task`). Did you remember that `shift()` is how we can grab the elements of an array starting at the beginning?

Take a look at the `printf()` statement here (in *line 5*). Notice that the code defines two string fields and specifies their width with negative numbers (`%-10s` and `%-16s`). That causes the fields to be populated left-justified. Here's what the program run looks like:

```
$ argdefaults.pl mike "build fire"
name: mike       task: build fire
```

SIMPLE CONDITION, COMPLEX TASK—USING `if/else`

Sometimes you want to do one thing if the test turns out to be true, something else if the test yields false. The construct for this looks like:

```
if (some_condition) {
    some instruction;
}
else {
    some other instruction;
}
```

In `argdefaults.pl`, we saw the program print a message if we got the correct input from the command line. If we don't have what we need there, it fails silently. Let's revise it to make it a little smarter.

ARG2DEFAULTS.PL

```
1  #!/usr/bin/perl
2  if (defined $ARGV[1]) {
3      $name = shift;
4      $task = shift;
5      printf "name: %-10s task: %-16s\n", $name, $task;
6  }
7  else {
8      print "syntax: $0 <name> <task>\n";
9  }
```

Now we can tell explicitly whether the program succeeds or fails because we get a message printed either way. The only thing still wrong is that most of the program is embedded in a block that runs if everything is okay, and the error message is left dangling at the end almost as an afterthought.

The best way to present this would be to have the test check for an error, and print a message if one is found. Otherwise, we'd want the program to proceed normally to do whatever it is supposed to do. I'll leave it as an exercise for you to revise this program to make the logic a little cleaner.

CASCADING CONDITIONS—USING `if/elsif/else`

There will be times when you want to check for a condition, and if it isn't true (or if it isn't false) you want to check for another condition. You may have many of these chained together with some action that should be performed in each case, and something that happens if none of our tests turn out right.

Here's a whimsical little program that demonstrates the syntax. It uses the less-than (<) operator to test the relationship between two numbers. We'll talk about that operator at greater length in the next Lab.

WHOPAYS.PL

```
 1  #!/usr/bin/perl
 2  $price = shift;
 3  print "Clerk: How will you pay for that?\n";
 4  if ($price < 100) {
 5     print "You: With cash.\n";
 6  }
 7  elsif ($price < 500) {
 8     print "You: With a credit card.\n";
 9  }
10  elsif ($price < 1500) {
11     print "You: With someone else's credit card.\n";
12  }
13  else {
14     print "You: Never mind, I'll wait for the sale.\n";
15  }
16
```

Can you see what happens here? We get a number from the command line. It is compared with successively larger values until we either locate the correct range and print our answer, or we get tired of testing and, of course, that makes our decision for us.

PIDGIN PERL

Moving from the ridiculous to the sublime (or, in the opinion of some, from the ridiculous to the perverse), there are a couple of ways we can state things more concisely when we want to set up conditional execution of code. The first of those is to use the "short-circuit" operators.

To understand the "short-circuit" operators, consider the following English sentences:

```
Take out your keys AND then start the car.
Present valid registration AND then take a ballot.
```

In each case, our sentences consist of two clauses. The first clause describes a course of action, and the second clause describes a course of action that is dependent upon the success of the first. If the first action failed, there would be little point in attempting the second one.

Now think about these sentences.

```
Use your key to open the door OR call AAA for help.
Present valid registration OR join the "new voter" queue.
```

In each of these cases, the second clause suggests a course of action that should be conducted only if the first action fails. If the first action succeeds, we are happy and have little motivation to attempt the second action.

This is how Perl will behave with respect to the logic operators we used in the last Lab. When you combine two statements with the (&&) or (||) operators, they will be evaluated using the rationale we've just considered.

■ FOR EXAMPLE

You might want to print an error message if there is no command-line argument.

```
defined $ARGV[0] || print "bad syntax!\n";
```

The message here prints only if the first clause is not true. Here's another one that's fairly common:

```
open (INPUT, "filename") or die "couldn't open filename";
```

You've seen this in our text already, and you'll see it many times in working Perl code. It's a perfect example of the most convenient way to take advantage of this shortcut. Because the open function will return "false" whenever the operation fails, we can easily determine whether we want the program to continue.

We can use the AND operator the same way. Here's one you've seen before:

```
m/CA/ && print;
```

This phrase tries to match the phrase "CA" somewhere in the value stored in the default variable ($_). If the variable contains that pattern, the print statement is called with its default behavior.

The plain language version is also useful.

```
defined $ARGV[0] and print "arg is $ARGV[0]\n";
```

This instruction inspects the first command-line argument and then prints a message if one is found.

Use these shortcuts wherever it's useful. Just be sure that you don't obscure the meaning of your code by doing it just "because you can."

THE CONDITIONAL OPERATOR

Another tribute to brevity often found in the Perl programming world is the use of the conditional operator. Here's the syntax:

```
expression1 ? val1 : val2;
```

The conditional operator is most often put to use with an assignment statement. The way it works is that the initial expression (`expression1`) is first evaluated. If it is true, the entire conditional expression evaluates to the value of `val1`. If the initial expression turns out to be false, then the entire phrase takes on the value in `val2`.

■ FOR EXAMPLE

You might want to set a variable, like debugging level, to a value taken from the command line if one exists, or to a default value if none is present. Here's how you might do that.

```
$debug = defined $ARGV[0] ? $ARGV[0] : 3;
```

This code will check for the existence of the initial command-line parameter, and if it exists, save its value in $debug. Otherwise, $debug becomes the literal value 3. As you can see from this, we can consolidate two operations from our debuglevel2.pl program into one. When you've become accustomed to this operator, its use will seem more elegant than an if/else construct that does the same job.

Before we move on, let's look at just one more example. In this one, we want to print a name that might be provided on the command line. If the name is present, we print that; otherwise, we use a default name.

```
print "Hello there, ",
    defined $ARGV[0] ? $ARGV[0] : "John Doe",
    ". It's good to see you!\n";
```

Determining the required value in the middle of a call to a function like print() or printf() is an excellent use of the conditional operator. You'll find this approach in common use by C, Java, awk, and Perl programmers alike.

LAB 6.2 EXERCISES

6.2.1 CONDITIONALLY EXECUTE ENTIRE BLOCKS OF CODE

a) What's wrong with this program?

CONDITION.PL
```
1  #!/usr/bin/perl
2  $value = 5;
3  if ($value < 10) then {
4      print "\$value is: $value \n";
5  }
```

b) Rewrite the program `arg2defaults.pl` from the Lab discussion to read a little easier (that is, write `arg3defaults.pl`). Have Check the program for the presence of command-line arguments. If none are found, print the syntax message. Otherwise, the main body of the program can execute.

**LAB
6.2**

_____

_____

Now, imagine that two things happen to our programs (`arg2defaults.pl` and `arg3defaults.pl`). The first thing is that the specifications change.

• There must be three command-line arguments: name, task, and data file.

• There must be an environment variable called "ARGLIB."

• The program must succeed at opening the file named in the third command-line argument.

If any of these conditions is not satisfied, we'll need to print an error message. Each error condition will require a different message. The other thing that changes is that the main body of the program will need to print a lengthy multi-line message.

c) Use this template to write the program described above.

A4DEFAULTS.PL

```
 1  #!/usr/bin/perl
 2
 3  # check for command-line args
 4  #
 5
 6  # to open the file, we'll say:
 7  open IN, "$ARGV[2]";
 8
 9  # Here's the message we'll print if everything is okay
10  print <<"EoMessage";
11  This program is ready to run.
12  The required library $ENV{ARGLIB} is present.
13  Entry for: $ARGV[0].
```

```
14 Task for: $ARGV[1].
15 Ready to read from file: $ARGV[2].
16 EoMessage
17
18 # we always close our files
19 close IN;
```

LAB
6.2

<hr>

6.2.2 USE THE SHORT-CIRCUIT OPERATOR

Read this program and describe what you think will print in each of the invocations that follow.

NESTED.PL
```
1  #!/usr/bin/perl
2  if (! defined $ARGV[0]) {
3     print "no arguments found\n";
4  }
5  else {
6     print "found an argument\n";
7     $name = $ARGV[0];
8     if (defined $ARGV[1]) {
9        $task = $ARGV[1];
10    }
11    else {
12       $task = "read documentation";
13    }
14    print "$name: $task\n";
15 }
```

a) $ **nested.pl tom**

b) $ `nested.pl tom give a haircut`

_____

_____

c) $ `nested.pl tom "give a haircut"`

_____

_____

d) $ `nested.pl`

_____

_____

e) Use the short-circuit operator to implement conditional debugging statements like we did in the `debuglevel2.pl` program. In this program (`debuglevel3.pl`), the word $debug should appear at the beginning of the line.

_____

_____

f) In Chapter 2, "The Nickel Tour," we saw how to use the `system()` function to run an external command. We learned that most programs will return an exit code of 0 when everything goes okay. Write a program (`execcheck.pl`) that runs an external command and prints a message as long as everything is okay. To test it, run the commands "`ls -1`" and "`ls -1/bogus/directory/name`" so that you can observe your program's behavior completely.

_____

_____

6.2.3 USE THE CONDITIONAL OPERATOR

a) Read this program and try to anticipate what it will print.

TWOCONDITIONS.PL

```
1   #!/usr/bin/perl
2   $name = "Bob";
3   $Task = "cut the grass";
4   print "Today, ", defined $name ? $name : "John Doe";
5   print " will have to ",
6      defined $task ? $task : "debug the program.\n";
```

_____

_____

b) Use the conditional operator to write a program (`setedi-tor.pl`) that prints out the value of the environment variable EDI-TOR, if it exists; otherwise, print the variable `VISUAL` if that exists, or else print the static value "`/usr/bin/vi`".

_____

_____

LAB 6.2 EXERCISE ANSWERS

6.2.1 ANSWERS

a) What's wrong with the program `condition.pl`?

Answer: The syntax for the `if` construct does not call for the word "then" to be part of the structure. This code should look like:

```
$value = 5;
if ($value < 10) {
   print "\$value is: $value \n";
}
```

In many other languages, it would be legal to omit the curly braces when the block to be executed consists of only one statement. This is NOT the case in Perl. You must always supply braces when you use the `if` construct.

Remember that there is an if construct (as seen in this example) and an if modifier (like we saw in the beginning of the chapter). They are different things. The former demands curly braces, and the latter does not use them at all.

LAB 6.2

   b) Rewrite the program `arg2defaults.pl` from the Lab discussion to read a little easier.

     Answer: This program would do the trick:

ARG3A-DEFAULTS.PL

```
1  #!/usr/bin/perl
2  if (! defined $ARGV[1]) {
3     print "syntax: $0 <name> <task>\n";
4  }
5  else {
6     $name = shift;
7     $task = shift;
8     printf "name: %-10s task: %-16s\n", $name, $task;
9  }
```

The reason this program is an improvement is that we can easily see the effect of the logic in one glance. If the main program body (*lines 6-8*) were 20 lines long, we might see only the test and the beginning of the conditional construct. When we finally reached the "else" clause, it would not be clear why that clause would be in effect. Here's another way it might have been written.

ARG3B-DEFAULTS.PL

```
1  #!/usr/bin/perl
2  unless (defined $ARGV[1]) {
3     print "syntax: $0 <name> <task>\n";
4  }
5  else {
6     $name = shift;
7     $task = shift;
8     printf "name: %-10s task: %-16s\n", $name, $task;
9  }
```

Perl allows a rich variety in syntax, some of it mildly redundant. We can use "unless" rather than "if" when it clarifies the meaning of our program. Programmers and "pundits" who claim that Perl is not readable have simply never read or written good code. The tools are there for you if you want to write programs that are clear and understandable.

c)   Write the program described above.

Answer: Here's a program that meets those specifications.

ARG4DEFAULTS.PL

```
 1  #!/usr/bin/perl
 2  # check for command-line args
 3  if (! defined $ARGV[2]) {
 4      print "syntax: $0: <name> <task> <datafile>\n";
 5  }
 6  elsif (! defined $ENV{ARGLIB}) {
 7      print "Library ARGLIB must be defined\n";
 8  }
 9  # to open the file, we'll say:
10  elsif (! open (IN, "< $ARGV[2]") ) {
11      print "cannot open data file $ARGV[2]\n";
12  }
13  else {
14      # Here's the message we'll print if everything is okay
15      print <<"EoMessage";
16  This program is ready to run.
17  The required library $ENV{ARGLIB} is present.
18  Entry for: $ARGV[0].
19  Task for: $ARGV[1].
20  Ready to read from file: $ARGV[2].
21  EoMessage
22
23      # we always close our files
24      close IN;
25  }
```

In *line 11*, the call to the open() function should return "false" if the call fails. This is normally checked by the careful programmer before proceeding with the remainder of the program. The print() function in *line 15* takes advantage of the "here document" that we studied earlier. A multi-line string would have done the job just as easily.

To test this program fully from the shell prompt, it is necessary to run it several times. Something like this:

```
$ arg4defaults.pl
...something happens
$ arg4defaults.pl fred mow the lawn datafile
...something happens
$ export ARGLIB="/usr/lib/arglib.so"
$ arg4defaults.pl fred mow the lawn datafile
...something happens
$ arg4defaults.pl fred "mow the lawn" datafile
...something happens (we presume that "datafile" doesn't exist)
$ arg4defaults.pl fred "mow the lawn" arg4defaults.pl
...something happens (nobody said it had to be a "real" data file)
```

6.2.2 ANSWERS

Read the nested.pl program and describe what you think will print in each of the invocations that follow.

a) `$ nested.pl tom`

Answer: The system prints:

```
found an argument
tom: read documentation
```

The program allows something interesting to be printed as long as there is at least one argument. If there is not a second argument, the program simply chooses a default and prints that.

b) `$ nested.pl tom give a haircut`

Answer: The system prints:

```
found an argument
tom: give
```

In this case, there are many available arguments, and the program really only cares about the first two. The remaining arguments are ignored.

c) `$ nested.pl tom "give a haircut"`

Answer: Now the system prints:

```
found an argument
tom: give a haircut
```

Because the phrase "give a haircut" is quoted, the program sees it as a single argument with embedded spaces. This is the outcome we were probably hoping to achieve with this program.

d) $ **nested.pl**

Answer: The system prints:

```
no arguments found
```

And that is what we wanted to happen when the program was run without any command-line arguments at all. Most of your programs should probably be written to treat an empty command line as one that is being offered by an operator who isn't familiar with the program's operation. Some programmers go as far as to require a dummy argument just to check that the operator has read some of the documentation.

e) Use the short-circuit operator to implement conditional debugging statements like we did in the debuglevel2.pl program. This time, the word $debug should appear at the beginning of the line.

Answer: Here's a program that will do the work:

DEBUGLEVEL3.PL
```
1  #!/usr/bin/perl
2  # get debug level from command-line
3  $debug = defined $ARGV[0] ? shift : 3;
4  # now print appropriate message(s)
5  $debug < 1 || print "high priority\n";
6  $debug < 3 || print "medium priority\n";
7  $debug < 9 || print "minimum priority\n";
```

This program will print each of the messages that is appropriate for a given debug level. The nice thing about this program is that every line that is associated with supporting debugging messages can be identified as a line that begins with the variable name $debug. In the next chapter, we'll see how to strip those lines from the program with a simple Perl instruction.

f) Write a program (execcheck.pl) that runs an external command and prints a message as long as everything is okay.

Answer: Here is one version that works.

EXECCHECK.PL

```
1   #!/usr/bin/perl
2   $pgm1 = "ls -l .";
3   $pgm2 = "ls -l /tmp/bogus/directory";
4   system ($pgm1) || print "program 1 succeeded\n";
5   system ($pgm2) && print "program 2 failed\n";
```

The way this program is written, it prints out a message after both external commands are run. Remember that a program that succeeds will return an exit code of 0. (In essence, nothing has gone wrong.) In Perl, we treat 0 as false, so we have to write our logic as "unless the external program returns true, print a message saying that we succeeded."

6.2.3 ANSWERS

a) Read the `twoconditions.pl` program and try to anticipate what it will print.

Answer: Here is what we see when we run the program:

```
$ twoconditions.pl
Today, Bob will have to debug the program.
```

The variable that represents name is set properly and when we test it in *line 4*, the value can be printed properly. Notice that in *line 3* a variable is set, but it is called `$Task`. That is not what we test for in *line 6*, and as a result, the default value, "`debug the program`" is what we see printed.

b) Use the conditional operator to write a program (`seteditor.pl`) that prints out the value of the environment variable `EDITOR` if it exists; otherwise, print the variable `VISUAL` if that exists, or else print the static value "`/usr/bin/vi`".

Answer: Here's a program that fulfills these requirements:

SETDEFAULTS.PL

```
1   #!/usr/bin/perl
2   print "Editor is set to: ",
3       defined $ENV{EDITOR} ? $ENV{EDITOR} :
4       defined $ENV{VISUAL} ? $ENV{VISUAL} : "/usr/bin/vi",
5       "\n";
```

It is legal, as you see here, to nest conditional operators. In essence, the statement that begins on *line 2* says, "print part of a message and then check to see if the EDITOR variable is set in the environment; if so, print that; otherwise check to see if the VISUAL variable is set, and if so, print that; otherwise print this static string and, no matter what, finish up with a newline character."

It's much more concise when we say it in Perl, isn't it? Just remember that conventional wisdom says that if you have to nest conditional operators more than two deep, you should examine the logic of your program. There's probably a better way to get the job done.

LAB 6.2 SELF-REVIEW QUESTIONS

1) One of the following statements will execute a block of code when at least two command-line arguments exist. Which is it?

   a) _____ `if {defined $ARGV[2]} then (print $msg);`
   b) _____ `if (defined $ARGV[1]) then (print $msg);`
   c) _____ `if (defined $ARGV[1]) {print $msg};`
   d) _____ `if (defined $ARGV[2]) {print $msg};`

2) True or False: When you use an `if` construct, the curly braces are mandatory around the code block.

   a) _____ True
   b) _____ False

3) If you want the "short circuit operator" to conditionally exit from the program when no second command line option exists, you would say:

   a) _____ `defined $ARGV[1] OR die "bad command\n ";`
   b) _____ `defined $ARGV[2] || die "bad command\n ";`
   c) _____ `defined $ARGV[1] or die "bad command\n ";`
   d) _____ `defined $ARGV[2] OR die "bad command\n ";`

4) The following instruction will have what effect?

   `$result = defined ARGV[0] ? "cmd" : "interactive";`

   a) _____ The variable `$result` will be set to 1 if the first command-line argument is undefined.

   b) _____ The variable `$result` will be set to "interactive" if the first command-line argument is undefined.

   c) _____ The value `$ARGV[0]` will be set to "result" if the first command-line argument is undefined.

   d) _____ The variable `$result` will be set to "cmd" if the first command-line argument is undefined.

5) The variable `$ARGV[0]` is set to 10. What will the following instruction do?

   `$result = ARGV[0] == 10? "cmd" : "interactive";`

   a) _____ The variable `$result` will be set to 1 if the first command-line argument is defined.

   b) _____ The variable `$result` will be set to "interactive".

   c) _____ The value `$ARGV[0]` will be set to "result".

   d) _____ The variable `$result` will be set to "cmd".

Quiz answers appear in Appendix A, Section 6.2.

L A B   6.3

TESTS THAT INVOLVE NUMBERS, STRINGS, AND FILES

LAB OBJECTIVES

After this Lab, you will be able to:

✓ Conduct Arithmetic Comparison Tests

✓ Conduct String Comparison Tests

✓ Conduct File Status Tests

Perhaps the most common occurrence of conditional execution involves the use of test operators available in Perl. You can test for equality in strings, you can test for specific relationships between numbers (that is, "is $var greater than $val?"), and you can test for the status of files (for instance, "is the file readable," or "is the file over 30 days old?").

In this Lab, we'll see how to use the rich collection of test operators defined in Perl.

LAB 6.3 EXERCISES

Almost every production program has several places where a numeric comparison of values would be helpful. The Perl language provides us with a rich set of numeric and string comparison operators.

We'll start with the operators that compare numeric values.

ARITHMETIC COMPARISON OPERATORS

Table 6.1 illustrates the arithmetic comparison operators.

Table 6.1 ■ Examples of the Arithmetic Comparison Operators

Operator	Meaning	Example
==	equal	# check for 6 cmd-line args print "wrong" unless $#ARGV == 5;
>	greater than	# check for 2 or more args print "okay" if $#ARGV > 1;
<	less than	# loop while $idx less than 4 while ($idx < 4) {print; ++$idx;}
>=	greater than or equal	# loop while cmd-line args remain while ($#ARGV >= 0) {$a = shift}
<=	less than or equal	# loop while $idx hasn't reached 10 do {++$idx} while ($idx <= 10);
!=	not equal	# exit if cmd-line arg count isn't 2 exit 1 if @ARGV != 2;

As you can see, these operators may be used on any variables or literal numeric values. You may also use these comparisons on string values, but remember that a string placed in a numeric context (which any of these operators creates) will be evaluated as 0 unless it consists only of legal digits.

STRING COMPARISON OPERATORS

A corresponding set of operators is provided to allow comparison of string values. These operators are shown in Table 6.2.

Table 6.2 ■ Examples of the String Comparison Operators

Operator	Meaning	Example
eq	equal	# check first arg for "-d" print "debug" if $ARGV[0] eq "-d";
gt	greater than	# is arg late in the alphabet print "later" if $ARGV[0] gt "middle";
lt	less than	# is arg early in the alphabet print "early" if $ARGV[0] lt "middle";

ge	greater than or equal	# print args in alphabetical order
		if ($ARGV[0] ge $ARGV[1]) {
		    print "$ARGV[1] $ARGV[0]";
		}

le	less than or equal	# print args in alphabetical order
		if ($ARGV[0] le $ARGV[1]) {
		    print "$ARGV[0] $ARGV[1]";
		}

ne	not equal	# exit if arg is not "-d" exit 1 if $ARGV[0] ne "-d";

The operators shown here take two strings and evaluate them the same way you might if your job were to put the operands in order for a dictionary. Well, there is one minor difference. The comparison is what we call ASCIIbetical. This means that the strings are compared using the ASCII values of their characters. This gives us something a little bit short of a pure "dictionary sort." Consider the following four values:

```
Hundred
hundred
Thousand
thousand
```

In the dictionary, these values should appear in the order shown above. In an ASCIIbetical comparison on the other hand, they would be sorted in the following order:

```
Hundred
Thousand
hundred
thousand
```

This is because the letters "H" and "T" both appear before either of their lowercase counterparts in the ASCII character set. (The ASCII value for "T" is 84 decimal, and for "h" it is 104 decimal. This means that all uppercase letters are naturally "less than" any lowercase letters.)

LAB 6.3

There is a quirk you should remember when you use the string comparison operators. If both of the operands are strings that contain only digits, these operators will still view them as strings. The number 2 will be later than the number 1000. (In other words, the statement "2 gt 1000" is true in Perl.)

FILE TEST OPERATORS

The last collection of operators that we'll explore here is the set that is used to make determinations about files. Each of these operators allows your program to check certain characteristics about files and directories.

These are unary operators; in other words, they expect only one argument, a filename. Most of them return "true" (non-zero) or "false" (zero), but some of them actually return a value that may have some meaning to your program. (For example, the operator returns the size of a file. Normally, we use this to determine that the file has a non-zero length, but we may actually want to know the number of bytes in the file.)

The list of operators shown in Table 6.3 is not comprehensive. These are the ones you'll find in widespread use and are certainly enough to get you started. Check the Perl documentation for a complete list.

Table 6.3 ■ File Test Operators

Operator	Function	Example
-e	file exists	`# does file exists?` `print "it does" if -e filename`
-z	file exists and is zero length	`# is this an empty file?` `print "empty" if -z filename`
-s	file exists and is non-zero length	`# is file non-zero in length?` `print "substance" if -s filename`
-r	file is readable	`# is this file readable by me?` `print "ok to open" if -r filename`
-w	file is writable	`# can I write to this file?` `print "ok to write" if -w filename`

-x	file is executable (or directory is accessible)	`# run it if we can`
		`system "$fname" if -x filename`
		`# do we have directory access?`
		`print "okay" if -x directoryname`

-f	file is an ordinary file	`# is this an ordinary file?` `print "plain file" if -f filename`
-d	file is a directory	`# is the file a directory?` `chdir $fname if -d directoryname`
-l	file is a symbolic link	`# is this a symbolic link?` `print "symlink" if -l filename`
-S	file is a socket	`# is this a socket?` `print "socket" if -S filename`
-T	file is a text file (true for empty files)	`# is this a text file?` `print "text" if -T filename`
-B	file is binary (true for empty files)	`# is it a binary file?` `print "binary" if -B filename`

There are a couple of quirks among the normally straightforward behavior of these operators. For instance, -z tests to see if we're looking at a zero-length file. It will return false if the file doesn't exist, even though some people might consider that to be a zero-length file. The -s operator returns the size of the file. This means that an expression using this operator will implicitly return false if the file is zero-length, and true if the file has some length other than zero.

The -T and -B operators will both return true for a zero-length file. Each of these operators makes its determination about the content of the file by inspecting the data. If the file contains no data, each operator concludes, "Sure, it's a text (or binary) file!"

This is why you should consider making more than one test on a file to determine its exact status.

LAB 6.3

Which brings us to a happy fact. There is a shortcut you can use when you have to make several tests against the same file. When you have already used a file test operator, you can refer to the statistics for that file with the special variable _. (That's the underscore character by itself.)

■ FOR EXAMPLE

The following program tests to see if a file is non-zero-length, readable by the current process, and whether its contents are strictly text.

FILEX.PL

```
 1  #!/usr/bin/perl
 2  @flist = qw{WhoAmI.class mrpts.tar.gz filex.pl};
 3  foreach $f (@flist) {
 4      print "name: $f   ";
 5      if ( -s $f && -r _ && -T _ ) {
 6          print "okay to edit $f\n";
 7      }
 8      else {
 9          print "NOT okay to edit $f\n";
10      }
11  }
```

This program begins by creating an array with three file names. The first appears to be the name of a Java class file, the second, a compressed tar file. The third file name is the script itself. Each of the file names is tested and if all three tests evaluate to true, then the announcement is made that the file is okay to edit as text.

Now it's time to try some of these tools in your own programs.

6.3.1 CONDUCT ARITHMETIC COMPARISON TESTS

a) Use the arithmetic test operators to write a program (`arg-count.pl`) that prints the message "okay" if the program is run with two or more command-line arguments.

_____

_____

b) Write a program (`threshold.pl`) that accepts one command-line argument and compares it to each of the values in an array you initialize in the program. (Initialize it with (1, 3, 5, 7, 11, 13, 17, 19) if you can't think of a group that you like.) When the command-line number is greater than a number from the set, we want to print the set member.

_____

_____

Barber Tom was ready to add some features to his "To Do" program.

The program would need to accept a new entry from the command line that would represent the priority of the item, separated by a colon from a short description (for example: `3:Trim Beard`*).*

For a starter, Tom decided to begin with a simulated database representing a set of pre-existing items. He would then have his program print the following report:

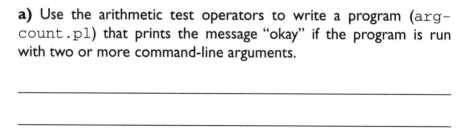

```
$ ipriority.pl "3:Trim Beard"
You added [Trim Beard] to the database with priority 3.
These tasks have a higher priority:
pri 1: Oil Change
pri 1: Pay Mortgage
```

```
pri 2: Dry Cleaning

pri 2: Get Groceries

These tasks have the same priority:

pri 3: Visit Ski Store

pri 3: Call Travel Agent
```

c) Use the template shown here to finish Tom's program (the template is called `ipri.pl`. The final program name should be `ipriority.pl`). It should take a command-line argument as shown in the example, and print a report as shown. The simulated database is included in the template.

LAB 6.3

IPRI.PL

```perl
1  #!/usr/bin/perl
2  # initialize simulated database
3  @dbase = (
4      "1:Pay Mortgage",
5      "1:Oil Change",
6      "2:Get Groceries",
7      "2:Dry Cleaning",
8      "3:Visit Ski Store",
9      "3:Travel Agent",
10     "4:Label Videotapes",
11     "4:Camera Battery",
12     "9:Update Home Page",
13 );
14
15 # Read and parse command-line arguments
16 die "Command-line Error" unless defined $ARGV[0];
17
18 # curse improperly formed command-lines (weakly)
19 ($new_pri, $new_task) = split /:/, $ARGV[0];
20 (defined $new_pri && defined $new_task) || die "Bad Argument";
21 # we should add more data integrity checks here...
22
23 # iterate through and compare the data
24 foreach $rec (@dbase) {
25     ($pri, $task) = split /:/, $rec;
26
27     # put our database record into an array
28     # if we'll need it for the report later
```

```
29 }
30
31 # create report
32 print "Added [$new_task] -- Priority: $new_pri\n";
33
34 print "These tasks have a higher priority:\n";
35 # now, print the array with higher priority entries
36
37 print "These tasks have the same priority:\n";
38 # now, print the array with equal priority entries
39
```

_____

_____

6.3.2 CONDUCT STRING COMPARISON TESTS

a) Write a program (dsort.pl) that reads a command-line argument, then compares it with each member of a wordlist defined in the program. Print out all of the wordlist members that should come before the command-line word.

_____

_____

Barber Tom believed that he would need code that could search for the existence of a given task in an established dataset. He wanted to at least limit the possibility of duplicate tasks.

b) Using the same dataset defined in the ipri.pl template file, write a program (dup_task.pl) that takes a command-line data record and searches for the task in the existing database. Print a message that declares whether or not the new record represents a duplicate task.

6.3.3 CONDUCT FILE STATUS TESTS

a) Write a program (`dircheck.pl`) that accepts a command-line argument and tests to see if the argument is the name of an existing directory. Also use the file test operators to determine whether the directory is readable and accessible (look for the read and execute permission on directories). Print a message reporting the status of each characteristic.

Tom decided that the next code fragment he should write would be one that searched for the existence of a database for a given person. In the final design, each person would have their own tasklist in a separate file. The ultimate program would have to determine whether the tasklist was present and ready to read.

b) Write a program (`dbcheck.pl`) that will consider the first command-line argument to be the name of a person. Use that name to form a filename of the form NAME.db where NAME is the command-line value. Print a report showing the file's size, age in days, read, write, and execute permissions, and whether or not the file is text or binary.

LAB 6.3 EXERCISE ANSWERS

6.3.1 ANSWERS

a) Use the arithmetic test operators to write a program (`argcount.pl`) that prints the message "okay" if the program is run with two or more command-line arguments.

Answer: This program actually represents a code fragment that will appear in many of your Perl programs. Here is one way to write it:

ARGCOUNT.PL
```
#!/usr/bin/perl
print "okay\n" if @ARGV >= 2;
```

Another way it could have been written:

ARGCOUNT2.PL
```
#!/usr/bin/perl
print "okay\n" if $#ARGV >= 1;
```

b) Write a program (`threshold.pl`) that accepts one command-line argument and compares it to each of the values in an array you initialize in the program. (Initialize it with (1, 3, 5, 7, 11, 13, 17, 19) if you can't think of a group that you like.) When the command-line number is greater than a number from the set, we want to print the set member.

Answer: This is an uncomplicated program to write. Here's one way you might do it:

THRESHOLD.PL
```
1  #!/usr/bin/perl
2  @primes = qw{1 3 5 7 11 13 17 19};
3  die "Bad Command Line" unless defined $ARGV[0];
4  print "primes smaller than $ARGV[0]!\n";
5  foreach $v (@primes) {
6     print "\n$v is smaller..." if $v < $ARGV[0];
7  }
```

The program begins by initializing a reference array; then in *line 3*, it checks for the presence of a command-line argument. If the program keeps running, there is an argument that can be used to compare to each element of the reference array. Any element of the array that is smaller than the number in the command line will be printed.

c) Use the template shown in the Exercise to finish Tom's program. It
    should take a command-line argument as shown in the example, and
    print a report as shown. The simulated database is included in the tem-
    plate.

    *Answer: This program is a little trickier and there are many possible ways you might
    have written yours successfully. Your program should behave the same way this one
    does:*

IPRIORITY.PL

LAB
6.3

```perl
1  #!/usr/bin/perl
2
3  # initialize simulated database
4  @dbase = (
5          "1:Pay Mortgage",
6          "1:Oil Change",
7          "2:Get Groceries",
8          "2:Dry Cleaning",
9          "3:Visit Ski Store",
10         "3:Travel Agent",
11         "4:Label Videotapes",
12         "4:Camera Battery",
13         "9:Update Home Page",
14         );
15
16 # Read and parse command-line arguments
17 die "Command-line Error" unless defined $ARGV[0];
18
19 # curse improperly formed command-lines (weakly)
20 ($new_pri, $new_task) = split /:/, $ARGV[0];
21 die "Bad Argument"
22    unless (defined $new_pri && defined $new_task);
23 die "Bad Priority" if $new_pri <= 0;
24
25 # iterate through and compare the data
26 foreach $rec (@dbase) {
27    ($pri, $task) = split /:/, $rec;
28 # put our database record in memory if we'll need it
29    push (@higher, $rec) if ($new_pri > $pri);
30    push (@equal, $rec) if ($new_pri == $pri);
31 }
32
33 # create report
34 print "Added [$new_task] -- Priority: $new_pri\n";
35 print "These tasks have a higher priority:\n";
```

```
36 foreach $rec (@higher) {
37    ($pri, $task) = split /:/, $rec;
38    print "pri $pri:  $task\n";
39 }
40 print "These tasks have the same priority:\n";
41 foreach $rec (@equal) {
42    ($pri, $task) = split /:/, $rec;
43    print "pri $pri:  $task\n";
44 }
```

**LAB
6.3**

In *lines 16-23*, you can see that we've tightened up the integrity checks made against the command-line argument. If the user supplies zero or a negative number as a priority, we declare that this is an invalid priority. If a non-numeric string is provided, it will evaluate to zero and that will also cause this message to be printed before we bail out.

In *lines 29 and 30*, you can see something that is typical of many Perl programs. We simply add information at the end of an array when we want to keep it for later reference. These lines form the heart of our "parsing loop."

Dynamically adding something to an array or a hash is a task that most Perl programmers perform many times. Try to make this second nature as you decide how you will solve a particular programming problem.

The loop starting in *line 36* illustrates the sort of routine we'll use to print the contents of the arrays built in the parsing loop.

6.3.2 ANSWERS

a) Write a program (`dsort.pl`) that reads a command-line argument, then compares it with each member of a wordlist defined in the program. Print out all of the wordlist members that should come before the command-line word.

Answer: The specification for this program is pretty simple. It could be written as sparsely as this:

DSORT0.PL

```
1 #!/usr/bin/perl
2 @wlist = qw{rocky daria scooby shaggy tick arthur bart fred};
3 die "No Args Present" unless defined $ARGV[0];
```

```
4  foreach $w (@wlist) {
5      print "$w\t" if $w le $ARGV[0];
6  }
7  print "\n";
```

Here's what it looks like when this program runs:

```
$ dsort0.pl homer
daria arthur bart fred
```

You might have wanted your program to be more elaborate. Here is an improved version that you might consider to be a bit more polished:

LAB 6.3

DSORT.PL
```
1  #!/usr/bin/perl
2  @wlist = qw{rocky daria scooby shaggy tick arthur bart fred};
3  die "No Args Present" unless defined $ARGV[0];
4  print "The following words come before $ARGV[0]:\n";
5  foreach $w (sort @wlist) {
6      print "\t$w\n" if $w le $ARGV[0];
7  }
```

The output from this looks a little bit more readable:

```
$ dsort.pl homer
The following words come before homer:
    arthur
    bart
    daria
    fred
```

The addition of a "header" line (*line 4*) to explain the significance of the data and a call to the sort() function (in *line 5*) makes the output much more useful.

b) Using the same dataset defined in the ipri.pl template file, write a program (duptask.pl) that takes a command-line data record and searches for the task in the existing database. Print a message that declares whether or not the new record represents a duplicate task.

Answer: This program has much in common with dsort.pl. *Take a look at this approach:*

DUPTASK.PL

```perl
1  #!/usr/bin/perl
2  # initialize simulated database
3  @dbase = (
4      "1:Pay Mortgage",
5      "1:Oil Change",
6      "2:Get Groceries",
7      "2:Dry Cleaning",
8      "3:Visit Ski Store",
9      "3:Travel Agent",
10     "4:Label Videotapes",
11     "4:Camera Battery",
12     "9:Update Home Page",
13 );
14 $match = 0;
15
16 # Read and parse command-line arguments
17 die "Command-line Error" unless defined $ARGV[0];
18
19 # curse improperly formed command-lines
20 ($new_pri, $new_task) = split /:/, $ARGV[0];
21 die "Bad Argument"
22     unless (defined $new_pri && defined $new_task);
23 die "Bad Priority" if $new_pri <= 0;
24
25 # iterate through and compare the data
26 foreach $rec (@dbase) {
27     ($pri, $task) = split /:/, $rec;
28     $match = 1 if $task eq $new_task;
29 }
30
31 # print the report
32 print "Adding [$new_task] -- Priority: $new_pri\n";
33 print "It was ",
34     $match == 1 ? "" : "not ",
35     "already in the database.\n";
```

Getting this to work was a simple matter of creating a boolean flag ($match in *line 14*). We set it to a non-zero value (essentially, "true") if a matching task is detected (*line 24*).

6.3.3 ANSWERS

a) Write a program (`dircheck.pl`) that accepts a command-line argument and tests to see if the argument is the name of an existing directory. Also, use the file test operators to determine whether the directory is readable and accessible (look for the read and execute permissions that control directory access). Print a message reporting the status of each characteristic.

Answer: This program represents a code fragment that you will need often. Let's see how we might do it simply:

DIRCHECK0.PL
```perl
1  #!/usr/bin/perl
2  die "Bad Command Line" unless defined $ARGV[0];
3  $nm = $ARGV[0];
4
5  if (-d $nm) {
6      print "$nm is a directory\n";
7  }
8  else {
9      die "$nm is not a directory\n";
10 }
11
12 if (-r $nm && -x _) {
13     print "$nm is accessible and readable.\n";
14 }
15 else {
16     print "$nm is not accessible and readable.\n";
17 }
```

In *line 12*, we take advantage of the fact that once we've conducted one file test on a given filename, we can reference the results with the special variable (_) that means "the last file we tested."

If you don't mind taking some shortcuts that might make your code less immediately obvious, you could write the routine like this:

DIRCHECK.PL
```perl
1  #!/usr/bin/perl
2  # see dircheck2.pl for a more traditional approach
```

```
 3  die "Bad Command Line" unless defined $ARGV[0];
 4  $nm = $ARGV[0];
 5
 6  print "$nm is ",
 7      -d $nm ? "" : "not ",
 8      "a directory.\n";
 9
10  print "$nm is ",
11      (-r _ && -x _) ? "" : "not ",
12      "accessible and readable by the current process.\n";
```

LAB 6.3

This approach is a little more efficient than the first program, but the performance gains are so small as to be nearly invisible. The real question is whether you can read this four months from now and quickly see what is happening in *lines 6-11*. The conditional operator can be a big help, but it can make the code more difficult to read at maintenance time.

b) Write a program (dbcheck.pl) that will consider the first command-line argument to be the name of a person. Use that name to form a filename of the form NAME.db, where NAME is the command-line value. Print a report showing the file's size, age in days, read, write, and execute permissions, and whether or not the file is text or binary.

Answer: The specification for this program leaves a lot of latitude with respect to the form of the output report. Here's one way that the program run might look (assuming the presence of a file called "bill.db"):

```
$ dbcheck.pl nobody
Bad Data Table Name at dbcheck.pl line
7.
$ dbcheck.pl bill
bill.db statistics:
     size: 19
     age: 0
     read: yes
     write: yes
     execute: no
     data type: text
```

In the first attempt, we give the name of someone for whom no data exists. In the second attempt, we name someone who does have a data file. (Or at least a file with the correct name exists.)

Here's the program that produces that output:

DBCHECK.PL

```
 1  #!/usr/bin/perl
 2  die "Bad Command Line" unless defined $ARGV[0];
 3
 4  # the command-line contains a name
 5  $dbname = $ARGV[0] . ".db";
 6  die "Bad Data Table Name" unless -e $dbname;
 7
 8  # otherwise, we're ready to print the file statistics
 9  print "$dbname statistics:\n";
10  print "\t size: ", -s _, "\n";
11  print "\t age: ", int(-M _), "\n";
12  print "\t read: ", -r _ ? "yes" : "no", "\n";
13  print "\t write: ", -w _ ? "yes" : "no", "\n";
14  print "\t execute: ", -x _ ? "yes" : "no", "\n";
15  print "\t data type: ", -T _ ? "text" : "binary", "\n";
```

In *line 6*, we test for the existence of the file. If we make it further than this in the program, the file exists and we can use the special variable along with several of the file test operators to observe the file's other characteristics.

LAB 6.3 REVIEW QUESTIONS

1) There are two command-line arguments. Which of the following
   instructions prints the number "100"?
   a) _____ `$val = $#ARGV == 2 ? 100 : 101;print $val;`
   b) _____ `$val = $#ARGV[2] == 1 ? 100 : 100;print $val;`
   c) _____ `print $#ARGV eq 1 ? 101 : 100;`
   d) _____ `$val = $#ARGV == 1 ? 100 : 101;print $val;`

2) True or False: The expressions `$result = 2 gt 100` and
   `$result = 2 > 100` both cause `$result` to be set to true.
   a) _____ True
   b) _____ False

3) One of the following statements will print "Okay." Which is it?
   a) _____ `print "Okay\n" if 32 % 4;`
   b) _____ `print "Okay\n" unless 6 < 16;`
   c) _____ `print "Okay\n" if "Staubach" gt "Bradshaw";`
   d) _____ `print 32 % 4 < 8 ? "Nokay\n" : "Okay\n";`

4) The following instruction will have what effect?
   `$result = -e /tmp/lock.$$ ? "Go" : "No";`
   a) _____ The variable `$result` will be set to `"No"` if a file named `/tmp/lock.$$` is executable.
   b) _____ The variable `$result` will be set to `"No"` if a file exists that has the name `"lock.PID"` where PID is the current process id.
   c) _____ The variable `$result` will be set to `"Go"` if a file exists that has the name `"lock.PID"` where PID is the current process id.
   d) _____ The variable `$result` will be set to true if a file exists that has the name `"lock.GO"`.

5) The variable $fname is set to "names.db" earlier in the program. What will the following instruction do?

```
print -T $fname, "\n";
```

    a) _____ Print the timestamp from the file "names.db" and then a newline.

    b) _____ Print 0 if "names.db" is a text file or an empty file.

    c) _____ Print 0 if "names.db" is a binary file or an empty file.

    d) _____ Print 0 if "names.db" is a text file but not if it's an empty file.

Quiz answers appear in Appendix A, Section 6.3.

LAB 6.3

C H A P T E R   6

TEST YOUR THINKING

In the chapter discussion, we looked at how to build a system that facilitates multiple levels of debugging output. Let's build code that can respond to 10 levels of "error severity." Our program should use a command-line model like this one:

```
$ dbugtalker.pl -x numeric_level
```

For instance, if you run the program with the following command-line, you would get messages of every severity up to level five:

```
$ dbugtalker.pl -x 5

problem at severity level 5

problem at severity level 4

problem at severity level 3

problem at severity level 2

problem at severity level 1

problem at severity level 0
```

1) Write a program (`dbugtalker.pl`) that prints warnings at every severity level from 0 through 9. Run the program with various levels to see how it behaves. (Be sure you test the values and $-1, 0, 9, 99, 255$, and -127.)

2) Write a program "`filewatch.pl`" that can read the names of files in the current directory, and then print a report indicating whether or not each file is readable, writeable, executable, text, or binary.

Perhaps your output could look like this:

Filename	Readable	Writeable	Executable	Text	Binary
WhoAmI.class	yes	yes	no	no	yes
debuglevel.pl	yes	yes	yes	yes	no
filewatch.pl	yes	yes	yes	yes	no

3) You learned in Chapter 4, "Arrays and Lists," that it's easy to iterate through an array, reading each item in turn. Now write a program that can read through the command-line arguments, watching for three different supported options. If an option -v is found, set the variable $verbose to the value 1. If an option -c is found, set the variable $config to the value 1. If the value -x is found, set the variable $dbuglevel to the value found in the next argument.

C H A P T E R 7

REGULAR EXPRESSIONS

<table>
<tr><td colspan="2" align="center">**CHAPTER OBJECTIVES**</td></tr>
<tr><td colspan="2">In this chapter, you will learn about:</td></tr>
<tr><td>✓ Standard Regular Expression Metacharacters</td><td>Page 298</td></tr>
<tr><td>✓ Perl Extended Metacharacters</td><td>Page 321</td></tr>
<tr><td>✓ Simulating a Switch Statement</td><td>Page 338</td></tr>
</table>

Perl is a language that was born in the shadow of the rich collection of utilities provided in UNIX to manipulate plain text. As a result, it borrows heavily from the functionality of tools like grep(1), sed(1), awk(1), and procmail(1). One thing that these tools have in common is the use of a system for matching patterns in text called "Regular Expressions."

In this chapter, we'll look at how to form a regular expression (or informally, a "regex"), and we'll see some examples of tasks that benefit from this powerful facility. Like most powerful language features, however, this will take some study, so get ready to focus in on, maybe even sometimes stare at, one line of code for 15 or 20 minutes at a time. (Be sure to stretch regularly.)

We'll start by revisiting the match operator and learning about the standard regular expression metacharacter set. We'll move on to the extended metacharacters which make Perl more powerful, and then we'll see how to take advantage of this to build a complex program control structure. Finally, we'll wrap this chapter up by looking at some other tools for manipulating text strings.

L A B   7.1

STANDARD REGULAR EXPRESSION METACHARACTERS

LAB OBJECTIVES

After this Lab, you will be able to:

✓ Use Regular Expressions to Match Partial Strings

✓ Use the Match Operator with the Default Variable

✓ Use the Binding Operator to Match in Any Variable

In Chapter 6, "Tests and Branching," we saw how to test a string for exactly the same content as another string. Now we will learn how to determine whether a partial string or string pattern is contained within a string value. The key to defining these patterns is a set of characters that allow us to state "regular expressions."

We'll also revisit the "match" and "substitute" operators. We'll see how we can use the "marking" operator to memorize part of a string matched by a regular expression.

Earlier, in Chapter 1, "Getting Started," we saw the match operator in use. We took advantage of the ability to search for a specific literal pattern within a string value. Did you remember that we can use `perl -n` to read each of the lines in a file named on the command line? We can do that in conjunction with the match operator to allow only certain lines to be printed. Let's review that.

THE MATCH OPERATOR

We used the match operator in a phrase that looked like this:

```
m/CA/ && print;
```

Now that we've talked about the boolean AND operator and short-circuit operation, you can already see part of how this works. In essence, this code says "If we match the string 'CA' then print."

Two questions beg for an answer. One is, "If we match the string 'CA' in what?" The other obvious question is, "Okay, then print what?" From what we saw of the program's operation in Chapter 1, "Getting Started," we might imagine that each line in succession is being searched for the target string and then `print()` emits the entire line if a match is detected.

The answer to both of our questions is related to the concept of the default input buffer ($_). We've seen this before, but let's just get a formal introduction right here. When we use the command-line option to Perl, each line from the file(s) named on the command line is read into $_ where it can be used by any functions that operate on the default variable. The match operator compares its pattern against the default variable unless we give it other instructions. So the pseudo-code for our previous program might look like this:

```
for each line in all of the named files
   read the line into $_
   print $_ if it contains the pattern /CA/
end for
```

Because Perl is designed to allow us to state things sparsely, we get all of that out of the following command line:

```
perl -ne 'm/CA/ && print;' file1 file2 file3
```

There is one more shortcut we can use in this program. It takes advantage of the fact that we usually use the forward slash (/) to delimit the pattern for which we search. The specification for the match operator says that we can use any delimiter we like. The slash is handy and usually doesn't conflict with any of the characters in our pattern. But we could use # or ! or ? if we like.

If you're willing to use the / as your delimiter however, you are allowed to omit the m from the match operator. This means that as long as we are going to take advantage of the default variable, our program can be as simple as:

```
/CA/ && print;
```

Yes! That's a complete Perl program. We must admit however, that it looks more like an awk(1) program and it *is* "Exhibit A" in the People's Case that Perl is a "write-only" language.

You might also recall that in Chapter 2, "The Nickel Tour," we saw how our program can open and process the file itself. Sometimes this is better than depending upon having exactly the right command line. Here's that code one more time:

FINDCAL.PL
```
1  #!/usr/bin/perl
2  open (IN, "<names.txt") or die "couldn't open file";
3  while (<IN>) {
4     /CA/ && print;
5  }
```

This works fine. Each line from the file "names.txt" is read into the default variable; you can search that for a specific pattern, and print it if you find the pattern. So what if you want to search for a pattern in something other than the default variable? Well, here's something you might want to know about.

THE BINDING OPERATOR (=~)

Officially named "the binding operator," the =~ allows us to conduct a pattern search on any scalar value. The Perl documentation tells us that it "binds a scalar expression to a pattern match." What that means in everyday terms is that it allows us to use the match operator on any value instead of just the default variable.

Some programmers informally call this the "scan" or the "contains" operator. Here is how it might be used:

```
$ARGV[0] =~ /Tom/ && print "$ARGV[0]\n";
```

One way to state this in English might be to say:

```
if the first argument contains "Tom" then print it
```

Or we might state it as:

```
scan the first argument for "Tom" and print on match
```

We'll see this operator a lot in our future programs because pattern matching is an important task in Perl. Before we lay the issue to rest, I want to tell you that the binding operator is also used with the substitution (s/original/substitute/) and the transliteration operators (tr/set1/set2/ or y/set1/set2/). We'll look at these before this Lab is finished.

Right now, we have to address the fact that so far we've used only literal strings directly when we've looked for matches. Perl offers us a well-developed collection of tools for matching patterns that are more useful than literal strings. These tools form something we call "regular expressions."

WHAT ARE REGULAR EXPRESSIONS?

Let's start with the simple and obvious. The string "CA" is itself a regular expression. Most characters stated in a regular expression simply represent themselves. In other words, the letter "C" means the letter "C" and so forth. The exceptions to this rule (the "metacharacters") are shown in the tables that follow. But even the characters that have special meaning in a regular expression can be included literally by preceding them with an escape character (\).

For instance, we will learn that the metacharacter "$" has a special meaning in a regular expression. But if we must search for a "$" in a string, we can simply "escape" the special meaning of the metacharacter. Suppose we want to look for the phrase that means "one hundred dollars" in the default variable:

```
/\$100/ && print;
```

This would do the trick for us. Let's look at the metacharacters that help us with our pattern-matching operations.

Table 7.1 ■ Standard Regular Expression Metacharacters

Metacharacter	Meaning	Example
. (period or dot)	Match any single character except newline	/.ob/ matches "bob", "rob", "lob" and portions of "knob", "Robert", and "Penobscott"
[abc123]	Match a single character from this set	/[RrBb]ob/ matches "bob", "Bob", and portions of "Robert", "Bobby" but it will not match in "Hobart" or "Penobscott"
		/log[0-9]/ matches "log1", "log8" and "log0", as well as portions of "log9.old" and "log5.txt" but not just "log".
[^abc123]	Match a single character not listed in the set	/log[^0-9]/ matches "loga", "logx" and "log-" but not "log1" or "log99"
$	Match end of line or end of string	/txt$/ matches "log.txt" but not "log.txtfile"
^	Match beginning of line or string	/^Rob/ matches "Robert", "Rob", and "Robert was here." but will not match "See Robert run."
		/^[^Rr]ob/ matches "Bob" and "Bobby K" but not "Go Bobby" or "Robert runs."
*	Match 0 or more of the preceding regular expression atom	/log[0-9]*/ matches "log1", "log10", "log9999" and simply "log"
+	Match 1 or more of the preceding regular expression atom	/log[0-9]+/ matches "log1", "log10", "log9999" but not "log"
?	Match 0 or 1 of the preceding regular expression atom	/html?/ matches "html" and "htm"
{quantity}	Match exactly "quantity" of previous regular expression atom	/log[0-9]{3}/ matches "log001", "log000" and "log123" but not "log1"

{min,max}	Match at least "min" but no more than "max" of the preceding regular expression atom	/log[0-9]{3,5}/ matches "log001", "log0011" and "log12345" but not "log35"	**LAB 7.1**

These are the standard regular expression metacharacters. This means that they are also used by many of the other utility programs on the UNIX system. In addition, many search facilities on the Internet support the use of regular expressions. The list is not comprehensive. There are some metacharacters that you'll learn about later. These are enough to get you on your way.

USING REGULAR EXPRESSIONS

So let's put some of these tools to use. We'll start by acknowledging the fact that most of the time we can restate a regular expression in English to help make more sense of it. For instance, look at the following regex:

```
[A-Z][a-zA-Z]*
```

If we were to restate this in English, we might say, "An upper case letter followed by zero or more instances of letters in any case."

Do this yourself a few times and pretty soon regular expressions will become second nature to you.

■ *FOR EXAMPLE*

Imagine that we have to parse the directory of a tar file. (A tar file, for those of you who don't see them often, is an archive that stores files, their directory, and their owner/permission information, along with some associated statistics. It is a common form of archive on the Internet.)

Here's a sample of the directory information stored in a tar file:

```
-rw-r--r-- sys/everyone   55808 1998-10-04 00:20 model.doc
drwxr-xr-x sys/everyone       0 1998-10-01 15:41 ch6/
drwxr-xr-x sys/everyone       0 1998-10-02 12:34 ch6/eg/
-rw-r--r-- sys/everyone      19 1998-12-12 20:29 ch6/eg/words
-rw-r--r-- sys/everyone     178 1998-11-25 13:56 ch6/eg/ednm.pl
```

```
-rw-r--r-- sys/everyone      68 1998-12-20 21:30 ch6/eg/argct.pl
-rw-r--r-- sys/everyone  110592 1998-12-21 22:30 ch6/ch06.doc
```

If we wanted to see only the lines that represent the names of Perl programs, we can form a regular expression that takes advantage of the fact that we are naming all of our programs with a ".pl" filename extension.

```
/\.pl$/ && print;
```

That's about all there is to it. In fact, let's see that as a complete command line program.

```
$ tar tvf somefile.tar | perl -ne '/\.pl$/ && print'
```

We can write a program that simulates manipulation of a tar file by embedding sample directory information in the code while we test and develop. Let's write a program that prints the name of each Perl program, and indicates whether it is executable or not. (A Perl program is executable if the read and execute permissions are set on.)

TARCHECK.PL

```
 1 #!/usr/bin/perl
 2 @flist = (
 3   "-rw-r--r-- sys/sys 55808 1998-10-04 00:20 model.doc",
 4   "drwxr-xr-x sys/sys     0 1998-10-01 15:41 ch6/",
 5   "drwxr-xr-x sys/sys     0 1998-10-02 12:34 ch6/eg/",
 6   "-rw-r--r-- sys/sys    19 1998-12-12 20:29 ch6/eg/words",
 7   "-rwxr-xr-x sys/sys   158 1998-11-15 18:39 ch6/eg/dbl.pl",
 8   "-rw-r--r-- sys/sys     0 1998-12-14 17:56 ch6/eg/mtfile",
 9   "-rw-r--r-- sys/sys   234 1998-11-15 18:43 ch6/eg/dbl2.pl",
10   "-rwxr-xr-x sys/sys   158 1998-11-15 18:39 ch6/eg/wp.pl",
11 );
12 foreach $line (@flist) {
13   if ($line =~ /\.pl$/) {
14     ($perm, $fname) = (split /\s+/, $line)[0,5];
15     print "Perl program: $fname\t";
16     print "Program is ",
17       $perm =~ /r.x/ ? "": "not ",
18       "executable\n";
19   }
20 }
```

The simulated data set is established in *lines 2-11*. The loop in *line 12* iterates over the lines in the data set, first checking that the line contains "the letters 'pl' followed immediately by the end of line." (We will allow the assumption here that these are the characteristics of a Perl program.) The code in *line 14* breaks the line into pieces and we keep the first and sixth fields as the permission string and the filename. The syntax for split begins to make more sense now that we know about regular expressions. The first argument is, in fact, a regular expression. We'll learn what "\s+" means in just a little while.

In *line 16*, we see a print statement that uses the conditional operator to search the permission string for a pattern that contains "the letter 'r' followed by any character then followed by the letter 'x,'" which is a reasonable indication that the program is set to be executable. (Note that these file permissions are applicable only on UNIX systems. The principles involved in matching patterns do apply to everyone, however.)

LAB 7.1 EXERCISES

7.1.1 USE REGULAR EXPRESSIONS TO MATCH PARTIAL STRINGS

FTP.LOG

```
1 127.0.0.1 admin [18/04/98:17:17] / "MKD news" 200 0 0
2 200.150.191.6 anon [05/06/98:15:43] / "RETR /feedback.htm" 200 1317 0
3 198.170.191.9 anon [05/06/98:15:43] / "RETR /robots.txt" 200 127 0
4 198.170.191.9 anon [05/06/98:15:44] /pix/mag "RETR padlock.gif" 200 896 0
5 198.160.191.5 anon [05/06/98:15:44] /pix/mag "RETR smag3.gif" 200 127 0
6 127.0.0.1 admin [18/04/98:20:16] / "MKD pub" 200 0 0
7 127.0.0.1 anon [05/06/98:15:44] /pix/mag "RETR tmag3.gif" 200 6929 0
8 198.160.191.5 anon [05/06/98:15:44] /pix/mag "RETR tmag1.gif" 200 6742 0
```

Here are eight lines that might appear in a log file. Determine which lines will be matched by the following regular expressions.

a) `/.*gif/`

_____

_____

b) /a*n/

_____

_____

c) /a.*n/

_____

_____

d) /a.{4} / #(expression ends with a space " " character)

_____

_____

e) /127/

_____

_____

f) /^127/

_____

_____

7.1.2 USE THE MATCH OPERATOR WITH THE DEFAULT VARIABLE

a) Write an instruction that would match blank lines in an input file. (Hint: It's a line where the beginning of the line is followed by the end of line.)

_____

_____

b) Write an instruction that would match a US zip code. To test it, use sample input that contains both simple five-digit zip codes and "zip plus four" style codes.

_____

_____

c) Write a program (`findimages.pl`) that reads in a file named on the command line and prints any lines that contain an absolute URL that refers to a GIF file or a JPG file. (It is permissible to assume in this Exercise that the only types of URL that interest us would be either an "http" or "ftp" URL. You may also assume that the files that interest us will have either `.gif` or `.jpg` as filename extensions.)

_____

_____

7.1.3 USE THE BINDING OPERATOR TO MATCH IN ANY VARIABLE

a) Write a short program (`argtest.pl`) that examines the first command-line argument. If the first argument is "-d", then assign the next argument to a variable to be used for a debug level.

_____

_____

b) Write a short program (`inputtest.pl`) that will prompt the operator for an input instruction and then compare it to each of four possible values. For now, pick the matching values arbitrarily and, after you find a match, simply print a message identifying the option chosen by the operator.

_____

_____

Barber Tom locked the door to the shop and turned to Uncle Larry. "You have to tell me all about the Storyteller's conference. Did you have a good time?"

"Yes, I did. But we'll have plenty of time to talk about that when we get to the pub. In the meantime, let's look at the progress you've made on your programming project." Larry spent a few moments studying code and muttering approving sounds before he spoke again. "Okay, you've got a good start here. Let's review what you've accomplished.

"You have a program that partially validates a user login.

"You have a program that accepts a new entry from the command line.

"You have a program that prints a report based upon the existing database."

Tom nodded. "That pretty much sums up what you asked me to do."

"Now it's time for the next step," Larry continued. "All of your programs use simulated data that's embedded into the code. This is a perfect place to start. Now we want to move that information into a file. Your new program is going to read the data in from a file, and combine all of the functions you've worked out into one program.

"And let's have the program write out a new data file through redirection. Here's a syntax model you can use.

```
todo001.pl <uname> <passwd> [-r | -a <task> <pri>] >newfile
```

"The way it breaks out is this.

"The first two arguments (username and password) are mandatory. They will be used to validate the user from a user data file. These may optionally be followed by a '-r' option, which tells the program to print a report showing all tasks for the identified user. Instead of the '-r' switch, the operator may provide a '-a' switch that indicates that the next two command-line options are a new task and its priority. Those should be added to the database.

"If neither the '-r' nor the '-a' switch is present, the program should simply validate the user and then print a report.

"For the time being, we'll have the program operator update the data file through the use of redirection. Later on, when your program is rock-solid, we'll have it write the information directly to a file.

"To get you started quickly, I'll give you three sample files that you can use. Two of them will contain sample data, and the third one is a template that forms a basis for your program."

Here are the files that Larry provided:

TODO.USERS
```
larry:lingo
tom:tonic
ellie:plasma
```

TODO.TASKS

```
larry:update autostory program:3
larry:read about file i/o:2
tom:order 12 gallons of Vitalis:1
ellie:find planet-related websites:2
tom:get more paper for clipboard:3
```

TODO-TEMPLATE.PL

```
#!/usr/bin/perl
# check command-line for validity
# validate username/password pair
   # open user data file
   # read user data into a hash
   # find command-line name/password in hash or exit
# check for runtime options (-r or -a)
# get existing task data
# write report if we're in that mode
# print out new data file if we're in that mode
```

c) Write the program that Tom is about to tackle (todo001.pl). It should comply with the syntax model shown previously.

_____

_____

LAB 7.1 EXERCISE ANSWERS

7.1.1 ANSWERS

FTP.LOG

```
127.0.0.1 admin [18/04/98:17:17] / "MKD news" 200 0 0
200.150.191.6 anon [05/06/98:15:43] / "RETR /feedback.htm" 200 1317 0
198.170.191.9 anon [05/06/98:15:43] / "RETR /robots.txt" 200 127 0
198.170.191.9 anon [05/06/98:15:44] /pix/mag "RETR padlock.gif" 200 896 0
198.160.191.5 anon [05/06/98:15:44] /pix/mag "RETR smag3.gif" 200 127 0
127.0.0.1 admin [18/04/98:20:16] / "MKD pub" 200 0 0
127.0.0.1 anon [05/06/98:15:44] /pix/mag "RETR tmag3.gif" 200 6929 0
198.160.191.5 anon [05/06/98:15:44] /pix/mag "RETR tmag1.gif" 200 6742 0
```

Determine which lines from the sample log file will be matched by the following regular expressions.

a) `/.*gif/`

Answer: Lines 4, 5, 7, and 8 all match this one.

In general, any line that contains the string "gif" will match this expression. Don't forget that although the phrase says, "any sequence of 0 or more of any characters followed by the string 'gif'", it is conceivable that a line with nothing more than "gif" will still match.

Never forget that the * in a regular expression means "it's okay if it's there, but it's also okay if it's not."

b) `/a*n/`

Answer: All of the lines match.

This was a very wicked trick question. If you were a little careless and interpreted this as, "'a' followed by anything and then followed by 'n'," you might have accidentally stumbled on the right answer.

What we have to remember is that the phrase actually means "zero or more 'a' characters followed by an 'n' character." That means that any line with an "n" would match (even if it had zero "a" characters just before the "n").

c) `/a.*n/`

Answer: All of the lines match.

In this case, we have the expression the way we probably ought to have it. It says, "The 'a' character followed by zero or more of any character, then followed by an 'n' character." The lines that have the word "anon" and the lines that have the word "admin" fit this description.

d) `/a.{4} /` # expression ends with a space character

Answer: Lines 1 and 6 match this phrase.

This time, we are explicit enough to get the "admin" lines without matching the "anon" lines. The phrase says, "The 'a' character followed by exactly 4 of any character, then followed by a space."

This illustrates that sometimes we have to be diligent, thorough, or creative to get the phrase that filters out everything except what we really want to see.

e) `/127/`

Answer: This phrase matches the lines 1, 3, 5, 6, and 7.

Lines 1, 6, and *7* contain the pattern at the beginning of the line in what appears to be an IP address. *Lines 3* and *5* contain the pattern elsewhere in the data on the line. Sometimes we have to try to be more precise.

f) `/^127/`

Answer: This pattern matched lines 1, 6, and 7.

This time we said, "the character string '127'" only when it appears at the beginning of the line.

7.1.2 ANSWERS

a) Write an instruction that would match blank lines in an input file. (Hint: It's a line where the beginning of the line is followed by the end of line.)

Answer: This instruction would match blank lines:
`/^$/`

Now there is a practical reason that we might want to match blank lines. It would seldom be to print the lines. But we might want to count them, or we might decide to delete them. For instance, look at the following command line.

```
perl -ne '/^$/ || print;' file1 >file1.new
```

This will create a new version of `file1` without any blank lines.

b) Write an instruction that would match a US zip code. To test it, use sample input that contains both simple five-digit zip codes and "zip plus four" style codes.

Answer: This instruction would do the trick:
`/[0-9]{5}-?[0-9]{0,4}/`

But there is a problem with it. This matching operation would be happy with a regular zip code or a zip-plus-four. But it would also match five digits followed by a hyphen. It would also match nine digits in a row, which probably isn't a zip code.

In essence, this expression says, "match five digits followed by an optional dash, followed by anywhere from zero to four additional digits." There may be a number of ways to fix it, but one interesting and useful way will be to use parentheses to "atomize" the dash and additional digit specification so that we can modify the whole phrase.

What we really want our expression to say is, "match five digits optionally followed by a dash and four additional digits." Here's the phrase we need for that:

```
/\b[0-9]{5}(-[0-9]{4})?\b/
```

c) Write a program that reads in a file named on the command line and prints any lines that contain an absolute URL that refers to a GIF file or a JPG file.

Answer:This is a program that would do the trick:

FINDIMAGES.PL

```
1  #!/usr/bin/perl
2  while (<>) {
3      /http:.*gif/i && print;
4      /http:.*jpg/i && print;
5      /ftp:.*gif/i && print;
6      /ftp:.*jpg/i && print;
7  }
```

This program takes a fairly simplistic approach (and that's a good place to start). If a line contains any of the patterns shown, the line will be printed. The problem is that if the line contains more than one of the patterns, it may be printed more than once.

Notice the use of the "i" modifier at the end of the match operator. This causes the match to ignore case differences between pattern and buffer. (Some people like to think of this modifier as providing a "case-insensitive" matching operation.)

If we're willing to work this a little bit, we can construct a phrase that prints each line only once whenever it contains any variation of the patterns shown. Take a look at this:

FINDIMAGES2.PL

```
1 #!/usr/bin/perl
2 while (<>) {
3     /[fh]t?tp:.*[jg][pi][gf]/i && print;
4 }
```

It's not pretty, but it works. Shall we render this in English? "An 'f' or an 'h' optionally followed by a 't' and then definitely followed by the string 'tp:' which may then be followed by zero or more of any characters, ultimately followed by a 'j' or a 'g' and then a 'p' or an 'i' and then at last by a 'g' or an 'f' at the end of the sequence." Ignore case while conducting the match.

Something tells me that you're hoping you might not have to do this very much. You won't, but if you practice working with regular expressions enough so that you can easily make them work, you'll be able to include them in your programs where another programmer might seek a less efficient solution. Perhaps you can fix the one we've just seen to pick up JPEG files when they have a '.jpeg' filename extension. Just keep on practicing.

7.1.3 ANSWERS

a)   Write a short program (`argtest.pl`) that examines the first command-line argument. If the first argument is "-d", then assign the next argument to a variable to be used for a debug level.

Answer: This program does the work we've been asked to do here.

ARGTEST.PL

```
1 #!/usr/bin/perl
2 die "usage: $0 -d debuglevel\n\t" unless defined $ARGV[1];
3 ($switch, $dlevel) = @ARGV if $ARGV[0] =~ /^-d/;
4 print "debug level is set to: $dlevel\n";
```

To keep things simple, this program doesn't work very hard at validating the command line. Ideally, it should probably take the approach we used in earlier programs. If the debug level isn't presented as an argument on the command line, we should assign a default. You remember how we did that before, and it *is* what you should do in your production code.

Our main focus here is in the regular expression that checks the first argument (*line 3*). You'll note that this one looks for a pattern that "follows the beginning of the line with the characters -d". This certainly does exactly what we were asked to do, but it isn't a very sophisticated check. In a later Lab in this chapter, we'll look at a more comprehensive way to process the command line without sacrificing simplicity.

b) Write a short program (inputtest.pl) that will prompt the operator for an input instruction and then compare it to each of four possible values. For now, pick the matching values arbitrarily and, after you find a match, simply print a message identifying the option chosen by the operator.

Answer: Here's a program that complies with these (fairly loose) specifications.

INPUTTEST.PL
```
 1 #!/usr/bin/perl
 2 print "
 3 Choose from among the following options:
 4    1) List Files
 5    2) View a File
 6    3) Delete a File
 7    4) Rename a File
 8
 9 Which: ";
10 $choice = <STDIN>;
11 if ($choice =~ /^1/) {
12    print "Here comes a list of files: \n";
13 }
14 elsif ($choice =~ /^2/) {
15    print "Ready to show you a file: \n";
16 }
17 elsif ($choice =~ /^3/) {
18    print "Ready to delete a file: \n";
19 }
20 elsif ($choice =~ /^4/) {
21    print "Ready to rename a file: \n";
22 }
```

Hey, this looks like the makings of a user shell! You'll note in *lines 2-9* that we use a multi-line string to print out the initial menu. There are other ways to accomplish this, but this one affords us ample control over layout and appearance.

We gather the user input in *line 10* but never bother to chomp() it. This is okay because we aren't going to do a direct equality check. Instead, we are going to inspect only the first character in the string they enter. You can see this happen in *lines 11, 14*, and so forth. Each time we check to only see if the input line from the operator will match an expression that begins with a specific digit that interests us.

The nice thing about this approach is that we could easily modify our test to allow the operator a variety of legal input options. Suppose they decide to type the first word from the menu option instead of the number? We can support that very easily. Here's how we would modify *line 17*, for instance, to allow that to work for them:

```
elsif ($choice =~ /^[3dD]/) {
```

This would allow them to type in the number, or the word "delete" in either case. (Unfortunately, it also allows them to type in any word that begins with "D" to get this option, but that's probably okay.) There's a limit to how much silliness your program should tolerate from the operator before it simply decides to break. Where you define that limit to be will depend upon your own personal reverence for civility.

c) c) Write the program that Tom is about to tackle (todo001.pl). It should comply with the syntax model shown in the Exercise text.

Answer: The following program is one way to write it:

TODO001.PL

```
 1 #!/usr/bin/perl
 2 # check command-line for validity
 3 die "syntax: $0 user passwd [-r | -a task priority]\n\t"
 4    if ! defined $ARGV[1];
 5
 6 # validate username/password pair
 7 $uname = shift;
 8 $passwd = shift;
 9 # open user data file
10 open UDATA, "<todo.users"
```

```
11     || die "couldn't open user data file.";
12 # read user data into a hash
13 while ($line = <UDATA>) {
14    chomp $line;
15    ($u, $p) = split /:/, $line;
16    $ubase{$u} = $p;
17 }
18 close UDATA;
19
20 # find command-line args in hash or exit
21 die "cannot find user $uname\n\t"
22    if ! defined $ubase{$uname};
23 die "cannot validate user password\n\t"
24    if $passwd ne $ubase{$uname};
25
26 # check for runtime options (-r or -a)
27 if (! defined $ARGV[0]) {
28    $mode = "report";
29 }
30 elsif ($ARGV[0] =~ /^-r/) {
31    $mode = "report";
32 }
33 elsif ($ARGV[0] =~ /-a/) {
34    $mode = "add";
35    $dummy = shift;
36    $newtask = shift;
37    $priority = shift;
38 }
39 else {
40    $mode = "report";
41 }
42
43 # get existing task data
44 open TDATA, "<todo.tasks"
45    || die "couldn't open task data file\n\t";
46 while ($line = <TDATA>) {
47    chomp $line;
48    push @tlist, $line;
49 }
50 # here's a cheaper way
51 # @tlist = <TDATA>;
52 close TDATA;
53
54 # write report if we're in that mode
55 if ($mode eq "report") {
```

```
56    foreach $t (@tlist) {
57        print "$t\n" if $t =~ $uname;
58    }
59 }
60
61 # print out new data file if we're in that mode
62 if ($mode eq "add") {
63     $newitem = join ":", ($uname, $newtask, $priority);
64     push @tlist, $newitem;
65     foreach $line (@tlist) {
66         print "$line\n";
67     }
68 }
```

This is a pretty long program and yours may be significantly different. Let's look at this one for techniques that you may want to harvest for your own code.

The first interesting code is in the loop that begins with *line 12*. Here you can see (again) how we read lines of data from a file and store them in a hash. The hash (called %ubase) is keyed to the first item from the data line (the user name) and contains the second item from the data line (the password). As soon as we've read the entire file, we close it. We won't need it any more.

The next block of code (*lines 20-24*) checks to see if the username and password from the command line are found in the legitimate user base. Then we continue to check the command line for additional options that might be found there. If we find the "-a" switch, we grab the next two items from the command line and save those for future reference (*lines 33-38*).

In *lines 43-52*, we read in the existing task list from its file and then close the file. Most of the work is contained in the loop that begins with *line 46*. You can see a suggestion in *line 51* for a way to replace the loop. As long as a file is known to be of a reasonable size, it can be read into an array with code as simple as that. (How large is a file "of a reasonable size"? It depends upon available memory. But in general, a file under one megabyte is usually a safe bet. Our data table here is definitely small enough.)

Once we're through with all of this setup, we can actually do the work that we came in here to do. In *lines 54-59*, you can see what we have to do if we've been asked to report on the data items for a particular person (that is, the one who logged in). This is a simple matter of testing each data item to see if it contains the user name. Note that this isn't entirely safe because we might have a user whose data item contains the name of the logged-in user. We'll have to fix that soon.

If we've been asked to add an item to the database, then we simply put the new data item at the end of the list (*lines 62-68*) and then print the contents of the entire list. Did you remember that `join()` is the opposite of `split()`?

If your program is nothing like this one at all, then run both of them and be sure they act in approximately the same way.

LAB
7.1

LAB 7.1 REVIEW QUESTIONS

Here is some output you might see on your own system.

```
-rw-r--r--    1 agentv    everyone     577 Jan  5 19:59 argswitch.pl
-rw-r--r--    1 agentv    everyone     170 Jan  4 08:30 argtest.pl
-rw-r--r--    1 agentv    everyone     771 Feb 20 14:40 tarcheck.pl
-rw-r--r--    1 agentv    everyone     727 Dec 23 11:26 tarcheck2.pl
-rw-r--r--    1 agentv    everyone     844 Jan  4 22:57 tardate.pl
-rw-r--r--    1 agentv    everyone    2414 Dec 21 23:18 tardir.txt
-rw-r--r--    1 agentv    everyone     344 Jan  4 14:35 todo-template.pl
-rw-r--r--    1 agentv    everyone     214 Jan  4 13:27 todopl.tasks
-rw-r--r--    1 agentv    everyone      38 Jan 13 22:53 todopl.users
-rw-r--r--    1 agentv    everyone    1461 Jan  5 20:21 todo001.pl
```

1) Which lines are matched by the regular expression: /tar*/?
   a) _____ 3, 4, 5 and 6
   b) _____ 3, 4, 5, 6, and 8
   c) _____ none of the lines
   d) _____ all of the lines

2) Which lines are matched by the regular expression /tar.*/?
   a) _____ 3, 4, 5 and 6
   b) _____ 3, 4, 5, 6, and 8
   c) _____ all of the lines
   d) _____ none of the lines

3) Which lines are matched by the regular expression /.*pl/?
   a) _____ all except 6, 8, and 9
   b) _____ 1, 2, 3, 4, 5, 7, and 10
   c) _____ all except 6
   d) _____ none of the lines

4) Which lines are matched by the regular expression /.*\.pl/?
   a) _____ 3, 4, 5 and 6
   b) _____ 1, 2, 3, 4, 5, 7, and 10
   c) _____ all except 6
   d) _____ none of the lines

5) Which lines are matched by the regular expression /pl$/?
   a) _____ all except 6, 8, and 9
   b) _____ 3, 4, 5 and 6
   c) _____ all of the lines
   d) _____ none of the lines

Quiz answers appear in Appendix A, Section 7.1.

L A B   7.2

PERL EXTENDED METACHARACTERS

LAB OBJECTIVES

After this Lab, you will be able to:

- ✓ Use Perl Extended Metacharacters
- ✓ Use the Perl Substitution Operator
- ✓ Use the Perl Transliteration Operator

Because many Perl programs are heavily involved in pattern-matching tasks, we are provided with additional tools that make life easier. Many of these extended metacharacters are concise ways to state expressions that can be formed with the traditional tools.

MORE METACHARACTERS

The following list of metacharacters constitutes a set that is not necessarily available in other UNIX utilities that process regular expressions. Many of them are defined only in Perl. You will find them to be very useful when you want to process text. So take a good look at Table 7.2.

Table 7.2 ■ Extended Regular Expression Metacharacters

Metacharacter	Description	Example
\s	a single whitespace character	same as [\t\n\f] (i.e., space, tab, newline, or formfeed)
\S	a non-whitespace character	same as [^ \t\n]
\d	a single digit character	same as [0-9]
\D	a non-digit character	same as [^0-9]
\w	a single "wordlike" character	same as [a-zA-Z0-9_]
\W	a non-wordlike character	same as [^a-zA-Z0-9_]
\b	the boundary between a word and non-word	similar to $, but it marks the end of a word. /bob\b/ would match "bob" but not "bobby"
\B	a boundary between two wordlike characters	the expressions /bob\B/ and /bob\w*/ are roughly equivalent in their meaning
(marked)	tag characters matched by expression within the parentheses for future use	/(\w+).html/ marks the word characters preceding the ".html" filename extension for future reference. The special variable $1 now holds that information.
|	alternative—match expression to the right or left of the metacharacter	/mar.*|ash.*/ would match patterns that contain "mar" or "ash"

A couple of these need further clarification. First of all, \w means "a word-like character," but the definition of what constitutes "wordlike" is more representative of a programmer's perspective than it is that of an English teacher. This is okay as long as we know about it in advance.

The \b and \B metacharacters are like $ and ^. We call these "zero-width assertions." These tools do not match a character, but the space between characters. So the phrase /sam\B\b/ has no meaning because there can be only one boundary between the last "m" and the next character.

The phrase shown in the example from the table (/bob\B/) could be read in English as "the letters b, o, and b, followed by a boundary that is not at the end of a word." The equivalent phrase could be stated as, "the letters b, o, and b, followed by one or more wordlike characters."

Let's look at a program that takes advantage of these tools.

TARCHECK2.PL

```
 1 #!/usr/bin/perl
 2 @flist = (
 3     "-rw-r--r-- sys/sys   234 1998-11-15 18:43 ch6/eg/db2.pl",
 4     # other data omitted here, same as before
 5 );
 6 foreach $line (@flist) {
 7     if ( $line =~ m!([-rwxstl]{10})\s+.*\s+.+/(.*pl)$! ) {
 8         print "file name: $2\t";
 9         print "perm string: $1\n";
10     }
11 }
```

Just look at that regular expression in *line 7*! This is a good example of why regular expressions and the tools that use them are widely feared. But you don't have to be afraid. Let's break this down together.

First, note that we're using the match operator in its full form with an alternative delimiter (!). This is because we're going to refer to the slash character (/) in our pattern and we don't want it to be mistaken for the end of the match operator.

Let's try to state this expression in English. "Ten characters, any of which may be from the set containing '-rwxstl' and that should be remembered as $1. That should be followed by one or more instances of whitespace, then followed by zero or more of any character, then followed by one or more whitespace characters. This should be followed by one or more of any characters immediately followed by the forward slash. This is to be followed by a memorized sequence consisting of zero or more of any character, immediately followed by the letters 'pl', the entire memororized sequence being stored in $2. The end of line should immediately follow."

Okay, so nobody could say that in one breath, but you can see from this that a regular expression can provide a powerful way to specify specific patterns in text.

There is a mystery here, however. We say "one or more instance of whitespace followed by zero or more of any character." Doesn't whitespace count as "any character"? Well, yes, it does, and the definition of the second clause in that phrase could include some whitespace characters. In fact, take a look at Figure 7-1 to see how the regular expression breaks down.

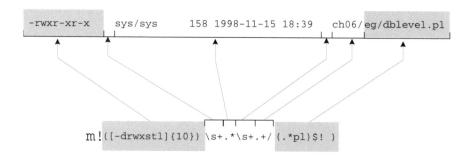

Figure 7.1 ■ Regular Expression Breakdown

One thing we can see from this diagram is that the portion that says "zero or more of any character" includes quite a lot of whitespace. But it doesn't include the space between the time and the beginning of the file-name. Why is that?

> *"Regular expressions are greedy."*

This means that a given portion of a regular expression will match the longest possible sequence of characters as long as the remainder of the regular expression can still be satisfied.

■ *FOR EXAMPLE*

If you have a regular expression as simple as:

```
/.*/
```

this means "zero or more of any character" and would match the entire string. On the other hand, the expression

```
/.*\s/
```

means that the `.*` matches a run of any characters only as long as it is followed by one whitespace character. We'll take a closer look at this during the Lab Exercises.

CIVILIZING REGULAR EXPRESSIONS

Fortunately, the Perl match operator allows you to break up regular expressions with whitespace and comments.

Take another look at the expression from *line 7* of `tarcheck2.pl`. Even though we are working with a text buffer that contains much whitespace and we actually refer to it explicitly in more than one place, there is no whitespace in the regex itself. So if we had a way of telling the match operator that whitespace is not to be treated literally as part of the pattern we seek, we should be able to have as much control over the visual presentation of the expression as we like.

The syntax for doing this is:

```
m/regular expression/x
```

So let's look at our line one last time:

```
if ( $line =~ m!([-drwxstl]{10}) # remember perms as $1
   \s+.*\s+.+/ # everything up to the last slash on the line
   (.*pl)$!x # save the filename in $2
   ) {
```

It's a little more readable here than it was before. This technique is something that will help you when you write code that you might want to maintain later. In fact, breaking the expression down this way suggests a much simpler way for us to have stated it. You can take a crack at that during the Lab Exercises.

SUBSTITUTION

Everything you've just learned about using regular expressions applies equally to the substitution operator.

We saw the substitution operator in Chapter 1, "Getting Started," so you might recall the syntax:

```
s/oldpattern/newpattern/
```

■ FOR EXAMPLE

Consider the following text file:

NOTIFY.TXT
```
Dear #WINNER#:
You have been selected as a winner. A two week
vacation in the name of #WINNER# and a guest...
```

If you had the job of writing a program that replaced the # encased string with a real name, you might write the following code:

NOTIFY.PL
```
1 #!/usr/bin/perl -p
2 # we'll expect the filename on the cmd-line
3 $winner = "Ed";
4 s/#.*#/$winner/;
```

One thing you can see from this is that it's legal to include a variable as part or all of the substitution pattern. A more important implication is this: If you mark part of the original pattern with parentheses, you can include it back into the substitution string.

■ FOR EXAMPLE

Let's work on the data that came from the directory listing of a tar file. Suppose we want to read in a line and print only the filename and its modification date. Here's a program that does it:

TARDATE.PL

```
 1 #!/usr/bin/perl
 2 @flist = (
 3 "-rw-r--r-- sys/sys        55808 1998-10-04 00:20 model.doc",
 4 # ... other lines as before ...
 5 );
 6 foreach $line (@flist) {
 7    $line =~ s/^.* # all the stuff up to the date
 8       (\d{4}-\d{2}-\d{2}) # the date itself into $1
 9       .*\s # all the stuff up to the last whitespace
10       (.*) # the filename into $2
11       $/$1   $2/x; # end of line and substitute pattern
12    print "$line\n";
13 }
```

Of course, we could have put the entire regular expression from the substitution on one line, but it would look like this:

```
$line =~ s/^.*(\d{4}-\d{2}-\d{2}).*\s(.*)$/$1   $2/;
```

You really have to decide for yourself which is more readable. Fortunately, most of the regular expressions you'll encounter will be much simpler than these.

TRANSLITERATION

Transliteration allows us to replace all occurrences of a specific character (or set of characters) with a different one (or one from a set of different ones). The syntax for the operator that allows us to do this is:

```
tr/oldcharacters/newcharacters/
```

Or, to make old-school `sed(1)` hackers happy, it can also be done with:

```
y/oldcharacters/newcharacters/
```

Each character of the input string is examined, and if the character appears in the string specified by "originalcharacters", it is replaced with its counterpart from "newcharacters" as defined by position.

■ FOR EXAMPLE

Take a look at this program that destroys all of the vowels in a message:

NOVOWELS.PL
```
1 #!/usr/bin/perl
2 $message = "There's a theory that we can understand
3 the essence of a message, even if we don't see any
4 vowels.  That's good news since vowels cause most
5 of the problems with spelling anyway.";
6 $message =~ tr/aeiou/12345/;
7 print "$message\n";
```

Each vowel in our original message is replaced by a digit that represents its position in the original list. Here are some other examples:

```
tr/A-Z/a-z/ # normalizes to lowercase
tr/a-z/n-za-m/ # simply shrouds original text (rot-13)
# if second list is too short, last character is replicated
tr/a-z/a-m/ # anything from n-z becomes m
# modify with 'd' to avoid last character replication
tr/a-z/a-m/d # anything from n-z is simply removed
```

You may find this operator to be of use in your programs. Let's give it a try.

LAB 7.2 EXERCISES

7.2.1 USE PERL EXTENDED METACHARACTERS

FTP.LOG
```
1 127.0.0.1 admin [18/04/98:17:17] / "MKD news" 200 0 0
2 200.150.191.6 anon [05/06/98:15:43] / "RETR /feedback.htm" 200 1317 0
3 198.170.191.9 anon [05/06/98:15:43] / "RETR /robots.txt" 200 127 0
4 198.170.191.9 anon [05/06/98:15:44] /pix/mag "RETR padlock.gif" 200 896 0
5 198.160.191.5 anon [05/06/98:15:44] /pix/mag "RETR smag3.gif" 200 127 0
6 127.0.0.1 admin [18/04/98:20:16] / "MKD pub" 200 0 0
7 127.0.0.1 anon [05/06/98:15:44] /pix/mag "RETR tmag3.gif" 200 6929 0
8 198.160.191.5 anon [05/06/98:15:44] /pix/mag "RETR tmag1.gif" 200 6742 0
```

Here are eight lines that might appear in a log file. Determine which lines will be matched by the following regular expressions.

a) `/127\b/`

_____

_____

b) `/127\B/`

_____

_____

c) `/127\s/`

_____

_____

d) `m!\d{2}/04/\d{2}!`

_____

_____

e) `/txt|htm/`

_____

_____

7.2.2 USE THE PERL SUBSTITUTION OPERATOR

a) Write a short program (`resolver.pl`) that will read the log shown in Exercise 7.2.1, and print the entire log. Change any occurrence of the IP address "127.0.0.1" to the word "localhost" whenever it occurs.

_____

_____

In the program `tarcheck2.pl`, we saw a lengthy regular expression that could stand some simplification. Take one last look at that expression and answer the question.

```
if ( $line =~ m!([-rwxstl]{10})\s+.*\s+.+/(.*pl)$! ) {
```

**LAB
7.2**

b) How could we simplify this expression so that it still accomplishes its goal?

_____

_____

c) Rewrite the `tardate.pl` program to extract the date and file-name as before. This time, however, take the date and change it so that it is presented in the (very American) format MM/DD/YY. Comment your regular expression.

_____

_____

7.2.3 USE THE PERL TRANSLITERATION OPERATOR

a) Write a short program (`rot13.pl`) that uses the Perl transliteration operator to change every occurrence of an alphabetic character (upper or lower case) for one that is offset by 13 places in the alphabet. (that is, "a" becomes "n" and "M" becomes "Z" and so forth.) Make sure that it works in both directions by sending some altered text back through the program to see it become the original text.

_____

_____

LAB 7.2 EXERCISE ANSWERS

7.2.1 ANSWERS

a) `/127\b/`

Answer: Lines 1, 3, 5, 6, and 7 all match.

This expression asks for the digits "127" to be followed by a word boundary. This is true in the instances of "127" in the IP addresses found near the beginning of the lines. But it's also true in a couple of the lines as incidental data.

This is a reminder to us that we might think that our regular expression will give us exactly what we want, but sometimes it gives us more. It's usually wise to check your regex against a fairly diverse set of data to see if there are any improvements that can be made.

Any line that contains a number that ends in "127" will be a match here. At the very least, we might anchor the pattern by asking for a word boundary at each end. Something like this:

`/\b127\b/`

That would cut out some of the potential anomalous occurrences of the pattern.

b) `/127\B/`

Answer: None of the lines match this.

There is not an instance of the required digit sequence followed by a non-boundary. In each occurrence of the sequence "127" there is a "non-word character" following. That constitutes a boundary in every case.

c) `/127\s/`

Answer: Lines 3 and 5 match this phrase.

The occurrence of "127" in the IP address portion of the lines does not terminate with a whitespace character. Again, any numeric string that ends with "127" will cause a match here.

One important thing to note here is the difference between the use of a word boundary and the use of trailing whitespace. Sometimes a word boundary appears when a word is followed immediately with punctuation, as in a sentence. If your expression demands whitespace following such a word, it will fail. On the other hand, sometimes a pattern can appear in a context that isn't at the end of a word semantically (as in the case where it is part of a hyphenated word or a dotted IP address) but it will appear to be adjacent to a word boundary.

You do have to take these things into consideration for your more complex tasks.

d) `m!\d{2}/04/\d{2}!`

Answer: The lines that match this phrase are lines 1 and 6.

Note that because our regular expression uses forward slashes as part of the pattern to be matched, we chose alternative delimiters.

Let's put this one into English. "Two digits followed by a slash, followed by '04' and then another slash followed at last by two more digits." We could have repeated the "\d" metacharacter twice in a row instead of using the quantifier in braces (you know, {2}). In fact, this would have saved us a keystroke for each occurrence of that part of the pattern. There isn't any particular advantage to one approach or the other in this instance. It's best if you know about both alternatives.

e) `/txt|htm/`

Answer: This pattern matches lines 2 and 3.

It's an almost static expression; in other words, there are almost no metacharacters. We simply use the alternation character to say, "the string 'txt' or the string 'htm'," which turns out to be a pretty handy thing to be able to do.

7.2.2 ANSWERS

a) Write a short program (`resolver.pl`) that reads the log shown in Exercise 7.2.1 and prints the entire log. Change any occurrence of the IP address "127.0.0.1" to the word "localhost" whenever it occurs.

Answer: Here's a program that does the work.

RESOLVER.PL
```
1 #!/usr/bin/perl
2 open IN, "<ftp.log" || die "couldn't open ftp.log\n\t";
3 while (<IN>) {
4    s/127\.0\.0\.1/localhost/;
5    print;
6 }
7 close IN;
```

In *line 3*, you can see how we set up a loop to read all of the lines in the file, using the default variable (`$_`) for each line in succession. This makes the body of the loop a lot simpler because we can use the default behavior of both the substitute operator and the `print()` function.

b) How could we simplify the regular expression from `tarcheck2.pl` so that it still accomplishes its goal?

Answer: The original expression really was a little bit more than necessary. Let's take another look at it:
```
if ( $line =~ m!([-drwxstl]{10}) # remember perms as $1
\s+.*\s+.+/ # everything up to the last slash on the line
(.*pl)$!x # save the filename in $2
 ) {
```

With the expression broken down like this, it's actually easier to see where we can tighten it up. The first clause is fine. The last clause is okay, too; we have to have it that way. It's the stuff in the middle that is a little more verbose than we need.

The comment says "everything up to the last slash on the line." There's no reason that can't be simplified to " .*/", which will do the same thing, thanks to the greediness of regular expressions. So here's our final expression:

```
if ( $line =~ m! ([-rwxstl]{10}) .*/ (.*pl)$ !x) {
```

Because we continue to use the "x" modifier, we can introduce whitespace in the middle of our expression to make it easier to read.

c) Rewrite the `tardate.pl` program to extract the date and filename as before. This time, however, take the date and change it so that it is presented in the (very American) format MM/DD/YY. Comment your regular expression.

Answer: Here is one approach to the refit operation:

TARDATE2.PL
```
1 #!/usr/bin/perl
2 @flist = (
3     "-rw-r--r-- sys/sys    55808 1998-10-04 00:20 model.doc",
4     #...other data as before...
5 );
6 foreach $line (@flist) {
7     $line =~ s!^.* # all the stuff up to the date
8     \d{2}(\d{2})-(\d{2})-(\d{2}) # the date into $1,$2,$3
9     .*\s # all the stuff up to the last whitespace
10    (.*) # the filename into $4
11    $!$2/$3/$1   $4!x; # end of line and substitute pattern
12    print "$line\n";
13 }
```

Most of the work consisted of changing the pattern delimiters so that we could use a slash in the expression, and breaking the date into three separate components so that it could be shuffled about.

If this was a tough Lab for you, don't worry. You're not alone. Almost everyone needs lots of practice with regular expressions before it becomes natural. Just be sure to practice.

7.2.3 ANSWERS

a) Write a short program (`rot13.pl`) that will use the Perl transliteration operator to change every occurrence of an alphabetic character for one that is offset by 13 places in the alphabet.

**LAB
7.2**

Answer: Here's a program that will do the work.

ROT13.PL

```
1 #!/usr/bin/perl
2 while (<>) {
3    tr/a-zA-Z/n-za-mN-ZA-M/;
5    print;
6 }
```

No magic here. We use the <> operator so that the filename can be specified on the command line or the data to be "rotated" can be streamed into our program from a pipe. So we could run the program on its own source code like this:

```
$ rot13.pl rot13.pl
#!/hfe/ova/crey
juvyr (<>) {
   ge/n-mN-M/a-mn-zA-MN-Z/;
   cevag;
}
```

Does it work both ways? One way to find out would be to run the program and pipe the data to another instance of itself. (Talk about self-referential!)

```
$ rot13.pl rot13.pl | rot13.pl
```

I'll let you think about what you could do with this technique.

LAB 7.2 SELF-REVIEW QUESTIONS

1) Which expression will change the line endings "ist," "er," "ant," and "man" to the string "meister" (that is, the phrase "pocket fisherman" becomes "pocket fishmeister")?

   a) _____ s/er$|ist$|and$|man$/meister/

   b) _____ s/er|ist|and|man$/meister/

   c) _____ s/(er|ist|and|man$)/meister/

   d) _____ s/er$||ist$||and$||man$/meister/

Use this line as a model for the following questions.

```
-rw-r--r-- sys/whell   203 1998-12-21 10:55 ch06/eg/dsort0.pl
```

2) Which of these expressions will match only the filename from the input line?

    a) _____ `/\s[^\s]+$/`
    b) _____ `/[^\s]+$/`
    c) _____ `/[a-z0-9]+$/`
    d) _____ `/[a-z0-9./]+/`

LAB
7.2

3) Which of these expressions will match the file size (the third column) and preserve it in the variable $1?

    a) _____ `/^\D+(\d+)/`
    b) _____ `/\D+(\d+)$/`
    c) _____ `/^[0-9]+([0-9]+)/`
    d) _____ `/[a-z0-9./]+(\d+)/`

4) Which of these regular expressions will use substitution to display the date in `mm-dd-yyyy` format (i.e., the date from our example would become `12-21-1998`)?

    a) _____ `s/(\d{4}-\d{2}-\d{2})/$2-$3-$1/`
    b) _____ `s/(\d{4})-(\d{2})-(\d{2})/$2-$3-$1/`
    c) _____ `s/(\d{4}-)(\d{2}-)(\d{2}-)/$2$3$1/`
    d) _____ `s/(\d{4-})(\d{2-})(\d{2-})/$2$3$1/`

5) Which of the following lines will change the uppercase letters in a string to lowercase?

    a) _____ `tr/a-z/A-Z/`
    b) _____ `y/a-z/A-Z/`
    c) _____ `tr/A-Z/a-z/`
    d) _____ `tr/(\s+)/\L$1\E/`

Quiz answers appear in Appendix A, Section 7.2.

L A B   7.3

SIMULATING A SWITCH CONSTRUCT

LAB OBJECTIVES

After this Lab, you will be able to:

✓ Implement a Switch Construct

✓ Write a User Shell

In Chapter 6, "Tests and Branching," we saw how a cascading series of tests could be written using the `if/elsif/else` construct. If the sequence is very long, however (more than three or four tests), the entire block can become unwieldy and inelegant.

This is why many programming languages (C, Java, Bourne Shell, among others) implement something called a "switch construct." In Perl there is no official syntax to do this same thing. This is okay because we can easily implement one using other syntactical elements. In this Lab, we'll see how to do that, and we'll revisit the user shell from the last Lab to make it more streamlined.

THE MOCK SWITCH

In many other programming languages, a very useful construct is provided to solve the following requirement. We have a variable that may be set to a value from a finite set of possible values. Depending upon which value the variable holds, the program will execute a specific set of instructions.

If we wrote it in pseudo-code, it might look like this:

```
for some possible value of $var
   if $var is A: { do this code }
   if $var is B: { do this code instead }
   if $var is unidentified: { do this default code }
endfor
```

In Perl, we can simulate this sort of construct by using a handful of standard mechanisms from the language. And there is a benefit. In most of the other languages, the value that controls the execution of a switch must be an integer or a single character. In Perl, we can use any type of variable or, for that matter, any condition that we know how to test.

**LAB
7.3**

THE SIMPLE WAY

Here's some code we saw earlier that uses traditional Perl syntax.

WHOPAYS.PL
```
 1 #!/usr/bin/perl
 2 $price = shift;
 3 print "Clerk: How will you pay for that?\n";
 4 if ($price < 100) {
 5    print "You: With cash.\n";
 6 }
 7 elsif ($price < 500) {
 8    print "You: With a credit card.\n";
 9 }
10 elsif ($price < 1500) {
11    print "You: With someone else's credit card.\n";
12 }
13 else {
14    print "You: Never mind, I'll wait for the sale.\n";
15 }
```

With a program this short, the approach we take here is just fine. But when things get more complicated, it would be nice if we have a syntax that is easier to maintain. We can do that in Perl by taking advantage of two syntactic appendages. These are the label and the "do block."

LABEL AND DO BLOCK

To define a label, you need to use an identifier that follows the same rules we discussed in Chapter 3, "Variables, Large and Small." Common convention is to use uppercase only for labels, but there is no structural reason that you have to do this. It will simply make your code more easily read.

A do block is simply a block of code that is placed where a single instruction might appear. Its syntax looks like this:

```
do {
    # some code here
};
```

Note that there is a semicolon at the end of the block. If you remember that you're putting this wherever a single statement is allowed, you will probably see the logic of writing it this way. And think about this: You could write a statement with a conditional clause at the end. You could add a conditional clause at the end of a do block.

■ *FOR EXAMPLE*

```
do {
    print "We are very happy!";
    print "I mean, very, very happy!";
} if $bank_balance > 1000000;
```

You could write such a block with an `if`, `while`, or `unless` clause at the end. (We'll explore `while` and `unless` clauses in Chapter 8, "Loops and Other Repetitive Experiences.")

Using what we've seen here and some things we've already learned, we're ready to build a Perl switch.

AND NOW, A PERL SWITCH

Our switch will consist of a labeled block that contains a set of tests inside. The result of each test will be to execute some code and then exit the block using the `last` statement.

■ *FOR EXAMPLE*

It's easier to grasp if we just look at one.

WHOPAYS2.PL

```
 1 #!/usr/bin/perl
 2 $price = shift;
 3 print "Clerk: How will you pay for that?\n";
 4 SW1: {
 5    ($price < 100) && do {
 6       print "You: With cash.\n";
 7       last SW1;
 8    };
 9    ($price < 500) && do {
10       print "You: With a credit card.\n";
11       last SW1;
12    };
13    ($price < 1500) && do {
14       print "You: With someone else's credit card.\n";
15       last SW1;
16    };
17    # default case
18    print "You: Never mind, I'll wait for the sale.\n";
19    last SW1;
20 }
```

**LAB
7.3**

The heart of this program is the labeled program block that begins with *line 4*. The label that we choose is named arbitrarily. Many people use the label "SWITCH:" and you can certainly do that yourself. We avoided that here because sometimes people think that they have to use that exact label for this to work. It's just a name for the block.

The body of the block consists of simple conditional statements. (Okay, they're not that simple, but in essence, they're just a series of ordinary statements.) Each one is formed by using a boolean expression in conjunction with the short-circuit operator to control entry into any particular do block. When the instructions from a particular do block are finished, the final one (that is, last SW1;) causes execution to resume, starting at the end of the labeled block.

SWITCHING ON THE DEFAULT VARIABLE

Here's another example that may help clarify this approach.

LAB 7.3

USHELL0.PL
```perl
 1  #!/usr/bin/perl
 2  print "
 3   1) List Files
 4   2) View File
 5   3) Delete File
 6   4) Rename File
 7
 8   Which? ";
 9  chomp($_ = <STDIN>);
10  SWITCH: {
11              /^[1Ll]/ && do {
12                  print "you chose to list files\n";
13                  last SWITCH;
14              };
15              /^[2Vv]/ && do {
16                  print "you chose to view a file\n";
17                  last SWITCH;
18              };
19              /^[3Dd]/ && do {
20                  print "you chose to delete a file\n";
21                   last SWITCH;
22               };
23               /^[4Rr]/ && do {
24                   print "you chose to rename a file\n";
25                   last SWITCH;
26               };
27              # default behavior
28              print "I have no idea what you want\n";
29              last SWITCH;
30          }
31  print "and later on, we'll actually do that for you\n";
```

Using the default variable makes the syntax of the switch a lot cleaner. You may find this useful in your own programs from time to time.

LAB 7.3 EXERCISES

7.3.1 IMPLEMENT A SWITCH CONSTRUCT

a) Write a short program (`argswitch.pl`) that will inspect each of the arguments on the command line and set program options based upon what it finds. Here's the syntax model:

```
argswitch.pl [-v] [-d debuglevel] [-f filename]
```

You can use this template as a starting place:

```
   AS.PL
 1 #!/usr/bin/perl
 2 $debug = 0;
 3 $verbose = 0;
 4 $filename = 0;
 5 while ($arg = shift) {
 6    # decide what to do with the arguments
 7 }
 8 print "debug level: $debug\n";
 9 print "verbose flag: $verbose\n";
10 print "filename: $filename\n";
```

_____

_____

Uncle Larry knew that Barber Tom would be calling any time to talk more about his programming project. In the meantime, Larry thought he might do a little work on his story-generator program. The last version had allowed the variable parts of a story to be kept in a file, but the order in which the items could appear was critical.

Larry wanted to improve his program to allow for the values to appear in any arbitrary order, identified by a keyword. He wanted a file filled with lines that looked something like this:

```
monster=griffin
profession=cinematographer
```

He decided that he could seed the program with default values and then read the file, overriding any terms that were present in the file. The cool thing about this approach is that he could use one config file for many stories. If a particular line in the config file didn't apply to the story, it could be ignored. And if each story set up its own default values, the config file would not have to always provide every entry.

**LAB
7.3**

b) Using the `newstory.pl` program (from Chapter 2, "The Nickel Tour") as a foundation, write a new program, `cfg_story.pl` that reads from a configuration file named on the command line. Any lines that don't match the correct format should be ignored. Any terms that don't have a function should also be ignored.

Here's a sample config file:

CS.CFG
```
creature=human rights activist
kingdom=French Riviera
monster=celebrity photographer
trade=political consultant
kitchen_utensil=meat tenderizer
tool=pocket fisherman
```

Here's a template to get you started:

CS.PL
```perl
#!/usr/bin/perl
$cfg_file = defined $ARGV[0] ? $ARGV[0] : "story.cfg";
open IN, "$cfg_file" || die "couldn't open $cfg_file\n\t";

$CREATURE="Hobbit";
$KINGDOM="Mordor";
$MONSTER="Dragon";
$UTENSIL="fork";
$TRADE="innkeeper"
$TOOL="weeding hoe";

while (<IN>) {
    # do something with each line
    # using a switch to override any story terms
}
close IN;
# and now, the story, as before (or a new one)
```

_____

_____

7.3.2 WRITE A USER SHELL

It had finally happened! Barber Tom had turned down an appointment to leave more time for programming. This thing was starting to capture his imagination. He'd called to talk to Uncle Larry about how to make the program more interactive. He got some new ideas from the conversation. (Although it had been a short one; Larry had seemed vaguely distracted somehow.)

Tom decided to implement his project as a suite of programs. He'd envisioned a way that he might combine all of the activities into one monolithic program, but somehow, breaking things down into smaller pieces seemed more elegant, more "Perl-like."

So his next step was to write an interactive front-end for the "to-do" database. It would support all of the options he'd put into his earlier program (todo001.pl) but there would be no need for command-line arguments. Each thing the program needed to know, it would ask the operator to supply in real-time. Here's what it looked like on its first successful run.

```
$ itodo.pl
login: larry
password: lingo


   1) Report all of your tasks

   2) Add a task to the list

   3) List everyone's tasks


   Which? 2


Enter a description of the new task: Add new stories
Enter a priority for the new task (1-9): 2
```

```
larry:finish autostory program:3
larry:read about file i/o:2
tom:order 12 gallons of Vitalis:1
ellie:find planet-related websites:2
tom:get more paper for clipboard:3
randal:write roster management program:2
larry:Add new stories:2
```

**LAB
7.3**

a) Write the interactive front-end (`itodo.pl`) for Tom's project. It should do all of the things that his last program did.

_____

_____

LAB 7.3 EXERCISE ANSWERS

7.3.1 ANSWERS

a) Write a short program (`argswitch.pl`) that will inspect each of the arguments on the command line and set program options based upon what it finds.

Answer: Here is a version of the program that will work:

ARGSWITCH.PL
```
 1 #!/usr/bin/perl
 2 $debug = 0;
 3 $verbose = 0;
 4 $filename = 0;
 5 while ($arg = shift) {
 6     # decide what to do with the arguments
 7 SWITCH: {
 8             $arg =~ /^-v/ && do {
 9                 $verbose = 1;
10                 last SWITCH;
11             };
12             $arg =~ /^-d/ && do {
```

```
13              $debug = shift;
14              last SWITCH;
15          };
16          $arg =~ /^-f/ && do {
17              $filename = shift;
18              last SWITCH;
19          };
20      }
21 }
22 print "debug level: $debug\n";
23 print "verbose flag: $verbose\n";
24 print "filename: $filename\n";
```

Not too many surprises in this program. We start by explicitly assigning default values to the three settings we hope to manage from the command line. Then we loop through the arguments on the command line, comparing each new one to the possible values until we find a match (or not). When we find a match (as in *line 8*), we take the appropriate action for that particular argument.

This is a reasonable approach for a simple program when we know that the operator will usually follow instructions reliably. If the command line is not well-formed, this program can result in unexpected behavior. For instance, suppose that the operator supplies a command line that looks like this:

```
argswitch.pl -v -d -f filename
```

When the program encounters the "-d" switch, it will gobble up the next argument to be the debug level. That wouldn't hurt too much except that now the "-f" switch is gone and there will be no filename assigned.

If we need a more durable command-line model, we'll have to look for information about the `getopts()` function in the Perl documentation.

b) Using the `newstory.pl` program (from Chapter 2, "The Nickel Tour") as a foundation, write a new program, `cfg_story.pl`, that reads from a configuration file named on the command line.

Answer: Here's a program that does the work. Look carefully, there are a number of tricks hidden in this code.

CFG_STORY.PL

```
 1 #!/usr/bin/perl
 2 $cfg_file = defined $ARGV[0] ? $ARGV[0] : "story.cfg";
 3 open (IN, "$cfg_file") || warn "couldn't open $cfg_file\n\t";
 4
 5 $CREATURE="Hobbit";
 6 $KINGDOM="Mordor";
 7 $MONSTER="Dragon";
 8 $UTENSIL="fork";
 9 $TOOL="weeding hoe";
10 $TRADE="innkeeper";
11
12 while (<IN>) {
13    if (/^([^=]+)=(.*)$/) { # if we have a legitimate line
14       $k = $1; $v = $2;
15 SWITCH: {
16          $k =~ /creature/i && do {$CREATURE=$v; last SWITCH};
17          $k =~ /kingdom/i && do {$KINGDOM=$v; last SWITCH};
18          $k =~ /utensil/i && do {$UTENSIL=$v; last SWITCH};
19          $k =~ /monster/i && do {$MONSTER=$v; last SWITCH};
20          $k =~ /trade/i && do {$TRADE=$v; last SWITCH};
21          $k =~ /tool/i && do {$TOOL=$v; last SWITCH};
22       }
23    }
24    else {
25       warn "bad line from config file\n\t";
26    }
27 }
28 # and now, the story, as before (or a new one)
29 print << "EndOfStory";
30 Once upon a time, a very nice $CREATURE
31 was named Prime Minister of a lovely place
32 called $KINGDOM.  On a trip to the provinces,
33 he met a $MONSTER who had been cruel to the
34 people.  The $CREATURE found a clever
35 $TRADE who helped him run the $MONSTER
36 out of the country.  Then they gave every
37 person a new $UTENSIL or $TOOL. (Each one
38 had to choose.)  Everyone was happy except
39 for the $MONSTER.
40  --- The End ---
41 EndOfStory
```

The first technique of interest here is in *line 3*. You'll see that when we try to open the file, instead of exiting the program if the operation fails (normally we use the `die()` command here), we use a companion function, `warn()`. This one emits a message but allows the program to continue. In this case that's appropriate, because the program makes allowances for the case in which there is no input file (see *lines 5-10*).

Here we go again in *line 13*. This regular expression looks unwieldy at first glance, but it's not so bad. Perhaps it would be easier to read if we introduced some whitespace. Here's what we have:

```
if ( /^    ([^=]+) = (.*) $/x ) {
```

The expression might read, "Starting at the beginning of the line, find (and remember in $1) one or more instances of any character that is not an equal sign, followed by an equal sign. Following that, locate (and remember in $2) zero or more of any character, followed by the end of line."

Now why do you think we said "one or more instances of any character that is not an equal sign"? Remember greed? Suppose we have a line that looks like this:

```
setting=bob+mary=fred
```

In our line from the program, the parameter in this case would be equal to "setting" and the value would be equal to "`bob+mary=fred`", which is what we want. The letters that make up "setting" are all "non-equal signs." If we'd used a pattern like ".+" instead of "[^=]+", greed would have caused it to match all the way up to the equal sign just before "`fred`". This is the last time we'll worry about greed. You're on your own with it from here on.

The main body of the program comes in the switch construct that shows in *lines 15-27*. You can see that we've compressed each case in the switch to one line. The general rule is that we should stick to one instruction per line. In this case, it makes sense to compress because each of the cases is similar and they are very short.

It's also true that this construct is easy to maintain. Suppose we want to add a new case to the program. We simply copy and paste one of the lines that represents a case and then modify the new line. We can also easily "comment out" a case if we decide that it's a good idea. So in this instance, we've found a very good exception to the rule.

7.3.2 ANSWERS

LAB
7.3

a) Write the interactive front-end (`itodo.pl`) for Tom's project. It should do all of the things that his last program did.

Answer: Here's a program that works for Tom. It still needs work, but we'll talk about that after you've studied this code.

ITODO.PL

```
1  #!/usr/bin/perl
2  # get username/password from command-line if possible
3  if (defined $ARGV[1]) {
4      $uname=shift;
5      $passwd=shift;
6  }
7  # otherwise, make them type it now
8  else {
9      print "login: ";
10     chomp ($uname = <STDIN>);
11     print "password: ";
12     chomp ($passwd = <STDIN>);
13 }
14 # validate username/password pair
15     # open user data file
16 open (UDATA, "<todo.users")
17     || die "couldn't open user data file.";
18     # read user data into a hash
19 while ($line = <UDATA>) {
20     chomp $line;
21     ($u, $p) = split /:/, $line;
22     $ubase{$u} = $p;
23 }
24 close UDATA;
25
26 # find username/password in hash or exit
27 die "cannot find user $uname\n\t"
28     if ! defined $ubase{$uname};
29 die "cannot validate user password\n\t"
30     if $passwd ne $ubase{$uname};
31
```

```
32 # get existing task data
33 open (TDATA, "<todo.tasks")
34    || die "couldn't open task data file\n\t";
35 @tlist = <TDATA>;
36 close TDATA;
37
38 # time for a menu
39 print "
40    1) Report all of your tasks
41    2) Add a task to the list
42    3) List everyone's tasks
43
44    Which? ";
45 chomp ($_ = <STDIN>);
46 SWITCH: {
47    /^[1Rr]/ && do {
48       foreach $t (@tlist) {
49          print "$t" if $t =~ /^$uname/;
50       }
51    };
52    /^[2Aa]/ && do {
53       print "Enter a description of the new task: ";
54       chomp ($newtask = <STDIN>);
55       print "Enter a priority for the new task (1-9): ";
56       $priority = <STDIN>;
57       $newitem = join ':', ($uname, $newtask, $priority);
58       push @tlist, $newitem;
59       # (TODO) this simulates writing the file -- fix it
60       foreach $line (@tlist) {
61          print "$line";
62       }
63    };
64    /^[3Ll]/ && do {
65       foreach $line (@tlist) {
66          print "$line";
67       }
68    };
69 }
```

This program borrows heavily from the todo001.pl program. In doing so, it inherits some flaws that need to be corrected. Both programs have the names of their data files hard-coded. The user data file is called todo.users and the task list is called todo.tasks. That may be okay, but we should probably allow those names to be supplied on the command line. We can address that in a later revision of this program.

A lot of things can go wrong before we get to *line 35*, but if we make it that far, you'll note that we take the shortcut discussed earlier in the chapter. Reading the entire file into an array this way is often called "slurping the file" and it's okay as long as we know that the file isn't enormous.

The switch that begins in *line 46* looks a lot like a cross between the ushello.pl program and the "guts" of todo001.pl from before. That's no coincidence. Sometimes our best programs are based upon our earlier work. Just be careful not to get caught "cutting and pasting" carelessly.

One problem that is fixed is the one we discussed earlier about checking data items before they are printed in the report. In *line 49*, we print a data item if it contains the logged user, but only if that pattern is at the beginning of the line. So if Tom has a data item that reminds him to "call Larry," we won't print that item when Larry is logged in.

We've introduced a new problem with this program that will have to be fixed later. Option 3 allows the operator to dump the entire data table to the screen. In a later revision, we may want to limit that type of access to administrative users. For now, it's a handy debugging tool that the program developer can use.

One last thing that we'll want to fix is that the program offers only one chance for the operator to choose an activity. After a choice is made, the program does the work and then exits. Perhaps we should encase most of this thing in a loop! We'll do that in the next chapter.

LAB 7.3 SELF-REVIEW QUESTIONS

Using these lines as input, answer the following questions.

```
1 creature=human rights activist
2 kingdom=French Riviera
3 monster=celebrity photographer
4 trade=political consultant
5 utensil=meat tenderizer
6 tool=pocket fisherman
```

1) Which regular expression matches and marks the first two words after the equal sign?

    a) _____ `($twowords)  =  /=((\w+){2})/`
    b) _____ `($twowords)  =  /=\s*(\w+\s+\w+)/`
    c) _____ `($twowords)  =  /=(\w+{2})/`
    d) _____ `($twowords)  =  m/=\w+\s+\w+/`

2) Which regular expression matches and marks the word portion prior to the equal sign?

    a) _____ `$key  =  /^\s*(^\s+)\s*=/`
    b) _____ `$key  =  m/\S+=/`
    c) _____ `$key  =  /^\s*(\S+)\s*=/`
    d) _____ `$key  =  m(/\s*\S+\s*=/)`

**LAB
7.3**

Use this code to answer the next two questions.

```
SWITCH: {
   $response =~ /^[1Ll]/ && do {
      print "100: okay\n"; last SWITCH;
   };
   $response =~ /^[2Ee]/ && do {
      print "200: Simple error\n"; last SWITCH;
   };
   print "300: unknown error\n"; last SWITCH;
}
```

3) What value of `$response` will cause the program to print "100: okay" when the switch construct runs?

    a) _____ `$response = "^Line item";`
    b) _____ `$response = "List items";`
    c) _____ `$response = "do option 1L1";`
    d) _____ `$response = "Elegant Programming";`

4) What value of `$response` will cause the program to print "300: unknown error" when the switch construct runs?

    a) _____ `$response = "Line item";`
    b) _____ `$response = "List items";`
    c) _____ `$response = "do option 1L1";`
    d) _____ `$response = "Elegant Programming";`

Quiz answers appear in Appendix A, Section 7.3.

C H A P T E R   7

TEST YOUR THINKING

In the chapter discussion, we saw how to parse the output from the `tar` command to get information. Let's take that exploration a bit further. We might decide to do an analysis that requires us to read the lines from the tar file's table of contents and extract only the time of day, the size, and filename. With that information, we could print a report that shows total bytes for files modified in each time of day category (think one category per hour). The report might look like this.

```
$ taranalyze.pl
File modifications by hour
   Hour        Bytes     Count
00:00            74        1
01:00            99        1
02:00           512        2
09:00           468        1
10:00           335        1
11:00          1220        2 [and so forth...]
```

1) Write a program (`taranalyze.pl`) that prints a report that analyzes the component files by hour of day. At the end of the program, it should print a report that sums up the values for each category.

In a web page, the code that refers to an inline image looks something like this:

```
<img src="images/ball.gif" alt="Blue Ball">
```

The optional *alt attribute* (`alt="Blue Ball"`) is used to help non-graphical browsers display text that represents the image. It can also serve as a description intended for web cataloging facilities (such as Alta Vista, Yahoo, and now, you!).

2) Write a program that reads the standard input stream (or a list of files named on the command line) and extracts each image reference found. Print a report that shows the name of each file and the associated alt attribute, if one is found. (Do not worry about attributes that begin on one line and end on the subsequent line.)

Barber Tom thought about his user database for the To Do system. The password file kept the passwords right there in plain sight. He decided that he wasn't that interested in "security," but he did want to keep people out of each others' hair.

Shrouding the passwords with a rot-13 rotation would be plenty to keep people from accidentally noticing other people's passwords. He needed a password management program that could perform three functions. It would have to add new passwords to the file, replace passwords for existing users, and validate a user login from the password database. Here is the syntax model he finally decided to use.

```
pwmanage.pl [-a | -r] name passwd
```

3)   Write a program that validates a user login for the To Do system. It should support an option to add new passwords, replace existing passwords, or simply validate passwords for user logins.

LOOPS (AND OTHER REPETITIVE EXPERIENCES)

In this chapter, we'll see how to make program code repeat. In Perl, we have a rich variety of ways to control this. We can say, "repeat as long as *this* condition is true," or "repeat until *this* condition is true," or "repeat *N* times," or "repeat once for each member of *this* list."

We'll also see some tools that add flexibility to the way we build our loops. We can force a loop to end prematurely or continue to the next iteration without further delay. With these techniques in hand, you'll be ready to begin writing some very useful programs.

L A B   8.1

TRADITIONAL LOOPS

LAB OBJECTIVES

After this Lab, you will be able to:

✓ Use While and Until Loops

✓ Use the Foreach Loop

✓ Use the For Loop

In this Lab, we're going to look at all of the Perl loops that really are loops. There are four of these and you've already seen two and a half of them in earlier chapters. In a way, the four loops break down into two sets of near identical twins. The while() and until() loops are nearly mirror images of the same thing. (So you've seen one and a half of these two.) The for() and foreach() loops are related in a more distant fashion.

GOOD TWIN, EVIL TWIN:
THE while() AND until() LOOPS

The syntax for the while() and until() loops is nearly identical:

```
while (condition) {program block}
```

and

```
until (condition) {program block}
```

Like the conditional constructs that we studied in Chapter 6, "Tests and Branching," you must not omit the braces around the program block, and

under normal circumstances, the loop will be stated over several lines
with the program block indented for readability.

■ FOR EXAMPLE

Here's a block similar to what you've seen many times in this book
already:

```
while ($line = <STDIN>) {
    chomp $line;
    print "Heh heh, you said $line\n";
}
```

The loop continues as long as the condition evaluates to "true." The read
operation performed by the angle brackets evaluates to true until there is
no more data available. Here's another example of the loop:

TAPER.PL
```
1 #!/usr/bin/perl
2 $index = 5;
3 while ($index > 0) {
4    print ("*" x $index, "\n");
5    --$index;
6 }
```

You probably guessed what this program does if you recall the "string replication operator." The first time through the loop, we get five "stars" and
each time after that, we get one fewer than before.

```
$ taper.pl

* * * * *

* * * *

* * *

* *

*
```

The program itself is not very interesting, but we can use it to see how the
`until()` loop differs. This one does exactly the same thing:

UTAPER.PL
```
1 #!/usr/bin/perl
2 $index = 5;
3 until ($index <= 0) {
4    print ("*" x $index, "\n");
5    --$index;
6 }
```

The only thing that changes is the sense of the conditional test. That's really not much difference at all. On the other hand, sometimes the choice to have a loop continue while a condition is false (which is just what the until() loop allows) makes your code a lot easier to read. Consider the difference between these two:

```
while (! defined $stop_now) {
    do something;
}
```

and

```
until (defined $stop_now) {
    do something;
}
```

Use the variation that makes you happy; they're both logical and correct.

EVERYBODY GETS A CHANCE: THE foreach() LOOP

You saw the foreach() loop in Chapter 4, "Arrays and Lists." We'll most often use it when we want to process each of the items in a list. Let's review its form:

```
foreach $var (@list) {
    do something with $var;
}
```

This loop is run once for each of the items in @list. Inside the loop, $var is assigned to the current item from the list. In our earlier explorations, we used this loop to iterate through an array. Let's see that again.

■ *FOR EXAMPLE*

Here's something you might do to iterate through the command-line arguments.

ARGS.PL

```
1  #!/usr/bin/perl
2  $count = 1;
3  foreach $arg (@ARGV) {
4      print $count++, ". $arg\n";
5  }
```

This program simply prints a numbered list of arguments. You might want to do something more meaningful with the information provided by the program operator, so you could write a program like this:

ARGREAD.PL

```
1  #!/usr/bin/perl
2  # read the command-line arguments
3  foreach $arg (@ARGV) {
4      $arg =~ /^-v/ && ($verbose = 1);
5      $arg =~ /^-x/ && ($extended = 1);
6      $arg =~ /^-d/ && ($debug = 1);
7  }
```

This program compares the current argument to each of three supported options and sets a variable when an option is detected. It doesn't do anything with unsupported options and it displays a minor inefficiency because even when it detects that a particular argument is matched, it still compares the argument to the other possible options. We'll work on improving this a little bit later.

From this you can see how the foreach() loop can work its way through an array, but what isn't explicitly clear is that the loop can also work with a literal list. Consider this code:

```
foreach $number (1, 2, 3, 4, 5) {
    print "$number:", "*" x $number, "\n";
}
```

This is about as interesting as our taper.pl program from before. But it does establish two important things. The first is that you can use this type of loop to iterate through a literal list. This could be handy if you decided to do something silly like this:

```
foreach $consumed ( 0 .. 99 ) {
    print "$consumed bottles down the hatch
  brew one up, pour into cup,",
    $consumed+1, "bottles down the hatch!\n";
}
```

The other thing is that you can use this form of loop when you have a function (like `split()`) that creates a list. Let's look in this next program for words of wisdom.

WISDOM.PL
```
 1 #!/usr/bin/perl
 2 print "Type in your favorite saying and press ENTER:\n";
 3 $saying = <STDIN>;
 4 foreach $word (split /\s+/, $saying) {
 5     $total_words++;
 6     $table{$word}++;
 7 }
 8 print "total words: $total_words\n";
 9 foreach $entry (keys %table) {
10     printf "word: %-24s count: %-24s\n",
11         $entry, $table{$entry};
12 }
```

We take advantage of this technique twice in this program. First, in *line 4*, we set up a loop that iterates through each word in the input line. Later, in *line 9*, we iterate through a hash that we built (in *line 6*) while we were looking through those words.

The `foreach()` loop is one of the handiest and most commonly used loops in Perl. We can simulate its behavior with the other loops, but that would be more work—something we're trying to avoid.

START HERE, STOP THERE: THE `for()` LOOP

The last stop in our journey through the land of Perl loops is a visit with the `for()` loop. It actually works like the loop in C with the same name. So if you know how it works in C, you know how it works in Perl. If you don't know how it works in C, you will know in a little while. (Speaking of which, the `while()` loop is also identical to C. If you don't already know C, you're learning some of it as you learn Perl.)

Here's the syntax of the `for()` loop:

```
for (initialize; condition; post_process) {
    loop_body;
}
```

Before the loop begins, the instruction identified here as "initialize" is run. Immediately after that, the expression in "condition" is evaluated, and if it's true, the loop body is run. At the end of the instructions contained in the body, the "post_process" instruction is run and then "condition" is evaluated again. The loop terminates when the condition finally evaluates to false.

■ FOR EXAMPLE

This loop does what `taper.pl` did for us earlier. (Yes, I realize that wasn't much.)

```
for ($index = 5; $index > 0; --$index) {
    print "*" x $index, "\n";
}
```

Perhaps you'd like to do something more meaningful with it. Let's write a crude simulation of the UNIX `head(1)` program. For those of you who haven't used it recently, the `head(1)` utility prints out the first 10 lines from the file named on its command line. If no file is named, then it prints the first 10 lines from its standard input stream. An optional argument allows the program operator to specify a different number of lines to be printed. Our simulation optionally accepts a number as the first argument and prints that number of lines instead of the default 10. This program will not support a filename on the command line. You may decide to modify it later to do that.

PHEAD.PL

```
1 #!/usr/bin/perl
2 $lcount = defined $ARGV[0] ? $ARGV[0] : 10;
3 for ($idx=0; $idx<$lcount; ++$idx) {
4     $ln = <STDIN>;
5     print $ln;
6 }
```

It needs a lot of work to perform like the head(1) utility, but if you run it as designed, it will give you the first 10 lines, or the first *n* lines as provided for on the command line.

```
$ cat bigfile | phead.pl 12
```

This gives us 12 lines from the beginning of the file.

MORE PIDGIN PERL

There is another form of the for() loop that dates back to the early days of Perl. This one works just like the Bourne shell loop of the same name. In essence, it's a foreach() loop with a shorter name.

If you see a loop like this, then you'll know what's going on.

```
for (@listname) {
    # process list item stored in $_
}
```

Don't write code like this yourself, but be sure you know that you may see it from other programmers from time to time. (Some Bourne shell programmers never heal completely.)

LAB 8.1 EXERCISES

8.1.1 USE WHILE AND UNTIL LOOPS

It might be clear to you that any of the four loop types can be used for most jobs. Your choice of which loop to employ will be driven by habit, familiarity, and convenience. To see this in action, you could write four loops, one of each type that iterates through a short array and prints out each value.

a) Write a program (`fourloops.pl`) that uses one of each type of loop to iterate through a short array and print out each value.

_____

_____

In Chapter 7, "Regular Expressions," we looked at a program that formed the foundation of a user shell (`ushell.pl`). This program would display a menu, read the choice typed in at the console, and then print a message that acknowledged the request. We can easily encase the body of this program in a loop that allows the procedure to be repeated until the operator asks to exit from the program.

b) Revise the `ushell.pl` program by adding a new option to "exit." Encase the main body of the program in a loop that repeats the menu until the new exit option is chosen.

_____

_____

8.1.2 USE THE FOREACH LOOP

In the Lab discussion, we saw a program (`wisdom.pl`) that scanned a line of input and created a hash to count the number of occurrences of each word it found. Using this technique, you should be able to write a program that opens a file named on the command line and reads through it, compiling a hash that contains statistics about word frequency.

a) Write the program (`wordfreq.pl`) that builds a hash from the words found in a file named on its command line. Print a report at the end that shows each word and its frequency.

_____

_____

Barber Tom had just finished a trim for Coach Randal and was pushing the broom absentmindedly around the chair. They'd talked a bit about Tom's "To Do" project and Randal had already contributed some interesting ideas. Randal ran his hand over the back of his neck. "Have you put your interactive program into a loop yet?"

Tom set the broom in a corner. "Actually, I'm planning to spend some time reading about loops tonight," *he said.*

"Let me see if I can explain it so you can get started sooner. I like to think of it in terms of my players. When practice starts, I like to tell them, 'WHILE I talk with the other coaches about today's practice, I want to see you people stretching and warming up.' Then later in the day, my favorite, 'UNTIL I tell you to stop, I want to see you folks on that track, running laps.'"

Tom raised an eybrow, "You're tough."

"Yeah, but believe me, it pays off during the game. Now when I talk to my quarterbacks, I tell them, 'FOR EACH of the receivers on the first and second string, throw four pass patterns.'"

"So that," *he concluded,* " accounts for three of the four Perl loops."

Randal rubbed his chin and glanced over at the computer where he'd be sitting in a few minutes. "Hmmm, that sounds pretty simple."

"Yes, now the last loop is a little tougher to state in these terms, but think about it this way. I say, 'Okay, people, start counting at one, and if you haven't already run twelve, then I want you to run more windsprints. After you finish each one, if you still haven't done twelve, add one and keep going."

Tom looked skeptically at Randal, who cleared his throat and said, "Okay, so most analogies break down before you can get to the end. Just write a simple example of each type of loop. When you've done that, you'll almost certainly know which one to choose for your project. You know—I could stay and help you a bit."

Tom shook his head. "I don't think so. That is," *he smiled slyly,* "not unless you want me down there helping you decide whether to go for it on fourth and goal." *Randal turned toward the door immediately.* "I'll see you next week," *he said over his shoulder.*

Tom smiled as the door banged shut and he turned toward his computer. The smile left his face a moment later as he thought, 'Hey! He still owes me twelve bucks!'

b) Update Tom's program (`itodo.pl`) from Chapter 7 to allow the menu to be printed repeatedly until the exit option is chosen.

While the program is open for revision, go ahead and take care of these chores as well. Remove the code that reads the login information from the command line. Everyone will have to log in from a prompt now. Change the case that "simulates" writing out the updated data file so that it uses the `tr///` operator to "shroud" the data with a rot-13 rotation.

_____

_____

8.1.3 USE THE FOR LOOP

We learned earlier that we could read an entire file (of a reasonable size) into an array by "slurping" it with the angle-bracket operator used in an array context. You can use this approach to simulate the UNIX utility `tail(1)`. (For those not familiar with it, the `tail(1)` utility prints the last 10 lines from a file or from the standard input stream. The program operator has the option of specifying a command-line argument that indicates the number of lines that should be printed.)

The `for()` loop would be set to begin counting forward from the point that is 10 lines from the end of the file, and print out all of the remaining lines. You could use this simplified syntax model for the program:

```
ptail.pl [nlines] [filename]
```

a) Write a program (`ptail.pl`) that can display the final *N* number of lines from a file named on the command line.

If no file is named, the program should read STDIN; if two arguments exist on the command line, the first should be considered the number of lines to display. (The real `tail(1)` utility expects the first argument, when it exists, to be preceded by a "–" or "+" sign. This program will not require that.)

_____

_____

b) Write a program (`fullweek.pl`) that accepts a positive integer *N* as a command-line argument and prints all the numbers between 1 and *N* that are evenly divisible by 7. Print an error message if the argument is not numeric or if the number is smaller than 1.

_____

_____

LAB 8.1 EXERCISE ANSWERS

8.1.1 ANSWERS

a) Write a program (`fourloops.pl`) that uses one of each type of loop to iterate through a short array and print out each value.

Answer: Here's an example of how you might have written this program:

FOURLOOPS.PL

```
1 #!/usr/bin/perl
2 @characters = qw{fred barney tick arthur};
3
4 # while loop
5 $idx = 0;
6 while (defined $characters[$idx]) {
7    print "element $idx: $characters[$idx++]\n";
8 }
9 print "\n";
10
11 # until loop
12 $idx = 0;
13 until (! defined $characters[$idx]) {
14    print "element $idx: $characters[$idx++]\n";
15 }
```

```
16 print "\n";
17
18 # foreach loop
19 foreach $c (@characters) {
20     print "element: $c\n";
21 }
22 print "\n";
23
24 # for loop
25 for ($idx = 0; $idx < @characters; ++$idx) {
26     print "element $idx: $characters[$idx]\n";
27 }
```

Actually, for a task of this magnitude, there isn't any one loop that turns out to be more convenient or more effective than the others. If you need to keep track of an element's position in the array as you process it, then you might consider using the `until()` or the `for()` loops with an independent index variable. If you don't care about the relative position, but merely want to be sure that you see each member of the list, then you might select the `foreach()` loop as the logical choice.

When the task that you're attempting grows in size or complexity, you may see a benefit to a particular approach and when that happens, you'll know what to do. In the meantime, go with what you know!

b) Revise the `ushell.pl` program by adding a new option to "exit." Encase the main body of the program in a loop that repeats the menu until the new exit option is chosen.

Answer: This program (`u2shell.pl`) takes care of this requirement as well as advancing a couple of other objectives for this project.

U2SHELL.PL

```
1 #!/usr/bin/perl
2 $done = 0;
3 until ($done) {
4     print "
5       1) List Files
6       2) View File
7       3) Delete File
8       4) Rename File
9       5) Exit
10
11      Which? ";
```

```
12    chomp($_ = <STDIN>);
13  SWITCH: {
14      /^[1Ll]/ && do {
15        print "you chose to list files\n";
16        #system ("ls -A");
17        last SWITCH;
18      };
19      /^[2Vv]/ && do {
20        print "you chose to view a file\n";
21        print "filename: ";
22        chomp($fn = <STDIN>);
23        #system ("cat $fn");
24        last SWITCH;
25      };
26      /^[3Dd]/ && do {
27        print "you chose to delete a file\n";
28        print "filename: ";
29        chomp($fn = <STDIN>);
30        #system ("rm $fn");
31        last SWITCH;
32      };
33      /^[4Rr]/ && do {
34        print "you chose to rename a file\n";
35        print "old filename: ";
36        chomp($fn = <STDIN>);
37        print "new filename: ";
38        chomp($newfn = <STDIN>);
39        #system ("mv $fn $newfn");
40        last SWITCH;
41      };
42      /^[5EeQqXx]/ && do {
43        print "You chose to exit. Thanks for playing\n";
44        $done = 1;
45        last SWITCH;
46      };
47      # default behavior
48      last SWITCH;
49    }
50    print "and later on, we'll actually do that for you\n";
51  }
```

There really wasn't much to change here. We simply added a control variable ($done in *line 2*) and then set up the loop to continue until that variable is set to true. The new menu option (supported by the case defined in *lines 42-46*) allows the operator to choose to exit from the program.

While we "had the hood open" on this one, it made sense to update it in some other ways. For instance, in the cases for the first four menu items, we added dialogs where they would be appropriate (see *lines 28-29*), and we added calls to the system() function that remain commented out just now. Later on, we'll activate those lines to bring this program to life.

8.1.2 ANSWERS

a) Write the program (wordfreq.pl) that builds a hash from the words found in a file named on its command line. Print a report at the end that shows each word and its frequency.

Answer: Here's a program that does the job.

WORDFREQ.PL
```
1  #!/usr/bin/perl
2  while (<>) {
3     @words = split;
4     $total_words += @words;
5     foreach $w (@words) {
6        $wtable{$w}++;
7     }
8  }
9  print "Total Word Count: $total_words\n\n";
10
11 printf "%24s  %12s\n", "Word", "Frequency";
12 foreach $e (keys %wtable) {
13    printf "%24s  %12s\n", $e, $wtable{$e}
14      if $wtable{$e} > 2; # dampen noise
15 }
```

If you wrote your program anything like this one, you got the chance to use "nested loops." Inside the main while() loop, you needed to have another loop (*lines 5-7*, a foreach() that iterated through the list of words from the current line).

To produce the report for this program, we needed another foreach() loop (*lines 12-15*) to iterate through the contents of the hash that contains the statistics. You might also have noticed in this example that we used the printf() function to get the output to align nicely.

While printing the report, it turns out to be nicer if we eliminate the display of words that appear only one or two times in the input data. If you eliminate *line 14*, you can see what happens when we report on every single word. (If you do this, use a small input file the first time.)

b) b) Update Tom's program (itodo.pl) from Chapter 7 to allow the menu to be printed repeatedly until the exit option is chosen.

> *Answer: This is the part of the program that contains significant changes from* itodo.pl. *The entire program is available at this book's companion website.*

ITODO2.PL

```
 1  #!/usr/bin/perl
 2  # login/user validation/read task data
 3
 4  $done = 0;
 5  until ($done) {
 6      # time for a menu
 7      print "
 8          1) Report all of your tasks
 9          2) Add a task to the list
10          3) List everyone's tasks
11          9) Quit
12
13          Which? ";
14      chomp ($_ = <STDIN>);
15  SWITCH: {
16          /^[1Rr]/ && do {
17              foreach $t (@tlist) {
18                  print "$t" if $t =~ /^$uname/;
19              }
20              last SWITCH;
21          };
22          /^[2Aa]/ && do {
23              print "Enter a description of the new task: ";
24              chomp ($newtask = <STDIN>);
25              print "Enter a priority for the new task (1-9): ";
26  $priority = <STDIN>;
27              $newitem = join ':', ($uname, $newtask, $priority);
28              push @tlist, $newitem;
29              # simulates writing out the file -- fix it later
30              foreach $line (@tlist) {
31                  $line =~ tr/a-zA-Z/n-za-mN-ZA-M/;
32                  print "$line";
33                  $line =~ tr/a-zA-Z/n-za-mN-ZA-M/;
```

```
34              }
35              last SWITCH;
36          };
37          /^[3Ll]/ && do {
38              foreach $line (@tlist) {
39                  $line =~ tr/a-zA-Z/n-za-mN-ZA-M/;
40                  print "$line";
41                  $line =~ tr/a-zA-Z/n-za-mN-ZA-M/;
42              }
43              last SWITCH;
44          };
45          /^[9Qq]/ && do {
46              $done = 1;
47              last SWITCH;
48          };
49      }
50  }
```

The major program loop begins in *line 5*. (Line numbers, of course, apply only to this program listing. The full program contains several lines prior to the start of the loop. To avoid excessive repetition, we've omitted those lines here.)

One of the two other major changes are the addition of *lines 26* and *28*, which shroud the data before it is printed out. (This happens in another of the cases at *lines 34* and *36*.) Now it might seem mysterious that we translate the characters before we print them and then translate them again afterward. The truth is that in this sort of loop (the `foreach()`), if you make any changes to the data in the utility variable (`$line` in *line 26*, for instance), then the data in the underlying array is actually altered. If we fail to "rotate" it back to the original value, the data in our table will not be what we originally put in there.

We won't see this program again for a while, but maybe, with it fresh in your mind, you'd like to add one more feature that shrouds only the lines of data that belong to other people when the data table is printed out. This would be a simple matter of testing each line before it is printed to see if it belongs to the logged-in user, and shrouding the line if it doesn't.

8.1.3 ANSWERS

a) Write a program (`ptail.pl`) that can display the final *N* number of lines from a file named on the command line.

Answer: Here's a short program that does the job.

PTAIL.PL
```perl
1 #!/usr/bin/perl
2 $lcount = defined $ARGV[1] ? shift : 10;
3 @lines = <>;
4
5 for ($idx = @lines - $lcount; $idx < @lines; ++$idx) {
6    print $lines[$idx];
7 }
```

There's not much code here because we've specified the program pretty simply. If there are two command-line arguments, we strip the first one off and store it in `$lcount` (*line 2*). It's in *line 3* that we get a tremendous amount of mileage out of a little bit of code.

If there is a file name on the command line (or several, for that matter), we slurp them all into the array `@lines`. If there are no file names, we get the content from STDIN.

The `for()` loop (*lines 5-7*) is easy at this point. We simply calculate the starting point in the array and then print everything that remains until we reach the end of the array.

This program will work only on files of a reasonable size, and it doesn't support some of the other functions of the `tail(1)` program, but it does a good job for a program of its size.

b) Write a program that accepts a positive integer *N* as a command-line argument and prints all the numbers between 1 and *N* that are evenly divisible by 7. Print an error message if the argument is not numeric or if the number is smaller than 1.

Answer: This little program will do the job for you.

FULLWEEK.PL

```perl
1 #!/usr/bin/perl
2 die "usage: $0 <positive-integer>\n\t"
3         unless $ARGV[0] =~ /^[1-9]\d*$/;
4 for ($idx=1; $idx<=$ARGV[0]; ++$idx) {
5    print "$idx\n" if ($idx % 7 == 0);
6 }
```

The test in *line 3* throws out non-numeric input as well as negative numbers and numbers that begin with 0. Because of the way we form the loop in *line 4*, we could have ignored the possibility of words or negative numbers on the command line. If the program operator supplied either of those, the loop would never get started due to the test ($idx<=$ARGV[0]). The program would fail silently. (And accurately. There are no integers between 1 and bogus_argument, for instance, that are divisible by 7.)

We conduct the command-line validation as a civility to the operator; it's our only chance to print a message showing the correct usage of the program. (It's also true that the program specification required that we print a message in response to bad input.)

LAB 8.1 REVIEW QUESTIONS

1) Which of the following lists the four types of Perl loops?
   a) _____ `for()`, `foreach()`, `whichever()`, and `while()`
   b) _____ `for()`, `foreach()`, `until()`, and `while()`
   c) _____ `forsome()`, `foreach()`, `forever()`, and `while()`
   d) _____ `for()`, `forevery()`, `until()`, and `while()`

2) Which loop is most natural for cycling through the elements of an array?
   a) _____ `for()`
   b) _____ `while()`
   c) _____ `foreach()`
   d) _____ `forevery()`

3) Which loop is most natural for reading through a stream of data from a file or pipe?
   a) _____ `for()`
   b) _____ `while()`
   c) _____ `whichever()`
   d) _____ `foreach()`

4) Which syntax correctly forms a `for()` loop?
   a) _____ `for($idx=1;$idx<5;++$idx){ loop_body() }`
   b) _____ `for($idx=1,$idx<5,++$idx){ loop_body() }`
   c) _____ `for($idx=1:$idx<5:++$idx){ loop_body() }`
   d) _____ none of these

Quiz answers appear in Appendix A, Section 8.1.

L A B 8.2

UNUSUAL LOOPS

LAB OBJECTIVES

After this Lab, you will be able to:

✓ Use the "Looplike" Modifiers and the do { } Block

✓ Write Nested Loops

In this Lab, we'll see how Perl allows us a convenient syntax that allows one line to be repeated some number of times, much as we've done with the loops we saw in the last Lab.

We'll also look at what some people call the "fifth" of the Perl loops. This construct (the do{} block) works a lot like a loop but doesn't share all of the characteristics of the "real loops."

We'll wrap up by looking more closely at the business of putting one loop inside another or "nesting loops." We did that rather incidentally in an earlier program, but we'll look at it formally here.

REPEAT "JUST THIS"

Programmers familiar with C or Java may be frustrated at the fact that Perl demands braces around our loops even when they consist of a single line of code. Those other languages allow the convenience of omitting the braces for such a simple loop. Unfortunately, that convenience introduces some ambiguity that causes interesting problems, many of which don't appear until too late in the program development cycle.

To avoid this, Perl provides a different mechanism to allow you to write simple one-statement loops. A Perl statement may be modified by a `while()` or `until()` clause much the way we can modify a statement with one of the conditional constructs.

■ *FOR EXAMPLE*

If you want to print the numbers from 0 through 10, you can write:

```
print $idx++, "\n" while ($idx <= 10);
```

Or, perhaps, more substantially:

```
print $ln while ($ln = <STDIN>);
```

This code, of course, will print any lines received from the standard input stream until the end-of-file marker is seen. What if you want to print an array backwards?

```
$idx = $#array; # get highest index in use
print $array[$idx] until (--$idx < 0);
```

In all three of these examples, you could have written the procedure differently. Most times, the ability to use these modifiers is just a way to simplify your code. Use it when it seems logical to you.

MAKING A do{} BLOCK INTO A LOOP

We already looked at the `do{}` block when we talked about how to build a switch construct. We discovered that you can put such a block wherever it is legal to put a single Perl statement. Because that's true, you may surely modify such a block with a `while()` or `until()` clause the way you might with an ordinary statement.

■ *FOR EXAMPLE*

You might ask your program operator for a directory name:

```
do {
```

```
    print "Enter a legal directory name: ";
    chomp ($fname = <STDIN>);
} until (
```

Or maybe you're ready to revise one of your interactive programs from an earlier Lab.

```
do {
    # print menu
    # get/process input
} while (! $done);
```

You'll find many places where you'd rather use a `do{}` block than a simple `while()` or `until()` loop. The choices are available so that you can make your code more readable if you want to do that. Perl is NOT a "write-only" language. Some Perl *programs* are "write-only," but the issue is in the hands of the codesmith.

BENEATH THIS CLOWN'S MASK LIES ANOTHER CLOWN'S MASK

We saw an example earlier of nested loops when we had a loop that read lines of input, and a loop inside that to iterate through the list of the words in each line. Let's take a closer look. From what you saw, it should be clear that you may certainly have one loop inside another.

■ FOR EXAMPLE

We can print a simple grid with this little bit of code:

GRID.PL
```
for ($idx=0; $idx<9; ++$idx) {
   for ($idy=0; $idy<5; ++$idy) {
      print "* ";
   }
   print "\n";
}
```

It is not clear why we would do this, but for what it's worth, here's the output:

```
$ grid.pl

*  *  *  *  *  *  *  *  *

*  *  *  *  *  *  *  *  *

*  *  *  *  *  *  *  *  *

*  *  *  *  *  *  *  *  *

*  *  *  *  *  *  *  *  *
```

Actually, while that program may not do anything useful, it does serve as a nice template for how we'll write a pair of nested loops that can deal with a two-dimensional data set.

You already know that there's no restriction on the type of loop that can be inside another loop. Again, that's just logical. The outer loop doesn't care what sort of code you put inside. It could be a conditional construct, a switch construct, or another type of loop.

Here's a quick example:

```
while (<>) { # outer loop
    @wlist = split;
    foreach $word (@wlist) { # inner loop
        # do something to $word
    }
}
```

Note that we indent the body of the inner loop even further than the other parts of the outer loop. This makes it easier to visualize the logic of the program, and easier to debug.

LAB 8.2 EXERCISES

8.2.1 USE THE "LOOPLIKE" MODIFIERS AND THE *do{}* BLOCK

The UNIX cat(1) program takes the data from its input stream, or from the filename(s) on the command line, and prints that data to the standard output stream. It provides a handy means to "dump" a file (or a series of them) for the UNIX system operator.

From what you've learned in this chapter, you should be able to write a Perl program that does this in one line of code (not counting the `#!/usr/bin/perl` line).

> **a)** Write the "one line cat program" (`oneline.pl`) using the looping modifiers.

 If you have trouble getting it down to one line, start with whatever number of lines you need to get it working. Then look at your program to see if you can reduce it by using fewer lines.

In an earlier example, we saw a program (`taper.pl`) that printed nine stars on a line, then eight on the next one, and so forth, until only one star was printed on the final line. If you wanted to write it to operate in the opposite fashion (that is, first one star, then two, until you end up with nine stars on the last line), you can write the whole program in one statement.

> **b)** Write a one-line program (`taperup.pl`) that works in the opposite direction from its predecessor, as described in this Exercise.

As we've seen before, a tar file is an archive of files that stores the data for each of its component files as well as much of the information about every one. It is a very common format on the Internet as well as for collections of files that are shared among UNIX users. The utility for managing tar files (`tar(1)`) is strictly command-line controlled. This is fine because it lends itself easily to automation (from crontab entries and make files, for instance) but for the casual system operator, it is sometimes difficult to remember the runtime options.

**LAB
8.2**

As a reminder, here are three of the most common tar file operations:

```
$ tar tvf <tarfile name>   # table of contents
$ tar cvf <tarfile name> <files to add> # create tar file
$ tar xvf <tarfile name> [<files to extract>] # extract files
```

> **c)** Using a `do{}` block, write an interactive front-end program (`itar.pl`) that prints a menu for common tar file operations (create, table of contents, and extract files).

_____

_____

8.2.2 WRITE NESTED LOOPS

> **a)** Using a pair of nested loops, you could print out a multiplication table. Write a program (`mtables.pl`) that prints a multiplication table (for multiples of 1 through 12) for each number presented on the command line.

_____

_____

Imagine a data file that contains lines that you need to extract. The problem is that the lines can be identified only as those that lie between a pair of line-length marker tokens. For instance, look at this data:

```
we don't want this line
```

```
START
we do want this line
STOP
but not this line
START
this line on the other hand, we do want
STOP
but not this line, it's a bad one
```

If you want to clip out the lines that lie between "START" and "STOP" as well as the marker lines themselves, you might decide to use nested loops. The outer loop would read lines from the file, and if the current line is the starter token, you want an inner loop that reads more lines until you see the stop token. (This is not the only way to accomplish the task, but it suits our purpose here.)

b) Write the program (`startnstop.pl`) that reads a data set like the one shown in this Exercise and prints out only the lines between the marker tokens.

For simplicity, instead of reading the data from a file, why not put the data into an array to start with? Later, when you get it perfect, you can easily modify the program to work with a file named on the command line.

LAB 8.2 EXERCISE ANSWERS

8.2.1 ANSWERS

a) Write the "one line cat program" (`oneline.pl`) using the looping modifiers.

Answer: Here's the program:
```
print while (<>);
```

Okay, so it looks like something we did in Chapter 1. Your production code should probably be less sparse than this. But you can see why Perl has been banned from some programming contests. It makes many jobs trivial.

While this doesn't fare well as a model for well-documented code, it does compare very favorably with the number of lines of C code that are used to implement the original UNIX cat(1) program.

b) Write a one-line program (taperup.pl) that works in the opposite direction from its predecessor, as described in this Exercise.

Answer: The key to this program is that we can increment a variable that has never been defined and it will become one. So the program looks like this:

TAPERUP.PL
```
#!/usr/bin/perl
print "*" x ++$idx, "\n" until ($idx >= 5);
```

Unless you wrote this program, it might be a bit difficult to parse visually at first glance. Parentheses might help a bit.

```
print (("*" x ++$idx), "\n") until ($idx >= 9);
```

Fortunately, you won't have to write that many one-line programs. So in a way, this requirement is artificial. On the other hand, you might find it convenient to write "one-line loops" from time to time. Now you know how to do it.

c) Using a do{} block, write an interactive front-end program (itar.pl) that prints a menu for common tar file operations (create, table of contents, and extract files).

Answer: This program is very similar to a couple of the programs we've already seen.

ITAR.PL
```
1 #!/usr/bin/perl
2 do {
3 # some status information
4    print "current directory: ";
5    system "pwd";
6    print "known tar files:\n";
7    system "ls *tar";
```

```
8
9  # now the menu
10    print "
11        C>reate a new tar file
12        D>irectory from tar file
13        E>xtract file from tar file
14        Q>uit
15
16        Which? ";
17    chomp ($_ = <STDIN>);
18
19 SWITCH: {
20      /^[Cc]/ && do {
21          print "Name of new file: ";
22          chomp ($tname = <STDIN>);
23          print "Files to add: ";
24          chomp ($files = <STDIN>);
25          system "tar cvf $tname $files";
26      };
27      /^[Dd]/ && do {
28          print "Name of tar file: ";
29          chomp ($tname = <STDIN>);
30          system "tar tvf $tname";
31      };
32      /^[Ee]/ && do {
33          print "Name of tar file: ";
34          chomp ($tname = <STDIN>);
35          system "tar xvf $tname";
36      };
37      /^[Qq]/ && do {
38          $done = 1;
39      };
40    }
41 } while (!$done);
```

This entire program consists of one do{} block. It isn't visually elegant when it runs, but it could be a little friendlier to the casual system operator than the traditional tar(1) program. The main thing this program proves to us, however, is that a single do{} block can form the cleanest wrapper for a menu-based interactive utility.

The block will repeat as long as the variable $done is not set to a non-zero value. We don't even need to initialize it. For simple programs like this one, there's no problem with taking advantage of that. Just be sure, if your version of the program becomes vastly more complex that you take more positive control of your variables (that is, initialize your variables to avoid surprising side effects).

8.2.2 ANSWERS

a) Write a program (`mtables.pl`) that prints a multiplication table (for multiples of 1 through 12) for each number presented on the command line.

Answer: This might seem like a trivial job, but if you want it to look good, you'll have to fiddle with it a bit.

MTABLES.PL

```
 1 #!/usr/bin/perl
 2 die "usage: $0 integer1 [integer2 ...]"
 3      unless defined $ARGV[0];
 4 #print header
 5 print "      ";
 6 for ($m=1;$m<=12;++$m) {
 7    printf "%4d ", $m;
 8 }
 9 print "\n";
10 # now the tables
11 foreach (@ARGV) {
12    printf "%4d ", $_;
13    for ($idx=1; $idx<=12; ++$idx) {
14       printf "%4d ", $_ * $idx;
15    }
16    print "\n";
17 }
```

The outer loop for this program (*line 11*) iterates once for each command-line argument, storing the current value in the default variable. The inner loop (*line 13*) iterates once for each integer between 1 and 12. Notice how the use of `printf()` can result in nicely formatted output.

The program is sensitive to the quality of the data presented on the command line. You might want to enhance it by inspecting the arguments a little more closely. Nothing breaks if the program operator puts a word or fractional number among the arguments, but the output might look a lit-

tle strange. As always, you have to balance the importance of the program
with the likelihood that bad data will be present.

b) Write the program (startnstop.pl) that reads a data set like the
one shown in the Lab exercise and prints out only the lines between
the marker tokens.

Answer:This program does the trick:

STARTNSTOP.PL

```
 1 #!/usr/bin/perl
 2
 3 # define a sample data set
 4 @sdata = (
 5 "we do not want this line\n",
 6 "START\n",
 7 "This line, we do want\n",
 8 "STOP\n",
 9 "not this line though\n",
10 "START\n",
11 "but this one belongs\n",
12 "STOP\n",
13 "we do not like this one, sam I am\n",
14 );
15
16 while ($news = shift @sdata) {
17    if ($news =~ /^START$/) {
18       $d .= $news;
19       until (! defined $sdata[0] ||
20             ($news = shift @sdata) =~ /^STOP$/) {
21          $d .= $news;
22       }
23       $d .= $news;
24       # omit newline to eliminate blank line between blocks
25       # print "$d";
26       print "$d\n";
27       $d = "";
28    }
29 }
```

The sample data set defined in *lines 3-14* includes explicit newline characters in the data to simulate lines in a file. If we had slurped lines from a
file into @sdata, the content would be much as we've defined it here. (In
fact, you can easily modify this program to use the sample data when no

command-line argument is present; otherwise, you could use the <> operator to slurp the lines into the array.)

The main outer loop begins in *line 16* and reads a line of data at a time. Inside the body of this loop, if we see that the line matches the start token, we have more work to do; otherwise, we don't have to do anything, just go back to the top of the loop and get another line.

When we do get a match, though, we want to add the line we've read into the target string ($d). Our next step is to create a loop that reads more lines until the stop token is found (or until we hit the end of the data). This loop is defined on *lines 19* and *20*. If we fail to check for an end-of-data condition in this loop, the program will break if there is a start token but no stop token prior to the end of the data stream. As we read each additional line of data, we add it to the target string (*line 21*).

Because the loop ends when we see the stop token, we have to be sure to add that to the target string (in *line 23*) before we print it. This program offers us a choice (*lines 24-26*) about whether we want to see a blank line between discrete occurrences of the target data.

LAB 8.2 REVIEW QUESTIONS

1) Which of the following shows the correct syntax for the do{} block?
   a) _____ do { loop body } while ($something_true)
   b) _____ do { sleep } perchance ($to_dream);
   c) _____ do { loop body } until ($something_true)
   d) _____ do { loop body } while ($something_true);

2) True or False: A do{} block can be modified by if(), unless(), while(), or until() clauses.
   a) _____ True
   b) _____ False

   Examine the following code and answer the related questions.

```
for ($idx=1;$idx<=5;++$idx){
    printf "%2d: ", $idx;
    foreach (1..$idx) {
        print "x";
    }
    print "\n";
}
```

3) How many total lines will be printed?
  a) _____ 5
  b) _____ 10
  c) _____ 15
  d) _____ none

4) How many total "x" characters will be printed?
  a) _____ 5
  b) _____ 10
  c) _____ 15
  d) _____ 4

5) How many "x" characters will be written if the first line is altered to read as follows?
```
for ($idx=1;$idx<5;++$idx){
```
  a) _____ 5
  b) _____ 10
  c) _____ 15
  d) _____ 4

Quiz answers appear in Appendix A, Section 8.2.

L A B   8.3

ADVANCED LOOP CONTROL

LAB OBJECTIVES

After this Lab, you will be able to:

✓ Use `last`/`next`/`redo` to Control Loops

✓ Write "Infinite Loops" and Use the **`continue{}`** Block

In this Lab, we'll look at some examples of tools that extend your control over loop execution. We'll see how to end a loop prematurely, proceed directly to the next iteration, or restart the current iteration. We'll look at a reason why you may intentionally write an infinite loop, and we'll see how to do it elegantly. And we'll wrap up by looking at the construct that allows you to "wrap up" your loop very nicely.

THREE "TRAFFIC SIGNALS" FOR LOOPS

Perl provides three tools that allow us to employ "advanced routing" instructions in our loops. These tools take the form of Perl commands. They are shown in Table 8-1.

Table 8.1 ■ Loop Control Directives

Directive	Explanation	Example

`next`	"Move along." Proceed to the beginning of the loop and begin the next iteration.	```# print lines that contain "CA"```
		```while (<>) {```
		   ```next unless /CA/;```
		   ```print;```
		```}```

`last`	"That's it!" Proceed to the next instruction following the end of the loop.	```# watch for exit value```
		```until ($done) {```
		   ```print "number or```
		   ```chomp ($val = <STDIN>);```
		   ```last if $val == -1; #we're done!```
		   ```#...otherwise, do something...```
		```}```

`redo`	"Start again." Proceed to the beginning of the loop and repeat the current iteration.	```# get another input line```
		```until ($cows_come_home) {```
		   ```$line .= <STDIN>;```
		   ```last if $line =~ /END/;```
		   ```redo if $line =~ /BEGIN/;```
		```}```

Any of these tools can simplify the logic for a loop. Instead of having to maintain control variables (like $done or $continue), you can simply test for conditions that would indicate that the loop should stop, or iterate again, and do that directly.

■ *FOR EXAMPLE*

Imagine that you want to print a numbered listing of a file or input stream, skipping any blank lines. Here is a short program that will do it.

NOBLANKS.PL

```
#!/usr/bin/perl
while (<>) {
   next if /^$/;
   print ++$idx, ": $_";
}
```

We could not have used the variable "$." to facilitate line numbering because it represents the line number from the *input stream*. We want the numbering to be a function of the output data for a nice, neat printout.

The value of the approach we've taken appears when you want to choose between moving on to the next line or conducting some additional processing on the current line. Now suppose something slightly different were happening. You want to print out all of the lines from a file until you see a terminator line. (We'll use "=cut" as our terminator this time.)

■ FOR EXAMPLE

To process all of the lines from a file until a line consisting of "=cut" is encountered:

```
#!/usr/bin/perl
while (<>) {
   last if /^=cut$/;
   # otherwise, process the lines
}
```

Actually, we've seen the last command in our "switch" statement. Here, we see it break out of a loop, but it can also be used to break out of a labeled program block. We'll see some other implications of that in a moment.

There's one other command that belongs to this family. You'll see it less frequently than its siblings, but there will be occasions when you'll want to use the redo command.

■ *FOR EXAMPLE*

Suppose that you want to "build up" a string through concatenation until you find a token that tells you that all of the relevant data has been read.

```
#!/usr/bin/perl
until ($done) {
    $target .= <>;
    redo unless $target =~ /END$/;
    print $target; last;
}
```

**LAB
8.3**

Be careful here! This loop looks great at first glance. But it has a fatal flaw. Let's trace it through and see if we can spot it.

We start by adding the data from the default input stream to the end of the variable `$target`. That makes good sense. Then, unless `$target` ends with the pattern "END", we go to the beginning of the loop and add more data to the end of our string buffer. We continue to do this and eventually we see the terminator and we can stop the loop after we print the data in `$target`.

What happens if we do not "eventually" see the terminator? Well, we never set the control variable `$done`, so the loop continues, even after the input stream is exhausted. We have created a potential "infinite loop" but left no way to exit from it. We'll talk more about infinite loops in a bit, but let's fix this code right now.

THE eof() FUNCTION

We can fix our infinite loop problem by checking for an "out-of-data condition" before we read another line of input. The `eof()` function allows this. It can tell us if there is no data remaining in the input stream. If we check just after we read, we can tell when our most recent read operation consumed the last of the data.

SIMPLESCAN.PL
```
1 #!/usr/bin/perl
2 until ($done) {
3     $target .= <>;
4     last if eof;
```

```
5    redo unless $target =~ /END$/;
6    print $target; last;
7 }
```

By making this change, we cause the program to test for an out-of-data condition as soon as we finish reading a line. If we detect that data is exhausted, we leave the loop (and thus the program). This does introduce the problem that if the final line is the termination token, we still do not print the output. We can fix that, but we'll do it in a little while when we look at this problem again.

LABELS AND ROUTING

Under ordinary circumstances, `last` and `next` deal with the innermost enclosing loop. (The same is true for `redo`.) That's great because it keeps things simple, but you can use any of these three commands to exert control over higher level enclosing loops when you're dealing with a nested construct. The key to doing this is to use a labeled loop over which you might want to exert direct control. Then any of `last`, `next`, or `redo` can accept a label name as an argument.

■ FOR EXAMPLE

If we write an abbreviated user menu program, we can see this approach in action.

NUMENU.PL

```
1 #!/usr/bin/perl
2 OUTER: until ($done) {
3    system "ls -CFA";
4    print "\nV>iew D>elete R>ename Q>uit -- Which? ";
5    $choice = <STDIN>;
6 SWITCH: {
7        $choice =~ /^[vVdDrR]/ && do {
8            print "Filename (or -1 to abort): ";
9            chomp ($resp = <STDIN>);
10           next OUTER if $resp =~ /^-1$/;
11           print "Operate on $resp\n\n";
12           last SWITCH;
13       };
14       $choice =~ /^[Qq]/ && do {
```

```
15            $done = 1;
16            next OUTER;
17        };
18    }
19 }
20 print "\n\nThanks for choosing Pshell!\n";
```

By itself, this program isn't very exciting, but it does demonstrate the technique for us. The program begins with a labeled loop in *line 2*. After we print an abbreviated menu (*line 4*), we look at the program operator's response and for any of the choices except for exit, we print a secondary prompt (*line 8*).

In that prompt, we offer the chance to start over again at the top by entering "-1" in place of a filename. In *line 10* we look for that input, and if we see it, we return to the top of the outer loop.

Now look at *lines 15-16*. We set the control variable to true and then return to the top of the outer loop. Can you guess how we might have consolidated that into one instruction? The answer has something to do with our next topic.

INFINITE LOOPS

We have already seen a couple of incidental examples of infinite loops. In one case, it was problematic because we would never have exited that loop under any circumstances. Most of the time when we see infinite loops, they are intentional. You already know how we can get out of such a loop when we are ready.

■ FOR EXAMPLE

Here's a loop similar to one we looked at in an earlier example:

```
until ($pigs_can_fly) {
    $doc .= <>;
    last if (($doc =~ m#</html>#) || eof);
}
```

We do have to be careful with this sort of loop. We must provide an inevitable set of conditions that will cause the loop to terminate. In this example, we look either for a token that indicates the end of an HTML document, or the end of the file. The latter condition is not guaranteed to occur, so we need to be sure that we provide a fail-safe exit condition.

There's one other issue that relates to this example. Earlier, when we talked about the `last` command, I mentioned that it's nice to avoid the use of an unnecessary variable. Here, for instance, we are planning to break out of the loop directly instead of setting a variable that will cause the test at the top of the loop to force termination. So we avoid the creation of a control variable that has only one brief purpose.

Or do we? Does the variable `$pigs_can_fly` ever actually get created in this example? In this case, the variable is never actually defined so we don't pollute our namespace or memory with a very transient resource. (That is true as well for our earlier examples where we said something like "`until ($done)`" at the top of the loop.)

In truth, infinite loops are common in programs that have interactive main loops designed to continue until some extraordinary condition occurs. Interactive menu-based programs such as we've seen here are examples of that. Another example might be a network server that waits for a connection request, handles the request, and then returns to waiting.

There are some "classic" forms of the infinite loop. You just saw my favorite; here are two others:

```
while (1) {
    # iterate until last
}
```

This one is considered idiomatic and self-explanatory:

```
for (;;) { # forever loop
    # iterate until last
}
```

It's also a good idea to use a comment to tag the top of a loop that is intentionally "infinite." All three of the examples we saw in this section pretty much make that intention clear, but it never hurts to reiterate a point in technical communication (which of course, is a large part of what a program really is).

CONTINUE BLOCK

There's an interesting addition to the loop syntax that isn't widely known or used, but you may find some use for it.

At the end of a `while()` loop, you can include a `continue{}` block. If your program reaches the bottom of the loop naturally, it will execute the content of the `continue{}` block. This will also happen if the `next` command is encountered in the body of the loop.

LAB 8.3

■ *FOR EXAMPLE*

Look at this simple `for()` loop:

```
for ($idx=1; $idx<10; ++$idx) {
    print "$idx \n";
}
```

This loop can be simulated exactly with this code:

```
$idx=1;
while ($idx<10) {
    print "$idx \n";
}
continue {
    ++$idx;
}
```

Now certainly the first loop is easier to read and its intent is clearer. On the other hand, the `while()` loop has so many useful features that you may want to do something that would seem logical to enclose in a `for()` loop, but that needs the convenience of a `while()` loop. (The most easily remembered instance would be "`while (<>)`" because you will use that so many times in Perl.) With a `continue{}` block, you can make a `while()` loop behave the way you'd like.

LAB 8.3 EXERCISES

8.3.1 USE LAST/NEXT/REDO TO CONTROL LOOPS

Take a look at this program and then answer the questions that follow:

CONTROL.PL

```
1  #!/usr/bin/perl
2  while (++$idx > 0) {
3      print "current value: $idx   ";
4      print "N>ext L>ast R>edo -- Which? ";
5      chomp ($choice = <STDIN>);
6      $choice =~ /^[nN]/ && next;
7      $choice =~ /^[lL]/ && last;
8      $choice =~ /^[rR]/ && redo;
9  }
10 print "Thanks!\n";
```

a) Does this loop have any natural exit condition?

_____

_____

b) If the "current value" is 3, what value will be printed next if you choose the R>edo option?

_____

_____

c) Rewrite this program to use a `for()` loop.

_____

_____

Now it's time to use what you've learned. You can write a program that calculates prime numbers (whole numbers evenly divisible only by themselves and 1) if you start with the following assumptions:

- The numbers 1, 2, and 3 are prime. If we're searching, our search can begin with the number four.
- There will never be a factor for a number *N* that is greater than *N*/2.
- The modulus operator will return 0 if a number is evenly divisible by a given factor. (That is to say, if we have a test number *N*, and a test factor *F*, the expression "N % F == 0" will be true if the number is evenly divisible.)

d) Write a program (`primes.pl`) that will read a number from the command line and use two loops to calculate all of the prime numbers less than that value.

**LAB
8.3**

8.3.2 WRITE "INFINITE LOOPS" AND USE THE `continue{}` BLOCK

a) Modify the `ushell2.pl` program to use a self-proclaimed "forever" loop at the outer loop level. Also, change it so that it actually performs the tasks chosen from the menu.

b) Rewrite the `primes.pl` program to use a labeled loop. This should simplify the code and eliminate the `$not_prime` variable.

We can take advantage of a side effect of the transliteration operator (`tr///`) to write a program that counts specific letters in a data stream. In a scalar context, the operator evaluates to the number of characters translated.

For instance:

```
$line = "a bird in the hand";
$acount = $line =~ tr/a/a/;
$ecount = $line =~ tr/e/e/;
print $acount; # we should get 2
print $ecount; # we should get 2 as well
```

c) Write a program (`vowelcount.pl`) that reads lines of text and counts occurrences of each of the vowels. Store the results in a hash. As a `continue{}` block for the loop, print a report for the current line and destroy the hash prior to the next iteration.

**LAB
8.3**

LAB 8.3 EXERCISE ANSWERS

8.3.1 ANSWERS

Look at the `control.pl` program and answer the questions that follow:

a) Does this loop have any natural exit condition?

Answer: No, there is none. Under natural circumstances, the loop can exit when the variable $idx is set to some value less than or equal to 0. Because the program uses the pre-increment operator to increase the variable each time through the loop, it is set to 1 the very first time it is tested. It only increases after that, so it can never be less than 0.

This is an example of a loop that should probably be marked as "infinite" or "forever" with a comment at the top. The code itself may seem to make that self-evident, but you can never know what will seem "self-evident" in six months. It's funny how old scripts (and old assumptions) can come back to haunt you.

b) If the "current value" is 3, what value will be printed next if you choose the R>edo option?

Answer: The next thing printed should be the number 3 again.

Because the `redo` command returns to the top of the current iteration of the loop, we'll not have a chance to increment the `$idx` variable. It will remain at 3 until we choose the option that lets the program issue a `next` command.

c) Rewrite this program to use a `for()` loop.

Answer: Here's one way you can do that.

CONTROL2.PL

```
 1 #!/usr/bin/perl
 2 for ($idx=1; $idx > 0; ++$idx) { # forever
 3    print "current value: $idx   ";
 4    print "N>ext L>ast R>edo -- Which? ";
 5    chomp ($choice = <STDIN>);
 6    $choice =~ /^[nN]/ && next;
 7    $choice =~ /^[lL]/ && last;
 8    $choice =~ /^[rR]/ && redo;
 9 }
10 print "Thanks!\n";
```

The only thing that changes here is *line 2*. It is probably very important to tag this one with a comment. The fact that this loop runs forever is obvious only upon a careful reading. A brisk casual reading will yield only the information that *"this is a loop on $idx."*

A handy way to tag this loop as unusual would be to omit the test clause.

```
for ($idx=1 ;; ++$idx) { # forever
```

Writing it like this would have really made it stand out.

d) Write a program (`primes.pl`) that will read a number from the command line and use two loops to calculate all of the prime numbers less than that value.

Answer: Here's a program that does the trick.

PRIMES.PL

```
 1 #!/usr/bin/perl
 2 # $0: prints prime numbers less than $ARGV[0]
 3 die "usage: $0 <number>" unless defined $ARGV[0];
 4 foreach $candidate (4 .. $ARGV[0]) {
 5    $not_prime = 0;
```

```
 6    foreach $factor (2 .. int ($candidate / 2)) {
 7        next if ($candidate % $factor != 0);
 8        $not_prime = 1;
 9        last;
10    }
11    print "$candidate is prime.\n" unless $not_prime;
12 }
```

The loop that starts in *line 4* iterates through all of the integers up through the number named on the command line. You could have written a `for()` loop here:

```
for ($candidate=4; $candidate<=$ARGV[0];++$candidate) {
```

I like the `foreach()` loop better for this. It's easier to see at a glance exactly what the range of the loop is to be.

The inner loop is set in *line 6* where we select the range of numbers from 2 through a value equal to one-half of the number being tested. (The `int()` function? Oh, that takes the expression given as its argument and returns only the integer part of the number represented by that expression.) If we get a 0 result from our modulus operation (*line 7*) at any time on our way through the inner loop, we have a non-prime number and we can exit the inner loop. We use the `last` command to get us back to the top of the outer loop.

8.3.2 ANSWERS

a) Modify the `ushell2.pl` program to use a self-proclaimed "forever" loop at the outer loop level. Also, change it so that it actually performs the chosen tasks for the program operator.

Answer: Only two major things need to be changed to make this happen. The first is to change these lines:
```
$done = 0;
until ($done) {
```
into this one line:
```
for (;;) { # forever
```

The other thing that needed to be changed is that the lines that contained calls to the `system()` function needed to be activated by removing the comment character from the beginning of each of those lines.

It seems wise to change the rm(1) command so that it works in "interactive mode." By writing the line this way, we can be sure that the system will prompt the program operator one last time before removing a file completely.

```
system ("rm -i $fn");
```

Can you think of how we might change the rename command so that the program operator can bail out before actually committing to the name change?

LAB 8.3

b) Rewrite the primes.pl program to use a labeled loop. This should simplify the code and eliminate the $not_prime variable.

Answer: Here's the program when you fix it up that way.

PRIMES2.PL
```
 1 #!/usr/bin/perl
 2 # $0: prints prime numbers less than $ARGV[0]
 3 die "usage: $0 <number>" unless defined $ARGV[0];
 4 CANDIDATE: foreach $candidate (4 .. $ARGV[0]) {
 5    foreach $factor (2 .. int($candidate / 2)) {
 6       next if ($candidate % $factor != 0); # not divisible
 7       next CANDIDATE; # it was evenly divisible
 8    }
 9    # if we made it through the inner loop,
10    print "$candidate is prime.\n";
11 }
```

We no longer need to keep track of a variable that indicates whether the number is prime or not. We can reach the bottom of the main outer loop only if we never find a factor during our search.

This is another case where we can tighten up the code nicely by using an advanced control mechanism, but we should feel even more strongly compelled to comment the routine.

c) Write a program (vowelcount.pl) that reads lines of text and counts occurrences of each of the vowels. Store the results in a hash. As a continue{} block for the loop, print a report for the current line and destroy the hash prior to the next iteration.

Answer: Here's what that program might look like.

VOWELCOUNT.PL

```perl
1  #!/usr/bin/perl
2  while (<>) {
3      chomp;
4      printf "line %3d:%8s: ", $., substr($_,0,7);
5      $stats{a} = tr/a/a/;
6      $stats{e} = tr/e/e/;
7      $stats{i} = tr/i/i/;
8      $stats{o} = tr/o/o/;
9      $stats{u} = tr/u/u/;
10 }
11 continue {
12     foreach $k (keys %stats) {
13         printf "%2s->%3d ", $k, $stats{$k};
14     }
15     print "\n";
16     undef %stats;
17 }
```

This program begins each iteration of the main loop by printing out some identifying information about the current line (*line 4*). We see a line number and the first fragment of the line as provided by the substr() function. (The latter is simply a flourish that helps us to be sure that the information we're getting is accurate—Oh, the substr() function? It wants to be given two arguments, a base string and a place to start. It will return the portion of the base string that begins at the start point and with a length equal to the optional third argument if you supply it. When no run length is supplied, it returns the remainder of the base string.)

In *lines 5-9*, we count the number of occurrences of each vowel and store it explicitly in the hash named %stats. Now it looks like we could have used a loop instead of putting five individual instructions in our code. The problem that prevents us from using a loop is that we cannot get the tr/// operator to interpolate variables for us. That is to say, the phrase:

```perl
$count = tr/$v/$v/;
```

will fail, or worse, it will give us misleading information. (It yields the count of the number of times that the characters '$' and 'v' are encountered.) There is something we can do about this. The Perl function called eval() allows us to provide a string that it will execute as a Perl instruction. So you could rewrite those five instructions as a loop that looks like this:

```
foreach $t (qw{a e i o u}) {
    $stats{$t} = eval "tr/$t/$t/";
}
```

In this example, the string "`tr/$t/$t/`" is evaluated (and thus the variable $t is interpolated) before `eval()` executes the code for us.

LAB 8.3 REVIEW QUESTIONS

1) Which of these is not a "forever" loop?
   a) _____ `for(;;){ loop_body() }`
   b) _____ `while(true) { loop_body() }`
   c) _____ `while(1) { loop_body() }`
   d) _____ `until ($pigs_can_fly = 0) { loop_body() }`

Use this numbered code listing to answer the questions that follow:
```
1 while (++$idx > 0) {
2    print "current value: $idx   ";
3    print "N>ext L>ast R>edo -- Which? ";
4    chomp ($choice = <STDIN>);
5    $choice =~ /^[nN]/ && next;
6    $choice =~ /^[lL]/ && last;
7    $choice =~ /^[rR]/ && redo;
8 }
9 print "Thanks!\n";
```

2) Which line will execute next if the program operator chooses the "N" option?
   a) _____ line 1
   b) _____ line 2
   c) _____ line 9

3) Which line will execute next if the program operator chooses the "L" option?
   a) _____ line 1
   b) _____ line 2
   c) _____ line 9

4) Which line will execute next if the program operator chooses the "R" option?

    a) _____ line 1

    b) _____ line 2

    c) _____ line 9

5) True or False: In order to break out of several levels of nested loops, the Perl `break()` statement can take a numeric argument.

    a) _____ True

    b) _____ False

Quiz answers appear in Appendix A, Section 8.3.

**LAB
8.3**

C H A P T E R   8

TEST YOUR THINKING

1) Write a program that generates 20 random numbers between 1 and 59. Then print 20 lines, each with a number of stars equal to the associated random number.

2) Write a program (`wordhist.pl`) that will read an entire file (or other data stream) and compile a report on any word that occurs more than five times. It should consist of an outer loop to read lines of data, and an inner loop to iterate through the array, looking for new words, and counting the ones that it already knows. If a word ends with a punctuation character, strip that off so that the word itself can be counted.

3) Write a program (`guessme.pl`) that uses a loop to enclose the body of an old number-guessing game. Initialize a target number and then get successive guesses from the program operator. After each guess, report whether the number is higher or lower than the target. When the number is finally guessed, report the number of tries that it took. Offer a new game after the target number is guessed. Allow the operator to exit the program instead of guessing at any time.

4) Write a program that prints out multiplication problems to be answered by the program operator. Allow command-line options that control the maximum value for operands, and the number of problems that will be displayed. At the end of the program, or with each new problem, print the elapsed time information.

FILES: OUTSIDE AND IN

In this chapter, we look at the "ins and outs" of handling files. Our first discussion deals with the things that characterize the file from the outside, its "statistics." We look at how to manipulate files by copying, moving, and renaming them. Then we'll delve into the issues that surround reading and writing files.

Along the way, we'll discover that the techniques we use to write files (or read them) can also be used to send information to another process or other, even more interesting places.

L A B   9.1

FILE META-INFORMATION (FILE STATISTICS)

LAB OBJECTIVES

After this Lab, you will be able to:

✓ Use **stat()** to Get Information About a File

✓ Read the Contents of a Directory

✓ Compile a Report Showing Large or Old Files

Because Perl was born largely of the same culture that gave us UNIX, the importance of the file as a fundamental building block is similar. Perl has very good support to allow you access to the information that defines a file from the outside. In UNIX, files are characterized by their size, their creation and modification time, their owner, their access permissions, and several other attributes.

FILE STATISTICS AND stat()

We can easily inspect these file attributes with the stat() function.

■ *FOR EXAMPLE*

To get the statistics for a file whose name is stored in $filename, you could use the instruction:

```
($dev, $ino, $mode, $nlink, $uid, $gid, $rdev,
    $size, $atime, $mtime, $ctime, $blksize, $blocks)
    = stat $filename;
```

As you can see from this, stat() returns a list. The names we choose here to constitute the elements of the list are arbitrary, but these particular choices are somewhat mnemonic. They help remind us of the order and meaning of the attributes returned by the stat() function.

Table 9.1 lists the attributes along with a brief description of their meaning. Some of the attributes may not apply to every operating system. If you don't understand what a particular attribute is, don't worry about it. There is a reasonable possibility that it doesn't apply to your platform. If you actually need to use any of the attributes that are listed, you'll become aware of its meaning as it is required.

Just be sure you know that stat() will return something for each of these file characteristics and you are free to pick out and use the ones that have some meaning for you.

Table 9.1 ■ File Attributes Returned by stat()

	Attribute	Meaning
0	Dev	Filesystem Device Number
1	Ino	File Inode Number
2	Mode	Mode (Permissions and File Type)
3	Nlink	Number of Links (Names)
4	Uid	File Owner (Numeric User ID)
5	Gid	Associated Group (Numeric Group ID)
6	Rdev	Special File Device Identifier
7	Size	File Size (in Bytes)
8	Atime	Most Recent Access Time
9	Mtime	Most Recent Modification Time
10	Ctime	Inode Change Time
11	Blksize	Filesystem Block Size
12	Blocks	Blocks Allocated

There are some other points that are worthy of note. The three time values will be expressed in a number that is the number of seconds since midnight of January 1, 1970 (the UNIX epoch). The time value that represents the date of the most recent inode change ($ctime in our example) is often viewed mistakenly as the file's creation time. Most of the time, it works out that way, so the mistake is entirely forgivable.

For most purposes, the indicator of file size ($size in our example) is more useful than the count of allocated blocks. The elements represented here as $blocks and $blksize are usually available only on BSD breeds of UNIX.

Because the stat() function returns a list, we can store that in an array. The instruction looks like this:

```
@info = stat "filename.txt";
```

You can also take advantage of list slicing notation to retrieve only the values that interest you:

```
($owner, $size, $mtime) = (stat "filename.txt")[4,7,9];
```

Let's see a program that takes advantage of this.

BIGFILES.PL
```
1 #!/usr/bin/perl
2 $threshold = 10000;
3 #$threshold = 1000000;
4 while (defined $ARGV[0]) {
5    $fn = shift;
6    $size = (stat $fn)[7];
7    printf ("%10d %s\n", $size, $fn) if $size > $threshold;
8 }
```

For this example, we set the file size threshold to 10,000 in *line 2* because that will make it easier to test. We can set the threshold up to a higher number (as in *line 3*) when we put the program into production.

The loop in *line 4* runs as long as there are remaining command-line arguments, taking each one in turn and using stat() to determine its size. The file name and size are printed (*line 7*) if the size is above the defined threshold.

Just like the file test operators we observed in Chapter 6, "Tests and Branching," we can use the special entity _ (the underscore character by itself) to refer to the most recently inspected file. So we could replace *line 7* from our example with the following conditional block:

```
if ($size > $threshold) {
    printf ("%10d %48s", $size, $fn);
    printf ("%5s %5s\n", (stat _)[4], (stat _)[5]);
}
```

That would print the file's owner and group id after the size and filename.

READING A DIRECTORY

For our purposes, a directory is just a special type of file. When you use stat() on a directory, it returns information just as you would expect for an ordinary file. The most notable differences will be that it probably isn't a very large file, and the file mode will be a little bit different.

The "mode" of a file contains information about the type of file and its access permissions. You could decode the file's mode to find out if it is a directory, but there's an easier way. You might recall from Chapter 6, "Tests and Branching," that you can use a file test operator (-d) to determine whether or not a file is a directory.

Once you decide that this is the case, you can open the directory in much the same way that you can open a file. The only difference is that you use the opendir() function instead of open().

■ FOR EXAMPLE

Here's what it looks like when you open a directory called /usr/spool/mail to inspect the contents:

```
opendir (IN, "/usr/spool/mail") or
    die "couldn't open directory /usr/spool/mail";
```

The opendir() function expects you to provide a filehandle (IN for this example), and the name of a directory to open. If the function succeeds, you can read from that filehandle to learn the names of the files in the named directory.

The easiest way to see how this works is to look at this program that opens the current directory and reads the filenames into an array.

DLIST.PL

```perl
1 #!/usr/bin/perl
2
3 # open the current working directory
4 opendir (INDIR, ".") or die "$0: Cannot open .";
5
6 # read each file in directory
7 while ($fname = readdir INDIR) {
8    push @flist, $fname;
9 }
10
11 # it's polite to close filehandles
12 closedir INDIR;
13
14 # we need a report
15 printf "%24s  %12s  %5s  %5s\n", "Name", "Size", "UID", "GID";
16 foreach $fn (@flist) {
17    ($uid, $gid, $sz) = (stat $fn)[4,5,7];
18    printf "%24s  %12d  %5s  %5s\n", $fn, $sz, $uid, $gid;
19 }
```

Our program begins in *line 4* with an operation that opens a directory. The line ends with what should now look pretty much like a standard coda that allows the program to end if something goes wrong. The loop defined in *lines 7-9* goes through the directory getting one new filename with each read operation. Each filename is pushed onto an array in the body of the loop.

It's important to know how to write that loop, but it may not be necessary here. If all you want to accomplish is what you see here, you won't need a loop at all. When you put the `readdir()` function into an array context, it gives a list containing the names of all the files. So *lines 7-9* could look like this:

```perl
@flist = readdir INDIR;
```

Much simpler. You will still need to write that loop, however, if you plan to make some decision about whether or not to include the filename in the target array. For instance, if you want to include only files whose name matches a particular pattern, then you'd have to consider the loop.

The remainder of the program is similar to several we've seen before. We close the filehandle and then loop through the array, printing the filenames as well as some information about each file.

THE USUAL SUSPECTS—LARGE AND OLD FILES

Let's take what we've learned here and write a program that will create a report about files that are beyond a certain age or above a certain size. The size part is easy, we've done that earlier in this discussion. The age part will require a little bit of extra preparation. We'll need a couple of new functions that deal with time.

To start, we'll need a function that tells us the current system time. That function is called `time()` and it returns the current system time as a number of seconds since the UNIX epoch. So the difference between the return from `time()` and the most recent file access time would tell us how long it has been since the file has been opened.

All we need to do for our program, then, is to figure out the time and size thresholds, then do a little calculation to determine the number of seconds in the time threshold, and we'll be ready to start looking at files.

For our first run at this program, let's hardcode the directory list and the threshold values. We can allow those to be command-line choices for the operator when you revise it in the Exercises.

TUS1.PL

```
1  #!/usr/bin/perl
2
3  # set the limits in stone for now
4  $daysold = 180;
5  $toobig = 10000;
6  #$toobig = 1000000;
7  # @dirlist = qw{/tmp /var/mail /var/tmp};
8  @dirlist = qw{/tmp /usr/spool/mail /usr/tmp};
9
```

```
10 # we will always need these
11 $now = time; # get current time
12 $too_old = $daysold * 24 * 60 * 60;
13
14 # loop through directories
15 foreach $dir (@dirlist) {
16    unless (opendir IN, $dir) {
17       # continue loop if directory won't open
18       warn "$0: cannot open $dir";
19       next;
20    }
21    while ($candidate = readdir IN) {
22       next if $candidate =~ /^\.\.?$/; # skip directory refs
23       $fullname = $dir . "/" . $candidate;
24       ($sz, $atime) = (stat $fullname)[7,8];
25       push (@bigones, $fullname) if $sz > $toobig;
26       push (@oldones, $fullname) if $now - $atime > $too_old;
27    }
28 }
29
30 # Some reports
31 print "Large files in target region\n";
32 foreach $big (@bigones) {
33    print "$big\n";
34 }
35
36 print "\nOld files in target region\n";
37 foreach $old (@oldones) {
38    print "$old\n";
39 }
```

The first half of this program is probably self-explanatory. We start by hardcoding some threshold values (in *lines 3-7*) that are convenient for testing. In *line 6*, we offer an alternative threshold number that you might want to use if you are looking for large files.

The conditional construct formed by *lines 16-20* allows us to get a warning if one of our directories is inaccessible, but it doesn't end the program. The loop that reads each filename in the directory under current consideration is formed in *lines 21-27*. There are some amenities that you might add only after experimentation with the program, like the regular expression in *line 22* that cycles to the next iteration of the loop if we detect that the filename is '.' or '..' because those filenames refer to the current and parent directory. In this context, those are of little interest to us.

You'll also note that in *line 23* we have to construct a full pathname for the file that we want to inspect with `stat()`. If we fail to do this, `stat()` will report on the status of the filename only if it exists in the current working directory. For example, if the directory under current consideration is `/tmp` and we find a file there named `todo.txt`, when `stat()` runs, it will try to find a file with that name in the current directory.

The reports we build from the data are very simple right now. Later on, we might want to enhance that part of this program. Something tells me we'll see this project again.

LAB 9.1 EXERCISES

9.1.1 USE `stat()` TO GET INFORMATION ABOUT A FILE

In the discussion, we saw three ways to get information about a file using the `stat()` function. You could:

1)   Save each bit of information in a separate variable.

2)   Store everything in an array and retrieve it at your leisure.

3)   Run `stat()` and use list slice notation to get only the parts you will need.

At various times, each of these three options is appropriate for the task at hand. Let's start with a program that needs to print all of the available information about a file named on the command line.

> **a)** Write a program (`allinfo.pl`) that reads a filename on the command line, and then prints all of the information provided by `stat()` for that file.

_____

_____

b) Revise your program to create a new one (`manyinfo.pl`) that produces a similar report for each of the files named on the command line.

_____

_____

The mode for a file is a number that encodes the file's type, plus any access information associated with it. On the UNIX platform, this consists of read, write, and execution permissions for the file as well as a set of extended permissions that control special types of access.

WORKING WITH FILE MODES

Normally, we interpret the mode as an octal value. Working only with the last five octal digits of the number, we might see something like this:

```
70644
```

The first digit indicates the file type, the second one refers to any extended permissions that the file might have. (Read about those in your system documentation on the `chmod(1)` command.) The last three digits indicate the access permission for the file's owner, group, and others (those who are not in either of the first two categories). Figure 9.1 illustrates this relationship between the value and the meanings embedded within.

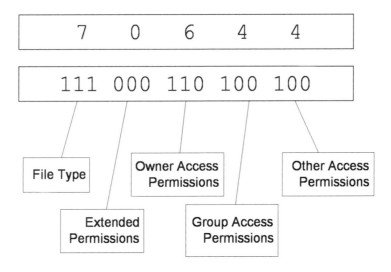

**Figure 9.1 ■ File type and permissions are embedded into the file's
mode value**

So our job, if we want to interpret the file's mode, is to trim it down so that we
see only the last five octal digits. We need to know how to specify an octal
number, how to display a number as an octal value, and how to see just part of
the number when we have a certain question about its meaning.

When you present a numeric value, if you begin with a 0 and follow that exclusively with legal octal digits (those between 0 and 7), the number is presumed
to be an octal value. When you want to display a number as an octal value, you
can use the printf() function.

Run this experiment from the command line to see how it works (for MS-DOS,
you will have to type the script into a file and run that instead).

```
$ perl -e
> $value = 0644;
> printf qq{value in decimal: %d\n},
$value;
> printf qq{value in octal: %o\n},
$value;
> '
```

```
value in decimal: 420
value in octal: 644
```

Given an octal value, we may have to do some special manipulation to inspect only certain parts. If we wanted to see only the portion of the previous number that refers to the owner access permissions, we could get rid of the other information in the number by using the "bitwise AND" operator. Take a look at the following code fragment:

```
$mode = 070644;
$owner_perms = $mode & 000700; # $owner_perms is now 0600 octal
$owner_perms /= 0100; # $owner_perms is now 06 octal
```

Figure 9.2 may give you an idea about how the first two lines work.

```
   111 000 110 100 100          (070644)

&  000 000 111 000 000          (000700)
   ─────────────────────────────────────
   000 000 110 000 000          (000600)
```

Figure 9.2 ■ The bitwise AND operator allows us to pick the portion of a number that is of interest.

The idea here is that the only bits that will be turned on (set to 1) in the resulting value are those that are turned on in both of the operands. The second operand in this expression is something we call a "bit mask." In the previous code fragment, we continue on to convert the value to a simple octal digit by using division between two octal numbers. It works as you might expect.

Let's put this together into a program that makes a closer inspection of a file's mode.

c) Write a program (`perms.pl`) that prints a report showing the octal digit for each of the owner, group, and other permissions on a file.

_____

_____

9.1.2 READING THE CONTENTS OF A DIRECTORY

In the discussion, we saw how to open a directory and read the contents into an array. Let's enhance that program a little bit.

a) Write a program (`dirlist.pl`) that improves upon `dlist.pl` by reading each of the directories named on the command line.

_____

_____

We saw that the time information stored for each file is represented by the number of seconds since the UNIX epoch. This makes it easy to compare relative age of files, and serves as a concise way to store time information. But for printing out information to be read by humans, it falls a little short.

USE `gmtime()` FOR HUMANS

Fortunately, Perl provides the `gmtime()` function that can convert a time stored in this fashion into a list of nine elements. Those can be used to construct a time specification that will be read by the operator of your program. Here's what it looks like when you use the function:

```
($sec, $min, $hour, $mday, $mon, $year, $wday, $yday, $isdst)
    = gmtime($mtime);
```

This code is idiomatic Perl; you'll find it in many programs that you're likely to encounter. The variable names used here help remind us of the meaning of each of the nine elements. A few of them beg for further explanation, though.

The variables $mon and $wday are populated with numbers that represent the month and weekday, respectively. Each of these is the sort of value that you might use to look up the text name in a zero-based array. As a result, the range of these values is 0-11 for $mon and 0-6 for $wday. The ninth value ($isdst) is used to designate whether the time under consideration is one that is subject to Daylight Savings Time.

There is one other way to use gmtime(). If you put it in a scalar context, it will return a text string that describes the time in terms of Greenwich Mean Time. You can try this for yourself right now.

If you want time formatted according to the program's local time zone, you can substitute the function localtime() in any of the examples that follow.

> **b)** Write a program (ftime.pl) that reads a directory name from the command line, and reports on each of the files by printing the name, size, and modification time in a human-readable form.

Now we're ready to represent our file information a little more rationally. We can get the file mode value, the number of links, the owner and group information, the size, the file's modification date, and its name, all from what we've learned so far.

Let's see what it will take to get a report from a directory that looks something like this:

```
$ dirlist2.pl .
40755   2   504   1000      1024 02/03 20:21 .
40755   3   504   1000      1024 02/03 20:13 ..
00744   1   504   1000       707 02/03 20:21 dirlist2.pl
00744   1   502   1000       610 02/02 15:01 all2info.pl
00744   1   504   1000       611 02/02 15:00 allinfo.pl
00744   1   501   1000       200 02/01 17:09 bigfiles.pl
```

c) Write a program (`dirlist2.pl`) that can read a directory named on the command line and produce a report as shown here.

_____

_____

9.1.3 COMPILE A REPORT SHOWING LARGE OR OLD FILES

In the Lab discussion, we looked at a program (`tus1.pl`) that could analyze a directory and report on files that are above a certain threshold size or that have not been accessed within a threshold time period. Let's enhance that program a bit here.

a) Rewrite `tus1.pl` to create a new program (`tus2.pl`) that accepts an optional threshold time (in days) and an optional threshold size (in megabytes) on the command line.

_____

_____

b) Enhance the `tus2.pl` program further to have it report not only the file's name, but also its size and date information.

_____

_____

LAB 9.1 EXERCISE ANSWERS

9.1.1 ANSWERS

a) Write a program (`allinfo.pl`) that reads a filename on the command line, and then prints all of the information provided by `stat()` for that file.

Answer: Here's one way you might write that program.

ALLINFO.PL

```
 1 #!/usr/bin/perl
 2 $fn = shift or $fn = $0;
 3 ($dev, $ino, $mode, $nlink, $uid, $gid, $rdev,
 4    $size, $atime, $mtime, $ctime, $blksize, $blocks) = stat $fn;
 5 print "\n\n";
 6 print "filename: $fn\n";
 7 print "filesystem device: $dev\n";
 8 print "inode: $ino\n";
 9 print "mode: $mode\n";
10 print "number of links: $nlink\n";
11 print "user id: $uid\n";
12 print "group id: $gid\n";
13 print "special device: $rdev\n";
14 print "size: $size\n";
15 print "access time: $atime\n";
16 print "mod time: $mtime\n";
17 print "creation time: $ctime\n";
18 print "block size: $blksize\n";
19 print "blocks used: $blocks\n";
20 print "\n\n";
```

There's not much surprise in this program. It plods very simplemindedly through the information that stat() returns. Remember that although our program announces "ctime" as the creation time for the file, it may hold a different value. Changes to the inode can occur after the file is created.

The real value in this program comes from what you observe when you run it on your particular platform. If you have access to do so, you should try this on as many different OS platforms as you can. (Try NT, Linux, Solaris, BSD, and anything else you can get your hands on, then compare the results.)

It's also instructive to see what it does when you feed it different files. How does the number of links change if you give it the name of a directory?

b) Revise your program to create a new one (manyinfo.pl) that produces a similar report for each of the files named on the command line.

Answer: Here's one way you might have written that program.

MANYINFO.PL

```
 1 #!/usr/bin/perl
 2
```

```
 3 #check command-line
 4 die "usage: $0 filename [filename ...]\t\n"
 5    unless defined $ARGV[0];
 6
 7 # set up loop over command-line args
 8 foreach $fn (@ARGV) {
 9    # ...same code as allfiles.pl from here on
10 }
```

With this program, you can see how easy it is to encase well-formed existing code in a loop when it suits your purpose. The minimum number of lines you might have changed is two (*line 8* and a line at the end of the program to terminate the loop). And to keep your code readable, you might have had to do a block indent.

Here's another way you might write this program to make it a little easier to maintain:

MANY2INFO.PL
```
 1 #!/usr/bin/perl
 2
 3 #check command-line
 4 die "usage: $0 filename [filename ...]\t\n"
 5    unless defined $ARGV[0];
 6
 7 @labels = qw{filename device inode mode linkcount uid gid
 8    minornum size atime mtime ctime blksize blocks};
 9
10 # loop over command-line args
11 foreach $fn (@ARGV) {
12    @info = stat $fn;
13    print "\n\n";
14    # loop over stat() info bits
15    for ($idx=0; $idx<@info; ++$idx) {
16        print "$labels[$idx]: $info[$idx]\n";
17    }
18    print "\n\n";
19 }
```

This program is shorter and would be easier to revise and extend. The array defined in *lines 7-8* defines the headings that should be printed for each corresponding bit of information. The information from stat() is read into an array because we know that we'll be printing all of it. With that done, we can use a loop to print the information out (*lines 15-17*). That cuts down on the length of the program considerably.

c) Write a program (`perms.pl`) that prints a report showing the octal digit for each of the owner, group, and other permissions on a file.

Answer: Here's a program that does the job.

PERMS.PL

```
 1 #!/usr/bin/perl
 2 #check command-line
 3 die "usage: $0 filename [filename ...]\t\n"
 4    unless defined $ARGV[0];
 5 foreach $fn (@ARGV) {
 6    $mode = (stat $fn)[2];
 7    printf "\nname %s\n", $fn;
 8    printf "mode value: %05o\n", $mode & 077777;
 9    printf "owner perms: %o\n", ($mode & 0700) / 0100;
10    printf "group perms: %o\n", ($mode & 070) / 010;
11    printf "other perms: %o\n", ($mode & 07) / 01;
12 }
```

The interesting parts of this program are in *lines 8-11*. First, we see the octal version of the mode value, but we look only at the last five digits. (Depending upon the platform, there may be information in the higher digits, but it may or may not be significant.)

After that, we look at the value of each of the three permission digits by doing first a bitmasking operation and then simple division. Later on, we'll have you break that information down further to inspect each of the individual permission bits (read, write, and execute). If you got this far with them, you're well on your way to making good use of the file mode value.

9.1.2 ANSWERS

a) Write a program (`dirlist.pl`) that improves upon `dlist.pl` by reading each of the directories named on the command line.

Answer: Here's a program that meets these requirements.

DIRLIST.PL

```
 1 #!/usr/bin/perl
 2 # check syntax
 3 die "usage: $0 directoryname [directoryname ...]\n\t"
 4    unless defined $ARGV[0];
 5
 6 # work through command-line args
 7 foreach $dir (@ARGV) {
 8    if (-d $dir) {
 9       # loop around if directory open fails
10       unless (opendir INDIR, $dir) {
11          warn "$0: Cannot open $dir";
12          next;
13       }
14       # read each file in directory
15       while ($fname = readdir INDIR) {
16          push @flist, $dir . "/" . $fname;
17       }
18       # it's polite to close filehandles
19       closedir INDIR;
20    }
21 }
22
23 # a report
24 printf "%24s  %12s  %5s  %5s\n", "Name", "Size", "UID", "GID";
25 foreach $fn (@flist) {
26    ($uid, $gid, $sz) = (stat $fn)[4,5,7];
27    printf "%24s  %12d  %5s  %5s\n", $fn, $sz, $uid, $gid;
28 }
```

This didn't take a lot of modification. We simply check that at least one command-line argument has been defined (*lines 3-4*) and then set up a loop (in *line 7*) to read through each directory named.

Using `printf()` in the report section (*lines 15-19*) makes everything come out nicely aligned.

b) Write a program (`ftime.pl`) that reads a directory name from the command line and reports on each of the files by printing the name, size, and modification time in a human-readable form.

Answer: Here's a program that will do the trick.

FTIME.PL

```
 1 #!/usr/bin/perl
 2 # check syntax
 3 die "usage: $0 directoryname\n\t"
 4    unless defined $ARGV[0];
 5 # open the directory
 6 $dir = shift;
 7 die "Cannot open $ARGV[0]\n\t" unless
 8    opendir IN, $dir;
 9 # get the contents
10 while ($fn = readdir IN) {
11    $fullname = $dir . "/" . $fn;
12    ($sz,$mt) = (stat $fullname)[7,9];
13    printf "%18s %10d %s\n", $fn, $sz, scalar (localtime($mt));
14 }
15 closedir IN;
```

This program looks a lot like several that we've seen already. The real differences show up in *line 12*, where we get the size and modification time from the return values of stat(). If you had to look at Table 9.1 again to remember which element was the size and which one was the time, that's okay. Using the reference material is an important part of being a Perl programmer.

On the other hand, if you wrote your program to use this idiomatic invocation of the stat() function, that's okay too.

```
($dev, $ino, $mode, $nlink, $uid, $gid, $rdev,
  $size, $atime, $mtime, $ctime, $blksize, $blocks)
  = stat $filename;
```

When you do this, you don't have to look for the exact elements that you want; everything is recorded in a variable and you can use the ones that you need. Either approach is okay in this context. Do it in the way that pleases you.

The other instruction of interest to us here is in *line 13*, where we take $mt and pass it to localtime(), which will render it as a string whenever we force it into a scalar context (which is, of course, what the scalar() function does for us in *line 13*).

c) Write a program (`dirlist2.pl`) that can read a directory named on the command line, and produce a report as shown in the Exercise text.

Answer: This program will print the report as required.

DIRLIST2.PL

```
 1 #!/usr/bin/perl
 2 # check syntax
 3 die "usage: $0 directoryname\n\t"
 4    unless defined $ARGV[0];
 5 # open the directory
 6 $dir = shift;
 7 die "Cannot open $ARGV[0]\n\t" unless
 8    opendir IN, $dir;
 9 # get the contents
10 while ($fn = readdir IN) {
11     $fullname = $dir . "/" . $fn;
12     # file stats
13     ($dev, $ino, $mode, $nlink, $uid,
14      $gid, $rdev, $size, $atime, $mtime,
15      $ctime, $blksize, $blocks) = stat $fullname;
16
17     # normalize the time
18     ($sec,$min,$hour,$mday,$mon,$year,$wday,$yday,$isdst)
19         = gmtime($mtime);
20
21     printf "%05o %3d %5d %5d %8d %02d/%02d %02d:%02d %s\n",
22         $mode & 077777,
23         $nlink, $uid, $gid, $size,
24         $mon+1, $mday,
25         $hour, $min, $fn;
26 }
```

For your own program, you may want to change the behavior of the syntax check in *lines 3-4*. In this program, we check for a command-line argument, and if none is present, we exit with a usage message. You may want to assume the current directory if none is supplied.

In *lines 13-15*, we gather the file status information into a group of named variables. We might easily have cut and pasted this from a variety of other programs. That would be the second best way to get this code into your program. In Chapter 10, "Functions: Programming in Polite Society," we'll look at a better way to do it.

Given the value for $mtime, we can use gmtime() to convert it to elements of a human-readable time specification (*lines 18-19*). From there, we're ready for a lengthy printf() call (in *lines 21-25*) that prints a line of the report as we want to see it. Pay particular attention to the field specifications for the date and time information in this statement. Each of the elements of the date and time are presented in a field with a width specifier of "02." Why not simply "2" instead? If you use a leading 0 in the width specification, the number will be presented with leading zeros where there is room.

9.1.3 ANSWERS

a) Rewrite tus1.pl to create a new program (tus2.pl) that accepts an optional threshold time (in days) and an optional threshold size (in megabytes) on the command line.

Answer: Here is the beginning of that program.

TUS2.PL (PARTIAL LISTING)

```
 1 #!/usr/bin/perl
 2
 3 =h1 Description
 4
 5 tus2.pl -- looks for large and old files
 6 within a certain set of likely directories.
 7
 8 =h1 Usage
 9
10 tus.pl [-t b<daysold>] [-s b<bigfilesize>]
11
12 =cut
13
14 # set defaults
15 $daysold = 180;
16 $megs = 10;
17 @dirlist = qw{/tmp /usr/tmp};
18
19 # what can we find on the command-line?
20 while ($_ = shift) {
21 SWITCH: {
22          /^-t/ && do {
23              $daysold = shift;
24              next SWITCH;
```

```
25              };
26              /^-s/ && do {
27                  $megs = shift;
28                  next SWITCH;
29              }
30          }
31 }
32
33 # we will always need these
34 $toobig = 1024 * 1024 * $megs;
35 $now = time;
36 $too_old = $daysold * 24 * 60 * 60;
37
38 # loop through directories
39 foreach $dir (@dirlist) {
40 # from here, identical to tus1.pl...
```

This program begins with a description block encased in POD markups (*lines 3-12*). We talked a little bit about this in Chapter 2, "The Nickel Tour," and this is a good time to start putting documentation into our programs when we expect to use them for any length of time. You might recall that POD directives always begin with an = sign in column one of a new line.

In this example, we mark two level one headers (=h1) and supply a paragraph for each one. The end of the POD content is marked with the =cut token. We'll see more POD content as we proceed with our exploration.

You will note that in *line 16*, we opt for expressing the threshold in megs instead of in bytes. A supporting instruction in *line 35* will convert this into a byte count more accurately than we would if we simply used base-10 reckoning to choose a threshold.

The "switch" construct in *lines 20-31* provides a place to check for command-line options that might override the default threshold we establish earlier in the program. This checking is delicate and we will have to learn to do better. For instance, if the program operator runs the program as:

```
tus2.pl -t -s 200
```

The program will not have a valid reading for the time threshold. Later on, we'll look at a more bulletproof way to process command-line options. (See Chapter 11, "Ends and Odds," for a more useful way to read from the command line.)

b) Enhance the `tus2.pl` program further to have it report not only the file's name, but also its size and date information.

Answer: To avoid unnecessary replication, only the last part of this program is shown here.

TUS3.PL (PARTIAL LISTING)

```
1 # same as tus2.pl up to here...
2 # Some reports
3 print "Large files in target region\n";
4 foreach $big (@bigones) {
5     ($sz, $atime) = (stat $big)[7,8];
6     ($min, $hr, $mday, $mon) = (gmtime $atime)[1..4];
7     printf "%02d/%02d %02d:%02d %11d %s\n",
8         $mon+1, $mday, $hr, $min, $sz, $big;
9 }
10
11 print "\nOld files in target region\n";
12 foreach $old (@oldones) {
13     ($sz, $atime) = (stat $old)[7,8];
14     ($min, $hr, $mday, $mon) = (gmtime $atime)[1..4];
15     printf "%02d/%02d %02d:%02d %11d %s\n",
16         $mon+1, $mday, $hr, $min, $sz, $old;
17 }
```

The accumulator arrays (`@bigones` and `@oldones`) store the complete pathname for each of the interesting files, so we can use `stat()` to collect information about them when it's time to produce the report. (See *lines 5 and 13*.)

With the access time information available, we can then use `gmtime()` to construct the details about the time that we want to display. (See *lines 6 and 14*.)

By now, you should be able to handle the file status information pretty well. You'll get one more chance to practice this before the chapter is over.

LAB 9.1 REVIEW QUESTIONS

1) The `stat()` function returns status information on a file. The three timestamps that are returned use which format to represent time?

   a) _____ the C language `struct time_t`

   b) _____ an integer that represents the number of seconds since the UNIX epoch, January 1, 1970.

   c) _____ an integer that represents the number of seconds since the discovery of Jupiter's "Red Spot."

   d) _____ a UNIX time string represented in terms of local time.

2) Which of the following code examples will accurately store a file's current byte count in the variable `$sz`?

   a) _____ `$sz = stat($filename);`

   b) _____ `@stats=stat($filename);$sz = $stats[6];`

   c) _____ `$sz = (stat $filename)[7];`

   d) _____ `$sz = stat ($filename, 7);`

3) True or False? The `readdir()` function behaves differently depending upon whether it is in a scalar or a list context. In a list context, it returns a list with the names from the open directory filehandle. In a scalar context, it returns the number of files in that directory.

   a) _____ True

   b) _____ False

Look at the following code and then answer the questions that follow:

DIRSTAT.PL

```
1 #!/usr/bin/perl
2 opendir PWD, "."
3    || die "Can't open local directory\n\t";
4 @fnames = readdir PWD;
5 close PWD;
6 foreach (@fnames) {
7    ($v1, $v2, $v3) = (stat $_)[2,7,9];
8 # sombody ought to be shot
9    print "Value 1 is: $v1\nValue 2: $v2\nValue3\n";
10 # no, shooting would be far too kind.
11 }
```

4) Which of the following describes the information stored in $v1, $v2 and $v3?

   a) _____ file permissions, name, and size.

   b) _____ file mode, size, and modification time.

   c) _____ too well-shrouded to be useful.

   d) _____ file permissions, size, and access time.

5) What information will be printed for each of the files in the current directory?

   a) _____ an integer that represents the file's type, permission set, and extended attributes, then an integer that represents the file's size in bytes, followed by an integer that represents the date of the most recent file modification.

   b) _____ three numbers that represent random pieces of information about the files.

   c) _____ an integer that represents the file's permissions followed by an integer that represents the file's creation date.

   d) _____ an integer that represents the file's type, permission set, and extended attributes, then an integer that represents the file's size in bytes.

Quiz answers appear in Appendix A, Section 9.1.

L A B   9.2

FUNCTIONS THAT MANIPULATE FILES

LAB OBJECTIVES

After this Lab, you will be able to:

✓ Remove/Rename Files

✓ Create/Remove Directories

✓ Change File Owner, Group, or Permissions

In this Lab, we'll look at some functions that Perl provides to manipulate files as entire units. We'll see how to rename and delete both files and directories. We'll see how to create a directory and how to manage file ownership, group assignment, and access permissions.

DELETE A FILE

To delete a file, you use the `unlink()` function. It expects to be given the name of a file or a list of filenames.

■ FOR EXAMPLE

Here are several ways that you might unlink files:

```
unlink "filename.txt";
$c = unlink qw{file1.txt file2.txt file3.txt};
unlink @ARGV;
unlink <*.txt>;
unlink;
```

The first example will delete a single file called `filename.txt`. The second example will remove all of the files in the supplied list. In that case, `$c` will be set to the number of files successfully removed. The third example removes files named on the command line.

The fourth example contains something that looks a little odd. The special phrase `<*.txt>` is one that allows Perl to construct a list of files that match the embedded wildcard pattern. The pattern is interpreted in the same way that it would be by the UNIX shell. (You can use that notation anywhere, not just with the `unlink()` function.)

The last example attempts to remove a file whose name is in `$_` if that holds a legal filename.

RENAME A FILE

To rename a file, Perl supplies a `rename()` function. Even a rocket scientist or brain surgeon could use this function. You supply it with two arguments, the old name, and the new name. If the file with the old name exists, the rename operation will be attempted.

The `rename()` function returns 1 if it succeeds, and 0 otherwise. If there is a problem, detailed information can be found in `$!` as an error code.

■ *FOR EXAMPLE*

To rename a file in the current directory, try:

```
rename "ushell3.pl" "filemgr.pl";
```

To rename a file by placing it in another directory:

```
rename "/usr/bill/ushell3.pl" "/usr/sally/ushell3.pl";
```

To check on the result of your operation:

```
rename ($old $new) || warn "problem: $! \n\t";
```

Several things can cause the operation to fail. You might not have write permission in the directory that contains the old file, you might not be able to write in the directory for the new name, the target directory may be on a different filesystem (in UNIX), or the old file may not exist. So it makes good sense to check on the return value of the function.

CREATE A DIRECTORY

It's easy to create a new directory; the function has the same name as the UNIX command. Use the `mkdir()` function to create a directory when you need to do so. The function expects to see the name of the new directory and a numeric mode that represents the file permissions.

Without going into all of the details of access permissions (take a look at your system documentation for `chmod()` if you're curious), let's just say that there are about three common modes that you might choose from.

Use `0755` to mean, "I can see this directory and add or remove files; anyone else can see it." (In this case, "I" means the operator of your program.) Use `0700` to mean, "I can see this directory and manipulate its contents. Others cannot see it." And use `0777` to mean, "Anyone can see this directory and add or remove files." There are other less common settings and when you need one of those, you'll know what value to use.

■ *FOR EXAMPLE*

To add a directory beneath `/tmp`, you would code:

```
mkdir ("/tmp/work", 0777) || die "Couldn't create /tmp/work";
```

REMOVE A DIRECTORY

You cannot remove a directory with the `unlink()` function unless special conditions are in effect. And the risk to the integrity of your filesystem is great if you don't know exactly what you're doing. Instead, you should use the `rmdir()` function, which can safely remove a directory. It expects to be given a filename, or it will remove the directory named in `$_` if that is a legal directory name.

This function returns `1` if it succeeds, `0` if it fails, and stores the error code in `$!` if things don't go well.

■ *FOR EXAMPLE*

To remove the directory we created in the last example, first it would have to be empty. Then you could code:

```
rmdir ("/tmp/work") || die "Couldn't remove /tmp/work";
```

As long as everything is nice and clean, this will work fine. In the exercises for this Lab, we'll let you write the code that tests for existing files and removes them before you remove the directory.

MANAGING FILE OWNERSHIP, GROUP, AND ACCESS

In our earlier discussion about file mode information, we touched on access permissions slightly. (Prentice Hall has a wonderful book on UNIX system administration that can help you with this if you don't understand it; pick up Joe Kaplenk's UNIX System Administrator's Interactive Workbook.) Perl provides functions to manage the characteristics of a file in a UNIX filesystem. The issue comes up a lot when you manage a website, an FTP site, or a source code tree that is kept on a UNIX server. Fortunately, if you know how to manage these characteristics from the shell prompt, you will find that it's almost the same in Perl.

To change ownership or group assignment of a file, Perl provides a chown() function. It expects to be given a list, the first two elements of which should be a numerical user id and group id. The remaining elements of the list should contain the names of the files to be altered.

■ *FOR EXAMPLE*

To change the ownership and group of files, you could use the chown() function like this:

```
chown 500, 500, 'file1.txt', 'file2.txt';
chown 500, 500, qw{file1.txt file2.txt};
chown 500, 500, @flist;
```

The first example changes two files (`file2.txt` and `file2.txt`) to be owned by the user with the UID of `500`. The files are also marked as being associated with the group that is identified by the GID of `500`.

The same thing happens in the second example to the files identified in the list, and in the third example to the files whose names are stored in the array `@flist`.

Changing access permissions is nearly as straightforward if you know how to specify file permissions in octal notation. (Again, if you aren't familiar with file permissions, just remember that there are three common ones for directories and programs, `0755`, `0700`, and `0777`; and there are three common ones for ordinary files, `0644`, `0600`, and `0666`. You can learn more about these in the documentation for the system `chmod(1)` command.)

The Perl `chmod()` function expects a list, the first element of which should be an octal number that represents the intended permission set; the remainder of the list should contain the names of files.

■ FOR EXAMPLE

You might want to set some of the files in your current directory to be private, readable and writable only by you.

```
chmod 0600, todo.txt, journal.txt;
```

You might decide to make all of the Perl programs in your directory executable only by you.

```
chmod 0700 <*.pl>;
```

Or you might decide to make all of the files readable and executable by everyone, but with nobody having write permission.

```
chmod 0555 <*.pl>;
```

Let's put all of this together in some programs.

LAB 9.2 EXERCISES

9.2.1 REMOVE/RENAME FILES

a) Write a "safe rm" program (srm.pl) that carefully removes files named on the command line. It should prompt the program operator before removing each one, and then unlink the file only if the response is affirmative.

_____

_____

The srm.pl program is an interesting starting place, but we need to do a little more work to it before it can really be useful. Instead of removing a file with unlink(), you might want to preserve it by renaming it as a hidden file in the current directory. On a UNIX system, a file can be hidden by giving it a name that begins with a '.' character. To ensure that a file renamed this way will get a unique new name, we could embed the current process ID at the beginning of the name, after the dot.

■ *FOR EXAMPLE*

Given the following facts:

```
Filename to be deleted:  facts.txt
Current Process ID: 9024
```

we would rename the file to be called:

```
.9024.facts.txt
```

The file would be hidden from normal directory listings and would not normally be included in groups formed by using wildcards (that is, it would not be one of the files in "*.txt").

Win32 programmers, this procedure will not result in the files being hidden when you rename them (unless you use Bash or ksh), but you should complete this Exercise anyway. It forms the basis for a later Exercise that will allow you to hide the files.

b) Write a revised version of `srm.pl` that renames the files instead of removing them. Make the files invisible, but still in the current directory, and embed the current PID so that a file that is "removed" several times can have several "undeletable" versions.

_____

_____

c) Write a program (`unsrm.pl`) that can find files that have been "removed" by the `srm2.pl` program and offer them for undeletion. If the undelete operation will trample an existing file, show the statistics on both files and prompt the operator to confirm the undelete.

_____

_____

9.2.2 CREATE/REMOVE DIRECTORIES

a) Write a program (`mytmp.pl`) that creates a directory under /`tmp` with a name that includes the current PID.

_____

_____

b) Write a program (`toastdir.pl`) that can remove a directory by checking first to see if it contains any files, and removing them, if necessary.

_____

_____

When we wrote the `unsrm.pl` program, a lot of code was dedicated to determining whether a file had been previously "removed" with the `srm2.pl` program. If the files had been in a special directory instead of stashed away in the current directory, it would be easier to get a listing of programs that are eligible for "undeletion."

We can simplify the entire process by creating a directory called `.wastebasket` when we want to safely remove a file with our "safe rm" program. If we want to support multiple versions of deleted files, we can change the name to include a prefix that represents the current date information.

■ FOR EXAMPLE

If the `date()` function returns the number:

`918203663`

and the file to be deleted is called:

`todo.pl`

then the file would be renamed to:

`.wastebasket/918203663.todo.pl`

c) Revise the `srm2.pl` program to use a hidden directory called `.wastebasket`, creating it if it doesn't exist. When a file is placed there, it should be renamed to include the date information as a prefix.

_____

_____

9.2.3 CHANGE FILE OWNER, GROUP, OR PERMISSIONS

a) Write a program (`onlyme.pl`) that reads a directory name from the command line and changes all files in that directory to be readable and writable only by the file owner (mode `0600`).

_____

_____

b) Enhance `srm3.pl` so that the `.wastebasket` directory is rendered inaccessible (set to mode `000`) after the files have been tucked away there.

_____

_____

LAB 9.2 EXERCISE ANSWERS

9.2.1 ANSWERS

a)   Write a "safe rm" program (`srm.pl`) that carefully removes files named on the command line.

Answer: Here's a short program that meets the specification.

SRM.PL

```
1  #!/usr/bin/perl
2  # syntax check
3  die "Usage: $0 file1 [file2 ...]\n\t"
4     unless defined $ARGV[0];
5
6  # loop through args
7  foreach $fn (@ARGV) {
8     print "Remove $fn?";
9     $response = <STDIN>;
10    $response =~ /^[yY]/ && unlink $fn;
11 }
```

This program is not terribly sophisticated, but you might find that it serves as a good foundation for a more useful program. Here we see it receive input from the program operator (*line 9*) and if the response begins with the letter "Y," the file under consideration will be removed (*line 10*) if it is possible.

Now if this doesn't seem very safe to you, it's not! You might want to check the operator's response more carefully. You might want to protect the file by simply moving it to a safe place instead of totally removing it from the system. (Hey, that sounds like the next Exercise!)

b) Write a revised version of `srm.pl` that renames the files instead of removing them.

Answer: Here is one program that does the work for us.

SRM2.PL

```
 1  #!/usr/bin/perl
 2  # syntax check
 3  die "Usage: $0 file1 [file2 ...]\n\t"
 4     unless defined $ARGV[0];
 5
 6  # loop through args
 7  foreach $fn (@ARGV) {
 8     print "Remove $fn?";
 9     $response = <STDIN>;
10     $response =~ /^[yY]/ && rename $fn, ".$$.$fn";
11  }
```

This one turned out to be pretty simple. We ask the program operator for confirmation (*line 9*) and then rename the file in *line 10* by constructing the target filename from the elements we discussed earlier.

c) Write a program (`unsrm.pl`) that can find files that have been "removed" by the `srm2.pl` program and offer them for undeletion.

Answer: Here is one version of a program that meets the stated requirements.

```
 1  #!/usr/bin/perl
 2  opendir (IN, ".") || die "Cannot open current directory\n\t";
 3  while ($fn = readdir IN) {
 4     next unless $fn =~ /^\./; # it's not a hidden file
 5     next if $fn =~ /^\.\.?$/; # it's a PWD or parent
 6     @nodes = split /\./, $fn; # first field will be empty
 7     next if $nodes[1] == 0; # first name-node is non-numeric
```

```
 8      $target = join ".", @nodes[2..$#nodes];
 9      print "undeleting: [$fn] to create: [$target]\n";
10      system "ls -l $fn $target";
11      print "undelete? [Yes/No] ";
12      $response = <STDIN>;
13      rename $fn, $target if $response =~ /^[yY]/;
14 }
```

This one turned out to be a little more involved. There might be a more concise way to do this, but it would probably be even harder to read. So we'll go through this example a little bit at a time. First, as we loop through the contents of the directory, we look at each file and if the file-name doesn't begin with a dot, we go on to the next file (*line 4*).

If our loop survives that check, we then make sure that we aren't looking at the filenames "." or ".." because those are not of interest to us. If we find one of those, we also return to the top and begin the next iteration of our loop.

When we're still in the loop, we now take the filename and split it into an array using the dot as the delimiter. Because the filename begins with a dot, the first field in the resulting array will be null. See how this works with a small sample of simulated data in Figure 9.3.

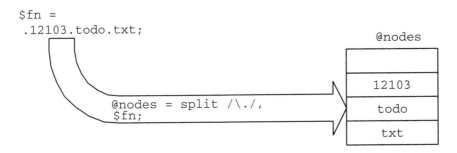

Figure 9.3 ■ Splitting the filename will yield one null element in the array.

So we look at the second element of the array ($nodes[1] in *line 7*) and if it evaluates numerically to 0, then we know that it isn't a process ID.

(There is a process on your UNIX system with PID of 0, but you can bet that it's NOT your Perl program.) We're assuming here that if the first part of the name is a string, it will look numerically like zero. So we'll go back to the top of the loop if the first useful information node is non-numeric.

At this point, we can't have an absolute guarantee that the file under consideration is a "safely deleted" file, but because we're going to be prompting the program operator, we can rely upon them for the remainder of the intelligence necessary to make this operation reliable. (I know that's a provocative stance, but you'll probably be the program operator yourself most of the time, and we're going to strengthen this program soon anyway, so everything will work out okay.)

In *line 8*, we take the name nodes beginning with the first one after the PID portion and assemble them back into a string using join(). We use *lines 9-11* to provide the operator with some information about the proposed changes, and if they grant approval, we restore the undeleted file in *line 13*.

We still need to improve this program to eliminate some of the guesswork, but taking this approach has proved instructive.

9.2.2 ANSWERS

a) Write a program (mytmp.pl) that creates a directory under /tmp with a name that includes the current PID.

Answer: There's not much to a program that does this.

MYTMP.PL
```
1 #!/usr/bin/perl
2 mkdir ("/tmp/$$.d", 0777) ||
3    die "Couldn't create /tmp/$$.d\n\t";
4 print "Created /tmp/$$.d\n";
```

In fact, most of this program listing consists of error checking (*line 3*) and a courtesy line that prints out a message about the details of the operation (*line 4*).

b) Write a program (`toastdir.pl`) that can remove a directory by checking first to see if it contains any files, and removing them if necessary.

Answer: This program is a little more elaborate than the last one. (BEWARE: This is also a very dangerous program. It removes files and directories without supervision, and with only a tiny bit of error checking. Your program must be much better than this unless you plan to use it only once and then destroy it.)

LAB
9.2

TOASTDIR.PL

```
 1 #!/usr/bin/perl
 2 die "usage: $0 directoryname\n\t"
 3    unless defined $ARGV[0];
 4 $dir = shift;
 5 opendir (IN, $dir)
 6    or die "$0: failed opening directory $dir\n\t";
 7 @flist = readdir IN;
 8 closedir IN;
 9 if (@flist > 2) {
10    foreach $f (@flist[2..$#flist]){
11        print "removing $dir/$f...\n";
12        unlink ("$dir/$f")
13            or die "$0: failed removing $dir/$f\n\t";
14    }
15 }
16 rmdir $dir
17    or die "$0: failed removing directory $dir\n\t";
```

What does this program do? Don't ever run a program unless you know the answer to that question. To do so begs for disaster.

The key to making this program easy to manage is reading the contents of the named directory into an array in *line 7*, and then checking to see if more than two entries are present (*line 9*). Look closely at *line 10* where we use list slicing notation to get the portion of `@flist` that starts after the second entry.

You might have used a `for()` loop here (starting your index at 2, and ending at `$#flist`), but the `foreach()` loop is usually a bit more convenient when you're dealing with an array. The `print()` statement in *line 11* is not entirely necessary, but you might want to leave that in as you test and revise your program. It's comforting to be able to see what's going on as you experiment.

When all of the component files have been removed (or if there were no component files), we can finally remove the directory in *line 16*.

c) Revise the srm2.pl program to use a hidden directory called .wastebasket, creating it if it doesn't exist. When a file is placed there, it should be renamed to include the date information as a prefix.

Answer: This program required a few tweaks to get it right. Here's one way you might have done it.

SRM3.PL

```
 1 #!/usr/bin/perl
 2
 3 # syntax check
 4 die "Usage: $0 file1 [file2 ...]\n\t"
 5    unless defined $ARGV[0];
 6
 7 # build the wastebasket if necessary
 8 $bname = ".wastebasket";
 9 mkdir ($bname, 0700) unless -d $bname;
10
11 # loop through args
12 foreach $fn (@ARGV) {
13    print "Remove $fn?";
14    $response = <STDIN>;
15    $tstamp = time;
16    $response =~ /^[yY]/ && rename $fn, "$bname/$tstamp.$fn";
17 }
```

Two lines had to be added to define the name for our special directory (*line 8*), and then create it, if necessary (*line 9*). A line is added to grab the current time information (*line 15*) and the job is finished with an alteration to the line that renames (and moves) the file (*line 16*).

9.2.3 ANSWERS

a) Write a program (onlyme.pl) that reads a directory name from the command line and changes all files in that directory to be readable and writable only by the file owner (mode 0600).

Answer: Here's one way to write that program.

ONLYME.PL

```
1 #!/usr/bin/perl
2
3 # check syntax
4 die "usage: $0 directoryname\n\t"
5    unless defined $ARGV[0];
6 $dir = shift;
7
8 opendir (IN, $dir)
9    || die "$0: couldn't open directory $dir\n\t";
10 @flist = readdir IN;
11 closedir IN;
12
13 # change to the target directory
14 chdir $dir || die "$0: Cannot go to $dir\n\t";
15 # rip out first two entries
16 splice @flist, 0, 2;
17 # and doctor the rest...
18 chmod 0600, @flist;
```

LAB
9.2

Through *line 11* in this program there are no surprises. This looks just like half a dozen programs we've examined so far. In *line 14* we have to try something new. Rather than get each filename entry and concatenate it to the end of the target directory name, we can go to the target directory and then all of the filenames will be legitimate without their full path-names.

If you remember how to use `splice()` to remove a slice from an array, then *line 16* should seem pretty straightforward. Then, thanks to the nice design of the `chmod()` function, fixing the permissions on a list of files is nearly trivial in *line 18*.

b) Enhance `srm3.pl` so that the `.wastebasket` directory is rendered inaccessible (set to mode `000`) after the files have been tucked away there.

Answer:This program does the trick.

SRM4.PL

```
 1 #!/usr/bin/perl
 2
 3 # syntax check
 4 die "Usage: $0 file1 [file2 ...]\n\t"
 5    unless defined $ARGV[0];
 6
 7 # build or unlock the wastebasket
 8 $bname = ".wastebasket";
 9 if (-d $bname) {
10    chmod 0700, $bname
11        || die "$0: Couldn't unlock $bname\n\t";
12 }
13 else {
14    mkdir ($bname, 0700)
15        || die "$0: Couldn't create $bname\n\t";
16 }
17
18 # loop through args
19 foreach $fn (@ARGV) {
20    print "Remove $fn?";
21    $response = <STDIN>;
22    $tstamp = time;
23    $response =~ /^[yY]/ && rename $fn, "$bname/$tstamp.$fn";
24 }
25 chmod 0000, $bname;
```

The major change to this program came in *lines 7-16*. There we look to see if the .wastebasket directory exists, and if so, we simply need to change the permissions to be accessible for a short while. If the directory doesn't yet exist, we create it with access permissions open for the program operator.

In *line 15*, we wrap things up by changing the mode back to 0000 so that the directory cannot be accessed inadvertently.

LAB 9.2 REVIEW QUESTIONS

1) Which function is used to remove a file?
   a) _____ remove()
   b) _____ mv()
   c) _____ rm()
   d) _____ unlink()

2) Which function is used to rename a file?
   a) _____ rename()
   b) _____ mv()
   c) _____ rn()
   d) _____ relink()

3) Which function is used to remove a directory?
   a) _____ rmdir()
   b) _____ mv()
   c) _____ rn()
   d) _____ dir_unlink()

4) True or False? The chmod() function works exactly like the UNIX command of the same name.
   a) _____ True
   b) _____ False

5) Which example shows a legal use of the Perl chown() function?
   a) _____ chown 500, 500, $filename;
   b) _____ chown 500, $filename;
   c) _____ chown root, $filename;
   d) _____ chown $filename, 500, 500;

Quiz answers appear in Appendix A, Section 9.2.

LAB 9.3

OPENING FILEHANDLES FOR READING AND WRITING

LAB OBJECTIVES

After this Lab, you will be able to:

✓ Open a File for Reading, Writing, or Appending

✓ Open a Pipe for Reading or Writing

✓ Open the Special DATA Filehandle

We've looked at how we can handle files from the outside. Let's turn our attention now to the things we can do with the content inside a file. In this Lab, we see how to read and write to an ordinary file, how to write to or read from a pipe associated with another system process, and we wrap up with a peek at how to use a special filehandle that allows us to embed data right in the program.

We actually started having our programs read from files as far back as Chapter 2, "The Nickel Tour." In that chapter, we saw how to open a file-handle and read the data a line at a time. Let's review that briefly.

OPEN A FILE FOR READING

If we want to read from a file, we need to open a *filehandle* to gain access to its contents. A filehandle is simply a variable that provides us with an access point for a file. Its name is formed using the standard Perl rules for identifiers, and there is no prefix as there is for scalar, array, and hash variable names. Convention is to choose a filehandle identifier that is all upper case, but you are not required to do that. It simply makes filehandle names easier to identify.

**LAB
9.3**

To get a filehandle, we use the Perl `open()` function. It expects us to provide a name for the filehandle, and a string that contains both the name of the file and the *open mode*. The mode identifies how you plan to use the file (read, append, or write).

■ *FOR EXAMPLE*

Here's how we've been opening a filehandle to read a file:

```
open IN, "filename" or die "$0: couldn't open filename\n\t";
```

In this example, the name `filename` identifies the file. There is no explicit indication of the mode; the default mode is to read from the named file starting at the beginning. Another way to write this would be:

```
open IN, "<filename" or die "$0: couldn't open filename\n\t";
```

This time we explicitly indicate the open mode instead of counting on the default. Throughout this book, we've relied upon the default. You will find that much of the production code you encounter will do the same thing. On the other hand, because you know the symbol to open a file in input mode, you will find that the other modes are pretty logical, too (that is, logical if you're familiar with the redirection mechanism used by the UNIX shells and the MS-DOS command processor).

OPEN A FILE FOR WRITING

To open a file for writing, we use almost the same code as we did for reading. The only difference is the open mode:

```
open OUT, ">filename" or die "$0: couldn't open filename\n\t";
```

When you open a file in this fashion, it will be created if it does not already exist. If it does exist, the file will be opened and the original data will be completely overwritten. Even if you close the file immediately without writing anything, the original data will be gone.

And speaking of closing the file, whether you open the file for writing or reading, you should always remember to close the file when you are finished.

```
close IN;
close OUT;
```

If you forget to do this, things might still work out in your favor. The file will be closed (almost always) when your program ends. Closing a file simply ensures that any data that may be buffered will be written to the file so that it is not left in an indeterminate state.

If we open a file for writing, we must be able to write to it. Look at these two statements:

```
print "Words you can use.";
print STDOUT "Words you can use.";
```

Both lines do exactly the same thing. You might have already guessed that STDOUT is the name of a filehandle, one that just happens to be open when your program starts. Notice that there is no comma after the filehandle name when we provide it explicitly to the `print()` statement.

You can write to any open filehandle this way.

■ FOR EXAMPLE

Let's see a short program that writes information to a file.

ANSWER3.PL
```
1 #!/usr/bin/perl
2 print "What is your name? ";
3 chomp ($nm = <STDIN>);
4 print "What is your quest? ";
5 chomp ($quest = <STDIN>);
6 print "What is your favorite color? ";
```

```
 7 chomp ($color = <STDIN>);
 8 open OUT, ">$nm.txt" or die "Couldn't open $nm.txt\n\t";
 9 print OUT "name: $nm\n";
10 print OUT "quest: $quest\n";
11 print OUT "color: $color\n";
12 close OUT;
```

In *lines 8-12,* we see how we would open a file, write some output to it, and then close it. If you decide to use `printf()` to produce your output, you can do almost exactly the same thing to make it happen.

```
        printf OUT "name: \n", $nm;
```

WRITE BY APPENDING

Instead of automatically overwriting your files each time you open them, you may wish instead to add new information at the end of the file. You can open a file for appending with a line that looks like this:

```
open OUT, ">>srvr.log" or die "Couldn't open srvr.log\n\t";
```

Here's a program that counts the number of files in the `/tmp` directory and then adds that information to the end of a log file.

TMPCOUNT.PL
```
1 #!/usr/bin/perl
2 $tmpcount = `ls -1 /tmp | wc -l`;
3 #$tmpcount = `VER` # for MS-DOS
4 open LOG, ">>tmpcount.log"
5    or die "couldn't open tmpcount.log\n\t";
6 print LOG $tmpcount;
```

On most systems, "`ls -1`" prints out filenames one per line. The "`wc -l`" command will print the number of lines read from the pipe in this example. The program is a little bit contrived so that it has a chance to run on both UNIX and MS-DOS systems. A more "real world" program might execute the `uptime(1)` program and log those results in a file. We'll see more of this technique when we work on the Lab Exercises.

OPENING A PIPE FOR READING

In our study of Perl so far, you've seen that we can simulate most system commands with well-chosen tricks from our Perl toolkit. Sometimes, however, the simplest way to get the information we need is to use a system command. We can capture all of the output from a command with the "backtick operator" as we did in the last example. But what do we do if there is too much output to handle all at once? Consider this sequence of instructions:

```
$input = `ls -1 /tmp`;
@inlines = split /\n/, $input;
foreach $1 (@inlines) {
    # do something interesting
}
```

This works fine as long as there are a reasonable number of files in the /tmp directory. But what if there were 12,000 files in there?

First, you would be reading the entire output of ls(1) into a string, and then you would be claiming another equal-sized stretch of memory to break it into an array. Now you might have enough memory for this, but your program is becoming terribly wasteful. And maybe you have enough memory to handle 12,000 files, but what about 120,000? Eventually, you'll find that there just isn't enough memory to handle the job if you're going to read everything into memory.

A saner approach would be to read the output from the ls(1) program one line at a time, handling each line as it comes. To do this, we can read from a filehandle connected to a pipe from the system command we need.

■ *FOR EXAMPLE*

This code would allow us "one line at a time access" to the same data as that of our last example:

```
open INLINES, "ls -1 |" or die "Cannot read input\n\t";
while ($1 = <INLINES>) {
    # do something interesting
}
```

Maybe you have a combination of system commands that you'd like to run in order to create an input stream for your Perl program.

```
foreach $dir (@ARGV) {
   open STREAM, "ls -l $dir|tail +2|grep -v root|"
      or die "couldn't open input stream\n\t";
   while (<STREAM>) {
      # do something with $_
   }
   close STREAM;
}
```

**LAB
9.3**

The commands in your pipeline stream will run, and the output from the final command will be available for your Perl program to read from the STREAM filehandle in this example. Here's something else you might try:

```
open TOC, "zcat stuff.tar.Z|tar tvf - |";
```

This would open a pipeline filled with the list of files that make up a compressed tar archive. Your program could then use the lines that are relevant to its operation.

OPENING A PIPE FOR WRITING

You can also open a filehandle on a pipe for writing. This will send your output data to a system command for further processing. On a UNIX system, this might be useful if you want to have your Perl program send a mail message.

```
open NOTIFY, "|mailx -s 'NOTICE' addressee\@somesys.org";
```

Of course, your system would have to implement the mailx(1) program. (On some versions of UNIX, this is simply the mail(1) program.) We assume here that you'll add the error-checking code at the end of your open() command.

■ *FOR EXAMPLE*

To write output to this pipeline (and thus, to the mail message), you could then have code like:

```
print NOTIFY, "You are being notified\n";
```

Your output goes to the pipeline and, when the filehandle is closed, the pipeline is closed and the message will be sent.

Here's another thing you might try:

```
open CMPOUT, "|compress -c >pgmout.Z"
    or die "Couldn't open compressed output pipe\n\t";
foreach $line (@in_some_massive_array) {
    print CMPOUT "line ++$idx: $line\n";
}
close CMPOUT;
```

This example writes lines of output to the compress(1) program. It, in turn, writes the compressed data to a file using shell redirection. This is a very handy approach when you have to write a very large amount of output and you would prefer it to be compressed on disk.

USING THE DATA FILEHANDLE

Perl provides a special filehandle that you can use to read from data embedded in the program file. Just like STDIN, the DATA filehandle is open when your program starts; you don't even have to call open() before you start reading from it.

Information read from the DATA filehandle comes from the lines of the program file that appear after a special token that Perl recognizes as an "end-of-script" marker. That token consists of two underscore characters, followed by the word "END" and then two more underscores, that is, __END__.

The best way to see this feature in action is to simply look at some code.

INDATA.PL
```
1 #!/usr/bin/perl
2 # read in username database
3 while (<DATA>) {
4     chomp;
5     ($nm, $pw) = split /:/;
6     $udb{$nm} = $pw;
7 }
```

```
 8 # prompt for login name, password
 9 print "login: ";
10 chomp ($login = <STDIN>);
11 print "password: ";
12 chomp ($passwd = <STDIN>);
13
14 # validate user identity and proceed
15 die "begone clueless unperson\n\t" unless defined $udb{$login};
16 die "begone foul imposter\n\t" unless $passwd eq $udb{$login};
17 print "Welcome honored guest.\n";
18
19 __END__
20 larry:lingo
21 tom:tonic
22 ellie:plasma
```

In *lines 3-6*, we see the login database read from the data at the end of the program file. This is stored in a hash so that after the program operator types in a username and password (*lines 8-11*), the program can validate the login information.

The ability to embed data in the program file serves two common purposes. In a case like we've just seen, it is convenient to maintain only one file with the program and data in one place. It can also be handy when you want to use a sample data set during the program development cycle.

A program that is designed to read from a (sometimes enormous) system data file can be cumbersome to test when it has to be run repeatedly. It can be tested with a tiny sample data set to check its behavior during the early development phase; you may be able to see how well it's working without waiting for lengthy run times.

LAB 9.3 EXERCISES

9.3.1 OPEN A FILE FOR READING, WRITING, OR APPENDING

a) Write a program (pcp.pl) that takes two command-line arguments, then opens the first for reading and the other one for writing. Then copy the contents of the first file into the second.

The first file should be checked first to ensure that it's a text file, and if the second file exists, the program operator should be prompted to authorize the overwrite.

_____

_____

b) Write an operator log program (`olog.pl`) that can open its log file for appending, prompt the program operator for a log entry, and then append the information to the log file.

_____

_____

Barber Tom set down his book and stared at the ceiling for a moment. The Perl approach to file I/O made pretty good sense to him. With this information, he could bring his To Do List project to its next logical state. As he was sitting down to begin writing code, he heard a knock at the window. It was Coach Randal.

"I was about to write some code for my project," Tom said as soon as they were both seated near the computer. "It already reads the task data from a file. Now I want to be able to update that file. So when somebody adds a task, we can write it into the file."

Randal asked, "Have you thought about extending the user login record so that you can give certain people the ability to add new users to the system? That should be pretty easy to do."

"Sure, a supervisor flag. That's a good idea. I'll bet I could do that pretty easily in this revision. Let's start with the last version of my program." Two heads bent to peer at the computer screen.

c) Update the `itodo2.pl` program to allow it to write the tasklist data out to a file, and extend the definition of the login database so that certain login identities can be allowed to see the entire task list and add new users.

___

___

9.3.2 OPEN A PIPE FOR READING OR WRITING

a) Write a program that can send a mail message using `mailx(1)`, `mail(1)`, `elm(1)`, or another mail client that can be run from the command line. (Win32 programmers can get a `mailx(1)` simulator from this book's companion website.)

___

___

Anyone who has spent some time poking around on the Internet has at some point encountered a thing called a "gzipped tar file." (UNIX hackers will have seen many of them.) There are several ways to extract the component files or read a table of contents from such a file, but here are two that will consistently work on *most systems* (assuming you have `tar(1)` and `gzip(1)`):

```
gzip -dc tarfile.tar.gz |tar xvf -   # extracts files
gzip -dc tarfile.tar.gz |tar tvf -   # table of contents
```

If you need a file of this type to practice with before doing the next Exercise, the companion website has all of the program examples from this book available in exactly this format, as well as more detailed discussion of tools like `gzip(1)` and `gtar(1)`.

b) Write a program (`tartoc.pl`) that can read the directory of a `gzip (1)` compressed tar file. It should find the tar file name on the command line and print out a report that identifies the number of component files, the largest file in the archive, and the number of directories.

c) Write a program (`cmplog.pl`) that can both read and write a compressed log file.

Simulate log information by generating 10 lines per session, each with a simulated time stamp and some random sentence. Your program should be able to read in the current log and append new log information, then write the file out again.

9.3.3 OPEN THE SPECIAL DATA FILEHANDLE

In a program from an earlier exercise (`tartoc.pl`), we read lines of data from the table of contents in a compressed tar file. It was convenient for reference purposes to include a few sample lines in a comment block.

We could do better if we want to use that data extract as a real sample during development (or testing) time. Instead of putting the information in a comment block, we could place it after a __END__ token and then read it with the DATA filehandle.

Doing this would mean that we could test the program with a known data sample until we are ready to expose our program to the cruelty of production data.

a) Rewrite the `tartoc.pl` program to read sample data from the DATA filehandle. Use a data sample that is rich enough to confirm that the logic of the program is sound.

Barber Tom listened to the phone ring at the distant end of the line and hoped that he'd find Larry at home, even though it was a Friday night. Just as he was about to give up, Tom heard the distant receiver lifted and a voice said absent-mindedly, "This is my phone."

Tom flinched. He was pretty sure he'd interrupted Larry at a programming task himself. "Larry, this is Tom. I hate to interrupt you, but I was wondering if you'd had a chance to look at my latest To Do List code?"

"Oh, Tom," Larry still sounded distracted. A pause, and then, "Oh yes. I just read through your programs this afternoon. You've made a lot of progress since we talked about this. What are you going to do next?"

Tom breathed out. "I'm ready to put in some code that will allow the supervisors to add a new login. And I've been thinking about moving the login database into the program itself to cut down on the number of files that have to be maintained. But there's a problem.

"I have one interactive program and one that runs completely from the command line. If I embed the data into one of them, then I'll have to replicate it in the other. And, for that matter, I don't like the fact that the code I use to validate a login identity is identical in two different programs. I know how you feel about duplicating code. But I don't know how to get around doing it that way."

The sound of Larry's voice carried a smile as he said, "I'm glad to hear that you've been listening to what I told you. What you really need is to code your validation routine as a function and keep it in a separate file. But I don't have time tonight to explain what you have to do. I'm working on a little project of my own.

"There is something you can do using what you already know. Write a program that expects two command-line arguments, a name and a password. Have it embed the

database to be checked at the end and read from that with the DATA filehandle just like we talked about before.

"It should exit after checking the name and password with an exit code of 0 to mean that no match was found, or 1 to indicate that the information is correct. Then you can call this new program from your interactive program or your command-line program. No duplication except for the line that calls the external program."

**LAB
9.3**

Tom mulled this over for a moment and then said, "Yeah, I think I can see that. In fact, I could probably take that approach to end up with only two entry points to the system. One that is interactive and one that is command-line driven. Hey, thanks for helping out. I know you're busy."

Larry didn't hesitate an instant. "It's no problem, Tom. In fact, what are you doing, programming on a Friday night like this? I think it's time for me to set my project aside until tomorrow. You should too. In fact, if you don't get yourself down to Mickey's pub before I do, I'm going to have him put my first round on your tab."

Tom did hang up the phone before he headed for his door. Larry would already have a two-block head start.

> **b)** Write a program that validates logins from the To Do List database using the DATA filehandle. It should take two command-line arguments, name and password. It should return an exit code of 1 when the first argument matches a legal username and the second argument matches the appropriate password. Otherwise, it should return 0.

_____

_____

LAB 9.3 EXERCISE ANSWERS

9.3.1 ANSWERS

a) Write a program (`pcp.pl`) that takes two command-line arguments, then opens the first for reading and the other one for writing. Then copy the contents of the first file into the second.

Answer: This program takes a fairly straightforward approach to the task.

PCP.PL

```perl
1 #!/usr/bin/perl
2
3 # check syntax
4 die "usage: $0 source_file target_file\n\t"
5    unless defined $ARGV[1];
6
7 # grab the filenames from the cmd-line
8 $src = $ARGV[0];
9 $tgt = $ARGV[1];
10
11 # only copy text files
12 die "$0 only copies text files\n\t"
13    unless -T $src;
14
15 # prompt if we're going to overwrite
16 if (-e $tgt) {
17    print "Overwrite $ARGV[1]? [y/n] ";
18    $resp = <STDIN>;
19    exit 0 unless $resp =~ /^[yY]/;
20 }
21
22 # ready to copy
23 open SRC, "<$src"
24    or die "failed to open source file\n\t";
25 open TGT, ">$tgt"
26    or die "failed to open target file\n\t";
27 while ($line = <SRC>) {
28    print TGT $line;
29 }
30 close TGT;
31 close SRC;
```

Hopefully, the use of comments in this program makes it easy to understand. You can see in *lines 12-13* where we test to see if the first file named on the command line is a text file. The construct from *lines 16-20* handles the case where we may need to overwrite the target file with our new data.

Once the target file is opened (*lines 25-26*), any data that was once in there will be gone. And you'll note that in *line 30*, we opt to close the target file first. We need to get that file closed so that it won't be corrupted, and if some unforeseen difficulty arises when we close the source file, we would like to know that the target file is already okay.

Because the program takes a plodding and simpleminded approach to the task, it is easy to read. Take a look at this next example. Don't write your own programs like this, but see if you can follow along with what it does.

PCP_BAD.PL
```
1 #!/usr/bin/perl
2 open TGT, ">" . pop;
3 print TGT while (<>);
```

This program makes a lot of assumptions, and works as long as the program operator gives it a completely perfect command line. Let's break it down. In the second line, we open a filehandle (TGT) by using pop() to get the last element from its default source (@ARGV). That value is appended to the ">" symbol to indicate that the file should be open for writing. The print() statement then feeds the filehandle with the content of the default variable ($_) as long as something can be read into it with the diamond operator (<>). No error checking takes place and the program depends upon the fact that the filehandle will be closed upon exit.

Don't write code of your own like this, but be sure that you can decipher it when someone else exhibits this sort of bad judgment.

b) Write an operator log program (olog.pl) that can open its log file for appending, prompt the program operator for a log entry, and then append the information to the log file.

Answer: Here is a short program that meets the specs.

OLOG.PL
```
 1 #!/usr/bin/perl
 2
 3 $logfile = "olog.txt";
 4 $now = gmtime(time);
 5 print "Type in the log information.\n";
 6 print "Use ~s on a line by itself to finish.\n";
 7 while (<STDIN>) {
 8    last if /^~s/;
 9    $msg .= $_;
10 }
11 open LOG, ">>$logfile" or die "Failed to open $logfile\n\t";
12 print LOG "$now\n$msg\n\n";
13 close LOG;
```

**LAB
9.3**

Without adding too much code, we were actually able to add a nice feature. In *line 4*, we grab the current system time. The prompts in *lines 5-6* and the loop that gathers input from the operator in *lines 7-10* probably don't contain any surprises for you at this point.

The log file is opened in *line 11*, and then a simple `print()` statement puts the information into the file (*line 12*).

c) Update the `itodo2.pl` program to allow it to write the tasklist data out to a file, and extend the definition of the login database so that certain login identities can be allowed to see the entire task list and add new users.

 Answer: The new program (`itodo3.pl`*) is reproduced entirely here as a foundation. As we enhance it further, this will be the reference point for changes.*

 Note that you will need the support files—todo.tasks, and todo.users. You may create these files manually, or you can get a complete collection of support files for this project from the companion website.

ITODO3.PL
```
 1 #!/usr/bin/perl
 2 # get them to login
 3 print "login: ";
 4 chomp ($uname = <STDIN>);
 5 print "password: ";
 6 chomp ($passwd = <STDIN>);
 7
 8 # validate username/password pair
```

```
 9 $validated = 0;
10     # open user data file
11 open (UDATA, "todo.users")
12     || die "couldn't open user data file.";
13     # read user data, looking for the login name
14 while ($line = <UDATA>) {
15     chomp $line;
16     ($name, $pass, $sup) = split /:/, $line;
17     next unless $uname eq $name;
18     ($validated = 1, last) if $pass eq $passwd;
19 }
20 close UDATA;
21 die "Unknown login\n\t" unless $validated;
22
23 # get existing task data
24 open (TDATA, "todo.tasks")
25     || die "couldn't open task data file\n\t";
26 @tlist = <TDATA>; #slurp!
27 close TDATA;
28
29 $done = 0;
30 until ($done) {
31     # time for a menu
32     print "
33         1) Report all of your tasks
34         2) Add a task to the list
35         3) List everyone's tasks
36         9) Quit
37
38         Which? ";
39     chomp ($_ = <STDIN>);
40 SWITCH: {
41         /^[1Rr]/ && do {
42             foreach $t (@tlist) {
43                 print "$t" if $t =~ /^$uname/;
44             }
45             last SWITCH;
46         };
47         /^[2Aa]/ && do {
48             print "Enter a description of the new task: ";
49             chomp ($newtask = <STDIN>);
50             print "Enter a priority for the new task (1-9): ";
51             $priority = <STDIN>;
52             $newitem = join ':', ($uname, $newtask, $priority);
53             push @tlist, $newitem;
```

```
54          # this loop writes out the file
55          open OUT, ">todo.tasks"
56             or die "Couldn't open task file\n\t";
57          foreach $line (@tlist) {
58             print OUT "$line";
59          }
60          close OUT;
61          last SWITCH;
62       };
63       /^[3Ll]/ && do {
64          foreach $line (@tlist) {
65             unless ($sup || (split /:/, $line)[0] eq $uname) {
66                $line =~ tr/a-zA-Z/n-za-mN-ZA-M/;
67                print "$line";
68                $line =~ tr/a-zA-Z/n-za-mN-ZA-M/;
69             }
70             else {
71                print "$line";
72             }
73
74          }
75          last SWITCH;
76       };
77       /^[9Qq]/ && do {
78          $done = 1;
79          last SWITCH;
80       };
81    }
82 }
```

The code that validates logins has been changed from the previous version. In *lines 8-21*, the user login data file is read line-by-line in an attempt to locate the name and password provided by the program operator. Because the information is needed only at the beginning of the program, it would be inefficient to read the file into a hash to use it only once.

The next noteworthy change in the program is in the case for adding a new task to the data table (*lines 47-62*). This is updated to allow the data to be written to a file (*lines 55-62*).

With "the hood open" on this program, a minor change was made to the case that lists all of the data items (*lines 63-76*). Now the items that belong to the person who is logged in will be shown in plain text, and the others will be lightly shrouded by doing a rot-13 on them. It's not really encryption, but it keeps casual eyes from accidentally encountering private information.

The addition of code in *line 16* to read a "supervisor" flag makes it possible to have the supervisor logins see all of the data in plain text. In a future revision, we'll extend the menu and add another case to facilitate the addition of new people to the user database.

9.3.2 ANSWERS

a) Write a program that can send a mail message using `mailx(1)`, `mail(1)`, `elm(1)`, or another mail client that can be run from the command line.

Answer: This program meets the requirements in the most basic way.

NOTIFY.PL
```
 1 #!/usr/bin/perl
 2 open MSG, "|mailx -s notification person\@mailbox.org"
 3    or die "Couldn't open pipe to mail client\n\t";
 4 print MSG qq{
 5    This is a test notice to tell you that you are
 6    being notified by email. You may be notified
 7    on a test basis again in the future. Had this
 8    been an actual notice, it would have had meaningful
 9    content.
10 };
11 close MSG;
```

There are really only two things here worthy of note, and they are both in *line 2*. The first is the demonstration of how to open a filehandle on a pipline that writes output to another program.

The other is more subtle. You'll note that there is an escaped character in the e-mail address for the `mailx(1)` command line. If we don't do this, the hostname from the e-mail address will appear to be the name of an array and Perl will become terribly confused.

b) Write a program (`tartoc.pl`) that can read the directory of a
gzip(1) compressed tar file.

Answer: This program illustrates one way you could go about doing this job. (Beware that your version of tar may produce a table of contents with a different format. If so, then you may need to modify this program to match the output from your version.)

TARTOC.PL

```
1  #!/usr/bin/perl
2
3  =datasample
4  -rw-r--r-- agentv/everyone  312 1999-02-06 11:07 olog.pl
5  -rw-r--r-- agentv/everyone  263 1999-02-06 11:06 olog.txt
6  drwxr-xr-x agentv/everyone    0 1999-02-06 13:20 todo.d/
7  =cut
8
9  die "usage: $0 tarfilename\n\t"
10    unless defined $ARGV[0];
11 open TOC, "gzip -dc $ARGV[0] | tar tvf - |"
12    or die "Couldn't open input pipe\n\t";
13
14 while ($listing = <TOC>) {
15    ($mode, $sz, $fn) = (split /\s+/, $listing)[0,2,5];
16    # increment accumulator
17    ++$rpt{'total'};
18    # check for largest file
19    if ($sz > $rpt{'max'}) {
20        $rpt{'max'} = $sz;
21        $rpt{'biggest'} = $fn;
22    }
23    # is it a directory?
24    ++$rpt{'dirs'} if $mode =~ /^d/;
25 }
26 close TOC;
27
28 print "tar filename: $ARGV[0]\n";
29 print "total number of files: $rpt{'total'}\n";
30 print "largest component file name: $rpt{'biggest'}\n";
31 print "largest component file size: $rpt{'max'}\n";
32 print "number of directories: $rpt{'dirs'}\n";
```

This program begins by showing a sample of the data that will be read from the pipe (*lines 3-7*). The technique of using a false POD instruction allows us to paste reference information straight into the program. This is a big help to the programmer who can then look at the format of the data as the code is being written.

In *lines 11-12,* we can see how the pipe is opened for input. (If the archive were originally created with the UNIX compress(1) program, it would have a filename extension of ".z" and you could simply substitute the command "compress" where it now says "gzip" without changing anything else.)

Each data line read from the pipe is split up in *line 15* and the next few lines analyze the information, updating the appropriate elements of a hash (%rpt) that keeps track of the statistics we'll need.

The program wraps up in *lines 28-32* by printing the statistics collected during the analysis. You can use this program as a model for any task that requires you to analyze a stream of information that comes from a program. (Common examples are sar(1), ps(1), truss(1), snoop(1), and crash(1).)

   c)   Write a program (cmplog.pl) that can both read and write a compressed log file.

   Answer: Here's one way you might write this program.

CMPLOG.PL

```
 1  #!/usr/bin/perl
 2  @cookies = (
 3     "Never pet a burning dog!",
 4     "There's too much blood in my caffeine system.",
 5     "Never eat anything bigger than your head.",
 6     "A flashlight is a case for holding dead batteries.",
 7     "Give me ambiguity or give me something else."
 8  );
 9
10  # read compressed log file
11  open CLOG, "gzip -dc cmplog.gz |"
12     or die "couldn't open logfile for reading\n\t";
13  @loglines = <CLOG>;
14  close CLOG;
15
16  # produce simulated log entries
17  $now = time;
18  foreach $t (1..10) {
```

```
19    $line = $now+$t . ":" . $cookies[rand (1000) % 4] . "\n";
20    push @loglines, $line;
21 }
22
23 # write it back to the log
24 open CLOG, "|gzip -c >cmplog.gz"
25    or die "couldn't open logfile for writing\n\t";
26 foreach $line (@loglines) {
27    print CLOG $line;
28 }
29 close CLOG;
```

The specification for this program left a lot of latitude, so your program probably looks very different. Let's look at how this one works.

An array is set up in *lines 2-7* simply to give us simulated log entries. The existing logfile is read in to an array called @loglines (*lines 10-13*). A loop (*lines 17-20*) runs 10 times, pushing a new entry onto the array each time, and then the whole thing is written back out to a pipe that over-writes the original log (*lines 23-28*).

Keeping a logfile in compressed form means that you can worry a little bit less about how much space it is going to consume. And you can see from this example that it is very easy to maintain a compressed log. (Other programs besides gzip(1) that can help you with this are the UNIX compress(1) program and Info-ZIP's zip/unzip utilities.)

9.3.3 ANSWERS

a)   Rewrite the tartoc.pl program to read sample data from the DATA filehandle. Use a data sample that is rich enough to confirm that the logic of the program is sound.

Answer: Here are the changes you'd make to get this approach to work:

TARTOC2.PL

```
1 #!/usr/bin/perl
2
3 =until_later
4 die "usage: $0 tarfilename\n\t"
5    unless defined $ARGV[0];
6 open TOC, "gzip -dc $ARGV[0] | tar tvf - |"
```

```
 7    or die "Couldn't open input pipe\n\t";
 8
 9 while ($listing = <TOC>) {
10 =cut
11 while ($listing = <DATA>) {
12    # body of this loop doesn't change
13 }
14 =until_later
15 close TOC;
16 =cut
17
18 # report printout remains identical
19
20 __END__
21 -rw-r--r-- agentv/staff 200 1999-02-01 17:09 bigfiles.pl
22 -rw-r--r-- agentv/staff 378 1999-02-06 16:27 notify.pl
23 drw-r--r-- agentv/staff   0 1999-02-02 20:02 tmp/
24 -rw-r--r-- agentv/staff 478 1999-02-02 20:02 dlist.pl
25 -rw-r--r-- agentv/staff 611 1999-02-02 15:00 allinfo.pl
26 -rw-r--r-- agentv/staff 950 1999-02-03 13:38 tus1.pl
27 drwxr-xr-x agentv/staff   0 1999-02-02 15:01 extras/
28 -rw-r--r-- agentv/staff 802 1999-02-02 14:28 manyinfo.pl
29 -rw-r--r-- agentv/staff 470 1999-02-02 14:35 many2info.pl
```

The section that was responsible earlier for opening the pipeline for reading (*lines 4-7*) is now commented out as a block along with the setup for the read loop so that we can use the embedded data instead.

This means that we must remember to comment out the line responsible for closing the pipe (*line 15* in this example). We use the same sort of commenting mechanism on both sections so that it will be easy to search for and remove later, when we're ready to put the code into production.

But there's a better way to do this. We could read the command line to look for a "simulated data" switch to indicate that sample data should be used for this run of the program. If the program detects that switch, it uses the DATA filehandle; otherwise, it opens the pipe and reads from that.

One way to accomplish this is to store the identity of the preferred file-handle in a scalar variable. This code fragment shows how the program would begin:

```
1  #!/usr/bin/perl
2
3  die "usage: $0 tarfilename\n\t"
4     unless defined $ARGV[0];
5  if ($ARGV[0] =~ /^-s$/) {
6     $in = DATA;
7  }
8  else {
9     open TOC, "gzip -dc $ARGV[0] | tar tvf - |"
10        or die "Couldn't open input pipe\n\t";
11     $in = TOC;
12  }
13
14  while ($listing = <$in>) {
```

**LAB
9.3**

In this example, *lines 6 and 11* are used to set $in to refer to the appropriate filehandle. The improvement here is that we can continue to use the sample data for testing, even after the program is thought to be complete. Also, there is no special maintenance work that has to be done to make the program ready for production.

You would need to add this line after the end of the read loop that begins in *line 14*.

```
close $in;
```

b) Write a program that validates logins from the To Do List database using the DATA filehandle.

Answer: This program does the trick. It exceeds the requirements by returning a special code for the login identities that are for supervisory privilege.

VALIDATE.PL
```
1  #!/usr/bin/perl
2
3  exit 0 unless defined $ARGV[1];
4  $nm = shift; $pw = shift;
5  while (<DATA>) {
6     ($n, $p, $s) = split /:/;
7     next unless $nm eq $n;
```

```
 8    next if $pw ne $p;
 9    exit 2 if $s >= 1; # it's a supervisor
10    exit 1; # it's a regular login
11 }
12 exit 0; # no matching login/password pair
13
14 __END__
15 larry:lingo:1
16 tom:tonic:1
17 ellie:plasma:0
18 randal:effort:0
```

Moving this code into a program by itself makes things a lot easier. Now both the command-line and interactive programs can use the same code and the same data. And if you decide to change the program so that the password information is shrouded (or even encrypted), you will have to make changes to one program only. The programs that depend on this one will be oblivious to design changes as long as the interface remains constant.

In order to use this program now, the code that calls it will look like this:

```
system "validate.pl larry lingo";
die "Sorry\n\t" unless $?; # die if return code was zero
$super if $? >= 2; # supervisor (or better) privilege
```

Three lines where we once had about 10.

LAB 9.3 REVIEW QUESTIONS

1) Which of the following examples shows the correct use of the `open()` function when used to open a file for reading?
   a) _____ `IN = open $fname, "r+";`
   b) _____ `open IN, "<$fname" && die "failed opening file";`
   c) _____ `open IN, "$fname" || die "failed opening file;`
   d) _____ `open IN, ">$fname" || die "failed opening file;`

2) To open a file for appending, which of these lines you would use?
   a) _____ `open LOG, ">>$fname" || die "no log file";`
   b) _____ `open LOG, "<<$fname" || die "no log file";`
   c) _____ `LOG = open ">>$fname", "a+" || die "no log file";`
   d) _____ `open LOG, ">$fname" || die "no log file";`

3) True or False? To open a filehandle for reading from a process pipeline, the following code would work:

```
open (PIPE, "ls -1 |") || die "no log file";
```

   a) _____ True
   b) _____ False

4) What will the following code accomplish?

```
open (PIPE,
   "|gzip -c |uuencode bigmsg.gz|mailx -s qq{bigmsg} root")
   || die "no log file";
```

   a) _____ It opens an output filehandle to create a file called `bigmsg.gz` if it succeeds.
   b) _____ It opens an input filehandle to read the compressed content of a file called bigmsg.gz if it exists.
   c) _____ It opens an output filehandle to create a compressed file and then encodes it for transport by mail to the root user.
   d) _____ It doesn't work, so it accomplishes nothing.

5) When information is read from the DATA filehandle, where does that information come from?

    a) _____ It reads from a file called `data.db` if it exists; otherwise from a file called `data.txt`.

    b) _____ It reads from any lines in the file after the __END__ marker.

    c) _____ It reads from the database file tied to the filehandle.

    d) _____ It creates a link to the neural network of any Starfleet android in the sector.

Quiz answers appear in Appendix A, Section 9.3.

CHAPTER 9

TEST YOUR THINKING

1) In Lab 9.1, we saw a program (`dirlist2.pl`) that can read the contents of a directory and report many of the details about each file and directory there. It works very much like the `ls(1)` program already. From what we learned in this chapter, you should be able to write a program (`dirlist3.pl`) that can produce output like that of the command "ls -l" when given a directory name.

```
$ dirlist3.pl .
drwxr-xr-x   3    504    1000      1024 02/27 06:15 .
drwxr-xr-x   3    504    1000      1024 02/03 20:13 ..
-rwxr--r--   1    504    1000       707 02/03 20:21 dirlist2.pl
-rwxr--r--   1    504    1000       610 02/02 15:01 all2info.pl
-rwxr-xr-x   1    504    1000      1233 02/27 06:15 dirlist3.pl
drwxr-xr-x   2    504    1000      1024 02/27 05:42 junkdir
```

2) The "safe rm" program (`srm.pl`) and the companion undelete program (`unsrm.pl`) still need some enhancements. Create a production version of these two programs, each of which works with a hidden `.wastebasket` directory.

Change `srm.pl` so that it supports a single option, "`-f`", which can suppress the prompting for confirmation on every file. Change `unsrm.pl` so that it works with the hidden `.wastebasket` directory scheme. The program should offer a prompt for any deleted files, and, if necessary, place them back in the original directory.

3) It's time to tie together the pieces of Barber Tom's "To Do List" program suite. Let's get everything into four files. The programs `todo2000.pl` and `td2.pl` will provide the interactive and command-line interfaces, respectively. The program `validate.pl` is used to check login information, and the task data itself is to be kept in `todo.tasks`.

In particular, make sure that the td2.pl program can support the following command-line model:

```
td2.pl name password [-r | -1 | -a "task:priority"]
```

Default behavior is to report on the tasks for the logged user. The -r option does the same thing explicitly. The -1 option lists all tasks in the database. The -a option allows a new task to be added.

C H A P T E R 10

FUNCTIONS: PROGRAMMING IN POLITE SOCIETY

CHAPTER OBJECTIVES

In this chapter, you will learn about:

✓ Declaring and Calling Functions   Page 482

✓ Function Arguments and Return Values   Page 498

✓ Building a Library of Functions   Page 520

You've already used functions extensively in the programming that you've done to get here (chomp(), print(), sort(), splice(), and pop(), among others). This chapter is about getting you to write your own functions. We'll learn about using functions (subroutines, procedures, or methods—whatever you want to call them) to isolate bits of code so that they can be reused without replication.

You see, an unschooled programmer rewrites the same code over and over again. Novice programmers at least cut and paste, taking some advantage of their previous efforts. Journeyman programmers write functions that can be reused directly. (Master programmers build reusable objects, and you can do that in Perl, but *that* discussion will have to wait for another book.)

In Perl, a function is a procedure (a group of program instructions) that is given a name so that you can execute it from many different places in your program. When you design a function well, you can even use it from within different programs.

L A B   10.1

WRITING AND EXECUTING FUNCTIONS

LAB OBJECTIVES

After this Lab, you will be able to:

✓ Declare and Call a Function

✓ Call a Function That Updates Variables

This Lab will show you everything you need to get started creating and using your own functions in your programs. We'll look at how you declare a function, how you execute it from anywhere in your program, and how you can get your functions to communicate with the programming environment from which they are called.

The first thing you should know is that you can declare a function anywhere in your program file. You can put it at the top, before any other code, or you can put it at the end, after the main portion of the program.

> **The Whole Truth**
>
> Something that doesn't become apparent when you first start working with Perl is that your program is actually read twice. The first time happens as soon as you execute the program. At that time, the code is "compiled" into a representation that Perl can use to execute the instructions more efficiently.
>
> With a few exceptions, none of the instructions are actually executed at this time. Everything just gets read. This is why you'll notice that if you have an error in the last line of the program, none of the earlier instructions run; you just get an error message. The error is encountered and detected before the first instruction can be run.
>
> When your functions are read, they are simply compiled and "remembered" for a later time when you actually call them. This is why you can declare the function at the end of the file, and even if you call it in the first or second line of your program, Perl knows what to do.

LAB
10.1

DECLARE AND CALL A FUNCTION

The name for your function must comply with the standard rules for identifiers in Perl (just like scalars, arrays, hashes, labels, and filehandles). Officially, the name of a function includes an ampersand character (&) at the beginning. We'll learn later that the ampersand is mostly optional in Perl 5, but for the moment, let's treat it as a firm rule.

The syntax for declaring a function looks like this:

```
sub function_name {
    # body of the function
}
```

When you are ready to use the instructions that form the body of the function, you simply call it like this:

```
&function_name();
```

Where this line falls in your main program, the appropriate instructions are run. Let's see this in practice.

■ *FOR EXAMPLE*

We've often had to print a message in our programs that shows the program syntax. Let's see how a function could help us with that.

UFUNCTION.PL
```
 1 #!/usr/bin/perl
 2 # function declarations
 3 sub usage {
 4    print STDERR "usage: $0 sourcefile targetfile\n";
 5    exit -1;
 6 }
 7 # main program begins
 8 &usage() unless defined $ARGV[1];
 9 print "Legal command-line was detected\n";
10 exit 0;
```

This program doesn't do much by itself, but you can see clearly here how we might declare and call a function. The other thing you can see is a secondary reason for defining a function. Even if we plan to call this procedure from one place only, when we isolate it, and refer to it with an intelligible name, we can make the main body of the program more readable. Look at how clean *line* 8 has become when compared with our earlier programs.

One side note about something that we see here that hasn't really come up before. In past examples, we've been using the die() function to print a message and exit the program. Here you'll note that we print the message to the STDERR filehandle. This is the proper thing to do with error messages. The die() and warn() functions do this automatically, so we don't worry about it most of the time. When you print error messages the way we do here, you should remember that STDERR is the proper destination. That way, even if ordinary output from the program has been redirected, any warnings will appear on the operator's terminal screen, as you would wish.

AMPERSANDS AND PARENTHESES: WHO NEEDS 'EM?

In our last example, we saw that a function can be called from the main program like this:

```
&usage() unless defined $ARGV[1];
```

That's the absolute, simple way to use a function. It works in Perl 4 and Perl 5. There's a certain convenience to it. Functions defined in the standard library don't have a leading ampersand, but programmer-defined functions do. (It helps us know at a glance who should be blamed for what happens when the function runs.)

In Perl 5, though, your programmer-defined functions can be called the same way as standard library functions. When you want to call them, you don't have to use an ampersand unless you feel like it. You could change that previous line to read:

```
usage() unless defined $ARGV[1];
```

This makes things a little bit less noisy. Believe me, as your programs grow more complex, the fewer unnecessary curlicues you use, the happier you'll be in general. But that invites another question.

Remember this line from a previous program?

```
foreach $item (reverse sort keys %hashname) {
```

Those standard library functions can be called without using parentheses. Can our programmer-defined functions work the same way? In a word, yes!

```
usage unless defined $ARGV[1];
```

Whether or not it's wise to omit the parentheses here is something that you'll have to decide for yourself. Leaving them in makes it clear to the human reader that the token ("usage" in this case) is the name of a function. Taking them out makes the line a little easier to read as a sentence. Certainly in the "reverse sort keys" example we saw earlier, it is handy to omit them.

FUNCTIONS AND PROGRAM VARIABLES

Because Perl is more inclined to offer guidelines instead of "rules," you might guess that a variable in your program will naturally be seen by functions in the same program. (There are ways to prevent this, or to work around it. In general, however, a variable can be seen, and changed, everywhere in your program.) We might say that the "scope" of a variable is naturally global.

This means that your function can alter the value stored in any variable that hasn't been explicitly hidden from view. While this is not the best way, it's one way that a function can communicate with its calling program.

■ FOR EXAMPLE

Here's a program that illustrates the concept.

VARTRAMPLE1.PL
```
1 #!/usr/bin/perl
2 $var = 100;
3 print "At first, \$var is: $var\n"; # prints 100
4 trample();
5 print "Afterward, \$var is: $var\n"; # prints 200
6
7 sub trample {
8    $var = 200;
9 }
```

The comments in *lines 3* and *5* hint at how this program will behave. This approach can be convenient in short casual programs, but we'll need a better mechanism for functions to use to send information back to "the world." Look for that mechanism in Lab 10.2, where we talk about function *return values*.

For now, we can take advantage of Perl's "free range approach" to variable scoping with one more example.

MAKEARRAY.PL
```
1 #!/usr/bin/perl
2
3 # main program -- check syntax
4 usage() unless defined $ARGV[0];
5 $dir = shift;
6 $, = ":"; # array separator
7
8 # run the function, then print the array it creates
9 d2array();
```

```
10 foreach $item (@dlist) {
11    print $item, (stat "$dir/$item")[8,9,10], "\n";
12 }
13 # end of main program
14
15 # prints usage information
16 sub usage {
17    print STDERR "usage: $0 directoryname\n";
18    exit -1;
19 }
20 # reads directory into array
21 sub d2array {
22    opendir INDIR, $dir
23       or die "couldn't open directory $dir\n\t";
24    @dlist = readdir INDIR;
25    close INDIR;
26 }
```

This program requires some attention to read. You'll have to jump around a bit. The main program only runs from *lines 4-12*. It checks the command line (*line 4*), grabs the first argument (*line 5*), calls the d2array() function (*line 9*), and then prints out the array (in *lines 10-12*) created by the function.

The function itself is interesting for two reasons. It can obviously see the $dir variable created in the main program (*line 5*). It creates an array (@dlist in *line 24*) that can be seen by the main program in *line 10*.

Again, this is not a good way to write all of your programs, but for the simple and short ones, it's very handy. Now let's see what you can do with this.

LAB 10.1 EXERCISES

10.1.1 DECLARE AND CALL A FUNCTION

a) Write a program (threeargs.pl) that contains a syntax_check() function. The function should test for the presence of three arguments and exit with a syntax message if they're not all present. The third argument should be the name of a directory, and if it is not, the function should print out a different message and then exit.

_____

_____

b) Write a program (threefns.pl) based on threeargs.pl. The command line should be identical, but this time, there must be three functions. The syntax_check() function should be as before, but if it detects that there are not three arguments, it should call another function, usage(), which prints out the syntax message and exits. If the third argument is not the name of a directory, a different function called nodir() should be called so that it can print out an appropriate message and exit.

_____

_____

c) Write a program with an arraydump() function that prints out the contents of an array named @tablet. Initialize the array and call the function, then read the contents of a file into the array and call the function again.

_____

_____

10.1.2 CALL A FUNCTION THAT UPDATES VARIABLES

It's time to return to the ushell.pl program for some more work. We're pretty close to being ready to finish this now. We need to break it into pieces to make it easier to maintain. In this iteration, we want to write a total of five functions. One should print the menu and get a response from the operator. It should then call one of the other four functions. They should support the four menu options (List, View, Delete, and Rename).

a) Write a new update to the `ushell.pl` program to have the five functions discussed here.

_____

_____

b) Now update your program to include a new menu option for editing a file. Fix the menu, add an option in the switch to support the new activity, and add the function that implements the actual code to call the editor.

If you are working from your own custom version of the program, go ahead and modify yours first. Then take the solution to the last Lab exercise and modify that as well. Having done both, decide which one is easier to update and maintain.

_____

_____

Uncle Larry closed his curtains and unplugged the telephone from the wall. He was ready to write the newest piece in his Storyteller program. This would be a story editor. Using his `cfg_story.pl` *program as a foundation, he would now break things into functions and make the program much more flexible.*

This version of the program would read the configuration information from a file as before. It would also read the base story from a file. (Both files could be named on the command line or use program defaults.) The tricky part to this proposition was that he would no longer place scalar variable references straight into the program text. Instead, he would use tokens that looked like this:

```
+CREATURE+
```

When the story was actually going to be shown, those tokens would have to be translated into the words stored in a hash called `%pluggables`.

The new part would be an editor. It would implement several commands, dump, list, add, insert, stats, and save. The dump command would show the entire story on screen. The list command would show only one line of the story. The add and insert commands would allow a new line to be put into the story. The stats command would print information about the story, such as number of lines and "pluggable" story components in use. And the save command would write the story to a file.

c) Update Uncle Larry's Storyteller program with the new story editor. Implement all of the functions described in the discussion.

LAB 10.1 EXERCISE ANSWERS

10.1.1 ANSWERS

a) Write a program (`threeargs.pl`) that contains a `syntax_check()` function.

Answer: This is one way to write that program.

THREEARGS.PL
```
1 #!/usr/bin/perl
2 syntax_check();
3 print "We made it!  Main program begins\n";
4
5 sub syntax_check {
6    die "usage: $0 arg1 arg2 directoryname\n\t"
7       unless defined $ARGV[2];
8    die "$ARGV[2] is not a directory!\n\t"
9       unless
10 }
```

Actually, there aren't that many ways to write this program differently. You can put the function (defined in *lines 5-10*) at the beginning instead of at the end. You could use different messages, or a different way or printing the messages.

Perhaps you would like to exit with a different exit code, depending upon the type of problem. (That would be a perfectly reasonable thing to want to do.) You could rewrite the `die()` statement in *lines 6 and 7* to look like this:

```
unless (defined $ARGV[2]) {
    warn "usage: $0 arg1 arg2 directoryname\n\t";
    exit -1;
}
```

Then rewrite the other statement to use an exit value of `-2` and you'd be in business.

b) Write a program (`threefns.pl`) based on `threeargs.pl`. The command line should be identical, but this time, there must be three functions.

Answer: Here is one way to write that program.

THREEFNS.PL
```
1  #!/usr/bin/perl
2  syntax_check();
3  print "We made it!  Main program begins\n";
4
5  sub syntax_check {
6      usage() unless defined $ARGV[2];
7      nodir() unless -d $ARGV[2];
8  }
9
10 sub usage {
11     warn "usage: $0 arg1 arg2 directoryname\n\t";
12     exit -1;
13 }
14
15 sub nodir {
16     warn "Whoa there!  $ARGV[2] is not a directory!\n\t";
17     exit -2;
18 }
```

Again, hopefully there were no big surprises for you in this solution. It is permissible (and common) to call one function from another one. Because we structured things this way, it was also easy to facilitate different exit codes for each failure case.

The problem is mildly contrived, but it does give you a chance to see that you can call functions from within one another. There is no theoretical limit to the depth of your function call stack. If you get too carried away, you may run out of memory, but within reason, you can do whatever you need to do.

c) Write a program with an `arraydump()` function that prints out the contents of an array named `@tablet`.

Answer: This program demonstrates the appropriate behavior.

ARRAYDUMP.PL

```
1 #!/usr/bin/perl
2
3 sub arrayprint {
4    foreach (@tablet) {
5       print;
6    }
7 }
8
9 @tablet = (
10   "When ten to the enemy's one, surround him.\n",
11   "When five times his strength, attack him.\n",
12   "If double his strength, divide him.\n",
13   "If equally matched, you may engage him.\n"
14 );
15
16 arrayprint();
17 open IN, $0 or die "trying"; @tablet = <IN>; close IN;
18 arrayprint();
```

This time we put the function at the beginning (*lines 3-7*). We initialize an array with some well-aged words of wisdom (*lines 9-14*) and then call the function. After that finishes, we open the file that contains the program source code and read that into the array (*line 17*). Then we call the function again to make sure that it notices and responds to the change in the data.

10.1.2 ANSWERS

a) Write a new update to the `ushell.pl` program to have the five functions discussed in the exercise.

Answer: Here's how that program will look now.

U4SHELL.PL

```
 1 #!/usr/bin/perl
 2
 3 # main()
 4 $done = 0;
 5 until ($done) {
 6    menuswitch();
 7 }
 8 print "Thanks for using PerlShell!\n";
 9 # end of main()
10
11 # supporting functions
12 sub menuswitch {
13    print "
14      1) List Files
15      2) View File
16      3) Delete File
17      4) Rename File
18      5) Exit
19
20      Which? ";
21    chomp($_ = <STDIN>);
22 SWITCH: {
23        /^[1Ll]/ && do { listfiles(); last SWITCH; };
24        /^[2Vv]/ && do { viewfile(); last SWITCH; };
25        /^[3Dd]/ && do { deletefile(); last SWITCH; };
26        /^[4Rr]/ && do { renamefile(); last SWITCH; };
27        /^[5QqXx]/ && do { $done = 1; last SWITCH; };
28    }
29 }
30 sub viewfile {
31    print "filename: ";
32    chomp($fn = <STDIN>);
33    system ("cat $fn");
34 }
35 sub listfiles {
36    system ("ls -A");
37    # you could do this more precisely yourself
38 }
39 sub deletefile {
40    print "you chose to delete a file\n";
41    print "filename: "; chomp($fn = <STDIN>);
42    unlink $fn;
43    # you could implement a safe rm here
44 }
```

```
45 sub renamefile {
46    print "you chose to rename a file\n";
47    print "old filename: "; chomp($fn = <STDIN>);
48    print "new filename: "; chomp($newfn = <STDIN>);
49    rename $fn, $newfn;
50 }
```

This is changed a lot from the program we wrote in Chapter 8. The main body of the program now occupies only *lines 4-8*. And even the `menuswitch()` function is a mere shadow of its former self (*lines 12-29*). And half of that is the actual text of the menu.

The switch that processes the operator's choice is so small because all it has to do is to call the appropriate function for the current choice. The actual details of how to implement that choice are left to the component functions.

By separating the code out into these functional pieces, we make it easy to extend the program to perform new tasks, as you'll see in the next exercise.

b)   Now update your program to include a new menu option for editing a file.

Answer: This really doesn't take a lot of code. You'll need a function like this one.

```
1 sub editfile {
2    print "you chose to edit a file\n";
3    print "which file? "; chomp($fn = <STDIN>);
4    # put an appropriate editor here
5    system "vi $fn";
6 }
```

You may need to modify *line 5* to invoke an editor appropriate for your system. (Win32 programmers can use "notepad" here to get the program working.)

You also need to update your menu, of course, and you'll need to modify your switch construct with a line like this one:

```
/^[5Ee]/ && do { editfile(); last SWITCH; };
```

Remember that if you insert a menu item, your switch might need a little more maintenance to make it right. (In other words, if you formerly had an exit option set to menu item number 5, you'll want to make sure that you change it both in the menu and the switch.)

c) Update Uncle Larry's Storyteller program with the new story editor. Implement all of the functions described in the discussion.

Answer: This program is too long to reproduce it its entirety here. The complete program is available on the companion website. Here are some of the important portions.

STORYED.PL (FRAGMENT—MAIN PROGRAM BODY)

```
1  #!/usr/bin/perl
2
3  # main()
4  init();
5  dumpstory();
6  getcmd();
7  # end main()
```

By moving most of the messiest code into functions, we can see the main program flow very clearly here. Essentially, the program reads in the configuration information and the base story (init() in *line 4* of this fragment), dumps the story to screen once, prompts the story maker, and responds to the request (getcmd() in *line 6*).

The main core of the getcmd() function is pretty clean as well. Look at this:

STORYED (FRAGMENT—COMMAND PROCESSOR)

```
1  sub getcmd {
2     until ($done) {
3        print "\nDump List Add Insert Stats Save Quit\n";
4        print "\nWhich? ";
5        chomp($_ = <STDIN>);
6  SWITCH: {
7            /^[Dd]ump/ && do { dumpstory(); last SWITCH };
8            /^[Ll]ist/ && do { listlines(); last SWITCH };
9            /^[Aa]dd/ && do { addlines(); last SWITCH };
10           /^[Ii]nsert/ && do { insertlines(); last SWITCH };
11           /^[Ss]tats/ && do { printstats(); last SWITCH };
12           /^[Ss]ave/ && do { savestory(); last SWITCH };
13           /^[Qq]uit/ && do { $done = 1; last SWITCH };
14        }
15     }
16  }
```

It looks pretty straightforward when the switch can be primarily concerned with executing the correct function. You can probably tell that adding a new option is easy here. Most of the work will be involved in creating the support function.

As for those supporting functions in this program, each one has small challenges that you need to meet. Space limitations prohibit listing all of them here, but below is the one that is responsible for showing the story (dumpstory()). To grasp its meaning, you need to know that the story itself is being kept in an array called @story and the parts of the story that are variable are being supplied from a hash called %pluggables. A scalar variable called $current tracks the active line number.

STORYED.PL (FRAGMENT—STORY DUMP ROUTINE)

```
1 sub dumpstory {
2     $lnumber = 1;
3     foreach (@story) {
4         s/\+([^+]+)\+/$pluggables{$1}/g;
5         printf "%4d: %s\n", $lnumber++, $_;
6     }
7 }
```

That regular expression in *line 4* looks like a mess, but, in essence, it is saying that whenever a word is completely encased in "+" signs, it should be replaced by something looked up in the %pluggables hash, using the encased word as a key.

So if the line contains the word "+KINGDOM+", then that token will be replaced by whatever is stored in $pluggables{KINGDOM}.

Lab 10.1 Review Questions

1) Which of the following is the correct way to declare a function called announce?

   a) _____ `function announce {`

   b) _____ `sub announce () {`

   c) _____ `sub announce {`

   d) _____ `subroutine announce () {`

2) True or False: A function cannot automatically see variables created in the main program.

   a) _____ True

   b) _____ False

3) Which of the following is not a legal way to execute the `announce()` function?

   a) _____ `&announce();`

   b) _____ `announce;`

   c) _____ `run announce();`

   d) _____ `announce();`

4) True or False: A function must be defined in a program before it can be executed.

   a) _____ True

   b) _____ False

   Quiz answers appear in Appendix A, Section 10.1.

L A B 10.2

FUNCTION ARGUMENTS AND RETURN VALUES

LAB OBJECTIVES

After this Lab, you will be able to:

✓ Pass Information to Functions as Arguments

✓ Have Functions Return Information

✓ Localize Variables to Their Function

In this Lab, we learn how to interact with our functions by passing them arguments and having them send back information with the `return()` statement. We also see how we can prevent inadvertent trampling of our global variables by localizing variables to make them available only within the function.

TALKING TO YOUR FUNCTIONS

Because we've been using functions in a lot of our program code, you've already seen that arguments can be passed to a function. The `split()` function is a good example. It can be given a regular expression and a string to split. You might call it in one of the following ways:

```
@tbl = split (/:/, $bigstring);
@tbl = split /:/, $bigstring;
```

Your own functions can be given arguments as well. For instance, the usage() function from our ufunction.pl program could be called in any of the following ways:

```
usage ("message string");
usage ("message string", -1);
usage ("message string", STDERR, -1);
usage "message string", STDERR, -1;
```

The problem is that our function will not automatically notice or do anything with the arguments that are being passed to it. That's easy to fix however. All we need to know is that inside a function there is a special array that contains all of the arguments that have been provided with the function as it was called.

The special array is called @_ and it should not be confused in any way with the default variable, which is called $_. The only relationship between them is that they share the same base name.

So let's see how to rewrite the usage() function to take advantage of the arguments that might be passed in to it.

■ FOR EXAMPLE

We're going to rewrite the function so that it expects a minimum of one argument. That is a message to be printed. If a second argument is present, that will be used as an exit value. A third optional argument will be the filehandle to which the message will be printed.

```
1 sub usage {
2     ($msg, $evalue, $handle) = @_;
3     $evalue = -1 unless defined $evalue;
4     $handle = STDERR unless defined $handle;
5     print $handle "Error: $msg\n";
6     print $handle "usage: $0 source target\n";
7     exit $evalue;
8 }
```

To deal with situations where the optional arguments are not present, *lines 3-4* assign defaults, if necessary. It's interesting to note here that a filehandle value can be saved in a scalar (*line 4*). If you haven't seen that before, I want you to notice it here.

The values that have been passed in to the function (or the defaults) are used in the code for *lines 5-7*. From this, you can see that it's easy to send information to functions, even when you want to leave a lot of flexibility.

FUNCTIONS THAT TALK BACK

We've seen that it's no problem to put information into a function, so how can it send information back to the calling program? Well, there are two answers to this: the easy one, and the easy one.

The first is related to something we've already seen. We saw in the last Lab that the "scope" of a variable is naturally global. The `vartrample1.pl` program used a function to change the value of a variable that was defined in the main program.

So one easy way for a function to communicate with the "outside world" is to simply have it alter data structures directly. But it's not the best way. If our function depends upon the existence of an array called `@story`, or a string scalar variable called `$name`, that function can work only in the exact context for which it is built. It destroys the modularity that you can achieve when you build functions correctly. We need a mechanism that can pass information back without playing blindly with global data structures.

That mechanism is provided in the form of the `return()` statement. Your function can use it to return a scalar value, a list, or even a hash.

■ *FOR EXAMPLE*

The return statement can be used in a number of ways:

```
return 100; # returns a scalar literal
return "Bob was here"; # a scalar string is okay too
return $info; # no problem if you want to send a variable
return @tbl; # an array is easy enough
return qw{bob carol ted alice}; # a list is okay
return %wordlist; # send a hash at no extra charge
return ("one", 1, "two", 2); # array or hash?  you decide
```

Your function can return data in any of the forms that you see in these examples. There are probably a couple of ways we left out, too. So this is the careful way for your function to present data that has been created or changed.

The final example is a bit intriguing. Is that an array or a hash being passed back? It really depends upon what you do with it when you get it.

WELL THEN, HOW DO YOU...

How do you get it anyway? The data that is returned from a function can be stored in a variable with a simple assignment statement, or it can be put directly into a context that needs the sort of data that the function delivers.

■ *FOR EXAMPLE*

Here are some examples of lines that call the hypothetical functions containing the `return()` statements shown previously:

```
$num = fn1(); # scalar literal
printf "%s\n", fn2(); # scalar string
$value = fn3(); # some scalar variable
foreach $item (fn4()) { # they sent an array
@names = fn5(); # they sent a list
@index = keys (fn6()); # this was a hash, keys gives a list
%comp = fn7(); # treat it as a hash
@comp = fn7(); # treat it as a list
```

Actually, this is no different from what you've been doing all along. That's how it is with Perl (or a spoken natural language). You sometimes find out that you've been doing the right thing from the start without necessarily having to learn the technical reasons about why it works.

Let's take one more crack at this with a short example.

BIGGEST.PL (A FUNCTION ONLY)
```
sub biggest {
   $largest = 0;
   foreach $n (@_) {
```

```
        $largest = $largest > $n ? $largest : $n;
    }
    return $largest;
}
```

Here's an example of code that would call the function:

```
$max = biggest ($v1, $v2, $v3);
```

LOCAL TRAFFIC ONLY—USING my AND local

We need to talk about protecting the integrity of global variables. In the first Lab of this chapter, we wrote a function (in the program array-dump.pl) that displayed the content of a global array called @tablet. If you looked at the complete code for storyed.pl, you saw that most of the functions manipulate a global array called @story.

We know now that there's no reason to work like this. In both programs, we can pass the array to any function when we're ready to use it. But there's another problem we have to solve. In the last example, we saw a function that uses a variable called $largest. What happens if the main program that calls this function has its own notion of the value that should be stored in a scalar called $largest? We already know the answer to that from seeing the vartramplel.pl program. The function will overwrite any value in the variables with the names it chooses. It's somewhat easy to manage all this if your main program and all of the functions are in the same source code file. But if some functions are in a separate file, you can't easily tell if your new variable names will trample an important pre-existing variable.

There are two ways to prevent this. They involve the use of the modifier keywords my (for lexical scoping) and local (for dynamic scoping). If you're interested only in the pragmatic basics about these, forget about terms like lexical scoping and dynamic scoping, just remember this rule of thumb.

You should probably use my *instead of* local *to limit the scope of your variables because* my *variables are faster and safer.*

To get a handle on this business of scoping, think about these three cases:

1. If you declare a variable by simply mentioning it and using it, the variable is global and it can be seen from anywhere in the program any time after this, inside or outside of the function where you declare it. (It's permanent and global.)
2. If you declare a variable to be `local`, it can be seen from anywhere within the scope of the function or program block where it is declared. If another function is called from within that scope, the variable will still be visible. (It's dynamically global.)
3. If you declare a variable to be `my`, it will be visible only from within its enclosing scope, no further. If you call a subordinate function, the variable will not be visible. (It's lexically local.)

Let's see an example of what it takes to scope a variable with these tools. We'll focus on `my` because that is what you'll probably need to use most. The syntax for the `local` modifier is similar.

■ FOR EXAMPLE

To declare a variable (or variables) to be `my`, you simply modify the name of the variable the first time you use it. If you plan to do several variables at once, you should enclose them in parentheses. (This can also serve as a list operator, if it's convenient.)

```
my $name;
my $name = "Ranger Bill";
my ($n1, $n2, $n3);
my ($f1, $f2, $f3) = @ARGV;
my @table;
my %namelist;
```

Any of these approaches will work to keep your function variables under control. As your programs grow and become more complex, this will become increasingly important. In fact, let's start right now with the rule that unless you have a compelling reason to do otherwise, all variables used in a function should be scoped as `my` variables.

LAB 10.2 EXERCISES

10.2.1 PASS INFORMATION TO FUNCTIONS AS ARGUMENTS

a) Write a function that takes a string as an argument, and then checks to see if the string is the name of a directory. The function should print a message indicating whether the provided string is, or is not, a directory.

_____

_____

We saw in the Lab discussion how it is legal to pass an array or a hash to a function as easily as a scalar value. Well, there is a little bit of a surprise that you may encounter if you are careless. Take a look at the following program and see if you can guess what it will print. (Beware, many experienced Perl programmers would go down in flames over this one.)

ARGSMASH.PL

```
1 #!/usr/bin/perl
2
3 @folks = qw{Will Samuel Woody Chet};
4 # We know what $folks[0] is right now
5 print "First folk is: $folks[0]\n";
6 smash(@folks);
7 # Do we know what $folks[0] is now?
8 print "First folk is: $folks[0]\n";
9
10 sub smash {
11     $_[0] = "Emmylou";
12 }
```

Hopefully, with all the foreshadowing there, you guessed that "Will" would turn into "Emmylou." The fact is, when you're looking at @_, you're looking at the original data, not a copy of the data contents. You shouldn't make changes to the contents of the argument list directly unless you mean for those changes to stick.

This is another compelling reason to be sure to grab a copy of the arguments at the beginning of your function.

> **b)** Write two functions, one that takes an array or list as its argument and prints the contents, and another that takes a hash as an argument and prints the content.

_____

_____

10.2.2 HAVE FUNCTIONS RETURN INFORMATION

> **a)** Write a function (`cookiemaker()`) that returns a string chosen at random from an array of sayings.

_____

_____

When a function tries to do something that fails, it is a good idea to return a value that indicates a failure of some sort. The trick to this (maybe the art to this) is that you cannot return something that looks like a normal response from the function. If your function is supposed to return a string, it might seem clever to return the value **99** to indicate failure. The headlines have been filled recently by stories about the work of programmers who took that misguided approach.

It is not uncommon to return an actual value (like `-1`) that indicates a failed operation when the response is both well-documented and carefully chosen. But Perl offers us a choice that will seldom go wrong. We have the "value" `undef`, which is similar to zero, but cannot be confused with the numeric value that means "nothing."

In almost all cases, your function should return `undef` when things don't work out and you need for the calling program to be aware of the failure. The next exercise will show you how this turns out to be doubly convenient.

b) Write a function that takes two filenames as arguments and is designed to return a number indicating the difference in bytes between the first and the second file. Return `undef` if either filename does not exist.

The number that should be returned is the number of bytes by which the first file would have to change to be identical in size to the second file. For example, if the first file is 200 bytes and the second one is 170 bytes, the return value should be -30.

_____

_____

c) Write a function that returns a list of files from a directory named in the first argument. It should return `undef` if the argument is not a directory name. If a second argument is provided, it should be used as a filename filter.

For example, if the function is called as `flist( "/tmp/projects", "*.html")`, then all of the files from that directory with an `html` extension should be included in the returned list.

_____

_____

10.2.3 LOCALIZE VARIABLES TO THEIR FUNCTION

In the following program, a global scalar variable ($mval) is set to a fixed number. Two functions are called, each of which creates its own privately scoped variable with the same name. Upon return from a call to each of the functions, the global variable is printed out again to ensure that its value remains unchanged.

Read the following program and try to anticipate what will happen when you run it.

NOTRAMPLE.PL

```
1 #!/usr/bin/perl
2
3 $mval = 127;
4 print "Start: mval is: $mval\n";
5 myvarset ();
6 print "After myvarset(): mval is: $mval\n";
7 localvarset();
8 print "After localvarset(): mval is: $mval\n";
9 print "That's all folks!\n";
10
11 sub myvarset {
12     my $mval = 256;
13     print "inside myvarset(): mval is: $mval\n";
14 }
15 sub localvarset {
16     local $mval = 512;
17     print "Inside localvarset(): mval is: $mval\n";
18 }
```

LAB
10.2

a) Inside the functions `localvarset()` and `myvarset()`, is the global value of $mval visible?

_____

_____

Add a new function (`underneath()`) to the program that illustrates the difference between dynamic and lexically scoped localization. The new function should simply print out the value of $mval. Have each of the existing functions call the new function.

b) When `underneath()` is called from `myvarset()`, is the original value of $mval used? How about from `localvarset()`?

_____

_____

You now have enough information to start putting the finishing touches on the `ushell.pl` program. The next two exercises will have you build function components that comprise the final elements you'll need to have built a comprehensive tool.

> **c)** Build a line editor function that can handle editing for reasonable-size files (that is, if it can edit a file of 2000 lines, that's good enough for this project).
>
> The function will expect a filename as an argument. It should open the file and slurp the contents into a buffer. This editor should normally add new lines at the end of the buffer, but must also support functions to delete, modify, and list lines from the edit buffer. Lines that begin with the tokens ~d, ~m, and ~l can indicate the commands.

_____

_____

Now, one more function you'll need is one that can present lengthy output in pages, when there's more than a screenful. (The UNIX utilities pg(1), more(1), and less(1) do this nicely, but you'll need a function of your own to do some of those things.)

> **d)** Build a paging function that can take a number (that represents screen size) and an array. It should present the number of elements from the array that it takes to "fill the screen."
>
> We can use the assumption that the array will be filled with lines of text that contain their own newline characters. So if the screen size is 24, then the function should present 23 elements and then offer a prompt that waits for further instructions. (Return can mean fill another screen, the minus sign means go backward by one screenful.)
>
> If the last element in the array has been displayed, there is no reason to prompt further. The function can exit.

_____

_____

LAB 10.2 EXERCISE ANSWERS

10.2.1 ANSWERS

a)   Write a function that takes a string as an argument and then checks to see if that string is the name of a directory.

> *Answer:We have given you two versions so you can look at some variations.*

```
1 sub isdir {
2    my $dirname = $_[0]; # arglist, not default variable
3    my $isword = -d $dirname ? "" : "not";
4    print "$dirname is $isword a directory\n";
5 }
6
7 sub isdir2 {
8    my $dirname = shift @_;
9    # @_ is actually the default here
10   # my $dirname = shift; # also legal
11   printf "%s is %s a directory\n", $dirname,
12       -d $dirname ? "" : "not";
13 }
```

The first version of the function declares and populates a variable ($dirlist) in *line 2*. Be careful to note that $_[0] is not related to $_. The former is element 0 of an array called @_ and the latter is the default variable.

Next, we have to determine whether the string is the name of a directory. That drives how we will form the message to be printed.

In the second variant (*lines 7-13*), we see a more elegant approach to the same problem. *Line 8* grabs the first element of the argument list by using shift(), which naturally operates on the argument list by default when it is used in a function. The cleanest line to use would have actually been the one offered in *line 10,* as long as we know what the default behavior is going to be.

No matter what, though, if you are going to use the arguments passed to a function, grab them right away when the function begins. Don't go 12 lines into a function and still be talking about $_[3] or running shift()

with the default argument. It's like walking around all day with your money in your hand so you won't have to use a wallet.

One last thing that suggests the latter function as the better of the two—by putting the file test directly into a clause of the `printf()` statement, we were able to eliminate the need for a second temporary variable. Not a big deal in a function this simple, but a worthy habit to promote. Always be on the lookout for places where crafting the code a little differently will allow you to avoid unnecessary variables.

b) Write two functions, one that takes an array or list as its argument and prints the contents, and another that takes a hash as an argument and prints the content.

Answer: Here is a program that contains and tests the required functions.

GROUPRINT.PL

```
1  #!/usr/bin/perl
2
3  # functions
4  sub arrayprt {
5     my @lst = @_;
6     foreach (@lst) {
7         print "$_\n";
8     }
9  }
10
11 sub hashprt {
12    my %stuff = @_;
13    foreach $k (keys %stuff) {
14        print "stuff-sub-$k: $stuff{$k}\n";
15    }
16 }
17
18 # main program
19 @names = qw{fred ralph archie};
20 %ages = ( fred=>10000, ralph=>99, archie=>79);
21 @fakehash = qw{bit culture musical roadkill};
22
23 print "\n"; arrayprt(@names); print "\n";
24 print "\n"; hashprt(%ages); print "\n";
25 print "\n"; hashprt(@fakehash); print "\n";
```

The functions that do the work are listed first here. There shouldn't be much surprise about the first one. It grabs the argument list into an array (*line 5*) and iterates through, printing each entry (*lines 6-8*).

The second function is a little more interesting. It takes the argument list and assigns it to a hash (*line 12*). This will work as long as there is an even number of elements in the argument list. When we go to test this in *lines 24* and *25*, we know that it will work okay the first time because we are putting a hash in there directly. In *line 25* we pass an array, but it does have an even number of arguments, so it can be coerced into a hash.

What really matters is how we use the data when we get it into the function. You have a lot of freedom and flexibility with that, but be careful. You're responsible for what happens.

10.2.2 ANSWERS

a) Write a function (`cookiemaker()`) that returns a string chosen at random from an array of sayings.

Answer: Here's an example of how you might do it.

COOKIEMAKER.PL

```perl
1 #!/usr/bin/perl
2
3 foreach (1..21) {
4    print cookiemaker(), "\n";
5 }
6
7 sub cookiemaker {
8    my @cookiesheet = (
9    "Bartender: pharmacist with a limited inventory.",
10   "Headline: Drunk gets nine months in violin case",
11   "Lottery: A tax on people who are bad at math.",
12   "Headline: Enraged cow injures farmer with ax",
13   "Help Wanted: Telepath—You know where to apply",
14   "Headline: Miners refuse to work after death",
15         );
16   my $choice = (rand 1024) % scalar(@cookiesheet);
17   print "$choice  ";
18   return $cookiesheet[$choice];
19 }
```

This one may have a couple of surprises. Look at *line 8* where we declare the array. It is declared as a my variable. The array cannot be seen outside of the function. In *line 16* where $choice is declared, you can see that it is also localized to the current function.

So the question might be, "How can we return $cookiesheet[$choice] when @cookiesheet and $choice are constrained in scope?" The answer is that in *line 18*, both of those names still have a meaning. So what gets passed back to the calling program is the data represented by the expression that uses those names.

b) Write a function that takes two filenames as arguments and is designed to return a number indicating the difference in bytes between the first and the second file. Return undef if either filename does not exist.

Answer: Here's a quick program that does the trick.

FSDIFF.PL

```
1 #!/usr/bin/perl
2
3 print "difference: ", fsdiff("fsdiff.pl", "storyed.pl"), "\n";
4 print "difference: ", fsdiff("storyed.pl", "story.base"), "\n";
5
6 sub fsdiff {
7     my ($file1, $file2) = @_;
8     return undef unless (-f $file1 && -f $file2);
9     my $f1size = (stat $file1)[7];
10    my $f2size = (stat $file2)[7];
11    return $f2size - $f1size;
12 }
```

The function shown here is actually pretty standard for how a good function might look. The working portions of the argument list are grabbed right at the top (*line 7*) and tested for integrity right away. If there's a problem, we deal with it before we go any further (*line 8*).

All of the variables are scoped to be local, so there's no chance of trampling any global variables. Probably the one thing we could do to tighten this up a bit is get rid of the transient utility variables declared in *lines 9* and *10*. We could conduct our calculations right in the return line and save ourselves a tiny bit of memory and stress on the namespace by doing something like this:

```
return (stat $file2)[7] - (stat $file1)[7];
```

c) Write a function that returns a list of files from a directory named in the first argument.

Answer: Here's a function like that and a program to test it.

FLIST.PL
```
 1 #!/usr/bin/perl
 2
 3 sub flist {
 4    my $fn = shift;
 5    return undef unless -d $fn;
 6    my $pattern = defined $_[0] ? shift : "*";
 7    return split /\s+/, `ls $pattern`;
 8 }
 9
10 @names = flist (".", "*pl");
11 print "@names", "\n";
```

This version of the function is a little weak, and the testing should be much more rigorous. Almost all of the action here is in *line 7*, where we use the backtick operator to get a list of files with the ls(1) command. (A stronger approach would be to simply open the directory and read it ourselves. It's not that hard, as you've learned.)

The list of files is split on whitespace to produce a list. A common mistake would be to assume that the output from ls() in the backticks produces a list. Certainly, from the way we tested this function, the difference between getting back a list and getting back a long string is subtle.

A stronger function would seem to be in order here, and more thorough testing. There should be at least one call to the function with no arguments, a call with one argument, and a call with an argument that is an invalid filename. Don't fall into the habit of relaxing when your program works the first time. It's easy to become complacent and miss an important flaw in your code.

10.2.3 ANSWERS

a) Inside the functions localvarset() and myvarset(), is the global value of $mval visible?

Answer: The simple answer to this is "no." If you ran the program and came to that conclusion, then you're right. When the functions declare their own privately scoped variables, any global variables of the same name are naturally hidden. If you're happy with that answer, then you're excused. The fishin' hole is really nice this time of year.

If you're interested in taking this a bit further, however, read on. It turns out that all of the variable names you put into your program are kept in something called the "symbol table." All the variables, that is, except those that you declare to be my variables.

When you refer to a variable, first a my variable of that name is sought. If none is found, then the symbol table is examined and if the variable is there, it will be used.

Every variable in the symbol table has a longer, more formal name than the one we've been using. The name for the global value $mval, for instance, is actually $main::$mval. If you refer to that explicitly in your function, the global value will be used instead of the my value.

When you use local, it's a little different. The easiest way to visualize what happens with local is to imagine that a new variable is created in the symbol table that hides the original one. When the function ends, the new variable is destroyed, leaving the original one visible and intact.

You can modify the notrample.pl program by adding two lines to watch how this behaves. Or you can go on the next exercise.

b)   When underneath() is called from myvarset(), is the original
value of $mval used? How about from localvarset()?

Answer: Two questions, two answers. Yes and no!

When myvarset() creates its own private version of the variable, the new variable is not added to the symbol table. It is simply referenced inside the myvarset() function. When localvarset() creates a variable with the same name, it is temporarily added to the symbol table and remains there until the localvarset() function ends.

By this point, you should know enough about this issue to determine when it is okay to suspend the rule we considered in the Lab discussion. *"Use my variables in your function because they're faster and more predictable unless you have a good reason to do otherwise."*

c) Build a line editor function that can handle editing for reasonable-size files.

Answer: Here's an example of a function that meets the required specs.

EFUNCTION.PL (FRAGMENT —ONLY THE EDITOR FUNCTION)

```
1 sub editfile {
2 # variable setup and syntax check
3   my ($filename, $done, $line_no, @buff);
4   $done = 0;
5   $filename = shift;
6   return undef unless -f $filename;
7 # slurp the file into the buffer show the top
8   open IN, $filename; @buff = <IN>; close IN;
9   $line_no = $#buff + 1;
10  bufferdump(1,10, @buff);
11
12 # prompt and go
13  print "Enter lines to be added, ~h for editor help\n";
14  until ($done) {
15      printf "%5d:", $line_no;
16      $_ = <STDIN>;
17      if (/^~[dlewhq]/) {
18 SWITCH:   {
19              /^~d/ && do { # delete
20                  print "Which line number? ";
21                  chomp($_ = <STDIN>);
22                  splice @buff, $_, 1;
23                  bufferdump ($_-5, $_+4, @buff);
24                  last SWITCH;
25              };
26              /^~l/ && do { # list
27                  print "Starting at which line number? ";
28                  chomp($_ = <STDIN>);
29                  bufferdump($_, $_+10, @buff);
30                  last SWITCH;
31              };
32              /^~e/ && do { # edit line
33                  print "Edit which line? ";
34                  chomp($_ = <STDIN>);
35                  $line_no = $_;
36                  printf "%s \n%5d:", $buff[$line_no], $line_no;
37                  $_ = <STDIN>;
38                  splice @buff, $line_no, 1, ($_);
39                  $line_no = $#buff+1;
```

```
40                      last SWITCH;
41                  };
42              /^~w/ && do { # write to file
43                  print "Current file: $filename\n";
44                  print "What filename? <RET> for default ";
45                  chomp($_ = <STDIN>);
46                  $filename = /^$/ ? $filename : $_;
47                  unless (open OUT, ">$filename") {
48                      warn "bad file $filename\n";
49                      last SWITCH;
50                  }
51                  print OUT @buff;
52                  last SWITCH;
53              };
54              /^~h/ && do { # help
55                  ehelp();
56                  last SWITCH;
57              };
58              /^~q/ && do { # quit
59                  $done = 1;
60                  last SWITCH;
61              };
62          }
63      }
64      else {
65          push @buff, $_;
66          ++$line_no;
67      }
68  }
69 }
```

It's pretty long, but there are a number of useful things that show up here. Starting in *line 3*, you can see that we declare the variables we'll need to use in the function. You are not required to declare everything in one place like you see here.

The existing file is opened and read into memory in *line 8*. The line is terribly provocative, however, because no error checking is done in the interest of brevity. Don't let your code go to production like this. If that file doesn't open, the rest of the program will behave badly, if it doesn't just blow up ceremoniously.

In *line 10*, we see a call to a function called `bufferdump()`. This is one that will have to be written; there is no such function in the Perl standard library. You might guess from what we see here that the function will expect to see a starting line, an ending line, and the buffer to be printed from. (Hmmm, wonder if that sort of function would be handy in other contexts?)

In *line 17*, the input line is examined to see if it begins with a supported command. If not (and you have to trace down to *line 64* to learn this), the input line is simply added to the end of the buffer. We could probably have used `unless()` here and avoided that particular bit of suspense.

Most of the cases in the switch construct that follows conduct fairly simplistic manipulations of the buffer. Notice the use of `splice()` in *lines 22 and 38* to accomplish deletion or replacement of a line. You may wish to also note that in three places (*lines 20, 28,* and *34*), the program prompts the operator to provide a number and in those cases, we `chomp()` the input before using it. If we had forgotten to do this, most of our operations would work anyway because when we go to look for a number, two digits followed by a newline are interpreted in the same way as the two digits by themselves. In *line 45*, the program gathers a filename from input and that will definitely need to be `chomp()`'d before we use it.

The rest of the time, we actually want to keep those trailing newline characters because they need to be both in the buffer and written to the file when it's time.

Overall, this function needs to be polished a bit more before it's completely ready, but you can use it as a starting place unless you prefer the version that you've written.

d) Build a paging function that can take a number (that represents screen size) and an array. It should present the number of elements from the array that it takes to "fill the screen."

Answer: This function does the trick reasonably well.

PERLPG.PL (FRAGMENT—PAGER FUNCTION ONLY)

```
1 sub pager {
2     my ($screensize, @buff) = @_;
3     my $hereline = 0, $done = 0;
4 MAINLOOP:
5     until ($done) {
6         foreach ($hereline .. $hereline+$screensize-2){
```

```
 7              if ($_ > $#buff) {
 8                  $done = 1; last MAINLOOP;
 9              }
10              print $buff[$_];
11          }
12          print ":";
13          chomp(my $input = <STDIN>);
14          if ($input =~ /^$/) {
15              $hereline = $hereline+$screensize;
16              print "\n";
17          }
18          if ($input =~ /^-/) {
19              $hereline -= $screensize;
20              $hereline = $hereline<0 ? 0 : $hereline;
21          }
22          if ($input =~ /^[qQxX]/) {
23              $done = 1;
24          }
25      }
26 }
```

The function starts by grabbing the argument list and putting it into the variables for screensize and a local buffer and declaring a couple of other utility variables that will be needed (*lines 2-3*).

The main loop (*lines 4-24*) is labeled so that we can easily break out of it when it's time in *line 8*. It begins with a small loop (*lines 6-11*) that dumps some of the input buffer to screen and then displays a prompt, waiting for the operator input.

The remainder of the function is concerned with reacting to the operator input. You can have as much or as little code as you like here. A call to an external help function would be fine, support for more options like a return to the top of the buffer, or a jump to a specific line number would be handy as well. You can probably see from this example how to add such functionality.

Get a copy of the program that contains this function from the companion website and play with it for awhile before you decide just how it should ultimately behave.

LAB 10.2 REVIEW QUESTIONS

1) Which of the following modifiers can localize a variable to be seen only within its enclosing scope?
   a) _____ `localize`
   b) _____ `privatize`
   c) _____ `my`
   d) _____ `private`

2) Which of the following uses of `local` will not compile?
   a) _____ `local ($action, $prevents, $global, $disaster);`
   b) _____ `local $val1;`
   c) _____ `local $val1, $val2, $val3;`
   d) _____ `local ($val1, $val2, $val3,) = @input;`

3) Should you modify your function variables with `my` or with `local`, as a general rule?
   a) _____ Use `local` most of the time because it's more portable.
   b) _____ Use either one, they are really synonyms.
   c) _____ Use `my` as a habit because it's faster and safer.
   d) _____ Use `local` for programs that you're not going to distribute, and `my` for programs that will be installed on many systems.

   Take a look at this code:

   ```
   sub alter {
       my $amount = 100;
   }
   ```

4) In this function, there is a variable called `$amount`. If the calling program also defines a variable called `$amount`, will it be changed when this function runs?
   a) _____ Yes
   b) _____ No

5) In the function shown before, if the variable is declared local, will the main calling program's variable `$amount` be changed when the function runs?
   a) _____ Yes
   b) _____ No

Quiz answers appear in Appendix A, Section 10.2.

L A B   10.3

BUILDING A LIBRARY OF FUNCTIONS

LAB OBJECTIVES

After this Lab, you will be able to:

✓ Put Functions into a Library for Reuse

✓ Manage Library Location with **@INC**

In this Lab, we'll tie everything together by learning how to write functions that might be reused by several programs. Then we'll take those functions and put them into a library that can be loaded by any program that needs to take advantage of the functionality.

We need to start by acknowledging one thing: We aren't going to see all of the story right here. There are two types of "libraries" that you can use in Perl 5. Traditional libraries are simply collections of functions that can be loaded when the program runs. You can use those with Perl 4 or Perl 5. "Perl modules" are specialized collections of functions and data structures (variables of whatever type) that are bound together in a way that is cohesive and protected from interference from (or with) the programs that use them.

 We won't have space to explore Perl modules here, but you will find additional information about them on the companion website.

PERL LIBRARIES

There's nothing special about the idea of Perl libraries. You've already done most of the work involved in building a library while you were wrestling with the exercises in the last Lab. There are really only three important things that you have to do if you want to use function libraries.

The first is to build sound functions. The first couple of functions we built in this chapter rely upon various assumptions about the program that will contain them. That makes them "not sound." They can be used only directly with the programs that they are designed for.

LAB 10.3

The last couple of functions you wrote, however, expect all of the data they need to be passed in through the argument list, and they pass information back to the caller with a `return()` statement when they are finished. Those functions are sound.

So that's the first of the three steps! Build solid functions that don't rely upon, or manipulate, global data structures.

The second step is to put the functions into a file of their own. The last line of that file should look like this:

```
return 1; # satisfy require
```

The comment is optional, of course, but you will see it in so much production code that you might think that it's mandatory. The important part is that the last line, the final thing that will be done when you use the `require()` statement to pull the library in, should evaluate to a nonzero value. This tells the main program that everything went okay when we read in the library.

Many times, you will find that programmers omit the `return()` statement itself.

```
1; # satisfy require
```

That's legal, it is just fine, and as long as you remember what it's there for, you should feel free to do it that way yourself.

LOADING A PERL LIBRARY

The third step is to bring the library into your main program, and it's very easy to do. Near the top of your program file, you should include a statement that looks like this:

```
require "utilities.pl";
```

This will load a file named `utilities.pl` and execute any code that happens to be in the file. Normally, the file consists of function definitions only and a single line at the end that returns a non-zero value.

Let's see what this looks like from the ground.

■ *FOR EXAMPLE*

Here are examples of both a library file and a program that loads and uses the library.

UTIL.PL (FRAGMENT)

```
 1 # utility functions
 2 #
 3 sub bufferdump {
 4     my ($start, $finish, @pad) = @_;
 5     # you've seen this before...
 6 }
 7
 8 sub pager {
 9     my ($screensize, @buff) = @_;
10     my $hereline = 0, $done = 0;
11 MAINLOOP:
12     # this is the same as before as well....
13 }
14 return 1; # appease require
```

To preserve space, we gutted the functions here; you've just seen them, anyway. (And of course, the complete listing is available on the companion website.)

Here's a program that uses the library.

USEUTILS.PL

```
1 #!/usr/bin/perl
2 require "util.pl";
3 @lines = <>; # slurp in files named on command-line
4 print "Here's a 5 line dump.\n";
5 bufferdump (0, 4, @lines);
6 print "Okay, let's page the stuff\n";
7 pager (12, @lines);
8 print "That's all folks!\n";
```

Actually, half of this listing is gravy. The only lines you need to see this work would be *line 2* to get the library, *line 3* to gather some data for your buffer, then *lines 5* and *7* to actually call the functions.

As you start to develop useful functions and gather them into libraries that can be reused, you'll start to have very simple main programs that do powerful things.

But we have a little more work to do, so let's get busy with it.

**LAB
10.3**

LOCATION, LOCATION, LOCATION

When your program uses `require()` to bring in a library file, Perl must know where to look for the library.

The clean way to give your library a central location that can be seen by all programs that might need it is to put the file in one of the directories contained in the special `@INC` array. When your Perl program begins, this array is already defined and it contains the location of library files that might be required. In fact, you should print it out the way you print out any Perl array just to see how it is currently defined on your system. (Go ahead, I'll wait.)

The Whole Truth

Need a hand with this? I used this command from my shell prompt:

```
perl -e "$,=qq{\n};print @INC;"
```

and I got output that looked like this:

```
/usr/local/perl/lib
/usr/local/perl/lib/site
```
.

On an MS-DOS system, you might see something like this:

```
c:\perl\lib
c:\perl\lib\site
```
.

Those directories are natural candidates for the appropriate place to put your own libraries. Particularly the directory called "site," because you can probably guess that it's intended to give you a place to collect things that are localized to your system.

You may not be able to put the library file into one of the directories that are naturally part of the @INC array. Among the various reasons, one of the most common is that you're going to be running a Perl program as a CGI script that doesn't have access to a lot of system directories.

This is not a problem because you can simply add directories to the array when your program is running (if you do it right), or you can use the -1 options to Perl to specify a list of directories in which library files might be found.

■ FOR EXAMPLE

To add directories to the array, it is a simple matter to add a line that looks like this:

```
push @INC, "/usr/local/customer/proplibs";
```

If you do that before you have a require() statement, your library from that directory will be found without trouble. You should consider encasing that statement in a special block, however, so that the modification to the include path takes place at program compile time. The block you want to use for this is called a BEGIN block. Here's what the top of a program will look like when you put these pieces in place.

LIBUSERTOP.PL (A PROGRAM FRAGMENT)
```
1 #!/usr/bin/perl
2 BEGIN {
3    push @INC, "/usr/local/customer";
4 }
5 require "customerlib.pl";
6
7 # program begins here...
```

LAB 10.3

Code that you put in the BEGIN block will be executed at compile time. The modification to the @INC directory doesn't have to be done then in order for require() to work. When you use a Perl module, however, you'll pull it in with the use() statement instead, and that statement runs at compile time. You'll need the include path to be updated in time for your Perl module to be found.

If you decide to use the command-line option to modify the library include path, that will automatically be done before anything else happens. So you could run your program as:

```
perl -I "/usr/local/customer" pgmname.pl
```

or you could even doctor the invocation line at the top of the script:

```
#!/usr/bin/perl -I /usr/local/customer
```

Personally, I tend to use the BEGIN block, but it doesn't have any inherent advantage over changing the Perl invocation line. In either case, you'll have to modify the script to make it ready to find its libraries. You've got three ways to do this. Choose the one that works best for you.

LAB 10.3 EXERCISES

10.3.1 PUT FUNCTIONS INTO A LIBRARY FOR REUSE

Take one more look at the natural output from the `ls(1)` command. Notice that every bit of information presented is available from the Perl `stat()` function (except the filename, which you probably used to run `stat()` in the first place).

```
-rwxr-xr-x   1 agentv   everyone    591 Feb   9 09:42 trample.pl
-rwxr-x---   1 agentv   staff      1474 May   2 07:56 perlpg.pl
drwxr-xr-x   1 agentv   everyone      0 Feb   8 10:33 samples.d
```

The trick, of course, is that you have to convert an octal number (the mode value) into the string that makes up the first field of this output. Also, take a look at the way that the timestamps for the files are rendered. You'll have to get the file modification time and convert it into two numbers, the hour and minute that the file was modified. Be sure to use leading zeros for this.

> **a)** Write two functions (`mode2string()` and `time2string()`). These functions should, respectively, convert mode and time information into the strings that we see when we run `ls(1)`. Add these functions to a library when they are finished.
>
> _____
>
> _____

It's time to create a library that you can reuse in your programs. The "safe rm" program and its companion undelete program from Chapter 9 are good candidates for library functions (if you retool them a bit). The simulated `ls(1)` program from that chapter can also be a useful function (especially now that you have a function to convert the mode and file timestamp). The editor and pager you built in the last Lab would be good choices to add to this library.

Here is a "test yoke" for a library that would contain all four of those functions. When you've finished assembling the pieces into your library, run this program and make sure that it works.

LIBTEST_YOKE.PL

```
 1 #!/usr/bin/perl
 2 require "utillib.pl";
 3
 4 print "Time for a directory listing:\n";
 5 ul_ls "/tmp"; # custom library function
 6
 7 # let's make a file that we can remove later
 8 open OUT, ">/tmp/junk.$$"; close OUT;
 9
10 ul_srm "/tmp/junk.$$";  # another library function
11 ul_unsrm "/tmp"; # another library function
12
13 ul_pg "$0"; # library function for paging output
14 ul_edit "$0"; # careful not to change anything important
15
16 __END__
17 just in case you add lines, they won't have to be
18 legal Perl syntax
```

**LAB
10.3**

b) Create a library that contains the four functions just discussed and use the provided test yoke to validate it.

_____

_____

10.3.2 MANAGE LIBRARY LOCATION WITH @INC

a) Move your new library to a central location in your file system (maybe somewhere like $HOME/lib) and modify the test yoke program to be able to find it. Use a BEGIN block to tell your program where to find the library.

_____

_____

b) Modify the original test yoke program again, this time by placing a command-line option in the Perl invocation line so that the program can find your new library.

LAB 10.3 EXERCISE ANSWERS

10.3.1 ANSWERS

a) Write two functions (`mode2string()` and `time2string()`). These functions should, respectively, convert mode and time information into the strings that we see when we run `ls(1)`.

Answer: This is how your functions might look.

CONVERTERS.PL (A LIBRARY FRAGMENT)

```
1  sub mode2string {
2     my $mval = shift;
3     my $typeval = $mval / 010000;
4     my $uperms = ($mval & 0700) / 0100;
5     my $gperms = ($mval & 0070) / 0010;
6     my $operms = ($mval & 0007) / 0001;
7
8     return sprintf "%s%s%s%s%s%s%s%s%s%s",
9     $typeval == 04 ? 'd' : '-',
10    $uperms & 04 ? 'r' : '-',
11    $uperms & 02 ? 'w' : '-',
12    $uperms & 01 ? 'x' : '-',
13    $gperms & 04 ? 'r' : '-',
14    $gperms & 02 ? 'w' : '-',
15    $gperms & 01 ? 'x' : '-',
16    $operms & 04 ? 'r' : '-',
17    $operms & 02 ? 'w' : '-',
18    $operms & 01 ? 'x' : '-';
19 }
20 sub time2string {
21    my @monthtable = qw{Jan Feb Mar Apr May Jun Jul Aug Sep Oct Dec};
22    my $timestamp = shift;
```

```
23    # normalize the time
24    my ($sec,$min,$hour,$mday,$mon,$year,$wday,$yday,$isdst)
25        = gmtime($timestamp);
26    return sprintf "%3s %2d %02d:%02d",
27        $monthtable[$mon], $mday,
28        $hour, $min;
29 }
```

The first function is the trickier of the two. You'll have to do a little "bit juggling" to extract the information you want from one single number. Most of this takes place in *lines 3-6*. To understand the code here, we can look at *line 4*. This line takes the value and first uses a bit mask and the bitwise AND operator to throw out all but one of the octal digits. Then it divides by an appropriate value so that the final result is something between 0 and 7. Later, in *lines 10-12*, that number is further deconstructed to decide how the actual elements of the mode string will look.

LAB 10.3

If this entire operation seems pretty byzantine to you, don't worry too much about it. You can take comfort in the fact that you won't have to do this sort of operation often, unless you choose to. Crusty old C programmers love this stuff. But you don't have to.

The function finishes up by constructing a carefully formatted string with a cousin of the `printf()` function. The `sprintf()` function operates just like its cousin but doesn't print the string to a filehandle. It simply returns the string to the calling function. Now that's civilized behavior for a function.

The second function is a little bit easier to read, and it illustrates an interesting point along the way. Look at the array formed in *line 21*. It contains month names, starting with January in element 0. Later on, in *lines 24 and 25*, we use `gmtime()` to get some date information and as we do, we populate a variable called `$mon`. How convenient that the function returns the month number in the range 0-11! This is also true for the weekday (something in the range 0-6) that we capture in `$wday`. Both values are designed to make it easy for you to grab a text name from a zero-based array.

In fact, because of that feature, constructing the string we want to return is simple.

b) Create a library that contains the four functions just discussed and use the provided test yoke to validate it.

Answer: Here's what the basic framework of that library should look like.

UTILLIB.FRAG (FRAGMENT OF FULL LIBRARY)

```
 1 # utility functions
 2 sub ul_pg {
 3    # paging function, as before
 4 }
 5 sub ul_ls {
 6    # list subdirectory function
 7 }
 8 sub ul_srm {
 9    # safe rm function
10 }
11 sub ul_unsrm {
12    # safe unremove function
13 }
14 sub ul_edit {
15    # editor as before (improved slightly)
16 }
17 sub ehelp {
18    # help screen -- supports edit function
19 }
20 sub bufferdump {
21    # buffer dump as before
22 }
23
24 return 1; # appease require
```

The actual code for the functions is not shown here in the interest of space. (You can get our version of the full library from the companion website.) The most important things are that you get the functions in the right place in the file, and that there be a line at the end to return a non-zero result to the calling program.

10.3.2 ANSWERS

a) Move your new library to a central location in your filesystem. (Maybe somewhere like $HOME/lib) and modify the test yoke program to be able to find it. Use a BEGIN block to tell your program where to find the library.

Answer: There isn't much to this; here's the beginning of the program.

```
1 #!/usr/bin/perl
2 BEGIN {
3    push @INC, "/home/tom/lib";
4 }
```

The whole point here is that once you get your library built, the things you'll have to do to use it are easy. Notice that we used `push()` to get the new directory into the array. This puts it at the end of the list. If you want to have your custom libraries found first when a search is conducted, you can use this line instead:

LAB 10.3

```
unshift @INC, "/home/tom/lib";
```

This stuffs your directory in at the top of the array.

b) Modify the original test yoke program again, this time by placing a command-line option in the Perl invocation line so that the program can find your new library.

Answer: Here's the line you'll need to use for this to work:

```
#!/usr/bin/perl -I /home/tom/lib
```

There is one benefit to this approach that can be handy when you have a suite of scripts that all need to look for libraries in a custom location. You can easily write a Perl program that can sweep through the entire suite of scripts and modify just that one line. I'll leave the construction of *that* script for your late-night amusement.

LAB 10.3 REVIEW QUESTIONS

1) If functions are isolated into a library, which of the following lines must appear in the library file?
   a) _____ `#pragma library_file`
   b) _____ `return 1;`
   c) _____ `#!/usr/bin/perl -1`
   d) _____ `use Library::Importer;`

2) How would you include a library called `utils.pl` in your Perl program?
   a) _____ `#include utils.pl`
   b) _____ `require "utils";`
   c) _____ `require "utils.pl";`
   d) _____ `use Library::utils`

3) If you download a library called `dateutils.pl` from the Internet, what directory should you place it in so that your programs can find it?
   a) _____ In your home directory.
   b) _____ In the `/usr/lib` directory.
   c) _____ In any directory whose name appears in the `@INC` array.
   d) _____ One copy must be in the same directory with each program that will use it.

4) True or False: When you use `require` to load a library, it will be loaded at run time.
   a) _____ True
   b) _____ False

5) When does the code in a BEGIN block run?
   a) _____ After libraries are loaded but before local subroutines are defined.
   b) _____ Before the `main()` function is executed.
   c) _____ Until the subsequent Parliamentary elections.
   d) _____ At program compile time.

   Quiz answers appear in Appendix A, Section 10.3.

C H A P T E R 10

TEST YOUR THINKING

1) Write a companion function for the `cookiemaker()` function. It should take the name of a cookie file and return an array consisting of the sayings.

2) Finish up the `ushell.pl` program now. Use the functions from the `utillib.pl` library to implement the actions selected by the program operator.

Barber Tom waited for Major Ellie to come through the door and then locked it behind her. He turned to face the room where his other friends were already seated. Larry reclined almost horizontally in one of the barber chairs, the one in which he did a lot of his thinking while the shop was slow. Coach Randal was fussing over the coffee pot, muttering something. His voice was nearly inaudible but the phrase, "...just cleaned this d—d thing once a year or so..." was loud enough to be heard by everyone.

Tom began, "You all know that I've been trying to get some use out of this old PC in here. The idea is to have a system that lets us maintain an online To Do List. I think everyone here has helped with different parts of this, so I wanted you all to be here to see the finished product.

"I ended up breaking the thing up into a suite of programs so that it can be operated from the command line or from an interactive shell. There's a central library of functions that supports interactive and command-line use. There are two data files, the authorization list and the actual To Do data.

"You will be able to add, delete, and edit tasks that are in the database. And you can print a report of all your tasks sorted by priority or date. If you'll gather here, I can show you how the menu for the interactive shell works. I'm hoping that you folks will have suggestions that I can use to improve the system."

Everyone moved toward the terminal and Tom typed a command to make the screen look like this:

```
1) Report your tasks by priority
2) Report your tasks by date
3) Add a new task
4) Delete a task
5) Edit one of your tasks
9) Quit
```

3)   From the pieces of this project that you've built earlier, write a finished suite
of programs that performs as Tom described. There should be an interactive
shell and command-line programs to accomplish administrative tasks. The
main functionality should be isolated to a library.

 If you want to see more comprehensive specifications before
you start, see the companion website.

CHAPTER 11

ENDS
AND ODDS

In this chapter, we wrap up with a grab-bag of topics that will help you as you program in Perl. We'll start by learning more about a mechanism that allows you to embed documentation right into your source code so that you need to maintain only one document base for both code and documentation.

We'll also look at a way to produce reports that is more powerful and orderly than using the meticulously tailored `printf()` statements that we've built in recent examples. With format specifications and the `write()` function, you can generate good-looking reports and do it with surprisingly little effort.

Our last stop in this chapter will feature a very quick look at the steps you'll use to take advantage of a Perl module. You've already written your own traditional libraries, so now we'll look at how you can also utilize the increasingly common form of libraries contained in modules.

L A B   11.1

USING POD TO EMBED MULTI-PURPOSE DOCUMENTATION

LAB OBJECTIVES

After this Lab, you will be able to:

✓ Write POD Content to Document Your Code
✓ Produce HTML and Man Pages from POD

We got a glimpse of POD content in Chapter 2, "The Nickel Tour," when we looked at how we could comment out an entire block of code easily. We learned that the Perl interpreter sees certain types of tokens (those beginning with an equal sign, "=" in the first column of a line) as a marker for embedded documentation.

When you embed certain sequences in your program (or in a file by themselves, for that matter), they can be used then to create documentation nearly automatically.

You can produce man pages, HTML pages, or simply plain text, as well as other formats. The key to this is a special set of *commands* that are ignored by the Perl interpreter (they're treated as comments). These commands can be used by certain *filter programs* supplied with Perl to produce the type of output that you'd prefer for your documentation. (For instance, there is a `pod2html` and a `pod2man` program.)

Designed for simplicity, the POD directives are few in number. They are listed in Table 11.1.

Table 11.1 ■ Pod command paragraph directives

Directive	Description
=pod	Begin a POD segment
=cut	End a POD segment
=head1 <heading>	Level 1 Heading
=head2 <heading>	Level 2 Heading
=over [4]	Begin an indented item list
=back	Terminate an item list
=item [*|1]	Mark an item in a list * character, make this a bulleted item; if followed by a digit, make this a numbered list
=for [html | text | roff]	Mark a paragraph as being for a special form of output. This is important only to the filter programs (that is, for html would be used only by pod2html)
=begin [html | text | roff]	Begin a segment (through the next =end directive) meant for a specific format
=end	Ends a specialized segment

Begin your documentation with either a =pod or a =head1 directive. At the end of the documentation, place a =cut directive. (The =cut may be omitted if the documentation simply runs until the end of the file.)

Table 11.1 shows the complete list of command paragraph directives in existence now, but you'll want to refer to the documentation as you develop your own documented programs. One thing that is difficult to divine from the existing documentation is the definition of a paragraph.

For the purposes of POD content, a paragraph is defined as being "some text immediately following a blank line and terminated with a blank line."

In the example you're about to read, you'll notice that the POD markup takes a lot of space because it's necessary to have blank lines between the structural elements.

Within a POD segment, you can have two types of paragraphs in addition to command paragraphs—ordinary paragraphs and verbatim paragraphs. Verbatim paragraphs will be included in the output documentation without any interpretation whatsoever. To create a verbatim paragraph, the first line should be indented with a leading space or a leading tab. There are no escape sequences in such a paragraph. This is handy because it allows you to paste a passage from your program's code directly into the POD; it will be reproduced without alteration as long as you indent it from the left margin by a space or more.

An ordinary paragraph will be any segment whose first line is not indented and that does not begin with one of the POD directives shown in Table 11.1. Within ordinary paragraphs, you may use special sequences that render text for emphasis and clarity. You can mark text as bold, italicized, filename, or literal code. There are a number of tools you may use for this, as listed in Table 11.2.

Table 11.2 ■ POD Special Formatting Characters

Special Formatting Character	Meaning
I<text>	Italicize text
B<text>	Bold text
C<code>	Code text
S<text>	Non-breaking space in text
F<filename>	Filename
X<index>	Index entry
L<location>	Link to location

There is a rich collection of variant links that you can use in your documentation (links to spots in the current document, in other documents, to specific sections of other documents, and many more) and not all of the special codes are shown in this table. See the `perldoc` man page for the complete and up-to-date list. The markups you see here will give you a place to start.

When your program is finished, and you have the POD section set up the way you want it, you can simply use one of the processor programs to produce output in the format you prefer. Let's look at a program that includes POD content.

HELLODOC.PL

```
 1  #!/usr/bin/perl
 2
 3  =head1 NAME
 4
 5  Documented Program
 6
 7  =head1 Synopsis
 8
 9  A verbatim paragraph would look like this. Everything
10  here will be reproduced exactly when you run the
11  processor, even if you B<embed> some of the items in
12  a special formatting code
13
14  =head2 Description
15
16  Ordinary paragraphs on the other hand, do allow B<embedded>
17  formatting codes that will be honored by most of the
18  processor I<programs> that know how to read B<POD>
19  content in your F<filename>.
20
21  You can also have bulleted lists by using C<=over>
22  and C<=back> along with the C<=item> directive.
23
24  =over 4
25
26  =item *
27  first item
28
29  =over 4
30
31  =item 1
32  nested items are
33
34  =item 2
35  allowed if you want them
36
37  =back
38
```

```
39 =item *
40 second item
41
42 =back
43
44 =head1 Author
45
46 Coach Randal
47
48 =cut
49
50 print "Hello Documentation Builder\n";
```

With your program set up in this fashion, you can produce an HTML version of the documentation by running the following command:

```
$ pod2html hellodoc.pl >hellodoc.html
```

By default, the pod2html program will emit the documentation on the standard output device. For most of us, that is the console screen. Using redirection, we can send the documentation to a file. It will look like what you see in Figure 11.1.

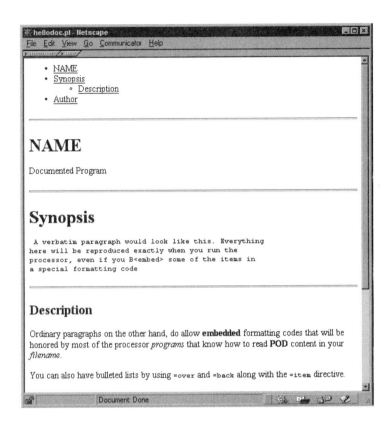

Figure 11.1 ■ POD documentation as an HTML file.

Some Perl programmers report different behavior from `pod2html` *on their systems. Your version of the program may have different options. Check your system documentation and the companion website for more information about how it might work on your system.*

Other POD filter programs include `pod2text`, `pod2man`, and `pod2latex`. If you need to produce output in one of these formats, the operation of those filters is nearly identical to what we've just done.

LAB 11.1 EXERCISES

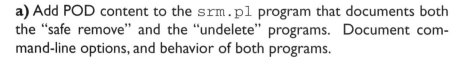

11.1.1 WRITE POD CONTENT TO DOCUMENT YOUR CODE

Find the `pod2man` program in your standard Perl distribution. (It's probably in the same directory that holds the Perl binary.) Open it and look it over to get some ideas about how you might structure your own documentation. Pay particular attention to what it says about the structure of a man page. This will help you with the first exercise.

a) Add POD content to the `srm.pl` program that documents both the "safe remove" and the "undelete" programs. Document command-line options, and behavior of both programs.

_____

_____

One particularly vital place to embed documentation is in your libraries. After code has been isolated to a library and has not been "worked" in a while, it is handy to have documentation that refreshes the memory about the correct usage of various functions, and maybe even offers a bit of information about the quirks.

b) Revise your `utillib.pl` library to include embedded documentation. You may choose any organizational structure for the documentation that you like, but if you're stuck, you may find it convenient to use the following organizational pattern:

```
NAME
DESCRIPTION
FUNCTION DEFINITIONS
    function1
    function2
ABOUT
    Revision Date
    Bugs
    Future Enhancements
    Author
```

11.1.2 PRODUCE HTML AND MAN PAGES FROM POD

POD content embedded in a program can be valuable for the developer and the maintenance programmer because it states in plain terms what the program is supposed to do and how it is supposed to be operated.

But the real magic comes from being able to turn it into documentation in a format useful to the intended user base.

> **a)** Use the `pod2man` program provided with the standard Perl distribution to produce man pages for the `srm.pl` and `unsrm.pl` programs. When your man page is finished, you may be able to view it with the following command:
>
> ```
> nroff -man filename
> ```

---

b) Use the `pod2html` program provided with the standard Perl distribution to create an HTML page documenting your `utillib.pl` library.

_____

_____

LAB 11.1 EXERCISE ANSWERS

11.1.1 ANSWERS

a) Add POD content to the `srm.pl` program that documents both the "safe remove" and the "undelete" programs.

Answer: Here is an example of how the first part of the newly revised program might appear.

SRM2000.PL

```
 1  #!/usr/bin/perl
 2
 3  =head1 NAME
 4
 5  srm.pl - safe remove program, a replacement for rm(1)
 6
 7  unsrm.pl - interactively undeletes files
 8
 9  =head1 DESCRIPTION
10
11  The C<srm.pl> program will delete the named files by
12  placing them in the hidden directory F<.wastebasket> with
13  the original basename and a filename extension that encodes
14  the current date and time.  If the F<.wastebasket> file
15  doesn't exist, it will be created.
16
17  The C<unsrm.pl> program will interactively offer for
18  B<undeletion> any files that currently occupy the hidden
19  F<.wastebasket> directory.
20
21  =head1 SYNOPSIS
22
```

```
23  srm filename [filename ...]
24  unsrm
25
26 =cut
27
28 # syntax check
29 die "Usage: $0 file1 [file2 ...]\n\t"
30    unless defined $ARGV[0];
31
32 # remainder of program is unchanged ...
```

Something you might have noticed when you looked at the POD content in the conversion program itself is that the major structural elements must be preceded and followed by a blank line. Later on, when we run the conversion programs, you will see that if you omit the surrounding blank lines, the conversion programs will not see the POD directives.

In this example, the POD content is at the beginning of the program, just like in the `pod2man` conversion program. One of the benefits of this approach is that the program maintainer will be able to see and read the documentation when the program is first opened in the editor.

Some programmers keep their POD information in a file separate from the code. It might even seem like a good idea when the documentation covers two different programs, as this one does. I think, however, that you'll find more value in combining the documentation and code. Try it both ways and decide this for yourself.

b) Revise your `utillib.pl` library to include embedded documentation.

Answer: This was a little bit bigger job, wasn't it? Here's how part of that documentation will look:

UTILLIB.PL
```
1 # utillib utility functions
2
3 =head1 NAME
4
5 utillib - library of file manipulation functions
6
7 =head1 DESCRIPTION
8
```

**LAB
11.1**

```
 9 This library contains various Perl functions suitable
10 for interactive manipulation of files and directories.
11 It forms the basis for the interactive program ushell.pl
12 but these functions could also be valuable for a suite
13 of command-line programs.
14
15 =head1 FUNCTION DESCRIPTIONS
16
17 The following functions are available as part of this library.
18
19 =head2 ul_pg
20
21 A pager that operates in a fashion similar to a crude version
22 of the F<pg(1)> program.  It expects to be given a screen size
23 and an array of lines, each of which must contain its own
24 newline character.
25
26 =cut
27
28 sub ul_pg {
29     # a function goes here
30 }
31
32 =head2 ul_ls
33
34 This function will print a directory listing similar to that
35 produced by the F<ls(1)> command when run with the C<-l> option.
36 It expects to be given a directory name.  It will do the rest.
37
38 =cut
39
40 sub ul_ls {
41     # a function goes here
42 }
43
44 =head1 ABOUT
45
46 =cut
```

For this sort of work, it makes sense not only to embed the documentation into the source code file, but also to intersperse it with the code so that the documentation for a function is near the function itself.

The benefit to the maintainer is that if it becomes necessary to update any of the functions, it will be very easy to update the documentation at the same time. Often the documentation is neglected later in a program's life-cycle. This, at least, stacks the odds in favor of the documentation.

11.1.2 ANSWERS

a) Use the `pod2man` program provided with the standard Perl distribution to produce man pages for the `srm.pl` and `unsrm.pl` programs.

Answer: You probably learned a lot more about man pages than you want to know as you did this. Here's the command line you might have used for this to work:

```
pod2man srm.pl > srm.1
```

The real issue would be based on whether you included the "mandatory" sections of a man page. This particular conversion program expects to see a section called "NAME" as a level one header. It also stubbornly insists that this section contain a line of text with an "isolated" dash somewhere. Your looking at the conversion program itself will probably be your best way to figure out how to get this right.

b) Use the `pod2html` program provided with the standard Perl distribution to create an HTML page documenting your `utillib.pl` library.

Answer: This is a little easier to produce because the conversion filter isn't as picky about structure. Here's the command you'll have to run:

```
pod2html utillib.pl >utillib.html
```

That additional freedom from format restrictions means that you'll have to spend more time thinking about how you want the final output to appear. You will find some standard templates on the Internet in various places that may help you get something that exhibits a fairly useful form. (Again, remember that the `pod2html` and `pod2man` programs may be different on your system. As more programmers begin to use POD, the conversion utilities may advance to include additional features. Who knows, you might even write an extension yourself.)

Figure 11.2 shows what an example final page might look like.

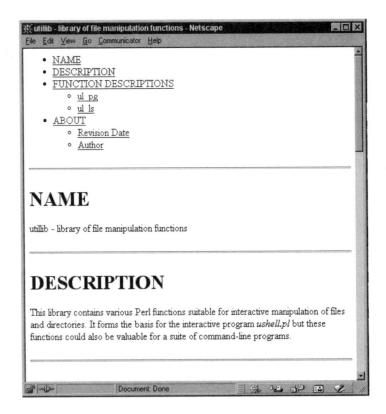

Figure 11.2 ■ HTML output from POD content is nearly automatic.

LAB 11.1 REVIEW QUESTIONS

1) The term POD stands for:
   - **a)** _____ nothing, not everything is an acronym.
   - **b)** _____ Particularly Obfuscated Data.
   - **c)** _____ Plain Old Documentation.
   - **d)** _____ Printing On Demand.

2) The identifying characteristic of POD content is:
   - **a)** _____ a ##POD## marker at the beginning and end.
   - **b)** _____ a line that begins with an = sign.
   - **c)** _____ the marker #<POD> at the beginning.
   - **d)** _____ the marker <<POD Begin at the beginning.

3) True or False: POD content must be in a separate file from the program it documents.
   - **a)** _____ True
   - **b)** _____ False

4) A verbatim paragraph allows a code fragment to be easily embedded in POD content. For a paragraph to be rendered verbatim in the final output, what characteristic it must exhibit?
   - **a)** _____ The first line must begin with a space.
   - **b)** _____ All lines in the paragraph must begin with a space.
   - **c)** _____ The paragraph must be embedded in a V<> tag.
   - **d)** _____ The paragraph must begin with =verbatim.

Quiz answers appear in Appendix A, Section 11.1.

L A B   11.2

USING FORMAT AND WRITE() FOR REPORTS

LAB OBJECTIVES

After this Lab, you will be able to:

✓ Use **format** and **write()** to Create a Report

✓ Use Advanced Report Features

We have often used `printf()` in our explorations to get formatted output in a way that is visually pleasing. In many circumstances, this is the best way to go about things. In other cases, we might find a better way with Perl. Let's take another look at a program from our past.

PLANET3.PL

```
 1 #!/usr/bin/perl
 2
 3 $au = 149.6;
 4 @ptable = qw{
 5   Mercury:57.9 Venus:108.2 Earth:149.6
 6   Mars:227.9 Jupiter:778.3 Saturn:1427
 7   Uranus:2870 Neptune:4497 Pluto:5900
 8 };
 9
10 # report header
11 printf "%10s  %18s  %18s\n",
12    "Planet", "Distance from Sun", "Distance in AU";
13 printf "%10s  %18s  %18s\n", "", "(Million KM)", "";
14 printf "%10s  %18s  %18s\n", "-"x10, "-"x18, "-"x18;
```

```
15
16 # report body
17 foreach $record (@ptable) {
18    ($p, $d) = split ':', $record;
19    printf "%10s  %18s  %18s\n", $p, $d, $d/$au;
20 }
```

Look closely at how the report header is formed in *lines 11-14*. Three printf() statements each form fields of 10, 18, and 18 characters wide. The body of the report is formed in *line 19*, where three fields of identical width are used for each line.

This method of specifying the look of a report takes a meticulous eye as well as a bit of trial and error. Experienced C programmers are accustomed to doing this and don't mind a bit. But you have a better way to do it in Perl if you want to. You need two things: a format specification and a write() statement in the right place.

FORMAT SPECIFICATION—VISUAL REPORT BUILDING

A format specification is essentially like a visual method of describing the look of a single line entry in the report you're planning to create. It is a little like a function in one respect. You may put it in your program at the beginning, at the end, or wherever you find it convenient. It will be read and remembered at program compile time, and available any time you need it during run time.

The name of a format should be the same as that of the filehandle with which it will be used. If we're going to be writing our report on STDOUT, we'll use a format with that same name. (We'll talk later about how to supercede this rule about format and filehandle names.)

A format specification consists of *picture lines* and *data lines*. A picture line is made up of literal information that will appear on each line of the report, and picture fields that will be populated with variable data. A data line must immediately follow any picture line that contains a picture field and must provide enough data to fill all of the picture fields contained in the preceding line.

The format specification is terminated with a period (".") on a line by itself.

■ *FOR EXAMPLE*

Here is a simple format specification that prints out two fields.

```
format STDOUT =
Planet: @<<<<<<<<<<<   Distance: @######.##
$planet, $distance
.
```

The two picture fields are those that look like @<<<<<<<<<<< and @######.## in the spec. The first of these indicates a left-justified text field with a width of 12 spaces. The second field indicates a numeric field with seven digits to the left of the decimal point and two on the right. In a picture field, the @ symbol and the symbols that follow it determine the width of the field and the type of data.

Table 11.3 describes the various types of picture fields that might be used.

Table 11.3 ■ Data Types Available in a Format Specification

Field Type	Meaning
@<<<<<<	left-justified string field
@>>>>>>	right-justified string field
@||||||	centered string field
@####.##	numeric field, aligned on decimal
^<<<<<<	left-justified multi-line field
^>>>>>>	right-justified multi-line field
^||||||	centered multi-line field

With our format defined, there's only one other thing we have to do in order to print our report.

"ANTICLIMAX" HE WROTE!

In our example format specification, we proclaimed that we would fill the picture fields on each line with the content of the variables $planet and `$distance`. So after we populate those variables with some information, what do we do to produce our report? We say `write()`. That's all.

Let's look at this in context to make better sense of it.

**LAB
11.2**

PLANET4.PL
```
 1 #!/usr/bin/perl
 2 %worlds = (
 3   Mercury => 57.9, Venus => 108.2, Earth => 149.6,
 4   Mars => 227.9, Jupiter => 778.3, Saturn => 1427,
 5   Uranus => 2870, Neptune => 4497, Pluto => 5900,
 6 );
 7
 8 foreach $planet (keys %worlds) {
 9   $distance = $worlds{$planet};
10   write;
11 }
12
13 format STDOUT =
14 Planet: @<<<<<<<<<  Orbital Distance: @######.##
15      $planet,                        $distance
16 .
```

This program works out to be a lot cleaner than the original, doesn't it? We can easily see what a line of the report will look like when we examine the format specification (*line 14*). The main program loop is not cluttered with fancy `printf()` pyrotechnics. Just one simple directive.

Here's what we get for our trouble:

```
Planet: Venus       Orbital Distance:       108.20

Planet: Jupiter     Orbital Distance:       778.30

Planet: Mars        Orbital Distance:       227.90

... and more ...
```

REPORT HEADERS

One problem with this output is that the labels for each field are repeated on every line. We can civilize this report by providing a header format.

It's constructed exactly like a body format; the only item that changes is
the name.

```
format STDOUT_TOP =
@<<<<<<<<<<     @<<<<<<<<<
"Planet",       "Distance"
.
```

This header specification could have contained only a picture line with
literal data (the headings "Planet" and "Distance"), but by putting picture
fields in place, the alignment can be guaranteed to match the body of the
report as long as we modify the body format spec now to look like:

```
format STDOUT =
@<<<<<<<<<<     @<<<<<<<<<
$planet,        $distance
.
```

And now we can expect output that looks like this:

```
Planet          Distance

Venus              108.20

Jupiter            778.30

Mars               227.90

... and more ...
```

Nothing changed in the rest of the program to produce this effect. By
simply changing the format specification and adding a header spec, the
report could be completely altered. When `write()` is called the first
time, a header is printed, and then the first body line. Each subsequent
call to `write()` will produce only a body line. The first time we call
`write()` after the page is full, another header will be written and then
the first body line of the subsequent page.

So how does `write()` know when the page is full? How does it know
how many lines there are on my page? How do those guys at the video
club know how large my TV is when they reformat the movie to fit my
screen? Nobody really knows the answer to that last question, but we *can*
answer the first two.

REPORT FORMAT SPECIAL VARIABLES

There are five special variables that are related to report formats. They each have default values and you are welcome to alter those if it suits your purpose. Table 11.4 describes the special variables.

Table 11.4 ■ Report format special variables

Special Variable	Meaning
$=	Lines per page
$-	Lines remaining on current page
$~	Name of current report format
$^	Name of current report format header
$%	Current page number

The last one ($%) can be rather handy in report headers. The others are mostly useful when you want to alter the natural behavior of the reporting mechanism. You'll have to try some of that yourself in the Exercises.

LAB 11.2 EXERCISES

11.2.1 USE `format` AND `write()` TO CREATE A REPORT

In Chapter 9, "Files: Outside and In," we saw how to extract directory information from a compressed tar file. You might recall that we used a command like this:

```
open TARDIR, "gzip -dc sample.tar.gz | tar tvf - |";
```

That gave us access to a data stream with the information from the compressed file. We can combine that technique with a format spec and the `write()` statement to get a report from a compressed tar file without disturbing it or making an uncompressed copy.

> **a)** Write a program (`tartoc4.pl`) that reads the table of contents from a tar file and produces a report.

For each file in the archive, the report should show the file datestamp, its size, and a cumulative byte count for files seen up to that point. The name of the file should be last. The report should look something like this:

```
Line #          Date      Bytes  Byte Total   Filename
       1    1999-02-01      200          200   bigfiles.pl
       2    1999-02-06      378          578   notify.pl
       3    1999-02-02        0          578   tmp/
       4    1999-02-02      478         1056   dlist.pl
       5    1999-02-02      611         1667   allinfo.pl
```

Major Ellie looked glumly at her calendar and realized that with all of the meetings and memos and phone mail, she'd had little time in the past weeks to fly, or to daydream about the her old friends, the planets, or even to work on her pet Perl programs. She looked at the calendar entries for the next two weeks and it all looked like more of the same.

Decisively, she launched a flurry of e-mail, canceling or declining meetings for the next two days. She changed the greeting on her voicemail to tell callers that she would be unavailable until three days hence. Then she sat back with a smile to stare at the wall for awhile as she pondered the next step in her solar system model program.

Planet	Orbital Distance (Million km)	Diameter (km)	Orbital Period (days)	Rotation Period (hours)
Mercury	57.9	4880	88	1416
Venus	108.2	12100	224.7	5832
Earth	149.6	12756	365.2	23
Mars	227.9	6794	687	24
Jupiter	778.3	142800	4328.9	9
Saturn	1427	120660	10752.9	10
Uranus	2870	51810	30660	16.8
Neptune	4497	49528	60225	16
Pluto	5900	2290	90520	153

With this information, she populated a hash composed of strings built up from the data she had in her table. As an example, the first element in the hash looked like this:

```
Mercury => "57.9:4880:88:1416",
```

At last, she wrote a program that printed a report from this data that looked visually like the chart she'd drawn by hand. (This would be the basis for a later program of hers that could report on even more planet data read from a file.)

LAB 11.2

b) Write the program that Major Ellie built (`planet_rpt.pl`).

_____

_____

11.2.2 USE ADVANCED REPORT FEATURES

When you build production reports, you can often expect to see hundreds, maybe even thousands, of lines of output. During development, you might find it convenient to have a tiny Perl program that can generate many lines to simulate production data. Here's one that gives 1000 lines.

```
perl -e 'foreach (1..1000) {print q{*} x rand 35, qq{\n}}'
```

This prints out 1000 lines, each with a random number of asterisks. If you run the command under the MS-DOS shell, you can simply change the single quotes to double quotes and the program will work just fine. You can use this approach to generate data for the next exercise. (Or feel free to use some other method to produce more than 100 lines of output.)

a) Create a program with a report header that includes the date and page number.

_____

_____

Most of the time we think of report formats as being for those sorts of reports that we send to a printer, or save to be printed later. But with a little creativity, you can use formats to create other sorts of output. Imagine that you wanted to produce a report that would be part of a webpage showing the contents of a compressed tar file.

You've already written a program that can gather the table of contents from a tar file and write a traditional report. Now let's see if you can update it to present the report in HTML format. The idea here will be to present each file-name along with a button that could be used to select it. Here's what your output file should look like:

TARTOC.HTML
```
<html><body>
<h1> File listing: sample.tar.gz </h1>
<-- your report should start here>
<form action="/cgi-bin/getfile.pl" method="post"><ul>
<li><input type="submit" name="pgm.pl" value="Get!">pgm.pl
<li><input type="submit" name="pgm2.pl" value="Get!">pgm2.pl
<li><input type="submit" name="README" value="Get!">README
<-- end of report>
</ul></form>
```

Figure 11.3 illustrates what will happen when this HTML is placed in a file.

Figure 11.3 ■ Output from your Perl program can be a webpage.

With the `tartoc4.pl` program you wrote before as a basis, you can write a program that produces output that ends up like this.

> **b)** Write a program (`tartoc2html.pl`) that can create an HTML page from a tar file listing.

_____

_____

LAB 11.2 EXERCISE ANSWERS

11.2.1 ANSWERS

> a) Write a program (`tartoc4.pl`) that reads the table of contents from a tar file and produces a report.
>
> *Answer: This program does the trick. (Again, remember that your version of tar may return a different table of contents. You may have to adjust your data collection routine appropriately.)*

TARTOC4.PL

```perl
1 #!/usr/bin/perl
2
3 die "usage: $0 tarfilename\n\t"
4    unless defined $ARGV[0];
5 if ($ARGV[0] =~ /^-s$/) {
6    $in = DATA;
7 }
8 else {
9    open TOC, "gzip -dc $ARGV[0] | tar tvf - |"
10       or die "Couldn't open input pipe\n\t";
11    $in = TOC;
12 }
13
14 while ($listing = <$in>) {
15    ($bytes, $dt, $fn) = (split /\s+/, $listing)[2,3,5];
16    $tbytes += $bytes;
17    write;
18 }
19 close $in;
```

```
20
21 format STDOUT_TOP =
22 @>>>>>   @>>>>>>>>>   @>>>>>>>>   @<<<<<<<<<   @<<<<<<<<<<<<<<<
23 "Line #", "Date",   "Bytes",    "Byte Total", "Filename"
24 .
25 format STDOUT =
26 @>>>>>   @<<<<<<<<<   @>>>>>>>>   @>>>>>>>>>   @<<<<<<<<<<<<<<<
27 ++$ln,     $dt,        $bytes,    $tbytes,     $fn
28 .
29
30 __END__
31 -rw-r--r-- agentv/staff 200 1999-02-01 17:09 bigfiles.pl
32 ... other data as before ...
```

This report presents five fields on each line. But look at how simple the main read loop is in *lines 14-18*. Three fields are extracted from the data stream (*line 15*). One field is calculated (*line 16*) and the call to `write()` takes care of everything else. The line number for the report is calculated as part of the format spec (see *line 27*).

Because the data line in a format spec consists of expressions that fill the picture fields, you can put calculations, function calls, or whatever else you like in there. You just have to make sure that you supply enough data to fill up the fields.

b) Write the program that Major Ellie built (`planet_rpt.pl`).

Answer: This simple program meets the minimum specifications for the Exercise. Initialization of the data is omitted here in the interest of space.

PLANET_RPT.PL (FRAGMENT)

```
1  #!/usr/bin/perl
2
3  # initialize the %pdata hash here...
4
5  foreach $pname (keys %pdata) {
6      ($dist,$diam,$orbit,$rotate) = split /:/, $pdata{$pname};
7      write;
8  }
9
10 format =
11 @<<<<<<<<<<<   @#####.#   @#######.#   @######.#   @#####.#
12 $pname,        $dist,     $diam,       $orbit,     $rotate
13 .
```

```
14  format STDOUT_TOP =
15  @<<<<<<<<<<<<   @<<<<<<<    @<<<<<<<<<<   @<<<<<<<<   @<<<<<<<
16  "Planet",      "Orbital",  "Diameter",  "Orbital",  "Rotation"
17  @<<<<<<<<<<<<   @<<<<<<<    @<<<<<<<<<<   @<<<<<<<<   @<<<<<<<
18  "",            "Distance", "(km)",                  "Period",   "Period"
19  @<<<<<<<<<<<<   @<<<<<<<    @<<<<<<<<<<   @<<<<<<<<   @<<<<<<<
20  "",            "(M km)",   "",           "(days)",   "(hours)"
21  @<<<<<<<<<<<<   @<<<<<<<    @<<<<<<<<<<   @<<<<<<<<   @<<<<<<<
22  "------------","--------","----------","---------","--------"
23  .
```

Your program could probably be a bit more complex. For one thing, this one presents the data in the internal storage order of the hash. You might want to take things a step further and choose a sort criterion.

The main program loop (*lines 5-7* in this listing) is very simple now. Essentially, the data is extracted from the hash, and then a call to write() presents the data in report form. The interesting part to us here is the construction of the format specifications.

Notice that the body format (*lines 10-13*) has no apparent name. When a name is not explicitly given, the default is STDOUT. This format understandably consists primarily of numeric fields. The nice thing about that kind of field is that it will align on the decimal, giving a very orderly look to the output.

The header format (*lines 14-23*) might be more complex than necessary. It would probably have been okay to have simply used literal information for the header. The benefit of using precise fields populated by literal strings is that it will be a little easier to keep the header uniform if changes are made during program maintenance. A little extra effort now might save a lot of effort later when the schedule is tight.

You can bet that Major Ellie's actual program is a lot more elaborate than this one, and I hope that yours is, too. Before you go on to the next Exercise, why not take a little time to see if you can enhance yours (or this one) by adding some features? Maybe you'll create something you'd like to bring to the companion website.

11.2.2 ANSWERS

a) Create a program with a report header that includes the date and page number.

Answer: Here is a program that does the thing.

DYNAHEADER.PL
```
1 #!/usr/bin/perl
2 $now = gmtime time;
3 foreach (1..1000) {
4     $line = "*" x rand 35;
5     write;
6 }
7 format STDOUT_TOP =
8 @<<<<<<<<<<<<<<<        @|||||||||||||||||||||||||||||        Page @>>>>
9 $now,                "Perl Program Report",                    $%
10 .
11 format STDOUT =
12     @<<<<<<<<<<<<<<<<<<<<<<<<<<<<<<<<<<<<<<<<<<<<<<<<<<<<<<<<<<
13     $line
14 .
```

Most of this program is a formality to test the behavior of report format headers. The loop in *lines 3-6* is a convenience to concoct some data that can be used as the body of the report. The real reason we're here is the format header specification in *lines 7-10*. In this, you can see that we include two variables and one literal string.

If you want to do so, it is permissible to have an expression where the variable $now appears that could calculate the time (or anything else) dynamically. As a substitute for *line 9*, for instance, you could have:

```
scalar(gmtime time),  "Perl Program Report",               $%
```

This would conduct the calculation each time the report header is generated.

b) Write a program (tartoc2html.pl) that can create an HTML page from a tar file listing.

Answer: The following program does the work and adds a couple of twists to enhance the output. (Your version of tar(1) may have different output. If that is the case, then you'll have to modify the program slightly to account for the differences in data.)

TARTOC2HTML.PL.

```
1  #!/usr/bin/perl
2
3  die "usage: $0 tarfilename\n\t"
4      unless defined $ARGV[0];
5  if ($ARGV[0] =~ /^-s$/) {
6      $in = DATA;
7      $tfilename = "default.data";
8  }
9  else {
10     $tfilename = $ARGV[0];
11     open TOC, "gzip -dc $tfilename | tar tvf - |"
12         or die "Couldn't open input pipe\n\t";
13     $in = TOC;
14  }
15
16  while ($listing = <$in>) {
17      ($bytes, $dt, $fn) = (split /\s+/, $listing)[2,3,5];
18      $fn = qq{"$fn"};
19      write;
20  }
21  close $in;
22  print  "</code></ul></form></body>\n";
23
24  format STDOUT_TOP =
25  <html><body> <h1> File listing: @<<<<<<<<<<<<<<<<<<<<<<<<<< </h1>
26                                  $tfilename
27  <form action="/cgi-bin/getfile.pl" method="post"><ul><code>
28  .
29  format STDOUT =
30  <li><INPUT TYPE="SUBMIT" NAME=@<<<<<<<<<<<<<<<<<<<<<<<< 10 VALUE="Get!">
31                                  $fn
32  @<<<<<<<<<  @#######. @<<<<<<<<<<<<<<<<<<<<<<<<
33  $dt,            $bytes,    $fn
34  .
35
36  __END__
37  -rw-r--r-- agentv/staff 200 1999-02-01 17:09 bigfiles.pl
38  ... [other data as before] ...
```

This turns out to be only a minor revision from the `tartoc4.pl` program. We grabbed the input file name (or create one) in *lines 7 and 10*. There is a minor change to *line 18* so that we can surround the individual filenames in double quotes. This is necessary for the reference to the filename as part of the HTML code.

Both the header and the body line format each consist of two lines. Using multiple lines per entry in the body is less common in printed reports intended for human consumption because multi-line reports are considered difficult to read. While creating HTML, this is no problem because a browser program will read the output we're creating here. The human who sees the report will see only what the browser renders from the code in our output. Using multiple lines per entry is just fine for this purpose.

The test for your program should be to run it and redirect the output to a file, and then use a browser to see the file. If you can get this right, you're almost ready to take on the tricky challenge presented by CGI programming.

LAB 11.2 REVIEW QUESTIONS

1) Where must a format specification be placed in your Perl program?
   a) _____ at the top of the program.
   b) _____ at the bottom of the program.
   c) _____ immediately prior to the `write()` statement.
   d) _____ any convenient place in the program .

2) How do you choose the name for your format specification?
   a) _____ The easiest thing is to call it by the same name as the file-handle with which it will be used.
   b) _____ Call it whatever you like as long as you use all caps.
   c) _____ Name it exactly the same as the program that contains it.
   d) _____ Call it whatever you like as long as you don't have a scalar variable with the same name.

3) Your program is going to print a report to the console. The format specification you've written is named STDOUT. What should you call the specification for the report header?
   a) _____ Call it `STDOUT_HDR`.
   b) _____ Call it `STDOUT_TOP`.
   c) _____ Call it `&STDOUT_TOP`.
   d) _____ Call it `STDOUT_H`.

4) Which of these is the special variable that represents the current page number in a report?
   a) _____ `$.`
   b) _____ `$pn`
   c) _____ `$%`
   d) _____ `$&`

Quiz answers appear in Appendix A, Section 11.2.

L A B   11.3

USING PERL MODULES

LAB OBJECTIVES

After this Lab, you will be able to:

✓ Use a Perl Module to Parse Command Lines

✓ Use a Perl Module to Recurse a Directory Tree

We talked a bit in Chapter 9, "Files: Outside and In," about traditional Perl libraries and about the increased popularity of the type of library called a *Perl module.* Beginning with Perl 5, it became possible to create a library that is protected from interference from (or with) the program that uses it.

Once you have grasped the fundamentals of Perl programming, you begin to see that the bulk of your work actually consists of using modules to perform tasks that someone has already solved in a systematic fashion. In this Lab, we'll look at two modules that you might find useful, and in doing so, I hope to make it easier for you to use any module that you might run across during your adventures with Perl.

USING A PERL MODULE—GENERAL RULES

You have to do these things to use a Perl module:

1. Install the module (unless it's part of the standard distribution).
2. Pull it into your program with the "use" directive.
3. Call the functions that it provides.

The first step may be easier than you think. Many Perl modules are presented as part of the standard distribution. The two that we'll look at in this Lab are in that category. Most of the others that you will have to install are accompanied by instructions that describe the steps you must conduct for a successful installation. If the module you need is not part of your standard distribution (or if it is, but for some reason is not installed on your system), you can find what you need at <http://www.cpan.org>, where most Perl modules can be obtained.

With your module properly installed, it is time for your program to load it. A line that looks like this will do the trick:

```
use Carp;
```

This causes the module (in this example, a module named "Carp") to be loaded into the program at compile time. If the module has already been loaded, this directive will simply be ignored. From this point on, any "public" functions and variables from that module are available to your program.

The third step above is to use the facilities provided by the module. Just what those facilities are is determined by the design and construction of the module. Just as each module usually comes with information about how to install, most modules are accompanied by documentation about the pieces of it that you can use. (And of course the module is written in Perl, so you will be able to read large parts of it, even now.)

If you couldn't find any documentation on the Carp module, you might still be able to tell that it contains a function named carp() and one called confess() and one called croak() by inspecting it directly.

WHERE DOES A MODULE LIVE?

After you've put a module into place, you should be able to find it somewhere in one of the directories contained in the @INC array. (If not, then you will have to locate it the hard way and either move it, or modify the @INC.) You will see a file with the module name and a .pm extension. (For instance, the "Carp" module mentioned before will be in a file called Carp.pm, located somewhere in one of the Perl library directories.)

Let's assume for a moment that your @INC contains a directory called /usr/local/perl/lib (or c:\perl5\lib on a Win32 system). If you look there, you should see the file called Carp.pm, along with a number of others. You will also see a number of subdirectories, including File/ and Getopt/, which, in turn, host modules of their own.

When a module name has more than one part (like File::Find and Getopt::Std), you can find that actual .pm file in the subdirectory indicated by the second part (or additional parts) of its name. So for our UNIX example in the last paragraph, if I go looking for the File::Find module, I might expect to see it in a file called /usr/local/perl/lib/File/Find.pm.

PARSING COMMAND LINES—THE EASY WAY

So let's put a Perl module to use. In the standard distribution, we get a module called Getopt::Std, which is designed to make it easy for us to read a command line formed in the traditional UNIX fashion. By that I mean that if you want your program to use a command line that functions in a fashion similar to ls(1), you might have to do a lot of work without this module.

■ FOR EXAMPLE

These four commands are all legal uses of ls(1)

```
ls -C -F
ls -CF
ls -1 -R -A
ls -1RA
```

Similarly, these commands accomplish the same thing with one version of the ps(1) command.

```
ps -f -u billybob
ps -u billybob f
ps -fu billybob
```

Parsing command lines in a way that allows that much flexibility could be tricky if you wanted to take the traditional plodding approach with conditionals and branching. The `Getopt` modules make it easy to write a program that works in this way, though.

■ FOR EXAMPLE

Let's write a simple program that accepts as many as four command-line options. Here's the syntax model:

```
testopts.pl [-v] [-x] [-f filename] [-u username]
```

This is how we could use the `Getopt::Std` module to process such a command line.

TESTOPTS.PL
```
1 #!/usr/bin/perl
2 use Getopt::Std;
3
4 getopts ('vxf:u:');
5 print "verbose on\n" if defined $opt_v;
6 print "extended mode\n" if defined $opt_x;
7 print "filename is $opt_f\n" if defined $opt_f;
8 print "username is $opt_u\n" if defined $opt_u;
```

The module is loaded in *line 2*. With that in place, we now have a function called `getopts()`. This function expects an argument consisting of a control string that contains all of the legal command-line options. In the control string, any options that are expected to be followed by an additional argument should have a colon character after them.

Look at the call to `getopts()` in *line 4*. From this, we should expect that the options 'v' and 'x' are to be simple options, while the 'f' and 'u' options are to be followed by additional information.

Here's what it looks like when we run the program:

```
1 $ testopts.pl -v -f bigfile -x
1 verbose on
1 extended mode
1 filename is bigfile
```

The same result would have occurred if we'd run it with any of the following command lines:

```
testopts.pl -vx -f bigfile
testopts.pl -vxf bigfile
testopts.pl -vxfbigfile
```

You can probably tell, from looking at the program and the result of the run, that any legal options detected by `getopts()` are stored in variables like `$opt_N`, where '*N*' is the identifier for the option. After `getopts()` runs, the options identified as legal will have been removed from the command line. If other information is present, it will remain in @ARGV for further processing.

RECURSIVELY WORKING A DIRECTORY TREE

While programming in Perl, a task that often comes up is that of conducting an operation on all of the files in a particular branch of the directory tree. For instance, suppose that, as a website administrator, you needed to go through your entire web document base to confirm that all of the documents are owned by the user "httpd" and that the permissions mode is 464 for every file.

In Perl, you'd have at least four different ways to go about it. The first would be to write all of the code necessary to read in the contents of each directory, check files that were found, and follow additional directories downward, looking at files in those places as well. (This really isn't that difficult to do in Perl and you know enough to do this, but there's a better way.)

Another way would be to use the UNIX `find(1)` command.

Once you form the correct `find(1)` command line, you could easily open a pipe to get the output from this command and process it in your Perl program. Or, you can take advantage of the `find2perl` program, which is designed to turn a `find(1)` command into a Perl program. (`find2perl` is part of the standard Perl distribution.) To use it, simply replace `find` in your command line with `find2perl`.

But possibly the simplest way to handle a task that must be conducted recursively over an entire branch of the directory tree is to use the

`File::Find` module, designed specifically for this sort of work. Let's take a look at a program that speaks a lot for itself.

■ FOR EXAMPLE

To use the `File::Find` module, you really need to know only a couple of things. After you load the module, you'll have access to a function called `find()`, which expects two things. It wants a *reference* to a function that will handle the operation you plan to conduct, and the name of one or more directories that will form the starting points for the tree traversal. (The short story about creating a reference to a function is that you simply escape the formal name of the function by using the \ character. There's a lot more to the story, but this is enough to get you to work on this activity.)

LAB 11.3

Take a look at the following program:

TUSFIND.PL

```
 1 #!/usr/bin/perl
 2 use File::Find;
 3
 4 $size_t = 500000;
 5 $age_t = 300;
 6
 7 find (\&wanted, "/tmp", "/usr/spool", "/usr/tmp");
 8
 9 =notes
10 ...inside the wanted() function ...
11 $File::Find::dir is the name of the directory under consideration
12 we are currently in that directory
13 $_ is the name of the file under current consideration
14 $File::Find::name is the fully qualified name
15 =cut
16
17 sub wanted {
18    ($size,$mtime) = (stat $_)[7,9];
19    ($size > $size_t) && do {
20       printf "bigone -- %9d  %s\n", $size, $File::Find::name;
21    };
22    (-M _ > $age_t) && do {
23       $now = localtime($mtime);
24       printf "oldone -- %s  %s\n", $now, $File::Find::name;
25    };
26 }
```

This program does draw deeply on things we talked about before and does one thing that is new to us. In *line 7*, where you see "\&wanted", we are not calling the function at that time. What we're doing is telling the find() function that, as it traverses the directory tree, it can use the wanted() function whenever it is considering a file and trying to decide whether to do anything about it.

We often refer to this sort of thing as a *callback* function. What we're saying to the find() function is, "Hey, when you get to a certain point, you're going to need a function that can do part of your work for you. Here is the function we want you to call."

The commentary in *lines 9-15* is there simply to give you some idea about what resources are available to you from within your wanted() function. When the function is actually called, these things will all be true.

The technique used in *line 22* may stir a dim recollection for you if you only vaguely recalled that the special entity _ (underscore) refers to whatever file was most recently tested with a file test operator or passed to the stat() function. The test operator in use here is the one that returns the number of days since the file was last modified, calculated from the time at which our program began.

You really have to work with this a few times before it becomes natural, but when you've done so, this will become a very powerful technique for which you may find many uses.

LAB 11.3 EXERCISES

11.3.1 USE A PERL MODULE TO PARSE COMMAND LINES

a) Write a program (simpleopts.pl) using Getopt::Std that examines the command line and simply prints information about what it finds there. The program should support the following options:

```
-x N = use debugging level N
-v = verbose mode
-c filename = use filename for config information
```

For any of the supported options, print a specific message, and then, after having checked for all of those, print what's left of @ARGV so you can see how getopts() treats unsupported options as well as other information found on the command line.

Test your programs with each of the following command lines:

```
simpleopts.pl -x 5
simpleopts.pl -v -x 2
simpleopts.pl -vx2 -c file1
simpleopts.pl -vx2 -c file1 file2 file3
simpleopts -vxc 5 filename
```

Uncle Larry sat in front of the keyboard and rubbed his hands together with satisfaction. His Storyteller program was now complete. He could run it from the command line and have it generate a story on the console or in a file, and it could generate either plain text or HTML output. The base story could be read from a file named on the command line or the general story embedded in the program would be used. And the config file with the variables could be named on the command line.

He ran his program (storymaker.pl) from the command line with no arguments to get a help message. This is what he saw:

```
usage: storymaker.pl -c cfgfile [-w] [-o ofile] [-s sfile]


   -w = produce HTML version of the story

   -c cfgfile = read variables from cfgfile

   -o ofile = write to ofile instead of console

   -s sfile = read story from sfile


When run with no options, show this help message.
```

b) Write your own version of storyteller.pl that behaves in accordance with the help screen shown here.

11.3.2 USE A PERL MODULE TO RECURSE A DIRECTORY TREE

a) Write your own version of "The Usual Suspects" (`tus2000.pl`) that recursively searches from each of a set of directories that you specify. It should allow a size and age threshold to be specified at the command line as options. It should allow a list of directories to be offered on the command line, or use its own default set.

_____

_____

b) Write a media hunter program (`mhunter.pl`) that will print a catalog of all .gif, .jpg, .mov, and .wav files. It should begin searching recursively from a directory name given on the command line. It should also allow additional file extensions to be named on the command line.

_____

_____

LAB 11.3 EXERCISE ANSWERS

11.3.1 ANSWERS

a) Write a program (`simpleopts.pl`) using `Getopt::Std` that examines the command line and simply prints information about what it finds there.

Answer: This is one way to write the program.

SIMPLEOPTS.PL

```
1 #!/usr/bin/perl
2 use Getopt::Std;
3
```

```
 4 getopts ("vx:c:");
 5 print "Verbose mode\n" if defined $opt_v;
 6 print "Debug level $opt_x\n" if defined $opt_x;
 7 print "Config file is: $opt_c\n" if defined $opt_c;
 8
 9 print "Here's the rest\n";
10 $, = "\n"; print @ARGV;
```

This short program checks for supported options in *lines 4-7* and then dumps the remainder of the argument list to console. You had several example command lines with which to test it. All but the last one are legitimate invocations and should do about what you'd expect. After the legal options have been detected, they are removed from the argument list. Anything that remains is still available.

You can see from the second test example (and others) that it's legal to "gang" the options as long as only one of the options expects an additional argument. (That is to say that –vx is okay, as long as the –v option does not require an argument of its own.)

In the last example, you can tell that if more than one of the options in a ganged set are going to expect additional arguments, the first one of that type is detected, and the remainder of the options set is read as the required argument.

If you need more precise handling of the command-line options or if you want to support a more complex syntax model, you should take a look at the module called Getopt::Long for details about how you can constrain options to accept only certain types of data or provide for mandatory additional arguments.

b) Write your own version of storyteller.pl that behaves in accordance with the help screen shown in the Exercise.

Answer: To conserve space, we print only the interesting segments of the program here. The complete source code is available at the companion website.

STORYMAKER.PL
```
1 #!/usr/bin/perl
2 use Getopt::Std;
3
4 # main()
5 getopts ("wc:o:s:");
```

```
 6 usage() unless defined $opt_c;
 7 exit -2 unless -f $opt_c; # check for config file
 8
 9 open IN, $opt_c || die "couldn't open config file $opt_c\n\t";
10 # read legitimate config file lines into %things
11 close IN;
12
13 # get story text into @story
14 if (defined $opt_s) {
15     # you know how to do this...
16 } # otherwise you read the story from DATA
17
18 # set up output device
19 if (defined $opt_o) {
20     open OUT, "> $opt_o" || die "Couldn't open file $opt_o\n\t";
21     select OUT;
22 }
23
24 # select output format
25 if (defined $opt_w) {
26     webstory();
27 }
28 else {
29     printstory();
30 }
31
32 close OUT;
33 # end of main()
34
35 sub printstory {
36     foreach (@story) {
37         s/\+([^+]+)\+/$things{$1}/g; # perform substitutions
38         printf "%s\n", $_;
39     }
40 }
41 sub webstory {
42     print << "EOHead";
43 <html><head>
44 <title>A Story That Could Happen To You</title>
45 </head><body><h1>A Story That Could Happen To You</h1>
46 EOHead
47     printstory();
48     print << "EOFoot";
49 <hr> This story brought to you by OpenLingo Productions
50 </body></html>
```

```
51  EOFoot
52  }
53
54  __END__
55  # you know what goes here...
```

This program begins as you would expect. The setup code in *lines 2-7* is much like what we've seen before. The fragment represented by *lines 9-11* simply reads legal lines in from the configuration file, just like we saw in our last version of this program. The code that follows, down through *line 20*, is all very much like things you've done several times now.

In *line 21*, however, we do something new. Here, we choose the OUT filehandle as the new default. By doing this, we can force simple print() and printf() statements to route their output to the newly select()'d filehandle. That simplifies the construction of the printstory() and webstory() functions presented in *lines 35-52*.

11.3.2 ANSWERS

a) Write your own version of "The Usual Suspects" (tus2000.pl) that recursively searches from each of a set of directories that you specify.

Answer: Here is a partial listing of the final program.

```perl
1  #!/usr/bin/perl
2  use Getopt::Std;
3  use File::Find;
4
5  sub usage {
6      die "usage: $0 [-o nDays] [-b nMB] [directory ...]\n";
7  }
8
9  # main ()
10 # determine settings
11 getopts("ob");
12 $age_t = defined $opt_o ? $opt_o : 90;
13 $size_t = 1024 * 1024 * defined $opt_b ? $opt_b : 5;
14
15 # set up directory list
16 @dlist = qw{/tmp /usr/tmp /var/spool};
17 foreach (@ARGV) {
18     push @dlist, $_ if (-d $_ && -x _);
```

```
19 }
20 # go check it out...
21 find (\&wanted, @dlist);
22 exit;
23 # end of main ()
24
25 sub wanted {
26     # this is the same as tusfind.pl
27 }
```

Your own program can be much better than this, of course. This example merely shows a foundation for what could be a very useful program to a system administrator or webmaster.

The usage() function in *lines 5-7* concisely shows the options that work with this program. You could easily add an option that allows the command-line directories to replace the default ones that are defined in the program (maybe -i to "ignore" or -r to "replace").

The code in *lines 12-13* sets program options to defaults or to the values provided on the command line. Little effort is made here to check the validity of the command-line input. It would probably be wise to make more complete checks on that data before it is used. Also, in spite of the clever use of the conditional operator to stuff all of this work into two lines, you might find it appropriate to spread this code out a little bit to allow more flexibility and readability.

The loop in *lines 17-19* does a better job of checking data before it is put to use. Notice that each argument left on the command line after the legal options have been removed is tested to ensure that it's a directory and that it's accessible to the program. In the interest of brevity again here, a directory that is not accessible or that doesn't exist is ignored and the program fails silently to consider it. You might want to beef this part of the program up to log an error message when a named directory cannot be used.

b) Write a media hunter program (mhunter.pl) that will print a catalog of all .gif, .jpg, .mov, and .wav files.

Answer: If not for the command-line processing, your program could be as simple as this:

MHUNTER0.PL

```
1  #!/usr/bin/perl
2  use File::Find;
3
4  @typelist = qw{wav gif jpg mov};
5  find (\&wanted, "/tmp");
6
7  sub wanted {
8      foreach $type (@typelist) {
9          /$type$/i && print "$File::Find::name\n";
10     }
11 }
```

**LAB
11.3**

Very simple, eh? Because the callback function will have access to the full pathname for the "current" file (as $File::Find::name) and the base name of the file (as $_), we can write very concise code to check for name patterns and print the filename.

Of course, we do need to meet the published specifications, so this full version will do. It's not much more complicated.

MHUNTER.PL

```
1  #!/usr/bin/perl
2  use File::Find;
3
4  sub usage {
5      die "usage: $0 basedir [extension ...]\n";
6  }
7
8  # main()
9  usage() unless defined $ARGV[0];
10 $basedir = shift;
11
12 # define media types
13 @typelist = @ARGV if defined $ARGV[0];
14 splice @typelist, 0, 0, qw{gif jpg mov wav};
15 # go find them
16 find (\&wanted, $basedir);
17 exit;
18 # end of main()
19
20 sub wanted {
21     foreach $ext (@typelist) {
22         print "$File::Find::name\n" if /$ext$/i;
23     }
24 }
```

By this time, you should have no trouble reading this program, even when it gets a little squirrelly in *lines 13-14* where it assigns values to the array that holds file type extensions. Your final version of this program should probably push the found filenames into an array to be presented in a more careful report.

If you find this program to be useful, you might want to look at the final version on the companion website for ideas about writing your own.

LAB 11.3 REVIEW QUESTIONS

1) To load a Perl module for use by your program, which of these lines would you use?
   a) _____ `use Modulename;`
   b) _____ `require Modulename;`
   c) _____ `load Modulename;`
   d) _____ `use::module Modulename;`

2) To be available for use, a Perl module must be in which of the following?
   a) _____ a sanitary single-use foil packet.
   b) _____ one of the directories in the `@INC` array.
   c) _____ the same directory as the Perl binary file.
   d) _____ any subdirectory below the current directory.

3) The `Getopt::Std` module allows command-line options to be read into variables of which of the following forms?
   a) _____ `$option_N` where *N* is the option.
   b) _____ `$flagN` where *N* is the option.
   c) _____ `$opt_N` where *N* is the option.
   d) _____ `$opt[N]` where *N* is the option.

4) Which of the following lines looks for the options "`-v`" "`-x`" or "`-f filename`"?
   a) _____ `getopt ('vxf');`
   b) _____ `getopts ('vxf');`
   c) _____ `getopt ('vxf');`
   d) _____ `getopts ('vxf:');`

5) When you use the `find()` function from the `File::Find` module, what name do you use to refer to the currently processing filename?
   a) _____ the filename is stored in `$fname`.
   b) _____ the filename is stored in the default variable.
   c) _____ the filename is stored in `$File::Find::filename`.
   d) _____ the filename is stored in `%File::Find{'name'}`.

Quiz answers appear in Appendix A, Section 11.3.

C H A P T E R   11

TEST YOUR THINKING

Barber Tom was terribly pleased with the reception of his "To Do List" system. He knew it wasn't because the program was some sort of engineering marvel, it was simply that his friends had wanted a system like this and he'd been the first one to "get around to doing it."

In order to make it a little easier to use, Tom decided to embed documentation into the program. Using POD markups, he built documentation primarily designed to create a set of help text files that could actually be read through his interactive menu system. But thanks to the flexibility of POD content, he could also create man pages for use while he used the command-line programs that made up his suite.

1)   1) Build a final revision to the To Do List system that includes POD documentation for all of the major parts. Documentation for the interactive shell should be written to produce text files that could be called from the menus. Documentation for the command-line tools should be designed primarily to produce man pages. When you've finished writing the documentation, create text files, man pages, and HTML pages so you can compare the differences between the three output types.

Major Ellie picked up the ringing phone and was pleased to find that Coach Randal was at the distant end. "I heard that you called me," Randal began. "Yes," replied Ellie. "I wanted to talk to you some more about our discussion on sorting. You see, I'm working on a program, and I need to be able to flexibly sort information on a field that is determined at run time."

"This isn't hard," Randal told her. "The key is something called a 'function reference.' What you do is write a function that acts the same way the evaluation block did in your earlier programs. It can assume that there will be two variables, $a and $b. It should return a value based upon the comparison of the two values.

"Once you have that right, simply take the formal name of the function (that means with the ampersand at the beginning), and slap a backslash in front of it, then put that in as the first argument when you call the `sort()` *function. Look, I'm e-mailing you two lines of code. I'll bet you can figure the rest out by yourself."*

Ellie frowned dubiously at her end of the line. But she said, "Okay, I'll take a look. Will you be around later if I have questions?" Randal said, "Yes, just call after practice today." Ellie grinned to herself, "Have you already sent that e-mail?" "Yes, it's on the way," Randal had just finished pressing the "send" button.

Ellie smiled, "Speaking of e-mail, did you get that special play diagram I sent you after your last game?" Randal breathed in, "You know, I—listen, one of my captains just walked in, I'll have to talk to you about that later." He dropped the line. Ellie opened her mailbox and found the following two lines of code:

```
sub byval { return $a <=> $b}
sort \&byval, qw{10 100 2 200 1000};
```

2) Take the information from Major Ellie's planetary data sheet and write a program that can report the information in order by any one of the characteristics.

3) Revise the "Media Hunter" program to act a little more intelligently. Instead of simply printing the name of each target file as it is found, store each name in one of a set of arrays. There should be one array for images, one for sounds, one for animations, and one for each other category that would interest you.

Before the program ends, print out a report that shows the component files for each category.

A P P E N D I X A

ANSWERS TO SELF-REVIEW QUESTIONS

CHAPTER 1
Lab 1.1 ■ Self-Review Answers

Question	Answer	Comments
1	b	The -v option to Perl will tell you the version as well as some of the details about how the binary was compiled.
2	b	The -e option tells Perl to execute the next argument as a script. The argument that follows the option should be a single-quoted string on most UNIX systems, and a double-quoted string when the MS-DOS prompt is your shell.
3	a	Your instructions can be executed once for each line of the input file(s) if you use the Perl -ne option. The most common use of this option is to select certain lines in an input stream to be printed.
4	c	Your instructions can be executed once for each line of the input file(s) before the line is finally printed when you use the -p option.
5	c	In Perl there are many ways to print a line, but the most common is to use the print() function.
6	b	In addition to the \n for newlines and \t for tabs, there are a number of other special escape characters used in Perl.
7	c	The match operator is one of the most important mechanisms used in Perl because so many activities involve pattern-matching.
8	d	The substitute operator is a handy way to edit the contents of a character string.

Lab 1.2 ■ Self-Review Answers

Question	Answer	Comments
1	c	The semicolon marks the exact end of a Perl statement. Several statements can exist on one line as long as each is terminated properly, and one statement can span several lines as long as it is eventually complete and terminated with the semicolon. The absolute final statement in a block may omit the semicolon, but it is not recommended as a habit.
2	a	Unless it appears as part of a quoted string, the # symbol means that the rest of the line should be ignored at run-time. (During development and maintenance programming time, however, you want to pay close attention to the content of such comments.)
3	b	There are occasionally other invocations that will work, and of course the one in your programs must actually point to the correct path for Perl.
4	b	You may put any Perl option switches that you want in the interpreter invocation. It is actually a good habit to use the -w option to have Perl print more detailed warnings when things don't look right.

CHAPTER 2
Lab 2.1 ■ Self-Review Answers

Question	Answer	Comments
1	a	The entire collection of arguments is held in a structure called @ARGV, and the first argument can be referred to with $ARGV[0]. The next argument is called $ARGV[1] and so forth.
2	b	The entire collection of environment variables is held in a structure called %ENV and any given environment variable can be referred to with a name that looks like $ENV{'VARNAME'}
3	c	Actually, there might be no right answer among your choices. There is the practical limit of available memory. Obviously you can only have as many arguments to the print() function as memory allows. I'm just betting that the limit of your patience comes up sooner than the limit to memory most times.

Lab 2.2 ■ Self-Review Answers

Question	Answer	Comments
1	c	The use of the *filehandle* STDIN in conjunction with the *angle bracket operator* provides one of two common ways to read from the keyboard. You will probably see <STDIN> appear in much of the code you encounter.

Lab 2.2 ■ Self-Review Answers (Continued)

Question	Answer	Comments
2	c	Whenever input is likely to contain a newline character at the end of a line, we may need to consider the necessity of stripping that character, especially if we are planning to do some comparisons or pattern matching.
3	d	The `system()` command executes external programs very nicely. Just be sure to watch your quotes whenever you try to pass a complex comment line as an argument to this function.
4	c	The *backtick operator* is a handy way to get program input by running an external command that is equipped to provide it.

Lab 2.3 ■ Self-Review Answers

Question	Answer	Comments
1	c	Whenever the *angle bracket operator* is used without an enclosed file-handle, it can read from the files named on the command line, or from STDIN. This is one of the handiest and most powerful syntactic mechanisms in all of Perl.
2	c	The only option that answers the question correctly is this one. But it is not a completely safe way to open a file. Option "d" is actually closer to the correct answer we would wish for. If it were not for the fact that it omits an important comma after the first argument to the `open()` function, this would be the best right answer. Option "b" is legal code, but it opens the file for writing.
3	a	I sure hope you got that one right. Most of the other options are syntactically legal, but they will not do anything like what you want here.
4	d	Again here, some of the other options contain legal code but not what you would be trying to do.

CHAPTER 3
Lab 3.1 ■ Self-Review Answers

Question	Answer	Comments
1	b	Perl doesn't differentiate between numeric and string data. The context in which you use the data will determine whether it is considered to be numeric or not.
2	d	The $ sign tells us that the named value is a scalar value. This is true whether the variable is a scalar variable itself, or some variable expression that yields a scalar value. You'll see more about this in Chapter 4, "Lists and Arrays."

Lab 3.1 ■ Self-Review Answers (Continued)

Question	Answer	Comments
3	d	Variable names should begin with a letter or an underscore. Treat this as a rule and your life will be much simpler.
4	a	It always pays to embed string information in quotes. There may be very rare situations in which you may omit them for readability or style reasons. But generally, you should always use quotes around a string to be safe.
5	c	Use the chomp() function to trim the trailing newline from a string. The return value from the function tells you how many characters were removed.

Lab 3.2 ■ Self-Review Answers

Question	Answer	Comments
1	b	If you remembered both that ** is the Perl exponentiation operator and that 10 to the 3rd power is 1000, you will have had no problem with this question.
2	a	To get this right, you would have to have recalled the use of the modulus operator (remainder from integer division of the operands), and the fact that the pre-increment operator will change the value of a variable *before* it is used in an expression.
3	b	Since the associativity of multiplicative operations is from left to right, the multiplication will occur and then the result from that will be divided by the value of $v3.
4	d	This one was a little tricky. You have to know that the decrement operator has about the highest precedence here. Then division is conducted ("--$v2 / $v3" is essentially 12 / 4). Finally the value in $v1 is reduced by that amount; the assignment operator has lowest precedence.
5	b	This question depended heavily upon order of precedence. The increment and decrement operators have the highest precedence, but they do their work first in an expression only if the pre-increment (or pre-decrement) variation is used.

Lab 3.3 ■ Self-Review Answers

Question	Answer	Comments
1	b	Since $power is set to a value that is numerically interpreted as 0, and since any positive integer raised to the 0th power is 1, that's what you get here.

Lab 3.3 ■ Self-Review Answers (Continued)

Question	Answer	Comments
2	b	The plus sign "+" and the string concatenation operator "." are like cousins. And as you can see here, neither one has a problem dealing with numeric data.
3	d	This example illustrates the concept that a series of digits followed by non-numeric information will be interpreted as a number consisting of the initial digits. The primary benefit of this is the case where a string contains a number followed by a newline character. Such a string would be interpreted the way you might like.
4	b	The -w option to Perl is one that you might want to consider using all the time. It will help keep your programs on track.

Lab 3.4 ■ Self-Review Answers

Question	Answer	Comments
1	b	In some languages, the name of the current program is embedded in the argument list. In Perl, a special variable is reserved to represent the name of the current program.
2	c	One easy way to remember this is to think about the question you might ask after an external program has run. "What happened?"
3	c	There are actually a couple of other choices that would work, but they are not the preferred way to send error messages. Use the model shown in answer "c" and you'll never go wrong.

CHAPTER 4
Lab 4.1 ■ Self-Review Answers

Question	Answer	Comments
1	b	A list is nothing more than a bunch of scalar values. Most lists are formed by a comma-separated list of values, but there are other ways that a list can be created.
2	a	An array is simply a variable that holds a list
3	c	Whenever you want to refer to an entire array, you simply precede the name with an @ sign. Or to say it another way, a variable name that begins with @ is meant to be seen as an array.
4	b	Although it is proper to precede the last item in a list in English with the word "and" you will never want to do that in a Perl array or list.
5	b	Always remember that an array uses 0 as the first index. You can change that behavior, but it's generally frowned upon.

Lab 4.2 ■ Self-Review Answers

Question	Answer	Comments
1	c	Sometimes you have to look for small things like the difference between parentheses and braces. Other times you have to look for big things like the fact that a $ precedes scalar data while a @ precedes a complete array.
2	b	The split() function is very helpful when you're dealing with a string that contains a series of words, or when you have data in a structured format (such as a colon-separated data record).
3	c	The sort() function can be easy to use as you see in our examples. It can also be used very flexibly if you're willing to do just a little bit of work. We'll talk about that more as you try new exercises.
4	b	The reverse() function simply inverts the order of elements in an array.
5	c	This shortcut is often taken when iterating through a list or array. You'll begin to see the real power of the approach when you get to Chapter 7, "Regular Expressions."

Lab 4.3 ■ Self-Review Answers

Question	Answer	Comments
1	b	This function is useful to help us get at the most powerful feature of Perl arrays: the fact that they are dynamically sized. The ability to build up an array through accretion will become important as we learn more Perl.
2	b	The pop() function is handy when we want to take items from a list in a "bottom up" fashion.
3	a	A queue can be handy for things like storing a list of tasks to be performed when a service is available, or stacking data so that it can be moved somewhere else.
4	b	Just remember that unshift() is the opposite of shift() (or the opposite of pop(), depending upon how you face). Imagine that you've used shift() to grab the first element from a list. If you changed your mind, you could unshift().
5	c	While splice() may be the most powerful of functions for dealing with an array or list, you can see that it also requires careful attention when used to its fullest capacity.

CHAPTER 5
Lab 5.1 ■ Self-Review Answers

Question	Answer	Comments
1	b	You can initialize a hash with a simple list containing key/value pairs, or you can use the Perl 5 hash syntax (key => value).
2	b	A hash may be printed when its name appears as an unquoted argument to print(). You probably won't like what you get though.
3	d	This is why. The keys and values are printed all together with no easy way to tell one from the other.
4	c	Remember that if the actual *thing* you are handling (like a hash element in this case) determines the variable name prefix. A hash element is a scalar and should be preceded with a $, while an entire hash is a collection of things and when named in aggregate, its name is preceded by a % sign.
5	d	Like the array, a hash is dynamic, and will come into existence the first time it mentioned constructively. You may declare a hash, and it may be anywhere in the program, but you are not required to do so.

Lab 5.2 ■ Self-Review Answers

Question	Answer	Comments
1	c	The elements of a hash can be retrieved as a collection of keys or a collection of values.
2	b	With three ways to get data from a hash, you should be able to do whatever you need, especially if you think creatively.
3	c	It's important to remember with each() that it will give you only the next key/value pair from the named hash.
4	a	While we can't get the size of a hash directly, we can determine it from the size of a list containing the keys (or values) from the hash.
5	d	The data inside a hash is simply a collection of scalar values. Whatever you know how to do with that sort of data can be done to an element of a hash.

CHAPTER 6
Lab 6.1 ■ Self-Review Answers

Question	Answer	Comments
1	d	Any simple statement can be modified to indicate that it should be executed only *if* (or *unless*) a certain condition is true.
2	c	This is a structure you might use (and will definitely see) a lot.
3	b	You can use parentheses almost anywhere and it's often free!

Lab 6.1 ■ Self-Review Answers (Continued)

Question	Answer	Comments
4	b	When you're testing for the logical conjunction of two conditions, use the double ampersand. The single ampersand (the bitwise AND operator) might yield a reasonable result in this example, but it is not likely to always do so.
5	a	The logical NOT operator (!) can be handy when you need to streamline the logic of your program.

Lab 6.2 ■ Self-Review Answers

Question	Answer	Comments
1	c	The difference between parentheses and braces is again important here.
2	a	The correct answer is "true," but you can be easily forgiven for holding an opposing opinion. An if() construct is one in which the condition is stated first, and then an arbitrary sized block of code can be executed if the condition is true. An if() modifier is a clause added to the end of an otherwise complete Perl statement.
3	c	You can use the symbolic OR operator (||) or you can use the English operator (or). In either case, the second element of an array is $array[1].
4	b	The conditional operator can sometimes make your code more streamlined. Does it make it harder to read?
5	d	Even if you decide not to use the conditional operator very much yourself, other programmers will do so. Be sure you can parse this code in your head.

Lab 6.3 ■ Self-Review Answers

Question	Answer	Comments
1	d	It's always important to remember that arrays indexes start at 0.
2	b	The first expression does yield true because, when compared as words, 2 is *larger* than 100.
3	c	When compared ASCIIbetically anyway, "Staubach" gt "Bradshaw" is true.
4	c	This technique is common with programs that act as network servers.
5	b	The ability to test for text content in a file is a powerful tool in Perl.

CHAPTER 7
Lab 7.1 ■ Self-Review Answers

Question	Answer	Comments
1	b	Remember what this expression says: "Somewhere in the line will be a 't' followed by an 'a' and then any number of 'r' characters."
2	a	This is probably what we were after in the last expression. We want the letters "tar" to be present, and they can be followed by a lot or a little of anything else.
3	c	Keep in mind that just because your search pattern ends with something doesn't mean that the string you're searching will necessarily have to end with that pattern to match. Anchor your expressions.
4	b	This time the expression is explicit enough to get what we're after because it mandates that the "`pl`" must be immediately preceded by a "`.`" character.
5	a	This time we solved the problem by anchoring the expression to the end of line.

Lab 7.2 ■ Self-Review Answers

Question	Answer	Comments
1	a	Hopefully you never have to do something like this.
2	b	The first choice looks pretty good, but if you look carefully, you'll see that it also matches the leading whitespace character.
3	a	Here we said, starting at the beginning of the input pattern, look for a run of non-digit characters followed by a run of purely digit characters (which we will mark and remember in $1).
4	b	Sometimes it takes a bit of patience to sort out a pattern like this. But go slow, and with some practice, you'll be building your own.
5	c	Converting the case of characters in a string is one of the two most common jobs for the transliteration operator.

Lab 7.3 ■ Self-Review Answers

Question	Answer	Comments
1	b	This is a good expression because it also matches when the equal sign is surrounded by whitespace.
2	c	The set of non-whitespace characters optionally surrounded by whitespace and then followed by an equal sign. Isn't that what we asked for?

Lab 7.3 ■ Self-Review Answers (Continued)

Question	Answer	Comments
3	b	It is not uncommon to check only the first few characters of a string when it is being used to select from among a few items.
4	c	Here's an example that proves the principle that a well-anchored regular expression has nothing to fear.

CHAPTER 8
Lab 8.1 ■ Self-Review Answers

Question	Answer	Comments
1	b	The variety of Perl loops is a big part of its strength.
2	c	This is not really a subjective question. The foreach() loop is specially designed to make it easy for you to work with lists and arrays.
3	b	The special feature of the while() loop for reading from a filehandle makes it the obvious first choice.
4	a	This is exactly how the same loop is written in C, C++, Java and even a couple of other languages.

Lab 8.2 ■ Self-Review Answers

Question	Answer	Comments
1	d	Sometimes punctuation is everything.
2	a	Isn't that an embarrassment of riches? You get all of these choices so that you can put your own particular *spin* on your code.
3	a	How many passengers will get off of the bus? The only real question here was, "How many times will that newline character be printed?" It's in the outer loop. Looks like five times.
4	c	That's what they call the "triangular number" for the number that represents the size of the outer loop.
5	b	The loop doesn't run for the number five, so that many fewer stars.

Lab 8.3 ■ Self-Review Answers

Question	Answer	Comments
1	b	Perl does not define a specific keyword for "tar" so placing the word in that context has the same effect as placing any arbitrary character string there.
2	a	The next command allows us to begin on the next iteration of the loop right away.

Lab 8.3 ■ Self-Review Answers (Continued)

Question	Answer	Comments
3	c	The `last` command makes it easy to drop out of the loop right away.
4	b	If we want to return to the beginning of this iteration of the loop, we can count on the `redo` command.
5	b	What `break` statement? Perl has a `last` command to do what the `break` statement does in other languages.

CHAPTER 9
Lab 9.1 ■ Self-Review Answers

Question	Answer	Comments
1	b	Perl uses this mechanism to represent time in a way that is impervious to the change in the millennium and that coincides with the timestamp information kept in many filesystems.
2	c	Remember that you can take all of the elements of the list that `stat()` provides for you, or you can get just the *slice* that interests you.
3	b	In a scalar context, `readdir()` returns the next filename from the directory being read.
4	b	The mode, size, and modification time are probably the most commonly used of a file's status information.
5	d	An error in the `print()` statement prevents the modification time from being printed. Now do you understand the comments embedded in the program?

Lab 9.2 ■ Self-Review Answers

Question	Answer	Comments
1	d	Remember that for C and Perl programmers, the function to remove a file is named for the system call, not for the UNIX command.
2	a	Sometimes the obvious answer is the correct one. Sometimes the answer points to itself.
3	a	This function will work only if the directory is empty.
4	b	The UNIX command of the same name offers a great deal more flexibility.
5	a	You must provide both owner and group information when you want to use the Perl `chown()` function. Also remember that on many UNIX systems, you may not change ownership of a file unless you are the root user.

Lab 9.3 ■ Self-Review Answers

Question	Answer	Comments
1	c	This is pretty close to how you will do it almost every time. The code shown in option "b" would have opened the file for reading, but then would exit the program if the open() call succeeds.
2	a	Fortunately this syntax is similar to that of the UNIX shell, so it's a little easier to remember how this is done.
3	a	That is how you are supposed to do it.
4	c	All you really have to do is look at both ends of the open mode string. If it starts with a pipe symbol, then we're opening the handle for writing. If it ends with a pipe symbol, then we're opening the handle for reading.
5	b	Being able to embed data into a program source code file is a big help to developers and system administrators alike.

CHAPTER 10
Lab 10.1 ■ Self-Review Answers

Question	Answer	Comments
1	c	The sub keyword is to remind us of the concept *subroutine*.
2	b	Unless the main program takes special steps, all of its variables are seen by any subroutines
3	c	Use or don't use the &, it's up to you. Use a parenthesized argument list or not, it's up to you (in Perl 5 anyway).
4	b	A function can be declared anywhere in the program. It will be seen when the program is compiled and will be available at run time.

Lab 10.2 ■ Self-Review Answers

Question	Answer	Comments
1	c	This is the most reliable and most efficient way to limit the scope of a variable.
2	c	If a group of variables are being declared to be local or my variables, they must be presented in a list.
3	c	This is really an easy rule to remember.
4	b	Protecting the value of global variables is exactly why we have the my modifier.
5	b	The main program variables can also be protected with the local modifier.

Lab 10.3 ■ Self-Review Answers

Question	Answer	Comments
1	b	While there are a couple of exceptions to the rule, you should probably be in the habit of providing this line at the end of all your function libraries.
2	c	The `require` statement will pull the library in for you and make its functions available.
3	c	It pays to know what the `@INC` directories are when you start to take advantage of third-party libraries.
4	a	That's exactly when it happens. The `require` statement pulls a library in at run time.
5	d	Anything in a BEGIN block will run during program compile time. It doesn't matter where you put the block, it will run before the first regular instruction in the program does.

CHAPTER 11
Lab 11.1 ■ Self-Review Answers

Question	Answer	Comments
1	c	In spite of how much you might have liked any of the other answers, this is the correct one.
2	b	When the Perl interpreter sees a line that begins with an = sign, it just ignores that line, and everything else until it sees a line with `=cut` by itself.
3	b	POD content can be in a separate file from the program it documents, but it is often much more convenient to keep it in the same file.
4	a	If the first line of a paragraph is indented, the paragraph will be rendered verbatim.

Lab 11.2 ■ Self-Review Answers

Question	Answer	Comments
1	d	Like functions, a format specification can appear at any location in the file that makes sense to you.
2	a	If you dream up a good reason to name your format spec differently from the filehandle to which it will be applied, you will know what to call it at that time. Until then, stick to the pavement.
3	b	Simply append the characters _TOP to a report specification name, and you now have a report header specification name.

Lab 11.2 ■ Self-Review Answers (Continued)

Question	Answer	Comments
4	c	Don't worry if you haven't memorized this one. It's so infrequently used that you may have to look it up every time you want to use it. There's no harm in that.

Lab 11.3 ■ Self-Review Answers

Question	Answer	Comments
1	a	For Perl modules, the use directive is preferred.
2	b	The module should be somewhere in the @INC path. Remember that a module with a multi-part name might be in a subdirectory of one of the @INC directories.
3	c	The variable will be set to 1 if the option is set on the command line, and it will contain a string if the option was one that takes additional arguments (such as -f filename, for example).
4	d	If you want to specify that a particular option takes an additional argument, it must be followed by a : in the string that is passed to getopts().
5	b	The base name of the file is in $_ and the full path is in $File::Find::name when you need absolute path information.

A P P E N D I X   B

PERL REFERENCE

B.I PERL FUNCTIONS

The following is a complete list of Perl functions and a short description of what they do.

abs

abs VALUE
Returns the absolute value of its argument ($_ is the default). Ignores signs.

accept

accept(NEWSOCKET,GENERICSOCKET)
Accepts a socket connection from clients waiting for a connection. The GENERICSOCKET, a filehandle, has been previously opened by the *socket* function, is bound to an address, and is listening for a connection. NEWSOCKET is a filehandle with the same properties as GENERICSOCKET. The *accept* function attaches GENERICSOCKET to the newly made connection. See accept(2)[1].

alarm

alarm(SECONDS)
alarm SECONDS
Sends a SIGALARM signal to the process after a number of SECONDS.
See alarm(3).[2]

atan2

atan(X,Y)
Returns the arctangent of X/Y in the range <pi>.

bind

bind (SOCKET, NAME)
Binds an address, NAME, to an already opened unnamed socket, SOCKET. See bind(2).

---

1. The encircled text is a reference to the like-named UNIX system call found in Section 2 of the UNIX manual pages.
2. The like-named UNIX library function is found in Section 3 of the UNIX manual pages.

binmode

> **binmode(FILEHANDLE)**
> **binmode FILEHANDLE**
> For operating systems that distinguish between text and "binary" mode (not UNIX). Prepares FILEHANDLE for reading in binary mode.

bless

> **bless (REFERENCE, CLASS);**
> **bless REFERENCE;**
> Tells the object referenced by REFERENCE that it is an object in a package (CLASS) in the current package if no CLASS is specified. Returns the reference.

caller

> **caller(EXPR)**
> **caller EXPR**
> **caller**
> Returns an array with information about the subroutine call stack, including the package, filename and line number. With EXPR, a number, goes back EXPR stack frames before current one.

chdir

> **chdir(EXPR)**
> **chdir EXPR**
> **chdir**
> Changes the present working directory to EXPR. If EXPR is omitted, changes directory to home directory. See chdir(2).

chmod

> **chmod (MODE, LIST)**
> **chmod MODE, LIST**
> Changes permissions of a list of files; first argument is the permission MODE number (octal); the remaining arguments are a list of file names. Returns the number of files changed. See chmod(2).

chomp

> **chomp(LIST)**
> **chomp(VARIABLE)**
> **chomp VARIABLE**
> **chomp**
> Chops off the last character of a string, VARIABLE, or the last character of each item in a LIST if that character corresponds to the current value of $/, by default set to the newline. Unlike chop (see below), it returns the number of characters deleted.

chop

> **chop(LIST)**
> **chop(VARIABLE)**
> **chop VARIABLE**
> **chop**
> Chops off the last character of a string, VARIABLE, or the last character of each item in a LIST and returns the chopped value. Without an argument, chops the last character off $_.

chown

> **chown(LIST)**
> **chown LIST**
> Changes owner and group of a list of files. First two elements in the list are the numerical uid and gid, respectively. The rest of the list are the names of files. Returns the number of files changed. See chown(2).

chr

> **chr NUMBER**
> Returns the ASCII value for NUMBER, e.g., chr(66) returns "B".

chroot

> **chroot (FILENAME)**
> **chroot FILENAME**
> Changes root directory for the current process to FILENAME, which is the starting point for pathnames starting with /. Must be superuser to do this. See chroot(2).

close

> **close(FILEHANDLE)**
> **close FILEHANDLE**
> Closes the file, socket, or pipe associated with FILEHANDLE.

closedir

> **closedir(DIRHANDLE)**
> **closedir DIRHANDLE**
> Closes a directory structure opened by *opendir*. See directory(3).

connect

> **connect(SOCKET, NAME)**
> Connects a process with one that is waiting for an *accept* call. NAME is a packed network address. See connect(2).

cos

> **cos(EXPR)**
> **cos EXPR**
> Returns the cosine of EXPR (in radians).

crypt

> **crypt(PLAINTEXT, SALT)**
> The password encryption function where PLAINTEXT is the user's password and SALT is a two character string consisting of characters in the set [a–zA–Z./]. See crypt(3).

dbmclose

> **dbmclose(%ASSOC_ARRAY)**
> **dbmclose %ASSOC_ARRAY**
> Breaks the binding between a DBM file and an associative array. Only useful with NDBM, a newer version of NDBM, if supported. (See untie). Also see dbm(3).

dbmopen

> **dbmopen(%ASSOC_ARRAY, DBNAME, MODE)**
> Binds a DBM or NDMB file to an associative array. Before a database can be accessed, it must be opened by *dbmopen*. The files *file.dir* and *file.pag* must exist. DBNAME is

the name of the file without the *.dir* and *.pag* extension. If the database does not exist and permission MODE is specified, the database is created. See dbminit(3). See tie.

defined

defined(EXPR)
defined EXPR
Returns a Boolean value, 1, if EXPR has a real value. Returns a Boolean value, 0, if EXPR does not have a real value. EXPR may be a scalar, array, hash, or subroutine. For a hash, checks only whether the value (not key) is defined.

delete

delete $ASSOC{KEY}
Deletes a value from an associative array. If successful, returns the deleted value; otherwise, an undefined value. If a value in %ENV is deleted, the environment will be modified. The *undef* function can also be used and is faster.

die

die(LIST)
die LIST
die
Prints the LIST to STDERR and exits with the value of $!, the system error message (errno). When in an *eval* function, sets the $@ value to the error message, and aborts *eval*. If the value of LIST does not end in a newline, the name of the current script, the line number, and a new line are appended to the message.

do

do BLOCK
do SUBROUTINE(LIST)
do EXPR
do BlOCK returns the value of the last command in the BLOCK.
do SUBROUTINE(LIST) calls a SUBROUTINE that has been defined.
do EXPR uses EXPR as a filename and executes the contents of the file as a Perl script. Used primarily to include subroutines from the Perl subroutine library.

dump

dump LABEL
Causes an immediate binary image core dump. Used for undumping a core file; *undump* is not part of this Perl distribution.

each

each (%ASSOC_ARRAY)
each %ASSOC_ARRAY
Returns a two element array, the key and value for the next value of an associative array, in random order.

eof

eof (FILEHANDLE)
eof()
eof
Returns 1 if next read on FILEHANDLE indicates the end of file. If FILEHANDLE is omitted, returns the end of file for the last file read.

eval

eval(EXPR)
eval EXPR

Evaluates expression as a Perl program in the context of the current Perl script. Often used for trapping errors. Eval is used to trap fatal errors. Syntax errors or runtime errors or those coming from the die function are returned to $@ variable. The $@ variable is set to null if there are no errors. The value returned is the value of the last expression evaluated.

exec

exec(LIST)
exec LIST

Executes a system command in LIST in context of the current program. Never returns. If LIST is scalar, checks for shell metacharacters and passes to /bin/sh. Otherwise, arguments are passed to the C function call, execvp. Does not flush output buffer.

exists

exists EXPR

Returns true if a specified key from an associative array exists, even if its corresponding value is undefined.

exit

exit(INTEGER)
exit INTEGER

Exits with script with status value of INTEGER. If INTEGER is omitted, exits with 0, meaning program exits with successful status. Non–zero status implies that something went wrong in the program.

exp

exp(EXPR)
exp EXPR

Returns e to the power of EXPR.

fcntl

fcntl(FILEHANDLE, FUNCTION, SCALAR)

Changes properties on an open file. Requires *"sys/fcntl.ph"*. The FUNCTION can duplicate an existing file descriptor, get or set file descriptor flags, get or set file status flags, get or set asynchronous I/O ownership, and get or set record locks. SCALAR is an integer for flags. See fcntl(2).

fileno

fileno(FILEHANDLE)
fileno FILEHANDLE

Returns the integer file descriptor for FILEHANDLE. Descriptors start with STDIN, STDOUT, STDERR, 0, 1, and 2, respectively. May not be reliable in Perl scripts if a file is closed and reopened. See ferror(3).

flock

flock(FILEHANDLE, OPERATION)

Applies or removes advisory locks on files. OPERATION specifies an operation on a lock for a file, shared locks, exclusive locks, or nonblocking locks. The OPERATION to remove a file is unlock. See flock(2).

fork

> **fork**
>
> Creates a new (child) process. The child is a copy of the parent process. Both child and parent continue execution with the instruction immediately following the *fork*. Returns 0 to the child process and the pid of the child to the parent.

format

> **format NAME =**
>   **picture line**
>   **value list**
>
>   **...**
>
>   **.**
>
> Declares a set of picture lines to describe the layout of corresponding values. The *write* function uses the specified format to send output to a named filehandle represented by NAME. If NAME is omitted, the default is STDOUT.

formline

> **formline PICTURE, LIST**
>
> An internal function used by formats to format a list of values according to the picture line. Can also be called directly in a program.

getc

> **getc(FILEHANDLE)**
> **getc FILEHANDLE**
> **getc**
>
> Returns the next character from the input file associated with FILEHANDLE. Returns a null string at EOF. If FILEHANDLE is omitted, reads from STDIN.

getgrent

> **getgrent**
> **setgrent**
> **endgrent**
>
> Iterates through */etc/group* and returns an entry from */etc/group* as a list, including group name, password, group id, and members.See getgrent(3).

getgrgid

> **getgrgid(GID)**
>
> Returns a group entry file by group number. See getgrgid(3).

getgrnam

> **getgrnam(NAME)**
>
> Returns a group file entry by group name. See getgrent(3).

gethostbyaddr

> **gethostbyaddr(ADDRESS, AF_INET)**
>
> Translates a network address to its corresponding names and alternate addresses. Returns the hostname, aliases, addresstype, length, and unpacked raw addresses. See gethostbyaddr(3). AF_INET is always 2.

gethostbyname

gethostbyname(HOSTNAME)

Translates a hostname to an entry from the */etc/hosts* file as a list, including the hostname, aliases, addresses. See gethostbyname(3). In scalar context, returns only the host address.

gethostent

gethostent
sethostent(STAYOPEN)
endhostent

Iterates through */etc/hosts* file and returns the entry as a list, including name, aliases, addresss type, length, and alternate addresses. Returns a list from the network host database,*/etc/hosts*. See gethostent(3).

getlogin

getlogin

Returns the current login from */etc/utmp*, if there is such a file. See *getlogin(3)*. If getlogin does not work, try:$loginname = getlogin || (getpwuid($<))[0] || die "Not a user here.";

getnetbyaddr

getnetbyaddr(ADDR, ADDRESSTYPE)

Translates a network address to its corresponding network name or names. Returns a list from the network database, */etc/networks*. See getnetent(3). In scalar context, returns only the network name. In scalar context, returns only the network name.

getnetbyname

gatnetbyname(NAME)

Translates a network name to its corresponding network address. Returns a list from the network database, */etc/networks*. See *getnetent(3)*. In scalar context, returns only the network address.

getnetent

getnetent
setnetent(STAYOPEN)
endnetent

Iterates through the */etc/networks* file and returns the entry as a list. Returns a list from the network database, */etc/networks*. See *getnetent(3)*. In scalar context, returns only the network name.

getpeername

getpeername(SOCKET)

Returns the packed *sockaddr* address of other end of the SOCKET connection. See getpeername(2).

getpgrp

getpgrp(PID)
getpgrp PID

Returns the current process group for the specified PID (PID 0 is the current process). Without EXPR, returns the process group of the current process. See *getpgrp(2)*.

getppid

> **getppid**
>
> Returns the PID of the parent process. If 1 is returned, that is the PID for init. Init adopts a process whose parent has died. See *getpid(2)*.

getpriority

> **getpriority(WHICH,WHO)**
>
> Returns the current priority, nice value, for WHICH—a process, a process group, or a user. WHO is relative to which group. A WHO value of zero, denotes the current process, process group, or user. See *getpriority(2)*.

getprotobyname

> **getprotobyname(NAME)**
>
> Translates a protocol NAME to its corresponding number and returns a list including the protocol name, aliases, and the protocol number. Returns a line from the network protocol database, */etc/protocols*. See *getprotoent(3)*.

getprotobynumber

> **getprotobynumber(NUMBER)**
>
> Translates a protocol number to its corresponding name and returns a list including the protocol name, aliases, and the protocol number. Returns a line from the network protocol database, */etc/protocols*. See getprotoent(3).

getprotoent

> **getprotoent**
>
> **setprotent(STAYOPEN)**
>
> **endprotoent**
>
> Returns a list from the */etc/protocols* database, including the protocol name, aliases, and the protocol number. If STAYOPEN flag is non–zero, the database will not be closed during subsequent calls. The endprotoent function closes the file. See *getprotoent(3)*. In scalar context, returns the protocol name.

getpwent

> **getpwent**
>
> **setpwent**
>
> **endpwent**
>
> Iterates through the */etc/passwd* file and returns the entry as a list, username, password, uid, gid, quotas, comment, gcos field, home directory, and startup shell. The endpwent function closes the file. See *getpwent(3)*. In scalar context, returns the username.

getpwnam

> **getpwnam(NAME)**
>
> Translates a username to the corresponding entry in */etc/passwd* file. Returns a list, including the username, password, uid, gid, quotas, comment, gcos field, home directory, and startup shell. See *getpwent(3)*. In scalar context, returns the numeric user ID.

getpwuid

> **getpwuid(UID)**
>
> Translates the numeric user id to the corresponding entry from the */etc/passwd* file. Returns a list, including the username, password, uid, gid, quotas, comment, gcos

field, home directory, and startup shell. See *getpwent(3)*. In scalar context, returns the username.

getservbyname

> **getservbyname(NAME,PROTOCOL)**
>
> From */etc/services* database, translates a port name to its corresponding port number as a scalar and, returns as an array, the service name, aliases, port where service resides, and protocol needed, from the */etc/services* database. See getservent(3). In scalar context, returns only the service port number.

getservbyport

> **getservbyport(PORT_NUMBER,PROTOCOL)**
>
> From */etc/services* database, translates a port number to its corresponding port name as a scalar and, returns as an array, the service name, aliases, port where service resides, and protocol needed, from the */etc/services* database. See getservent(3). In scalar context, returns only the service port number.

getservent

> **getservent**
>
> **setservent(STAYOPEN)**
>
> **endservent**
>
> Iterates through the */etc/services* database, returning the service name, aliases, port where service resides, and protocol needed. If STAYOPEN flag is non–zero, the database will not be closed during subsequent calls and endservent closes the file. See getservent(3). In scalar context, returns only the service port name.

getsockname

> **getsockname(SOCKET)**
>
> Returns the packed sockaddr address of the local end of the SOCKET connection. See getsockname(2).

getsockopt

> **getsockopt(SOCKET, LEVEL, OPTNAME)**
>
> Returns the requested options, OPTNAME, associated with SOCKET, at the specified protocol level. See getsockopt(2).

glob

> **glob EXPR**
>
> Performs filename expansion on EXPR as the shell does. Without EXPR, $_ is used. Uses the internal <*> operator.

gmtime

> **gmtime (EXPR)**
>
> **gmtime EXPR**
>
> Converts the results of the *time* function to a 9 element array with the Greenwich Mean time zone including the second, minute, hour, month day, month, year, weekday, yearday, and 1 if daylight standard time is in effect. See ctime(3) and timegm() in the Perl library module *Time::Local*.

goto

goto **LABEL**
goto **EXPR**
goto **&NAME**
Program branches to the LABEL and resumes execution. Cannot goto any construct that requires intialization, such as a subroutine or foreach loop. Goto never returns a value. The form goto &NAME substitutes the currently running subroutine with a call to NAME (used by the AUTOLOAD subroutine).

grep

grep(**EXPR, LIST**)
grep **BLOCK LIST**
Returns to a new array, any element in LIST where EXPR matches that element. Returns to a scalar, the number of matches.

hex

hex(**EXPR**)
hex **EXPR**
Returns the decimal value of EXPR interpreted as a hexadecimal string. Without EXPR, uses $_.

import

import **CLASSNAME LIST**
import **CLASSNAME**
Not a built-in function, but a class method defined by modules that will export names to other modules through the use function.

index

index(**STR, SUBSTR, POSITION**)
index(**STR,SUBSTR**)
Returns the position of the first occurrence of SUBSTR in STR. POSITION specifies a starting position for the substring in the string starting with base 0.

int

int(**EXPR**)
int **EXPR**
Returns the integer portion of EXPR. Without EXPR, $_ is used.

ioctl

ioctl(**FILEHANDLE,FUNCTION,SCALAR**)
Used to control I/0 operations, mainly terminal I/0. Requires *"sys/ioctl.ph"*. FUNCTION is an I/O request. SCALAR will be read or written depending on the request. See ioctl(2).

join

join(**EXPR, LIST**)
Returns a single string by joining the separate strings of LIST into a single string where the field separator is specified by EXPR, a delimiter.

keys

> **keys(%ASSOC_ARRAY)**
> **keys %ASSOC_ARRAY**
> Returns a normal array consisting of all the keys in the associative array.

kill

> **kill(SIGNAL, PROCESS_LIST)**
> **kill PROCESS_LIST**
> Sends a signal to a list of processes. The signal can either be a number or a signal name (signal name must be quoted). (Negative signal number kills process group.) See kill(2).

last

> **last LABEL**
> **last**
> The last command is comparable to C's break command. It exits the innermost loop, or, if the loop is labeled last LABEL, exits that loop.

lc

> **lc EXPR**
> Returns EXPR in lowercase. Same as \L \E escape sequence.

lcfirst

> **lcfirst EXPR**
> Returns EXPR with the first character in lowercase. Same as \l \E sequence.

length

> **length(EXPR)**
> **length EXPR**
> Returns the length in characters of scalar EXPR, or if EXPR is omitted, returns length of $_. Not used to find the size of an array or associative array.

link

> **link (OLDFILE, NEWFILE)**
> Creates a hard link. NEWFILE is another name for OLDFILE. See link(2).

listen

> **listen(SOCKET, QUEUESIZE)**
> Listens for connections on a SOCKET with a queue size specifying the number of processes waiting for connections. See listen(2).

local

> **local(LIST)**
> Makes variables in LIST local for this block, subroutine or *eval*.

localtime

> **localtime(EXPR)**
> **localtime EXPR**
> Converts the time returned by the *time* function to a 9–element array for the local timezone. See ctime(3).

log

log(EXPR)
log EXPR
Returns the logarithm (base e) of EXPR. If EXPR is omitted, returns log($_).

lstat

lstat(FILEHANDLE)
lstat FILEHANDLE
lstat(EXPR)
Returns a 14–element array consisting of file statistics on a symbolic link, rather than the file the symbolic link points to. The array consists of:
> device
> file inode number
> file mode
> number of hard links to the file
> user ID of owner
> group ID of owner
> raw device
> size of file
> file last access time
> file last modify time
> file last status change time
> preferred blocksize for file system I/O
> actual number of blocks allocated

See stat(2)

map

map (BLOCK LIST)
map (EXPR, LIST)
Evaluates BLOCK or EXPR for each element of LIST and returns the list value containing the results of the evaluation. The following example translates a list of numbers to characters. @chars = map chr, @numbers;

mkdir

mkdir(NAME, MODE)
Creates a directory, NAME, with MODE permissions (octal). See mkdir(2).

msgctl

msgctl(MSGID, CMD, FLAGS)
Calls the *msgctl* system call, allowing control operations on a message queue. Has weird return codes. (See System V IPC.) Requires library file *"ipc.ph"* and *"msg.ph"*. See also msgctl(2).

msgget

msgget(KEY, FLAGS)
Calls *msgget* system call. Returns the message queue id number, or if undefined, an error. (See System V IPC.) See also msgget(2).

msgrcv

msgrcv(MSGID, VAR, MSG_SIZE, TYPE, FLAGS)

Calls the *msgrv* system call. Receives a message from the message queue, stores the message in VAR. MSG_SIZE is the maximum message size and TYPE is the message type. (See System V IPC.) See also msgrcv(2).

msgsnd

msgsnd(ID, MSG, FLAGS)

Calls the *msgsnd* system call. Sends the message, MSG, to the message queue. MSG must begin with the message type. The *pack* function is used to create the message. (See System V IPC.) See also msgsnd(2).

my

my EXPR
my (EXPR1, EXPR2, ...)

Variables declared with the *my* function are made private, i.e., they exist only within the innermost enclosing block, subroutine, eval, or file. Only simple scalars, complete arrays, and hashes can be declared with *my*.

new

new CLASSNAME LIST
new CLASSNAME

Not a built-in function, but a constructor method defined by the CLASSNAME module for creating CLASSNAME type objects. Convention taken from C++.

next

next LABEL
next

Starts the next iteration of the innermost or loop labeled with LABEL. Like the C continue function.

no

no Module LIST

If a pragma or module has been imported with *use,* the *no* function says you don't want to use it anymore.

oct

oct(EXPR)
oct EXPR
oct

Returns the decimal value of EXPR, an octal string. If EXPR contains a leading 0x, EXPR is interpreted as hex. With no EXPR, $_ is converted.

open

open(FILEHANDLE, EXPR)
open (FILEHANDLE)
open FILEHANDLE

Opens a real file, EXPR, and attaches it to FILEHANDLE. Without EXPR, a scalar with the same name as FILEHANDLE must have been assigned that filename.

read	"FILEHANDLE"
write	">FILEHANDLE"
read/write	"+>FILEHANDLE"

append	">>FILEHANDLE"
pipe out	"| UNIX Command"
pipe in	"UNIX Command |"

opendir

opendir(DIRHANDLE, EXPR)

Opens a directory structure, named EXPR, and attaches it to DIRHANDLE for functions that examine the structure. See directory(3).

ord

ord(EXPR)
ord

Returns the unsigned numeric ASCII values of the first character of EXPR. If EXPR is omitted, $_ is used.

pack

$packed=pack("TEMPLATE", LIST)

Packs a list of values into a binary structure and returns the structure. TEMPLATE is a quoted string containing the number and type of value.

TEMPLATE is:
- a   An ASCII string, null padded.
- A   An ASCII string, space padded.
- b   A bit string, low–to–high order.
- B   A bit string, high–to–low order.
- h   A hexadecimal string, low nybble first.
- H   A hexadecimal string, high nybble first.
- c   A signed char value.
- C   An unsigned char value.
- s   A signed short value.
- S   An unsigned short value.
- i   A signed integer value.
- I   An unsigned integer value.
- l   A signed long value.
- L   An unsigned long value.
- n   A short in "network" order.
- N   A long in "network" order.
- f   A single–precision float in native format.
- d   A double–precision float in native format.
- p   A pointer to a string.
- x   A null byte.
- X   Back up a byte.
- @   Null–fill to absolute precision.
- u   A uuencoded string.

package

package NAMESPACE

A package declaration creates a separate namespace (symbol table) for NAMESPACE, the Perl way of creating a class. The NAMESPACE belongs to the rest of the innermost enclosing block, subroutine, eval or file. If the package declaration is at the same level, the new one overrides the old one.

pipe

> **pipe(READHANDLE, WRITEHANDLE)**
> Opens a pipe for reading and writing, normally after a fork. See pipe(2).

pop

> **pop(ARRAY)**
> **pop ARRAY**
> Pops and returns the last element of the array. The array will have one less element.

pos

> **pos (SCALAR)**
> **pos SCALAR**
> Returns the offset of the character after the last matched search in SCALAR left off, i.e., the position where the next search will start. Offsets start at 0. If the *$scalar* is as signed "hello" and the search is *$scalar =~ m/l/g*, the *pos* function would return the position of the character after the first 'l', position 3.

print

> **print(FILEHANDLE LIST)**
> **print(LIST)**
> **print FILEHANDLE LIST**
> **print LIST**
> **print**
> Prints a string or a comma separated list of strings to FILEHANDLE, or to the currently selected FILEHANDLE, or to STDOUT, the default. Retuns 1 if successful, 0 if not.

printf

> **printf(FILEHANDLE FORMAT, LIST)**
> **printf(FORMAT, LIST)**
> Prints a formatted string to FILEHANDLE or, if FILEHANDLE is omitted, to the currently selected output filehandle. STDOUT is the default. See printf(3). Similar to C's printf, except * is not supported.

push

> **push(ARRAY, LIST)**
> Pushes the values in LIST onto the end of the ARRAY. The array will be increased. Returns the new length of ARRAY.

q, qq, qw, qx

> **q/STRING/**
> **qq/STRING/**
> **qw/LIST/**
> **qx/COMMAND/**
> An alternative form of quoting. The *q* construct treats STRING as if enclosed in single quotes. The *qq* construct treats STRING as if enclosed in double quotes. The *qw* construct treats each element of LIST as if enclosed in single quotes, and the *qx* treats COMMAND as if in back quotes.

quotemeta

> **quotemeta EXPR**
>
> Returns the scalar value of EXPR with all regular expression metacharacters backslashed.

rand

> **rand(EXPR)**
> **rand EXPR**
> **rand**
>
> Returns a random fractional number (scalar) between 0 and EXPR, where EXPR is a positive number. Without *srand* generates the same sequence of numbers. If EXPR is omitted, returns a value between 0 and 1. See rand(3).

read

> **read(FILEHANDLE,SCALAR, LENGTH, OFFSET)**
> **read(FILEHANDLE, SCALAR, LENGTH)**
>
> Reads LENGTH number of bytes from FILEHANDLE, starting at position OFFSET, into SCALAR and returns the number of bytes read, or 0 if *eof*. (Similar to fread system call.) See fread(3).

readdir

> **readdir(DIRHANDLE)**
> **readdir DIRHANDLE**
>
> Reads the next entry of the directory structure, DIRHANDLE, opened by *opendir*. See directory(3).

readlink

> **readlink(EXPR)**
> **readlink EXPR**
>
> Returns the value of a symbolic link. EXPR is the pathname of the symbolic link, and if omitted, $_ is used. See readlink(2).

recv

> **recv(SOCKET, SCALAR, LEN, FLAGS)**
>
> Receives a message of LEN bytes on a socket into SCALAR variable. Returns the address of the sender. See recv(2).

redo

> **redo LABEL**
> **redo**
>
> Restarts a loop block without reevaluting the condition. If there is a continue block, it is not executed. Without LABEL, restarts at the innermost enclosing loop.

ref

> **ref EXPR**
>
> Returns a scalar true value, the data type of EXPR, if EXPR is a reference, else the null string. The returned value depends on what is being referenced, a REF, SCALAR, ARRAY, HASH, CODE, or GLOB. If EXPR is an object that has been blessed into a package, return value is the package (class) name.

rename

rename(OLDNAME, NEWNAME)

Renames a file OLDNAME to NEWNAME. Does not work across filesystem boundaries. If NEWNAME already exists, it is destroyed. See rename(2).

require

require(EXPR)

require EXPR

require

Includes file, EXPR, from the Perl library by searching the @INC array for the specified file. Also checks that the library has not already been included. $_ is used if EXPR is omitted.

reset

reset(EXPR)

reset EXPR

reset

Clears variables and arrays or, if EXPR is omitted, resets ?? searches.

return

return LIST

Returns a value from a subroutine. Cannot be used outside of a subroutine.

reverse

reverse(LIST)

Reverses the order of LIST and returns an array.

rewinddir

rewinddir(DIRHANDLE)

rewinddir DIRHANDLE

Rewinds the position in DIRHANDLE to the beginning of the directory structure. See directory(3).

rindex

rindex(STRING, SUBSTR, OFFSET)

rindex(STRING, SUSSTR)

Returns the last position of SUBSTR in STRING starting at OFFSET, if OFFSET is specified.

rmdir

rmdir(FILENAME)

rmdir FILENAME

Removes a directory, FILENAME, if empty.

s

s/SEARCH_PATTERN/REPLACEMENT/[g][i][e][o]

Searches for pattern and, if found, replaces the pattern with some text. Returns the number of substitutions made. The g option is global across a line. The i option turns off case sensitivity. The e option evaluates the replacement string as an expression, e.g., *s/\d+/$&+5/e;*

scalar

scalar(EXPR)

Forces EXPR to be evaluated in a scalar context.

seek

seek(FILEHANDLE, POSITION, WHENCE)

Positions a file pointer in a file, FILEHANDLE, from some position, relative to its postition in the file, WHENCE. If WHENCE is 0, starts at the beginning of the file; if WHENCE is 1, starts at the current position of the file, and if WHENCE is 2, starts at the end of the file. POSITION cannot be negative if WHENCE is 0.

seekdir

seekdir(DIRHANDLE, POSITION)

Sets the position for the *readdir* function on the directory structure associated with DIRHANDLE. See directory(3).

select

select(FILEHANDLE)
select

Returns the currently selected filehandle if FILEHANDLE is omitted. With FILEHANDLE, sets the current default filehandle for *write* and *print*. (See Formatting.)

select

select(RBITS, WBITS, EBITS, TIMEOUT)

Examines the I/0 file descriptors to see if descriptors are ready for reading, writing, or have exceptional conditions pending. Bitmasks are specified and TIMEOUT is in seconds. See select(2).

semctl

semctl(ID, SEMNUM, CMD, ARG)

Calls the *semctl* system call, allowing control operations on semaphores. Has weird return codes. (See System V IPC.) Requires library file *"ipc.ph"* and *"sem.ph"*. See also semctl(2).

semget

semget(KEY, NSEMS, SIZE, FLAGS)

Returns the semaphore id associated with KEY, or undefined if an error. (See System V IPC.) Requires library files *"ipc.ph"* and *"sem.ph"*. See also semget(2).

semop

semop(KEY, OPSTRING)

Calls the *semop* system call, to perform operations on a semaphore identified by KEY. OPSTRING must be a packed array of *semop* structures. (See System V IPC.) Requires library files "ipc.ph" and "sem.ph". See also semop(2).

send

send(SOCKET, MSG, FLAGS, TO)
send(SOCKET, MSG, FLAGS)

Sends a message on a SOCKET. See send(2).

setpgrp

> **setpgrp(PID, PGRP)**
>
> Sets the current process group for the specified process, process group, or user. See getpgrp(2).

setpriority

> **setpriority(WHICH, WHO, PRIORITY)**
>
> Sets the current priority, *nice* value, for a process, process group, or user. See getpriority(2).

setsockopt

> **setsockopt(SOCKET,LEVEL,OPTNAME,OPTVAL)**
>
> Sets the requested socket option on SOCKET. See getsockopt(2).

shift

> **shift(ARRAY)**
> **shift ARRAY**
> **shift**
>
> Shifts off the first value of the ARRAY and returns it, shortening the array. If ARRAY is omitted, the @ARGV array is shifted, and if in subroutines, the @_ array is shifted.

shmctl

> **shmctl(ID,CMD,ARG)**
>
> Calls the *shmctl* system call, allowing control operations on shared memory. Has weird return odes. (See System VIPC.) Requires library file "ipc.ph" and "shm.ph". See also shmctl(2).

shmget

> **shmget(KEY, SIZE, FLAGS)**
>
> Returns the shared memory segment id associated withthe KEY, or undefined if an error. The shared memory segment created is of at least SIZE bytes.
> Requires *"ipc.ph"* and *"shm.ph"*. (See System V IPC.) See also shmget(2).

shmread

> **shmread(ID,VAR, POS, SIZE)**
>
> Reads from the shared memory ID starting at position, POS for SIZE. VAR is a variable used to store what is read.The segment is attached, data is read from, and the segment is detached. Requires *"ipc.ph"* and *"shm.ph"*. (See System V IPC.) See also shmat(2).

shmwrite

> **shmwrite(ID,VAR, POS, SIZE)**
>
> Writes to the shared memory ID starting at position, POS for SIZE. VAR is a variable used to store what is written. The segment is attached, data is written to, and the segment is detached. Requires *"ipc.ph"* and *"shm.ph"*. (See System V IPC.) See also shmat(2).

shutdown

> **shutdown(SOCKET, HOW)**
>
> Shuts down a SOCKET connection. If HOW is 0 further receives will be disallowed. If HOW is 1,further sends will be disallowed. If HOW is 2, then further sends and receives will be disallowed. See shutdown(2).

sin

> **sin(EXPR)**
> **sin**
> Returns the sine of EXPR (expressed in radians). If EXPR is omitted, returns sine of $_.

sleep

> **sleep(EXPR)**
> **sleep EXPR**
> **sleep**
> Causes program to sleep for EXPR seconds. If EXPR is omitted, program sleeps forever. See sleep(3).

socket

> **socket(SOCKET, DOMAIN, TYPE, PROTOCOL)**
> Opens a socket of a specified type and attaches it to filehandle, SOCKET. See socket(2).

socketpair

> **socketpair(SOCKET, SOCKET2, DOMAIN, TYPE, PROTOCOL)**
> Creates an unamed pair of connect sockets in the specified domain, of the specified type. See socketpair(2).

sort

> **sort(SUBROUTINE LIST)**
> **sort(LIST)**
> **sort SUBROUTINE LIST**
> **sort LIST**
> Sorts the LIST and returns a sorted array. If SUBROUTINE is omitted, sorts in string comparison order. If SUBROUTINE is specified, gives the name of a subroutine that returns an integer less than, equal to, or greater than 0, depending on how the elements of the array are to be ordered. The two elements compared are passed (by reference) to the subroutine as $a and $b, rather than @_. See Array Functions. SUBROUTINE cannot be recursive.

splice

> **splice(ARRAY, OFFSET, LENGTH, LIST)**
> **splice(ARRAY, OFFSET, LENGTH)**
> **splice(ARRAY, OFFSET)**
> Removes elements designated starting with OFFSET and ending in LENGTH from an array, and if LIST is specified, replaces those elements removed with LIST. Returns the elements removed from the list. If LENGTH is not specified, everything from OFFSET to the end of ARRAY is removed.

split

> **split(/PATTERN/, EXPR, LIMIT)**
> **split(/PATTERN/, EXPR)**
> **split(/PATTERN/)**
> **split**
> Splits EXPR into an array of strings and returns them to an array. The PATTERN is the delimiter by which EXPR is separated. If PATTERN is omitted, whitespace is used as the delimiter. LIMIT specifies the number of fields to be split.

sprintf

> **$string=sprintf(FORMAT, LIST)**
> Returns a string rather than sending output to STDOUT with same formatting conventions as the *printf* function. See printf(3).

sqrt

> **sqrt(EXPR)**
> **sqrt EXPR**
> Returns the square root of EXPR. If EXPR is omitted, the square root of $_ is returned.

srand

> **srand(EXPR)**
> **srand EXPR**
> **srand**
> Sets the random seed for the *rand* function. If EXPR is omitted, the seed is the time function. See rand(3).

stat

> **stat(FILEHANDLE)**
> **stat FILEHANDLE**
> **stat(EXPR)**
> Returns a 13–element array consisting of file statistics for FILEHANDLE or file named as EXPR. The array consists of:
> > the device
> > the file inode number
> > file mode
> > number of hard links to the file
> > user ID of owner
> > group ID of owner
> > raw device
> > size of file
> > file last access time
> > file last modify time
> > file last status change time
> > preferred blocksize for file system I/O
> > actual number of blocks allocated
> See stat(2)

study

> **study(SCALAR)**
> **study SCALAR**
> **study**
> Uses a linked list mechanism to increase efficiency in searching for pattern matches that are to be repeated many times. Can only study one SCALAR at a time. If SCALAR is omitted, $_ is used. Most beneficial in loops where many short constant strings are being scanned.

sub

> **sub NAME BLOCK**
> **sub NAME**
> **sub BLOCK**

sub NAME PROTO BLOCK
sub NAME PROTO
sub PROTO BLOCK

The first two declare the existence of named subroutines and return no value. Without a block, **sub NAME** is a forward declaration. The **sub BLOCK** is used to create an anonymous subroutine. The last three are like the first three, except they allow prototypes to describe how the subroutine will be called. A prototype will notify the compiler that a subroutine definition will appear at some later time and can tell the compiler what type and how many arguments the subroutine expects. For example, *sub foo ($$@)*, declares that the subroutine *foo* will take three arguments, two scalars and an array. An error will occur if, for example, fewer than three arguments are passed.

substr

substr(EXPR, OFFSET, LENGTH)
substr(EXPR, OFFSET)

Returns a substring after extracting the substring from EXPR starting at position OFFSET and if LENGTH is specifie that many characters from OFFSET. If OFFSET is negative, starts from the far end of the string.

symlink

symlink(OLDFILE, NEWFILE)

Creates a symbolic link. NEWFILE is symbolically linked to OLDFILE. The files can reside on different partitions. See symlink(2).

syscall

syscall(LIST)
syscall LIST

Calls the system call specified as the first element in LIST, where the system call is preceded with &SYS_ as in &SYS_system call. The remaining items in LIST are passed as arguments to the system call. Requires *"syscall.ph"*.

sysread

sysread(FILEHANDLE, SCALAR, LENGTH, OFFSET)
sysread(FILEHANDLE, SCALAR, LENGTH)

Reads LENGTH bytes into variable SCALAR from FILEHANDLE. Uses the read system call. See read(2).

sysopen

sysopen(FILEHANDLE, FILENAME, MODE)
sysopen(FILEHANDLE, FILENAME, MODE, PERMS)

Opens FILENAME using the underlying operating system's version of the open call, and assigns it to FILEHANDLE. The file modes are system dependent and can be found in the Fcntl library module. 0 means read-only, 1 means write-only, and 2 means read/write. If PERMS is omitted, the default is 0666. See open(2).

system

system(LIST)
system LIST

Executes a shell command from a Perl script and returns. Like the *exec* function, except forks first and the script waits until the command has been executed. Control then returns to script. The return value is the exit status of the program and can be obtained by dividing by 256 or right-shifting the lower 8 bits. See system(3).

syswrite

> **syswrite(FILEHANDLE, SCALAR, LENGTH, OFFSET)**
> **syswrite(FILEHANDLE, SCALAR, LENGTH)**
> Returns the number of bytes written to FILEHANDLE. Writes LENGTH bytes from variable SCALAR, to FILEHANDLE, starting at position OFFSET, if OFFSET is specified. Uses the write system call. See write(2).

tell

> **tell(FILEHANDLE)**
> **tell FILEHANDLE**
> **tell**
> Returns the current file position, in bytes (starting at byte 0), for FILEHANDLE. Normally the returned value is given to the seek function in order to return to some position within the file. See lseek(2).

telldir

> **telldir(DIRHANDLE)**
> **telldir DIRHANDLE**
> Returns the current position of the *readdir* function for the directory structure, DIRHANDLE. See directory(3).

tie

> **tie (VARIABLE, CLASSNAME, LIST)**
> Binds a VARIABLE to a package (CLASSNAME) that will use methods to provide the implemention for the variable. LIST consists of any additional arguments to be passed to the new method when constructing the object. Most commonly used with associative arrays to bind them to databases. The methods have predefined names to be placed within a package. The predefined methods will be called automatically when the tied variables are fetched, stored, or destroyed, etc.
>
> The package implementing an associative array provides the following methods:
>   TIEHASH $classname, LIST
>   DESTROY $self
>   FETCH $self, $key
>   STORE $self, $key
>   DELETE $self, $key
>   EXISTS $self, $key
>   FIRSTKEY $self
>   NEXTKEY $self, $lastkey
>
> Methods provided for an array are:
>   TIEARRAY $classname, LIST
>   DESTROY $self
>   FETCH $self, $subscript
>   STORE $self, $subscript, $value
>
> Methods provided for a scalar are:
>   TIESCALAR $classname, LIST
>   DESTROY $self
>   FETCH $self
>   STORE $self, $value

Example:
```
$object = tie %hash, Myhashclass;
    while($key, $value)=each (%hash){
    print "$key, $value\n";  # invokes the FETCH method
$object = tie @array, Myarrayclass;
    $array[0]=5;  # invokes the STORE method
$object = tie $scalar, Myscalarclass;
    untie $scalar;  # invokes the DESTROY method
```

tied

tied **VARIABLE**

Returns a reference to the object that was previously bound with the *tie* function or undefined if VARIABLE is not tied to a package.

time

time

Returns a four–element array of non–leap seconds since January 1, 1970, UTC. Used with *gmtime* and *localtime* functions. See ctime(3).

times

times

Returns a four–element array giving the user and system CPU times, in seconds, for the process and its children. See times(3).

tr

tr/SEARCHPATTERN/REPLACEMENT/[c][d][e]
y/SEARCHPATTERN/REPLACEMENT/[c][d][e]

Translates characters in SEARCHPATTERN to corresponding character in REPLACEMENT. Similar to UNIX *tr* command.

truncate

truncate(FILEHANDLE, LENGTH)
truncate(EXPR, LENGTH)

Truncate FILEHANDLE or EXPR to a specified LENGTH. See truncate(2).

uc

uc **EXPR**

Returns EXPR (or $_ if no EXPR) in uppercase letters. Same as \U \E escape sequences.

ucfirst

ucfirst **EXPR**

Returns the first character of EXPR(or $_ if no EXPR) in uppercase. Same as \u escape sequence.

umask

umask(EXPR)
umask **EXPR**
umask

Sets the umask (file creation mask) for the process and returns the old umask. With EXPR omitted, returns the current umask value. See umask(2).

undef

> **undef(EXPR)**
> **undef EXPR**
> **undef**
> Undefines EXPR, an lvalue. Used on scalars, arrays, hashes, or subroutine names (&subroutine) to recover any storage associated with it. Always returns the undefined value. Can be used by itself when returning from a subroutine to determine if an error was made.

unlink

> **unlink(LIST)**
> **unlink LIST**
> **unlink**
> Removes a LIST of files. Returns the number of files deleted. Without an argument, unlinks the value stored in $_. See unlink(2).

unpack

> **unpack(TEMPLATE, EXPR)**
> Unpacks a string representing a structure and expands it to an array value, returning the array value, using TEMPLATE to get the order and type of values. Reverse of pack. See pack.

unshift

> **unshift(LIST)**
> **unshift**
> Prepends LIST to the beginning of an array. Returns the number of elements in the new array.

untie

> **untie VARIABLE**
> Breaks the binding (unties) between a variable and the package it is tied to. Opposite of tie.

use

> **use Module LIST**
> **use Module**
> **use pragma**
> A compiler directive that imports subroutines and variables from Module into the current package. LIST consists of specific names of the variables and subroutines the current package will import. The -m and -M flags can be used at the command line instead of *use*. Pragmas are a special kind of module that can affect the behavior for a block of statements at compile time. Three common pragmas are: *integer, subs*, and *strict*.

utime

> **utime(LIST)**
> **utime LIST**
> Changes the access and modification times on a list of files. The first two elements of LIST are the numerical access and modification times.

values

values(%ASSOC_ARRAY)
values ASSOC_ARRAY
Returns an array consisting of all the values in an associative array, ASSOC_ARRAY in random order.

vec

vec(EXPR, OFFSET, BITS)
Treats a string, EXPR, as a vector of unsigned integers. Returns the value of the element specified. OFFSET is the number of elements to skip over in order to find the one wanted, and BITS is the number of bits per element in the vector. BITS must be one of of a power of two from 1 to 32, e.g., 1,2,4,8,16, or 32.

wait

wait
Waits for the child process to terminate. Returns the pid of the deceased process and –1 if no child processes. The status value is returned in the $? variable. See wait(2).

waitpid

waitpid(PID, FLAGS)
Waits for a child process to terminate and returns true when the process dies, or –1 if there are no child processes, or if FLAGS specify non–blocking and the process hasn't died. $? gets the status of the dead process. Requires "sys/wait.ph". See wait(2).

wantarray

wantarray
Returns true if the context of the currently running subroutine wants an array value, i.e., the returned value from the subroutine will be assigned to an array. Returns false if looking for a scalar. Example: *return wantarray ? () : undef;*

warn

warn(LIST)
warn LIST
Sends a message to STDERR, like the *die* function, but doesn't exit the program.

write

write(FILEHANDLE)
write FILEHANDLE
write
Writes a formatted record to FILEHANDLE or currently selected FILEHANDLE (See select), i.e., when called, invokes the format (picture line) for the FILEHANDLE; with no arguments, either goes to stdout or to the filehandle currently selected by the *select* call. Has nothing to do with the write(2) system call. See syswrite.

y

y/SEARCHPATTERN/REPLACEMENT/[c][d][e]
Translates characters in SEARCHPATTERN to corresponding character in REPLACEMENT. Also known as tr and similar to UNIX *tr* command or *sed* y command.

B.2 COMMAND LINE SWITCHES

–a	Turns on autosplit mode when used with –n or –p, performing implicit split on whitespace. Fields are put in @F array.
	*date	perl –ane 'print "$F[0]\n";*
–c	Checks Perl syntax without executing script.
–d	Turns on Perl debugger.
–D	Sets Perl debugging flags. (Check your Perl installation to make sure debugging was installed.) To watch how Perl executes a script, use –D14.
–e command	Used to execute Perl commands at the command line rather than in a script.
-Fpattern	Specifies a pattern to use when splitting the input line. The pattern is just a regular expression enclosed in slashes, single or double quotes. For example, -F/:+/ splits the input line on one or more colons. Turned on if -a is also in effect.
-h	Prints a summary of Perl's command-line options.
–iextension	Enables in–place editing when using <> to loop through a file. If extension is not specified, modifies the file inplace. Otherwise renames the input file with the extension (used as a backup), and creates an output file with the original file name which is edited in place. This is the selected filehandle for all print statements.
–Idirectory	Used with –P to tell the C Preprocessor where to look for included files, by default /usr/include and /usr/lib/perl and the current directory.
–Idigits	Enables automatic line–ending processing. Chops the line terminator if –n or –p are used. Assigns $\ the value of digits (octal) to add the line terminator back on to print statements. Without digits specified, sets $\ to the current value of $/.(See special variables.)
-m[-]module	
-M[-]module	
-M[-]'module'	
-[mM]module=arg[,arg]...	
-mmodule	Executes the *use* module before executing the Perl script.
-Mmodule	Executes the *use* module before executing the Perl script. Quotes are used if extra text is added. The dash shown in square brackets means that the use directive will be replaced with *no*.
–n	Causes Perl to implicitly loop over a named file printing only lines specified.
–p	Causes Perl to implicitly loop over a named file printing all lines in addition to those specified
.–P	Causes script to be run through the C preprocessor before being compiled by Perl.
–s	Enables switch parsing after the script name but before filename arguments removing any switches found there from the @ARGV array. Sets the switch

	names to a scalar variable of the same name and assigns 1 to the scalar, e.g., *–abc* becomes *$abc* in the script.
–S	Makes Perl use the PATH environment variable to search for the script if the *#!/usr/bin/perl* line is not supported.
-T	Forces "taint" checks to be turned on for testing a script, which is ordinarily done only on setuid or setgid programs. Recommended for testing CGI scripts.
–u	Causes a core dump of script after compilation. (UNIX based).
–U	Allows Perl to do unsafe operations, e.g., unlinking directories if superuser.
–v	Prints Perl version information. (UNIX based.)
-V	Prints a summary of most important Perl configuration values and the current value of the @INC array.
–w	Prints warnings about possible misuse of reserved words, filehandles, and subroutines, etc.
–xdirectory	Any text preceding the #!/usr/bin/perl line will be ignored. If a directory name is provided as an argument to the -x switch, Perl will change to that directory before execution of the script starts.

INDEX